ODD SCHNOZZ AND THE ODD SQUAD

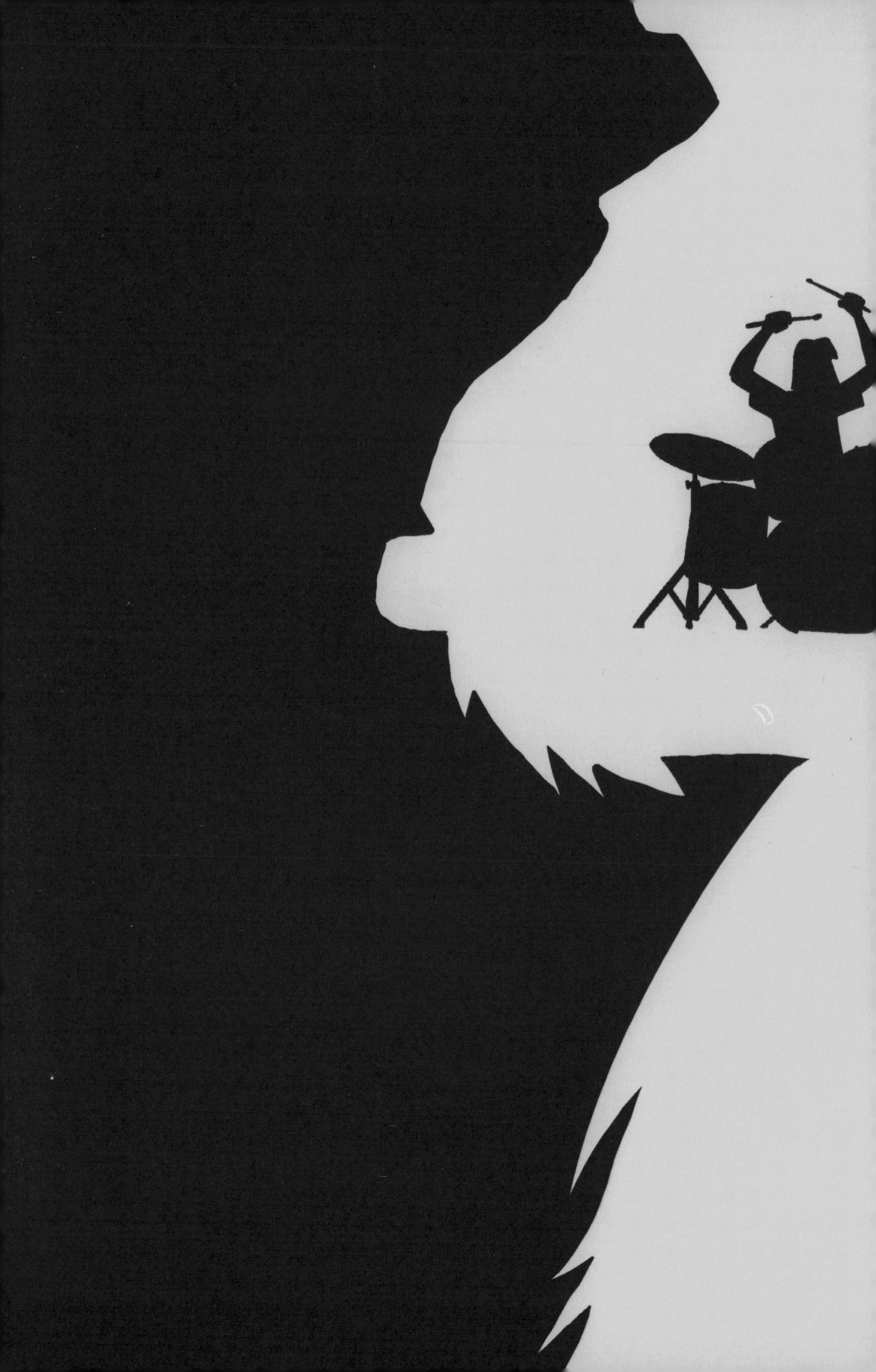

ODD SCHNOZZ
AND THE ODD SQUAD

written by **JEFFREY BURANDT**
illustrated by **DENNIS CULVER**
colored by **RAMON VILLALOBOS**

Lettered by Crank!
Edited by Robin Herrera and Jill Beaton
Logo Designed by Jason Storey
Book Designed by Fred Chao

Oni Press, Inc.
Joe Nozemack, publisher
James Lucas Jones, editor in chief
Tim Wiesch, v.p. of business development
Cheyenne Allott, director of sales
Fred Reckling, director of publicity
Troy Look, production manager
Hilary Thompson, graphic designer
Jared Jones, production assistant
Charlie Chu, senior editor
Robin Herrera, editor
Ari Yarwood, associate editor
Brad Rooks, inventory coordinator
Jung Lee, office assistant

1305 SE Martin Luther King Jr. Blvd.
Suite A
Portland, OR 97214

facebook.com/onipress
twitter.com/onipress
onipress.tumblr.com
onipress.com

First Edition: June 2015
ISBN: 978-1-62010-244-2
eISBN: 978-1-62010-245-9

Printed in China.

1 2 3 4 5 6 7 8 9 10

Library of Congress Control Number: 2014955107

I dedicate this book to Rilla Spiller Wright, aka Widdy, my grandmother who brought my mom and me into her home in Plano, TX, raised two generations of kids, and provided my first insight into code names. Also, please read this book in memory of my little brother, Christian Burandt, who left us heartbreakingly soon. I used to send him boxes and boxes of my old comic books and dreamed of giving him this volume, wherein a young boy named "Chris" befriends a cyborg cheetah before further adventures ensue. I love and miss you every day, Chris.

-JB

To my friend, Alexa, who helped me through a difficult time.

-DC

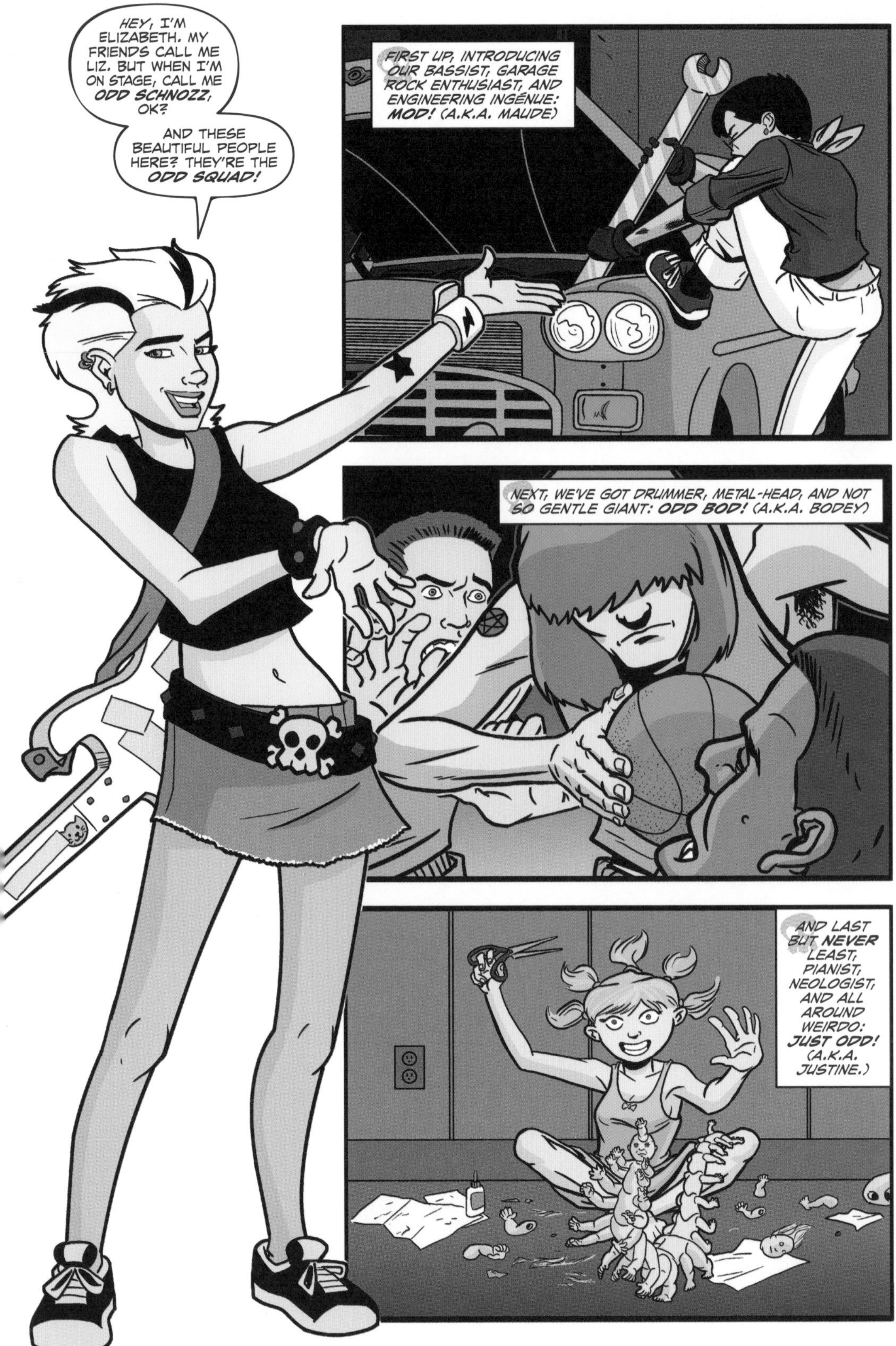

HEY, I'M ELIZABETH. MY FRIENDS CALL ME LIZ. BUT WHEN I'M ON STAGE, CALL ME ODD SCHNOZZ, OK?
AND THESE BEAUTIFUL PEOPLE HERE? THEY'RE THE ODD SQUAD!
FIRST UP, INTRODUCING OUR BASSIST, GARAGE ROCK ENTHUSIAST, AND ENGINEERING INGÉNUE: MOD! (A.K.A. MAUDE)
NEXT, WE'VE GOT DRUMMER, METAL-HEAD, AND NOT SO GENTLE GIANT: ODD BOD! (A.K.A. BODEY)
AND LAST BUT NEVER LEAST, PIANIST, NEOLOGIST, AND ALL AROUND WEIRDO: JUST ODD! (A.K.A. JUSTINE.)

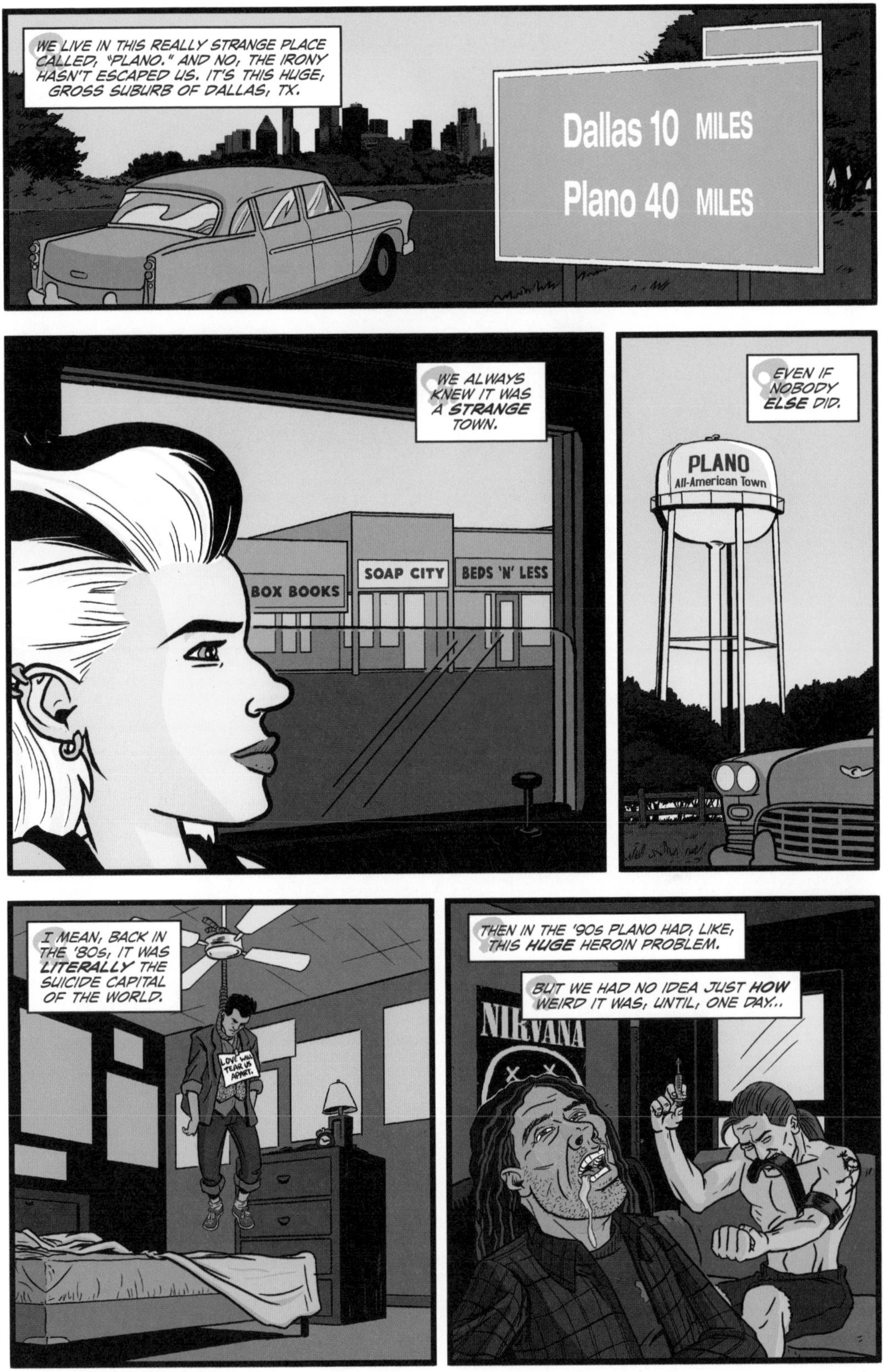

WE LIVE IN THIS REALLY STRANGE PLACE CALLED, "PLANO." AND NO, THE IRONY HASN'T ESCAPED US. IT'S THIS HUGE, GROSS SUBURB OF DALLAS, TX.
Dallas 10 MILES
Plano 40 MILES
WE ALWAYS KNEW IT WAS A STRANGE TOWN.
SOAP CITY
BEDS 'N' LESS
BOX BOOKS
EVEN IF NOBODY ELSE DID.
PLANO
All-American Town
I MEAN, BACK IN THE '80s, IT WAS LITERALLY THE SUICIDE CAPITAL OF THE WORLD.
LOVE WILL TEAR US APART.
THEN IN THE '90s PLANO HAD, LIKE, THIS HUGE HEROIN PROBLEM.
BUT WE HAD NO IDEA JUST HOW WEIRD IT WAS, UNTIL, ONE DAY...
NIRVANA

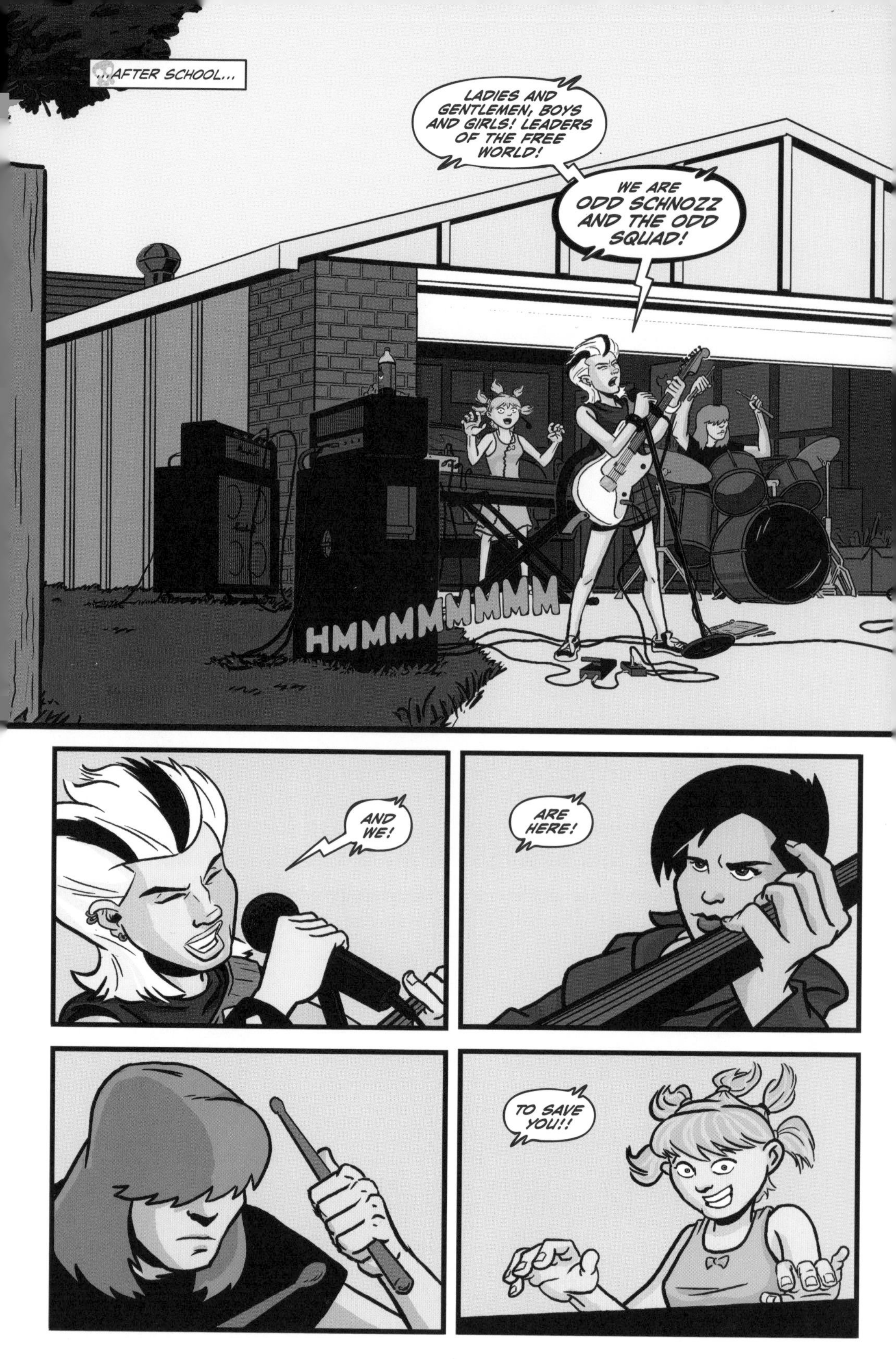
...AFTER SCHOOL...
LADIES AND GENTLEMEN, BOYS AND GIRLS! LEADERS OF THE FREE WORLD!
WE ARE ODD SCHNOZZ AND THE ODD SQUAD!
HMMMMMMMMMM
AND WE!
ARE HERE!
TO SAVE YOU!!

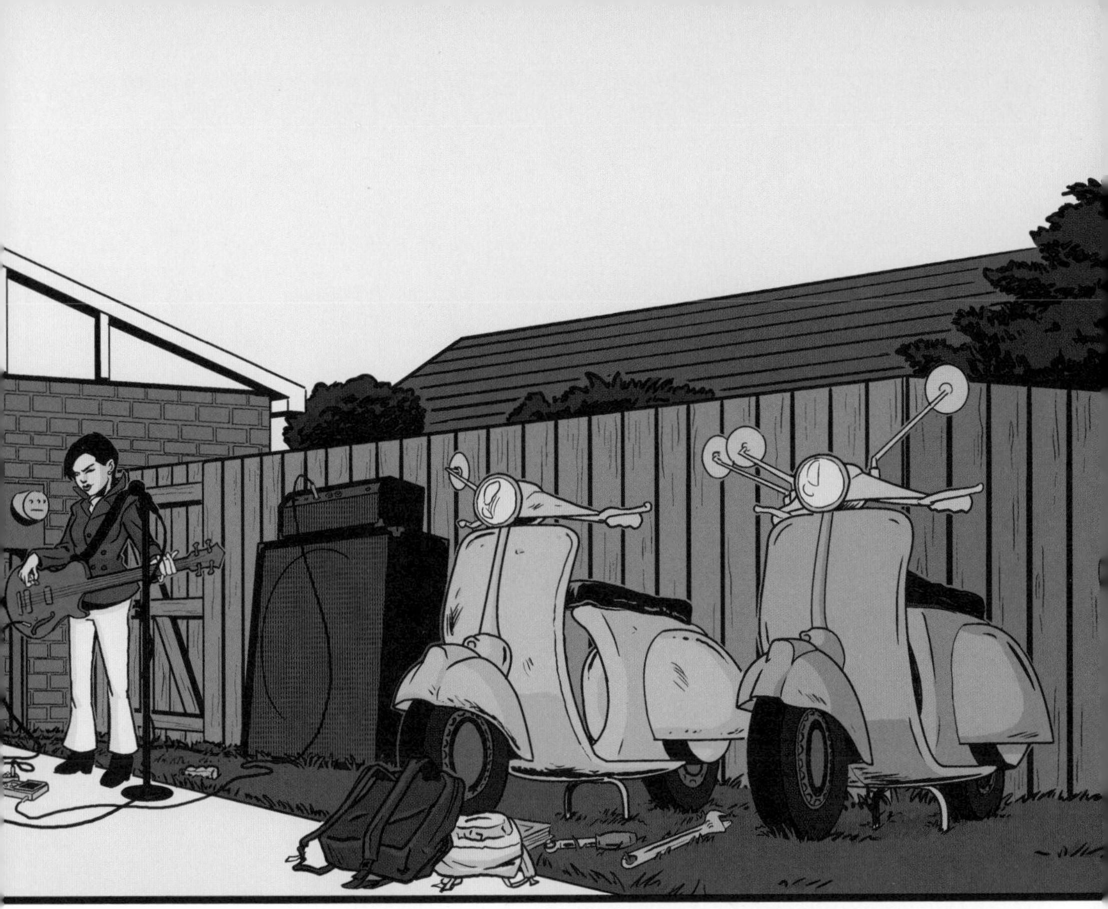

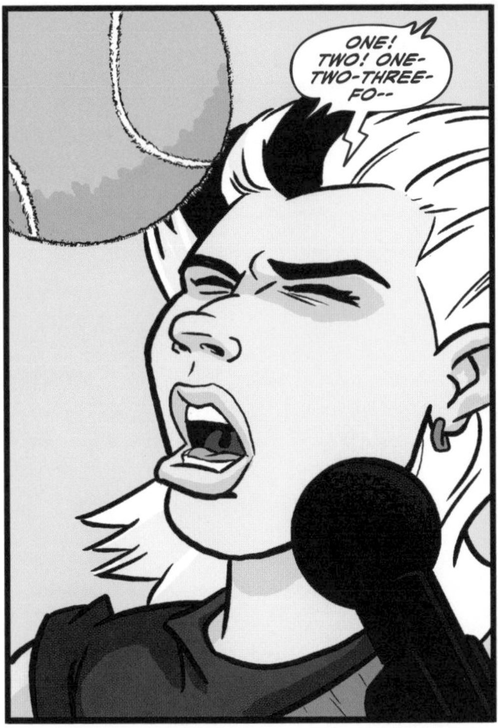
ONE! TWO! ONE-TWO-THREE-FO--

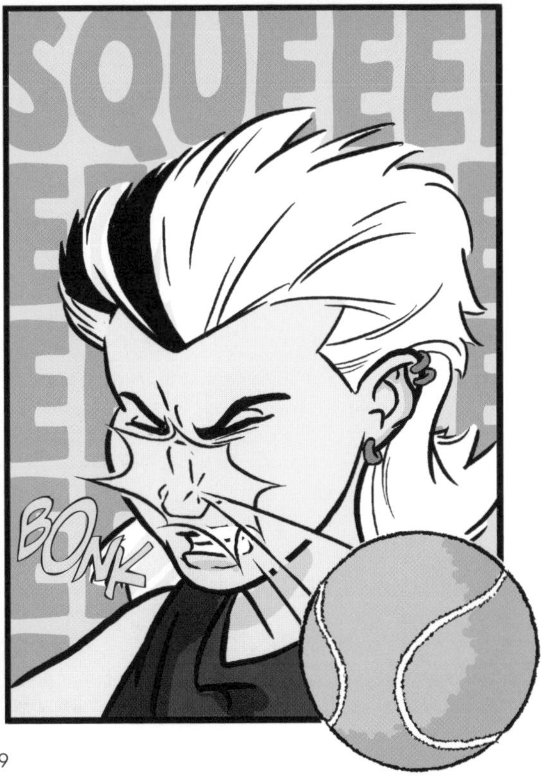
SQUEEE
BONK

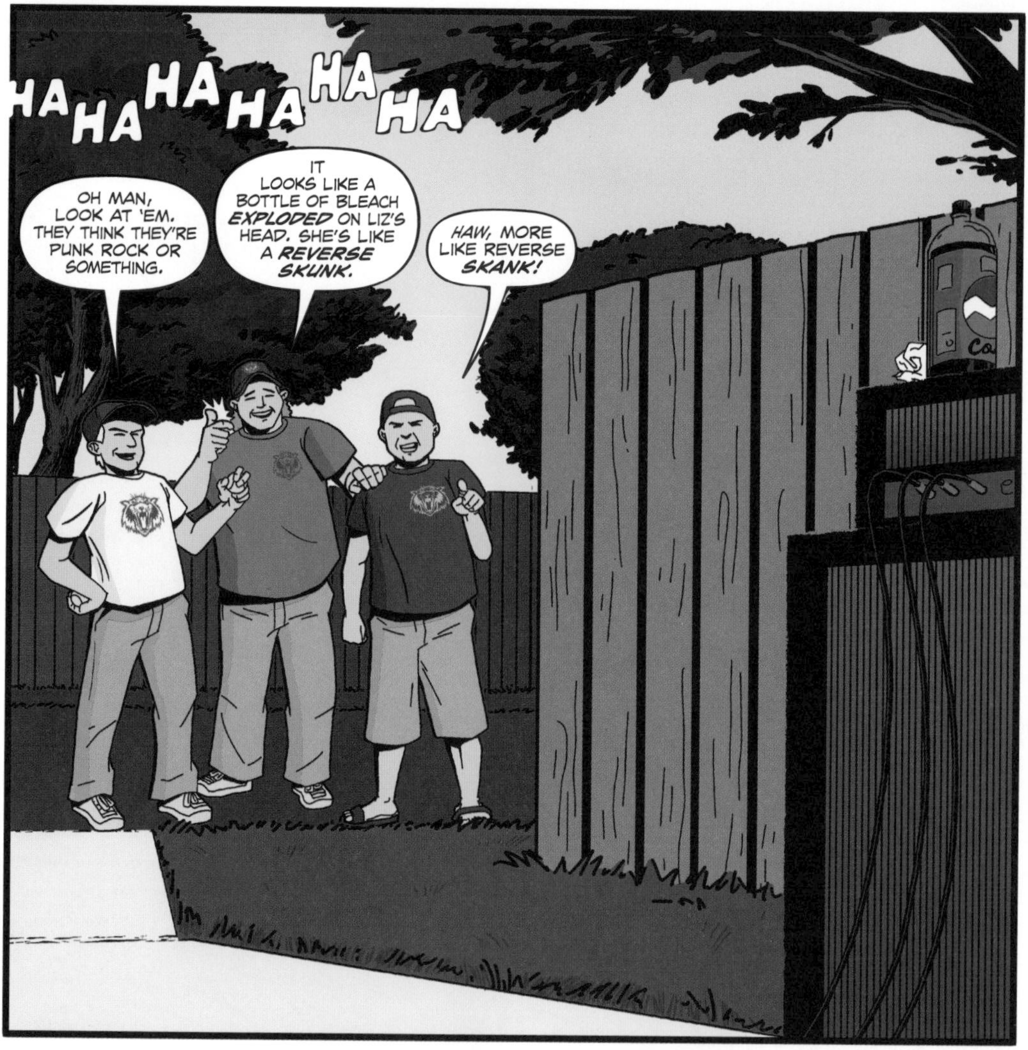
HA HA HA HA HA HA HA
OH MAN, LOOK AT 'EM. THEY THINK THEY'RE PUNK ROCK OR SOMETHING.
IT LOOKS LIKE A BOTTLE OF BLEACH *EXPLODED* ON LIZ'S HEAD. SHE'S LIKE A *REVERSE SKUNK.*
HAW, MORE LIKE REVERSE *SKANK!*

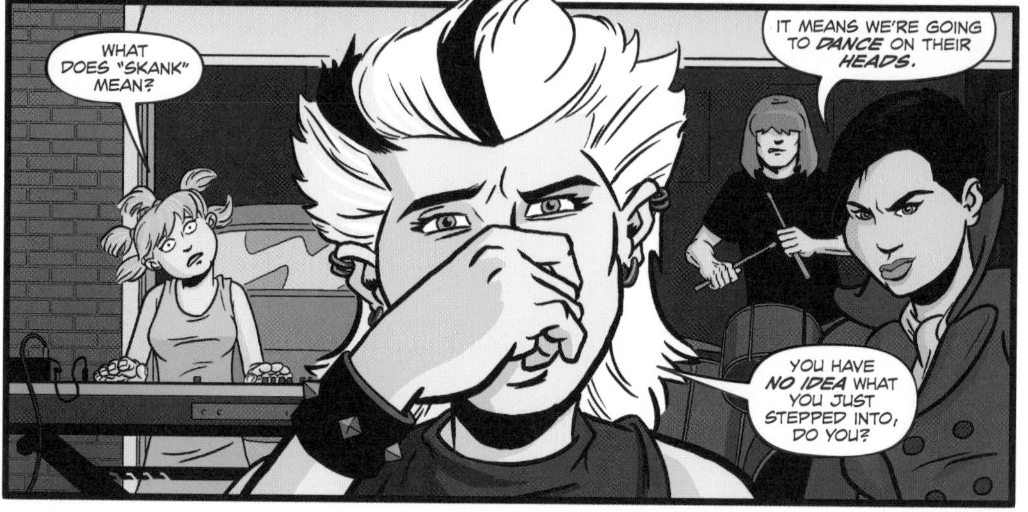
WHAT DOES "SKANK" MEAN?
IT MEANS WE'RE GOING TO *DANCE* ON THEIR *HEADS.*
YOU HAVE *NO IDEA* WHAT YOU JUST STEPPED INTO, DO YOU?

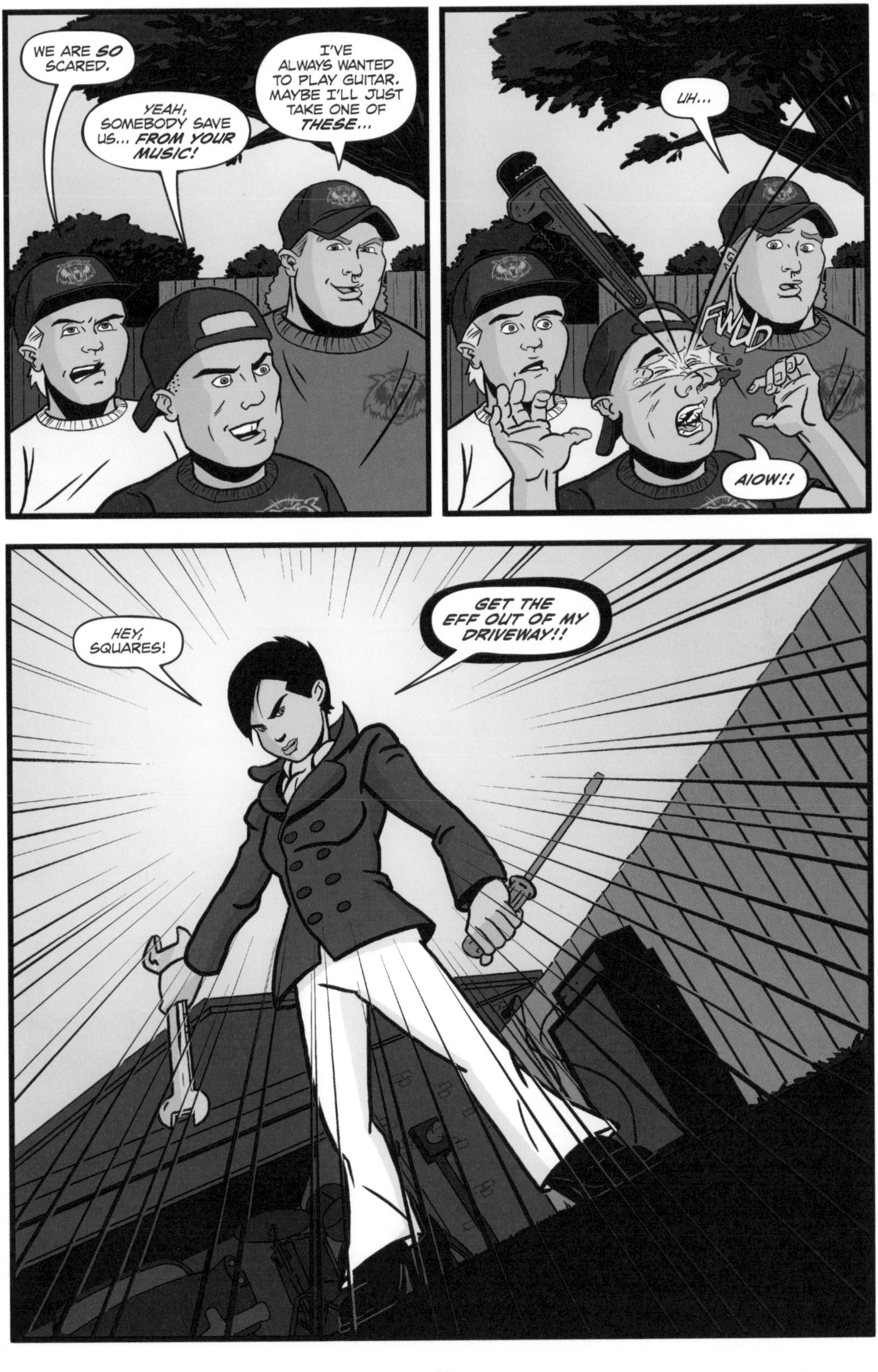
WE ARE SO SCARED.
YEAH, SOMEBODY SAVE US... FROM YOUR MUSIC!
I'VE ALWAYS WANTED TO PLAY GUITAR. MAYBE I'LL JUST TAKE ONE OF THESE...
UH...
FWUD
AIOW!!
HEY, SQUARES!
GET THE EFF OUT OF MY DRIVEWAY!!

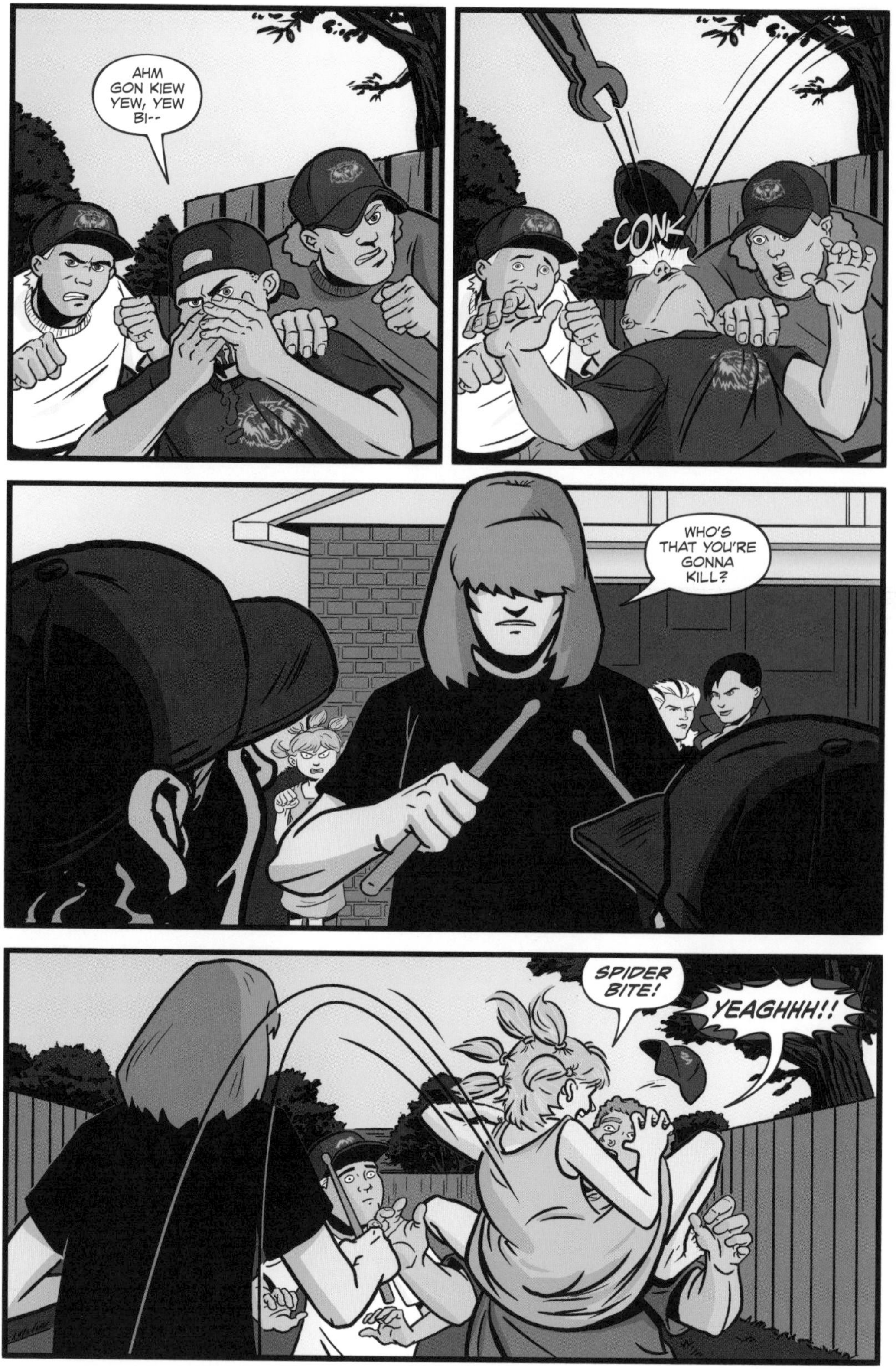
AHM GON KIEW YEW, YEW BI--
CONK
WHO'S THAT YOU'RE GONNA KILL?
SPIDER BITE!
YEAGHHH!!

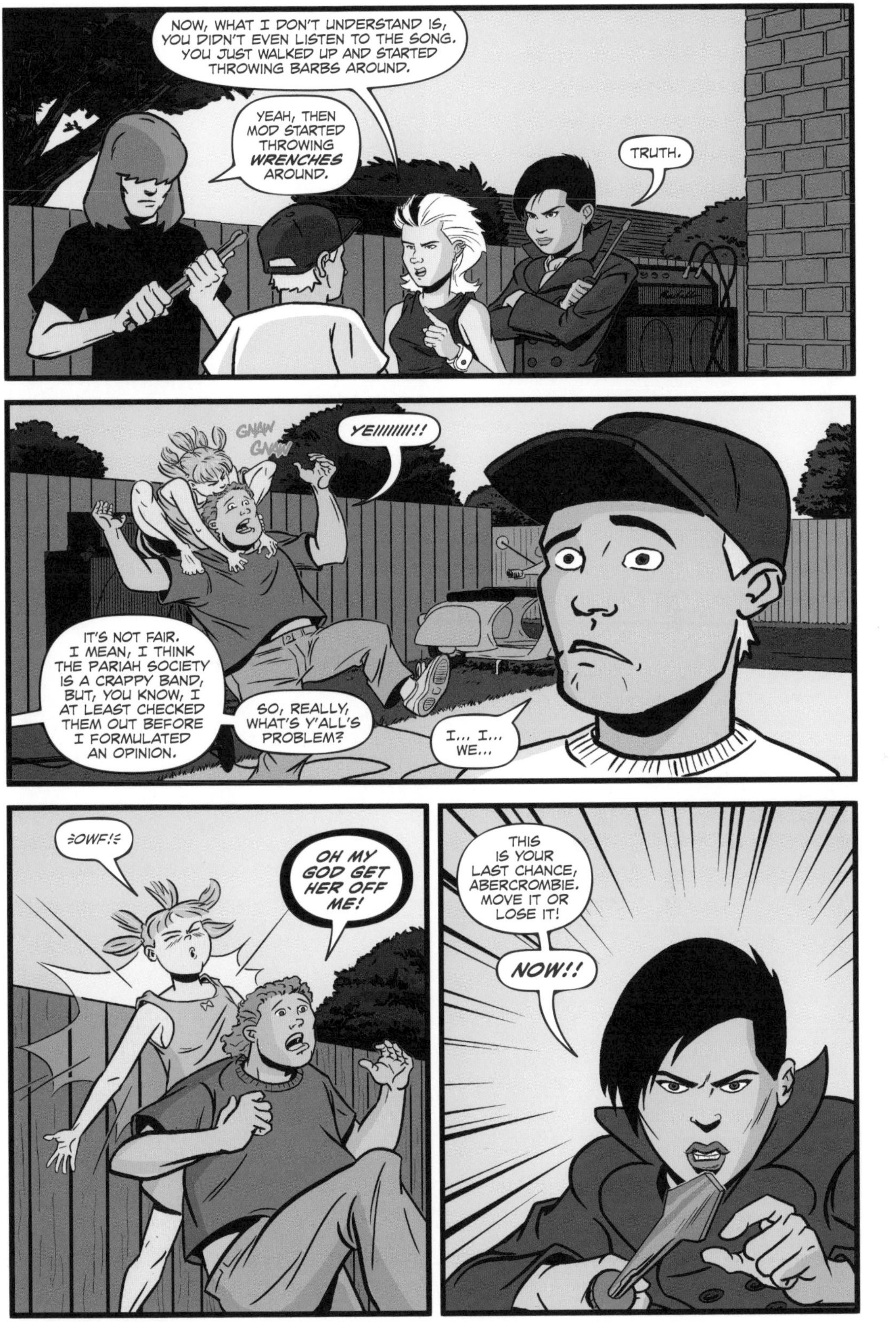
NOW, WHAT I DON'T UNDERSTAND IS, YOU DIDN'T EVEN LISTEN TO THE SONG. YOU JUST WALKED UP AND STARTED THROWING BARBS AROUND.
YEAH, THEN MOD STARTED THROWING *WRENCHES* AROUND.
TRUTH.
GNAW GNAW
YEIIIIIIII!!
IT'S NOT FAIR. I MEAN, I THINK THE PARIAH SOCIETY IS A CRAPPY BAND, BUT, YOU KNOW, I AT LEAST CHECKED THEM OUT BEFORE I FORMULATED AN OPINION.
SO, REALLY, WHAT'S Y'ALL'S PROBLEM?
I... I... WE...
OWF!
OH MY GOD GET HER OFF ME!
THIS IS YOUR LAST CHANCE, ABERCROMBIE. MOVE IT OR LOSE IT!
NOW!!

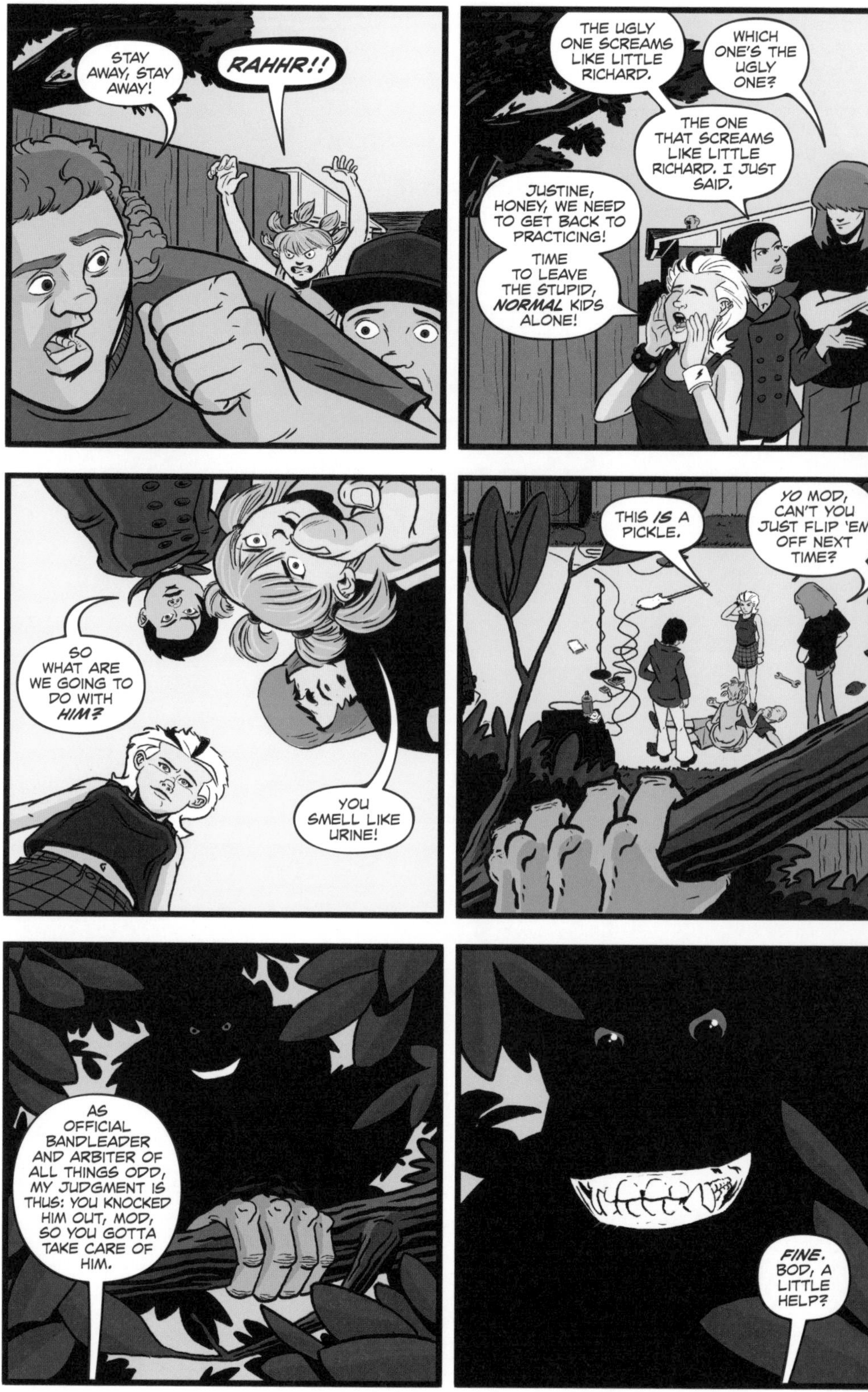
STAY AWAY, STAY AWAY!
RAHHR!!
THE UGLY ONE SCREAMS LIKE LITTLE RICHARD.
WHICH ONE'S THE UGLY ONE?
THE ONE THAT SCREAMS LIKE LITTLE RICHARD. I JUST SAID.
JUSTINE, HONEY, WE NEED TO GET BACK TO PRACTICING!
TIME TO LEAVE THE STUPID, NORMAL KIDS ALONE!
SO WHAT ARE WE GOING TO DO WITH HIM?
YOU SMELL LIKE URINE!
THIS IS A PICKLE.
YO MOD, CAN'T YOU JUST FLIP 'EM OFF NEXT TIME?
AS OFFICIAL BANDLEADER AND ARBITER OF ALL THINGS ODD, MY JUDGMENT IS THUS: YOU KNOCKED HIM OUT, MOD, SO YOU GOTTA TAKE CARE OF HIM.
FINE. BOD, A LITTLE HELP?

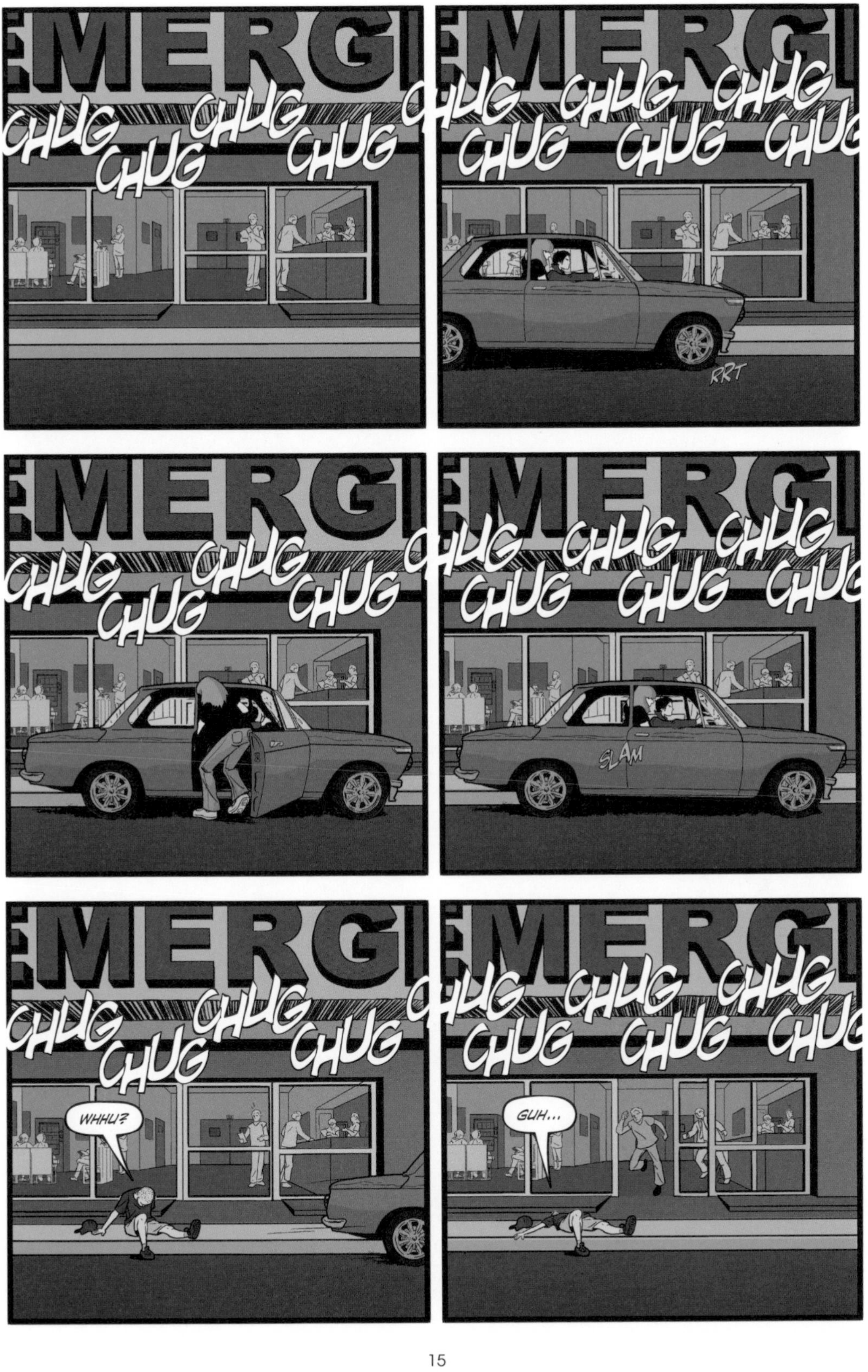
EMERG
CHUG CHUG CHUG CHUG CHUG
EMERG
CHUG CHUG CHUG CHUG CHUG CHUG
RRT
EMERG
CHUG CHUG CHUG CHUG CHUG
EMERG
CHUG CHUG CHUG CHUG CHUG CHUG
SLAM
EMERG
CHUG CHUG CHUG CHUG CHUG
WHHU?
EMERG
CHUG CHUG CHUG CHUG CHUG CHUG
GUH...

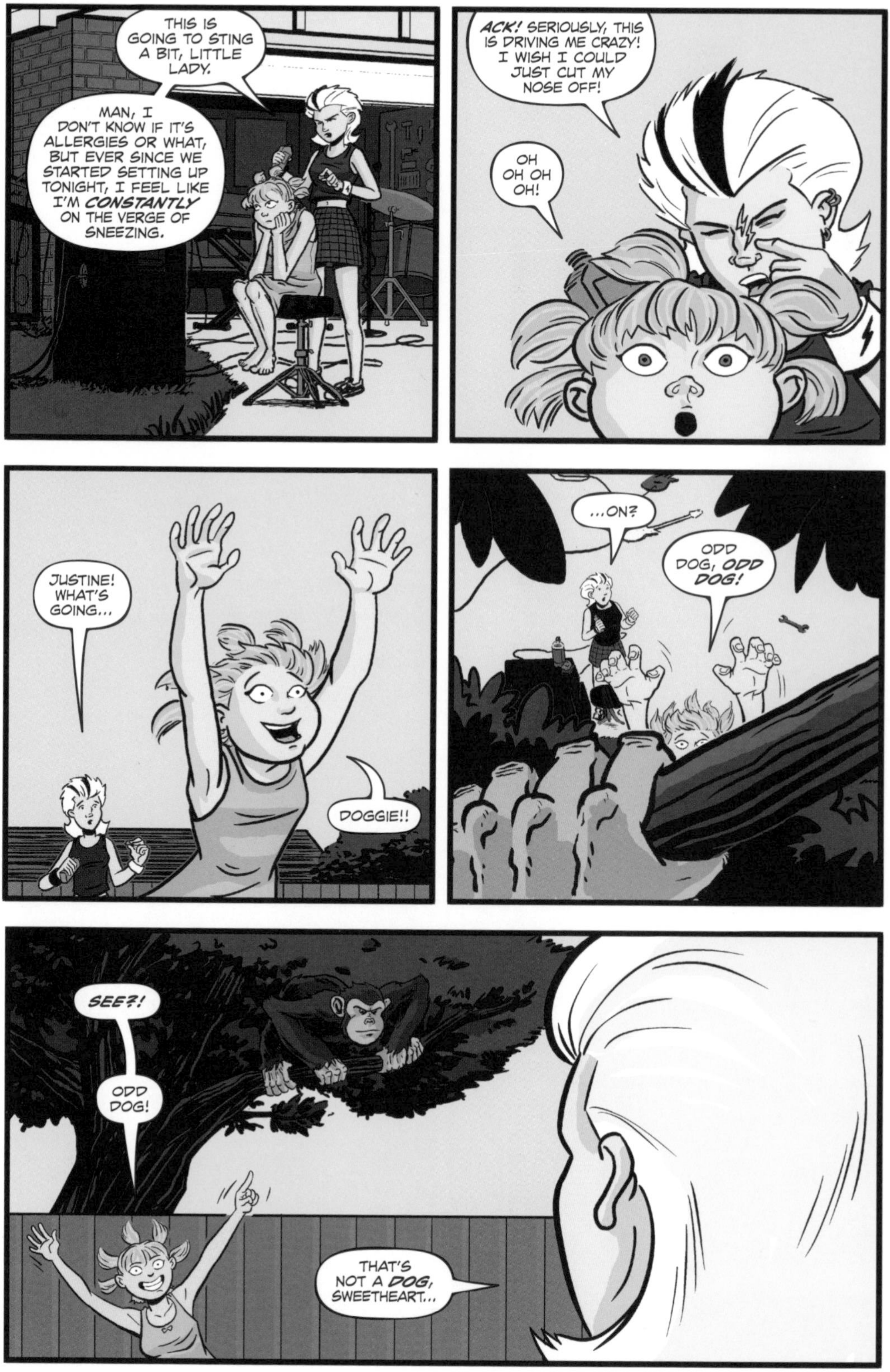
THIS IS GOING TO STING A BIT, LITTLE LADY.
MAN, I DON'T KNOW IF IT'S ALLERGIES OR WHAT, BUT EVER SINCE WE STARTED SETTING UP TONIGHT, I FEEL LIKE I'M CONSTANTLY ON THE VERGE OF SNEEZING.
ACK! SERIOUSLY, THIS IS DRIVING ME CRAZY! I WISH I COULD JUST CUT MY NOSE OFF!
OH OH OH OH!
JUSTINE! WHAT'S GOING...
DOGGIE!!
...ON?
ODD DOG, ODD DOG!
SEE?!
ODD DOG!
THAT'S NOT A DOG, SWEETHEART...

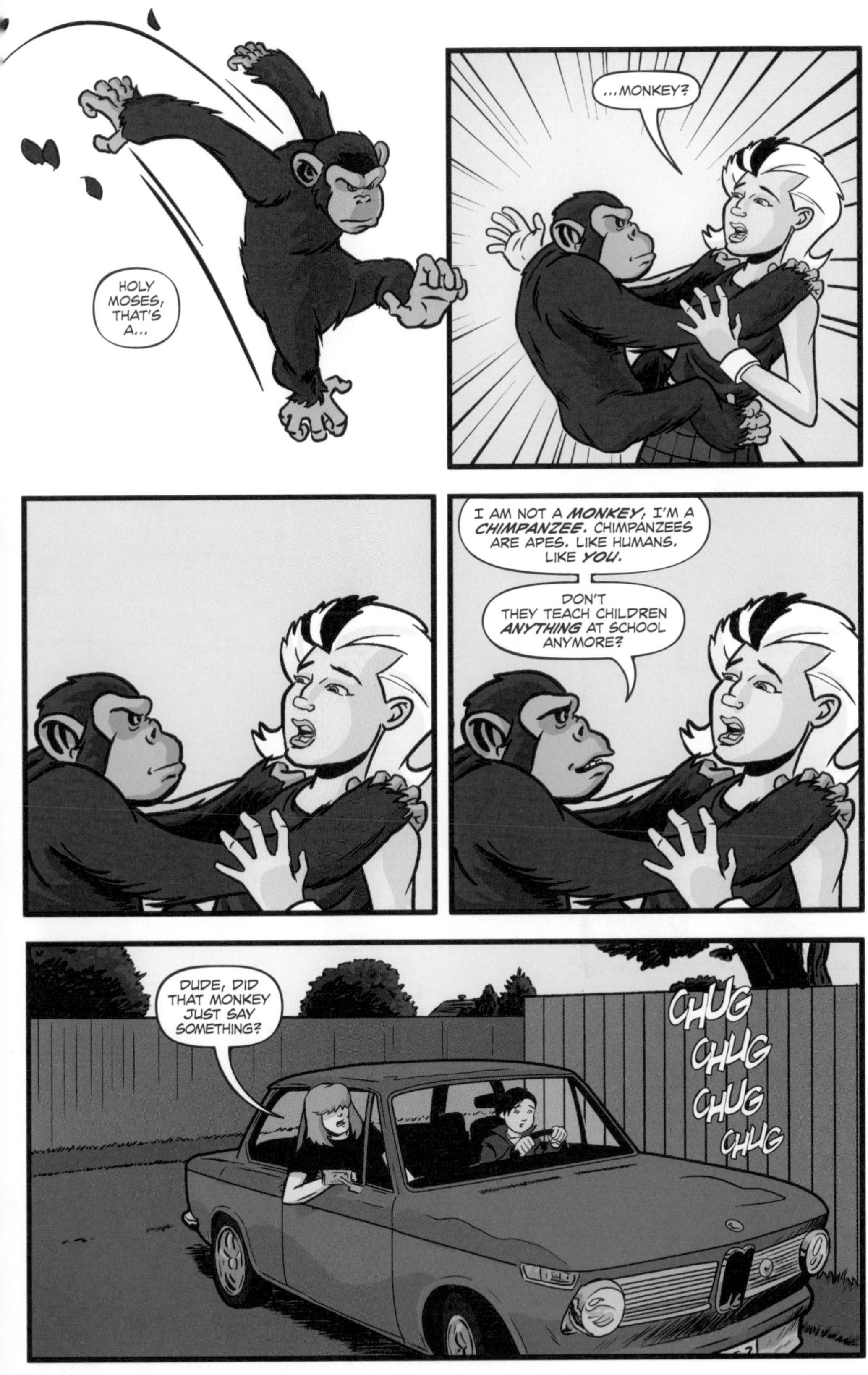
HOLY MOSES, THAT'S A...
...MONKEY?
I AM NOT A MONKEY, I'M A CHIMPANZEE. CHIMPANZEES ARE APES. LIKE HUMANS. LIKE YOU.
DON'T THEY TEACH CHILDREN ANYTHING AT SCHOOL ANYMORE?
DUDE, DID THAT MONKEY JUST SAY SOMETHING?
CHUG CHUG CHUG CHUG

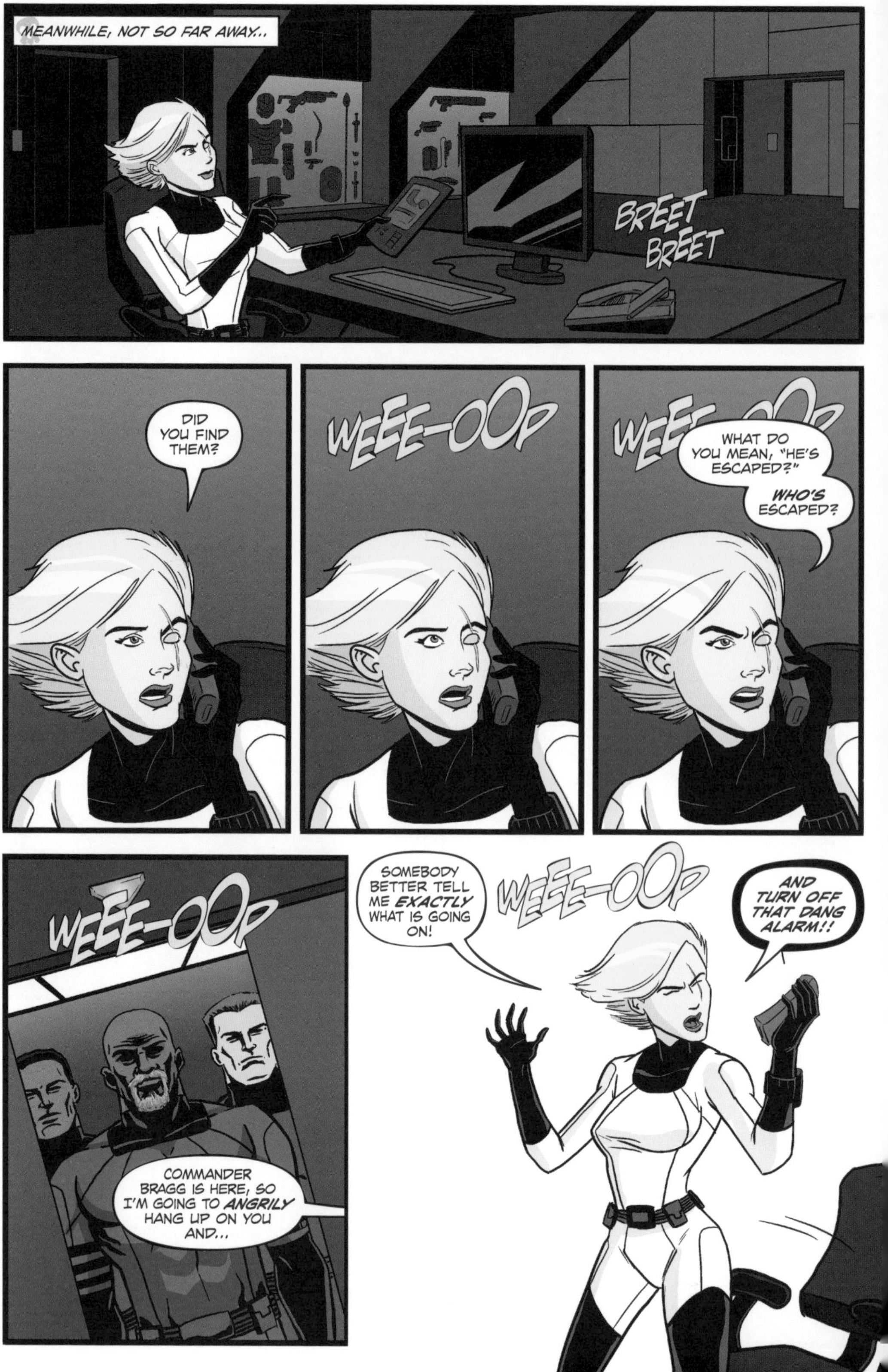
MEANWHILE, NOT SO FAR AWAY...
BREET BREET
DID YOU FIND THEM?
WEEE-OOP
WHAT DO YOU MEAN, "HE'S ESCAPED?"
WHO'S ESCAPED?
WEEE-OOP
COMMANDER BRAGG IS HERE, SO I'M GOING TO ANGRILY HANG UP ON YOU AND...
SOMEBODY BETTER TELL ME EXACTLY WHAT IS GOING ON!
WEEE-OOP
AND TURN OFF THAT DANG ALARM!!

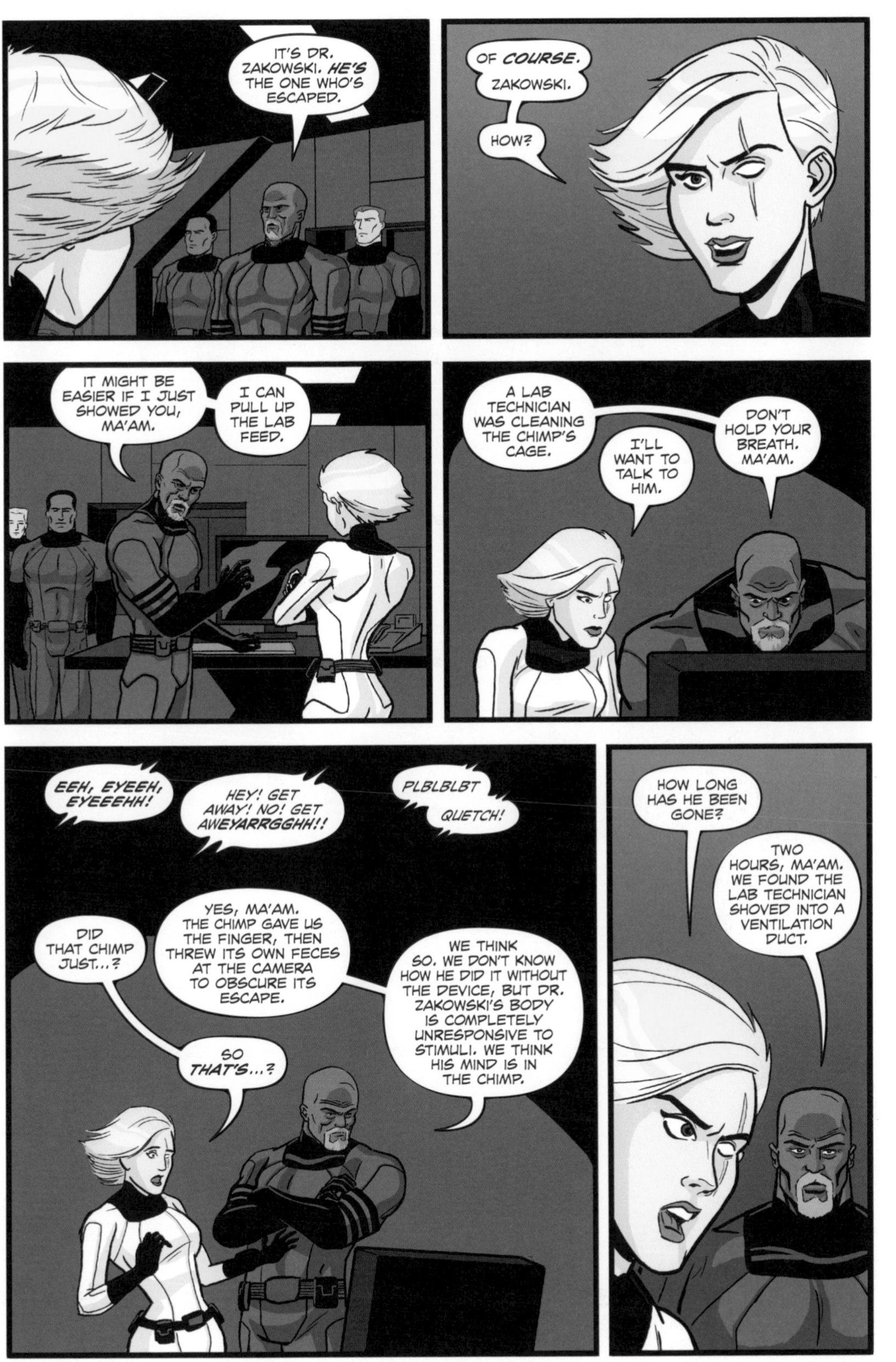
IT'S DR. ZAKOWSKI. HE'S THE ONE WHO'S ESCAPED.
OF COURSE.
ZAKOWSKI.
HOW?
IT MIGHT BE EASIER IF I JUST SHOWED YOU, MA'AM.
I CAN PULL UP THE LAB FEED.
A LAB TECHNICIAN WAS CLEANING THE CHIMP'S CAGE.
I'LL WANT TO TALK TO HIM.
DON'T HOLD YOUR BREATH. MA'AM.
EEH, EYEEH, EYEEEHH!
HEY! GET AWAY! NO! GET AWEYARRGGHH!!
PLBLBLBT
QUETCH!
DID THAT CHIMP JUST...?
YES, MA'AM. THE CHIMP GAVE US THE FINGER, THEN THREW ITS OWN FECES AT THE CAMERA TO OBSCURE ITS ESCAPE.
SO THAT'S...?
WE THINK SO. WE DON'T KNOW HOW HE DID IT WITHOUT THE DEVICE, BUT DR. ZAKOWSKI'S BODY IS COMPLETELY UNRESPONSIVE TO STIMULI. WE THINK HIS MIND IS IN THE CHIMP.
HOW LONG HAS HE BEEN GONE?
TWO HOURS, MA'AM. WE FOUND THE LAB TECHNICIAN SHOVED INTO A VENTILATION DUCT.

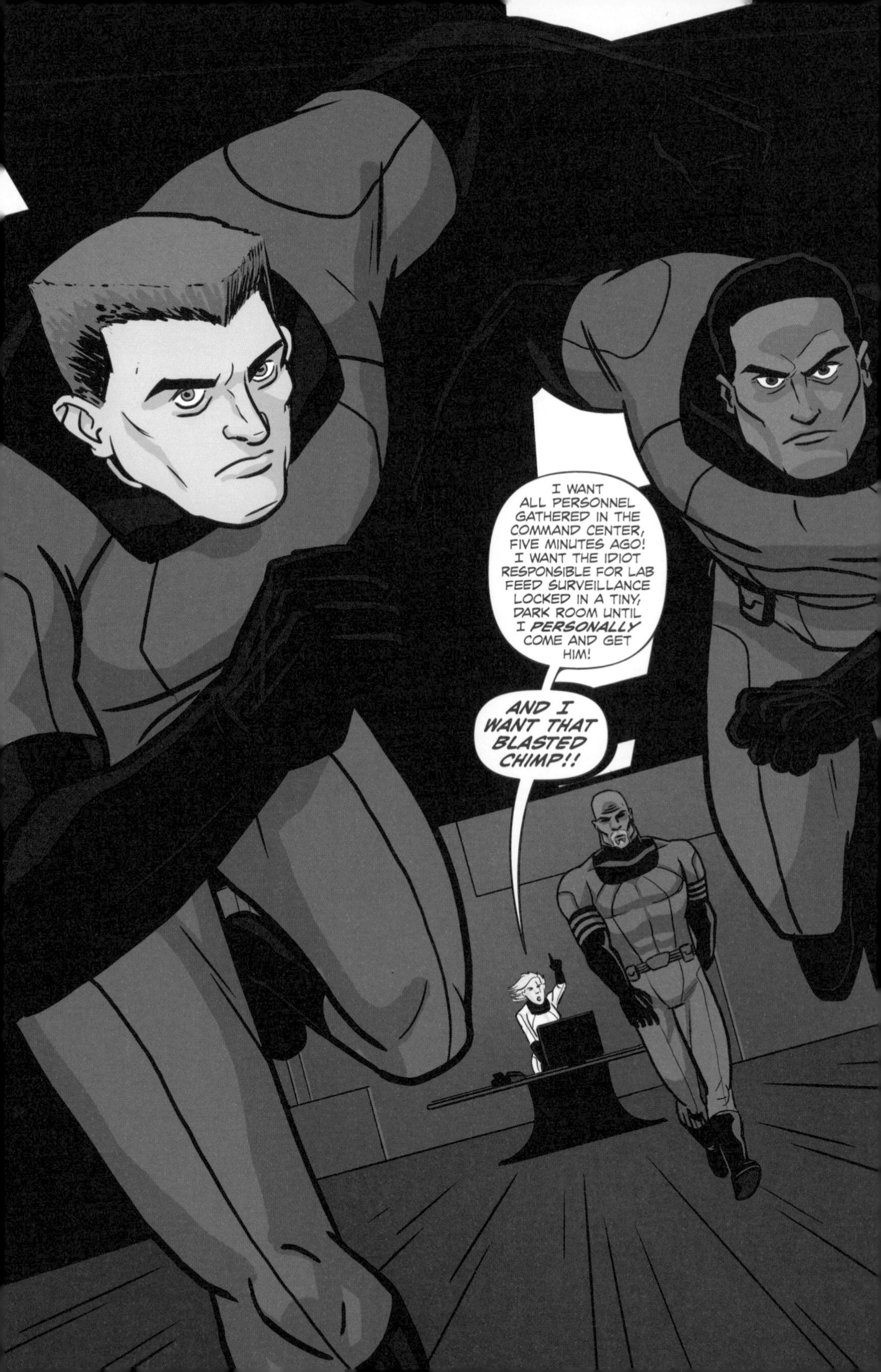
I WANT ALL PERSONNEL GATHERED IN THE COMMAND CENTER, FIVE MINUTES AGO! I WANT THE IDIOT RESPONSIBLE FOR LAB FEED SURVEILLANCE LOCKED IN A TINY, DARK ROOM UNTIL I *PERSONALLY* COME AND GET HIM!
AND I WANT THAT BLASTED CHIMP!!

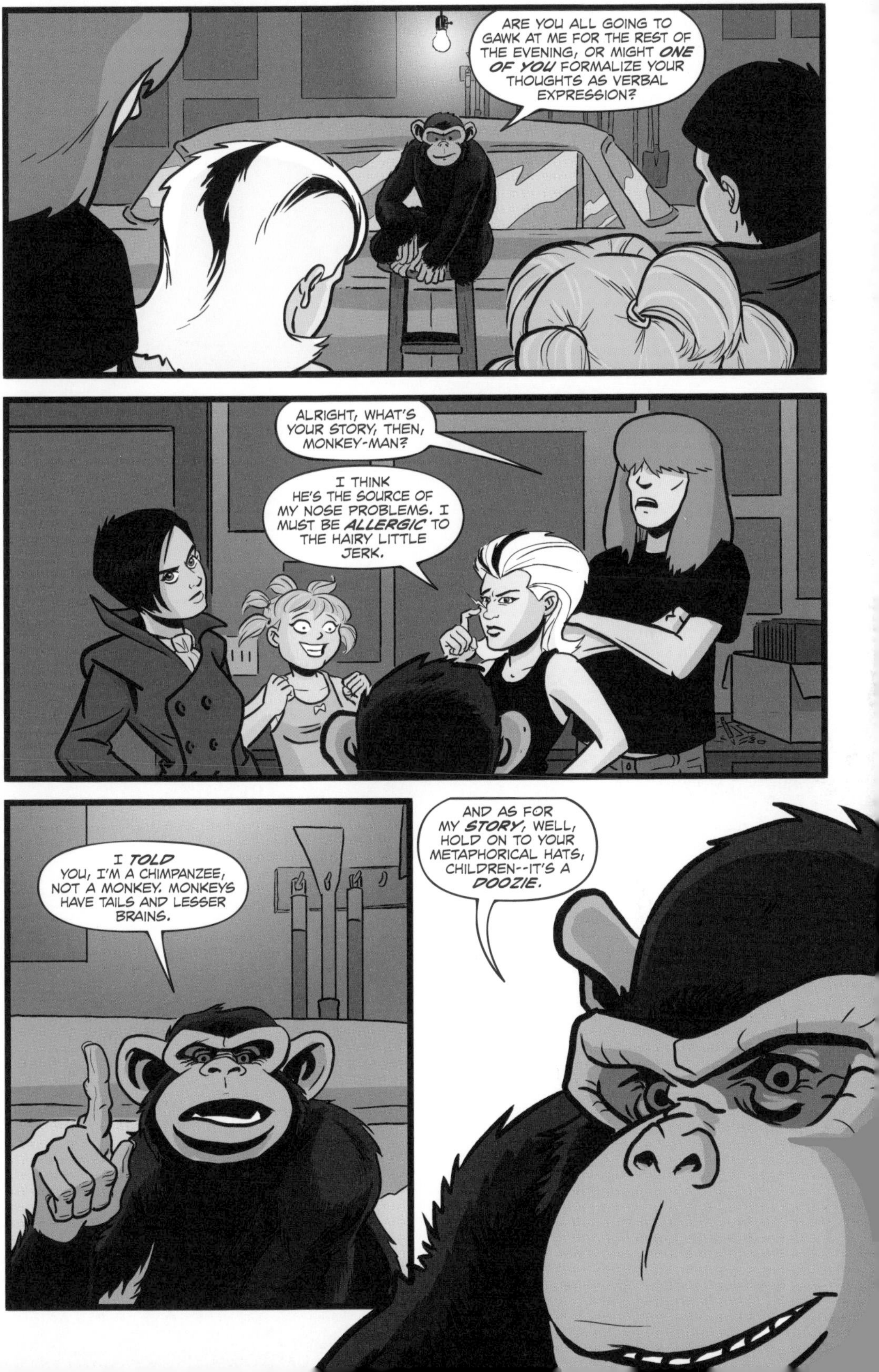
ARE YOU ALL GOING TO GAWK AT ME FOR THE REST OF THE EVENING, OR MIGHT ONE OF YOU FORMALIZE YOUR THOUGHTS AS VERBAL EXPRESSION?
ALRIGHT, WHAT'S YOUR STORY, THEN, MONKEY-MAN?
I THINK HE'S THE SOURCE OF MY NOSE PROBLEMS. I MUST BE ALLERGIC TO THE HAIRY LITTLE JERK.
I TOLD YOU, I'M A CHIMPANZEE, NOT A MONKEY. MONKEYS HAVE TAILS AND LESSER BRAINS.
AND AS FOR MY STORY, WELL, HOLD ON TO YOUR METAPHORICAL HATS, CHILDREN--IT'S A DOOZIE.

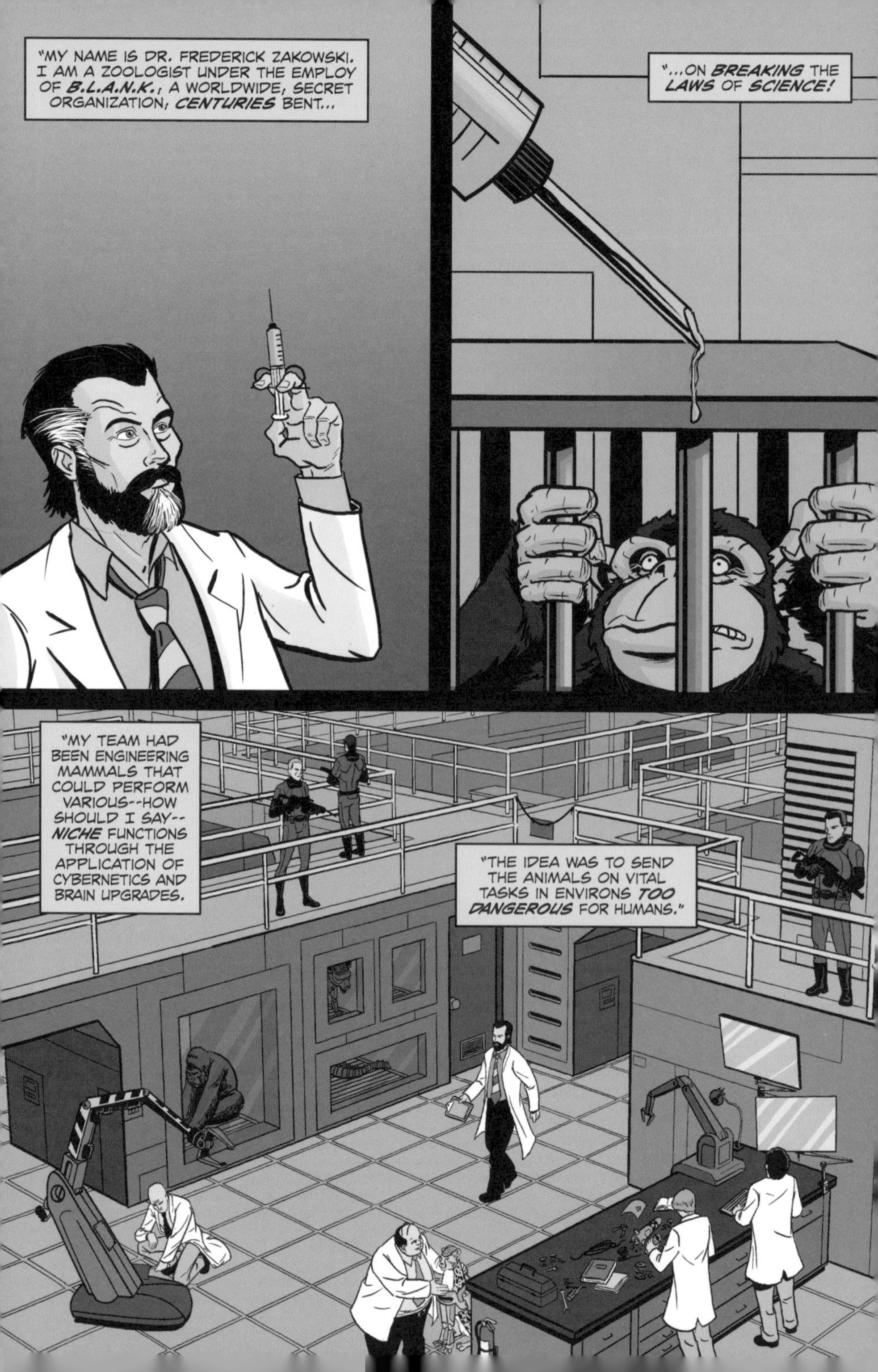
"MY NAME IS DR. FREDERICK ZAKOWSKI. I AM A ZOOLOGIST UNDER THE EMPLOY OF B.L.A.N.K., A WORLDWIDE, SECRET ORGANIZATION, CENTURIES BENT...
"...ON BREAKING THE LAWS OF SCIENCE!
"MY TEAM HAD BEEN ENGINEERING MAMMALS THAT COULD PERFORM VARIOUS--HOW SHOULD I SAY--NICHE FUNCTIONS THROUGH THE APPLICATION OF CYBERNETICS AND BRAIN UPGRADES.
"THE IDEA WAS TO SEND THE ANIMALS ON VITAL TASKS IN ENVIRONS TOO DANGEROUS FOR HUMANS."

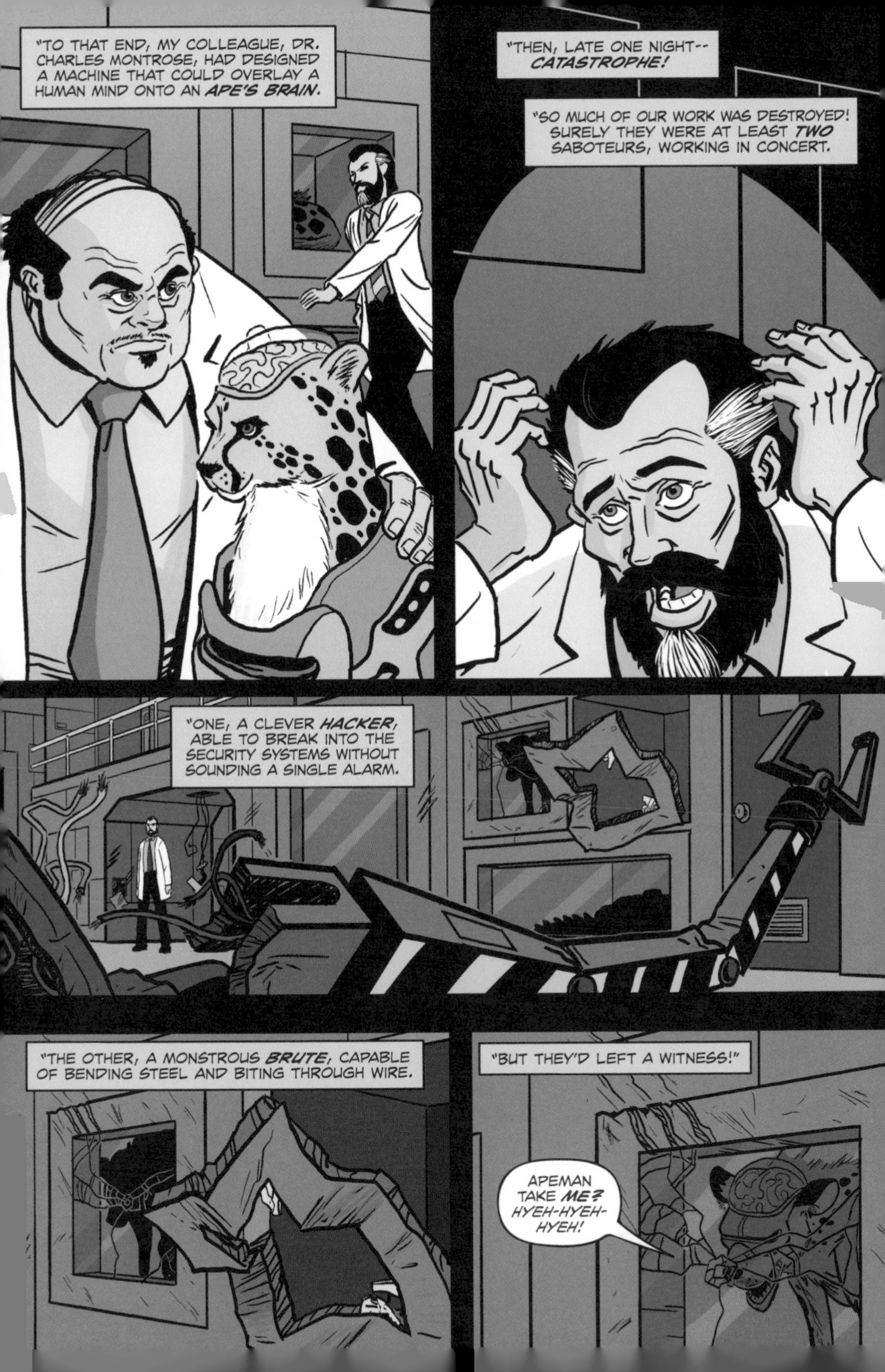
"TO THAT END, MY COLLEAGUE, DR. CHARLES MONTROSE, HAD DESIGNED A MACHINE THAT COULD OVERLAY A HUMAN MIND ONTO AN *APE'S BRAIN*.
"THEN, LATE ONE NIGHT-- *CATASTROPHE!*
"SO MUCH OF OUR WORK WAS DESTROYED! SURELY THEY WERE AT LEAST *TWO* SABOTEURS, WORKING IN CONCERT.
"ONE, A CLEVER *HACKER*, ABLE TO BREAK INTO THE SECURITY SYSTEMS WITHOUT SOUNDING A SINGLE ALARM.
"THE OTHER, A MONSTROUS *BRUTE*, CAPABLE OF BENDING STEEL AND BITING THROUGH WIRE.
"BUT THEY'D LEFT A WITNESS!"
APEMAN TAKE *ME? HYEH-HYEH-HYEH!*

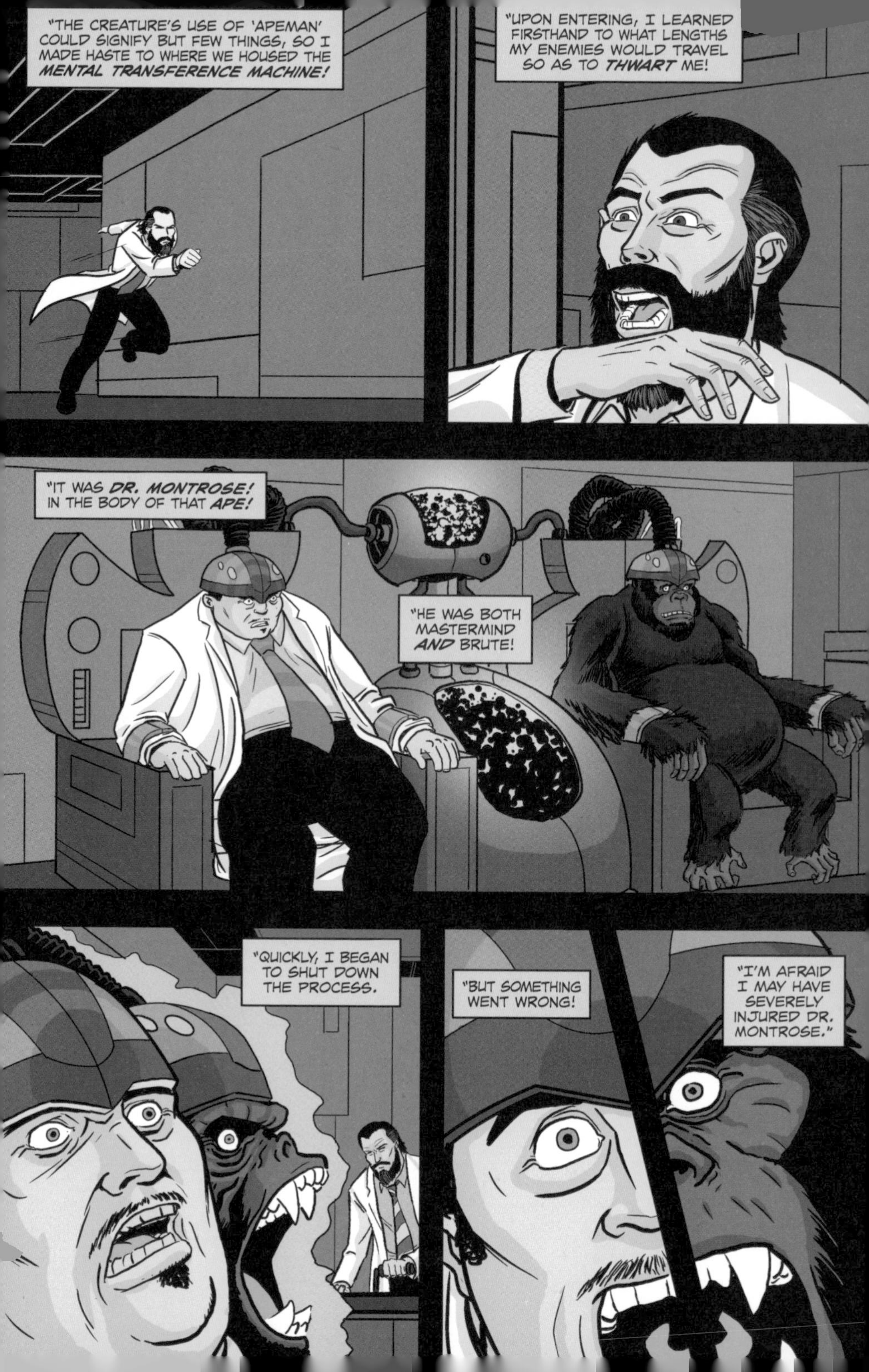

"THE CREATURE'S USE OF 'APEMAN' COULD SIGNIFY BUT FEW THINGS, SO I MADE HASTE TO WHERE WE HOUSED THE *MENTAL TRANSFERENCE MACHINE!*
"UPON ENTERING, I LEARNED FIRSTHAND TO WHAT LENGTHS MY ENEMIES WOULD TRAVEL SO AS TO *THWART* ME!
"IT WAS *DR. MONTROSE!* IN THE BODY OF THAT *APE!*
"HE WAS BOTH MASTERMIND *AND* BRUTE!
"QUICKLY, I BEGAN TO SHUT DOWN THE PROCESS.
"BUT SOMETHING WENT WRONG!
"I'M AFRAID I MAY HAVE SEVERELY INJURED DR. MONTROSE."

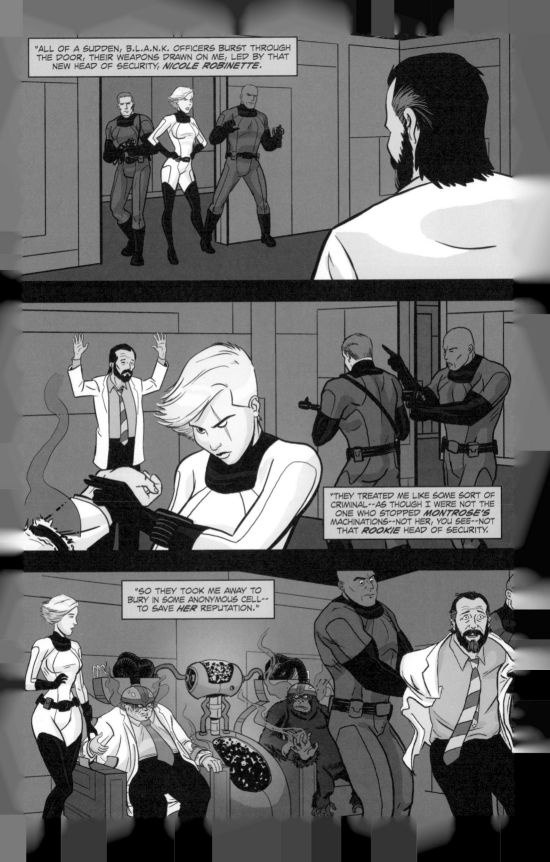

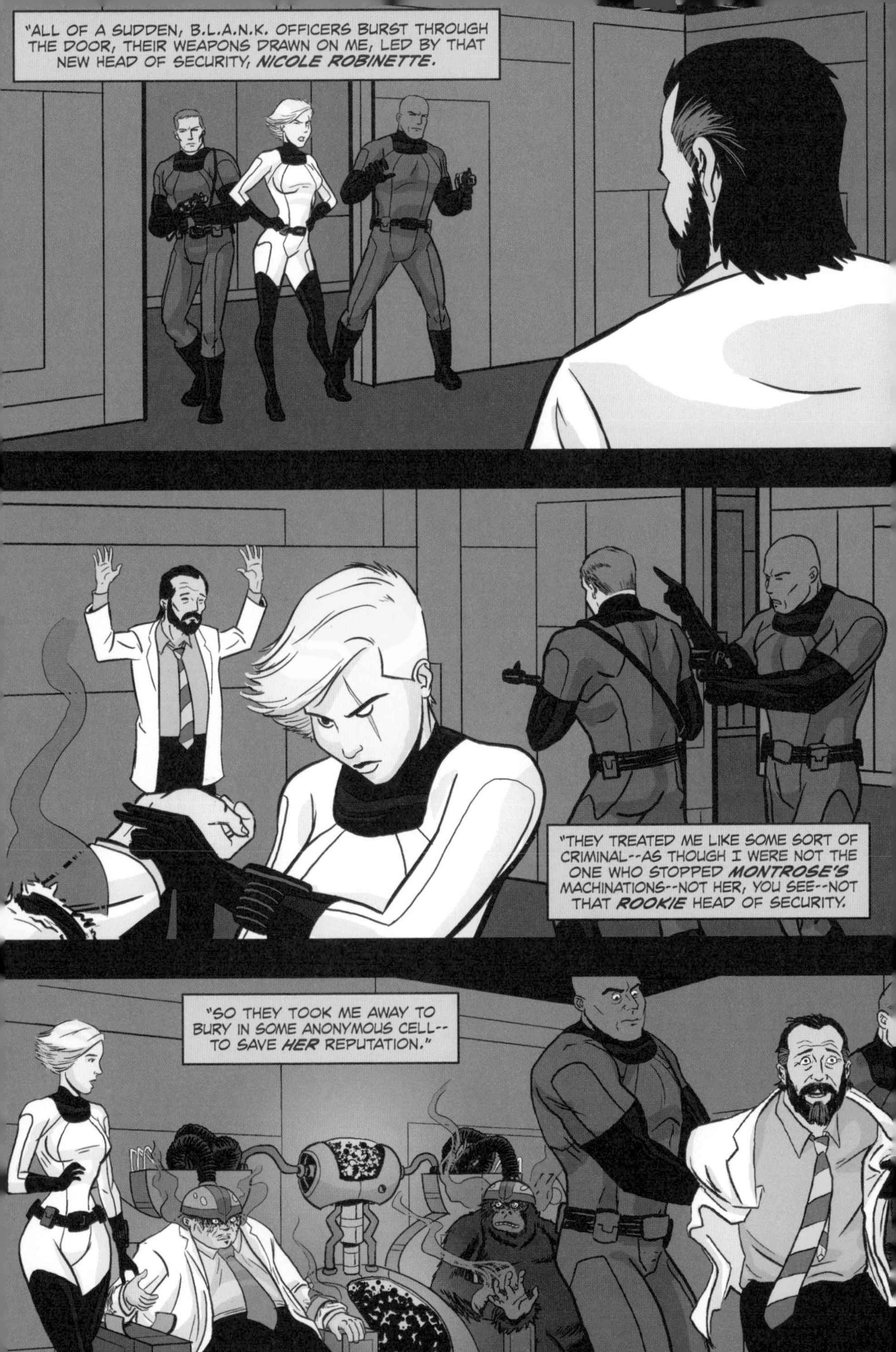
"ALL OF A SUDDEN, B.L.A.N.K. OFFICERS BURST THROUGH THE DOOR, THEIR WEAPONS DRAWN ON ME, LED BY THAT NEW HEAD OF SECURITY, NICOLE ROBINETTE.
"THEY TREATED ME LIKE SOME SORT OF CRIMINAL--AS THOUGH I WERE NOT THE ONE WHO STOPPED MONTROSE'S MACHINATIONS--NOT HER, YOU SEE--NOT THAT ROOKIE HEAD OF SECURITY.
"SO THEY TOOK ME AWAY TO BURY IN SOME ANONYMOUS CELL-- TO SAVE HER REPUTATION."

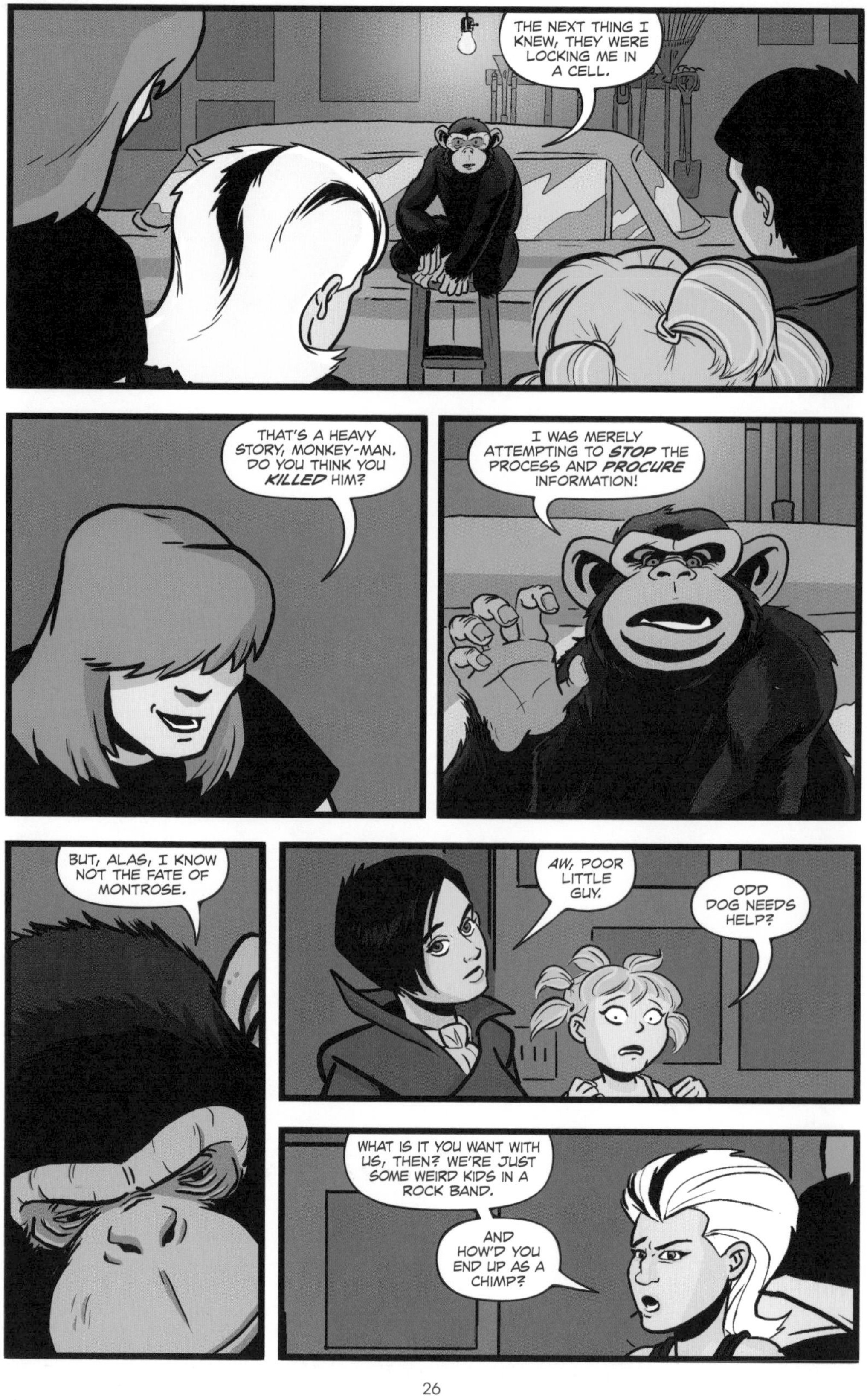
THE NEXT THING I KNEW, THEY WERE LOCKING ME IN A CELL.
THAT'S A HEAVY STORY, MONKEY-MAN. DO YOU THINK YOU *KILLED* HIM?
I WAS MERELY ATTEMPTING TO *STOP* THE PROCESS AND *PROCURE* INFORMATION!
BUT, ALAS, I KNOW NOT THE FATE OF MONTROSE.
AW, POOR LITTLE GUY.
ODD DOG NEEDS HELP?
WHAT IS IT YOU WANT WITH US, THEN? WE'RE JUST SOME WEIRD KIDS IN A ROCK BAND.
AND HOW'D YOU END UP AS A CHIMP?

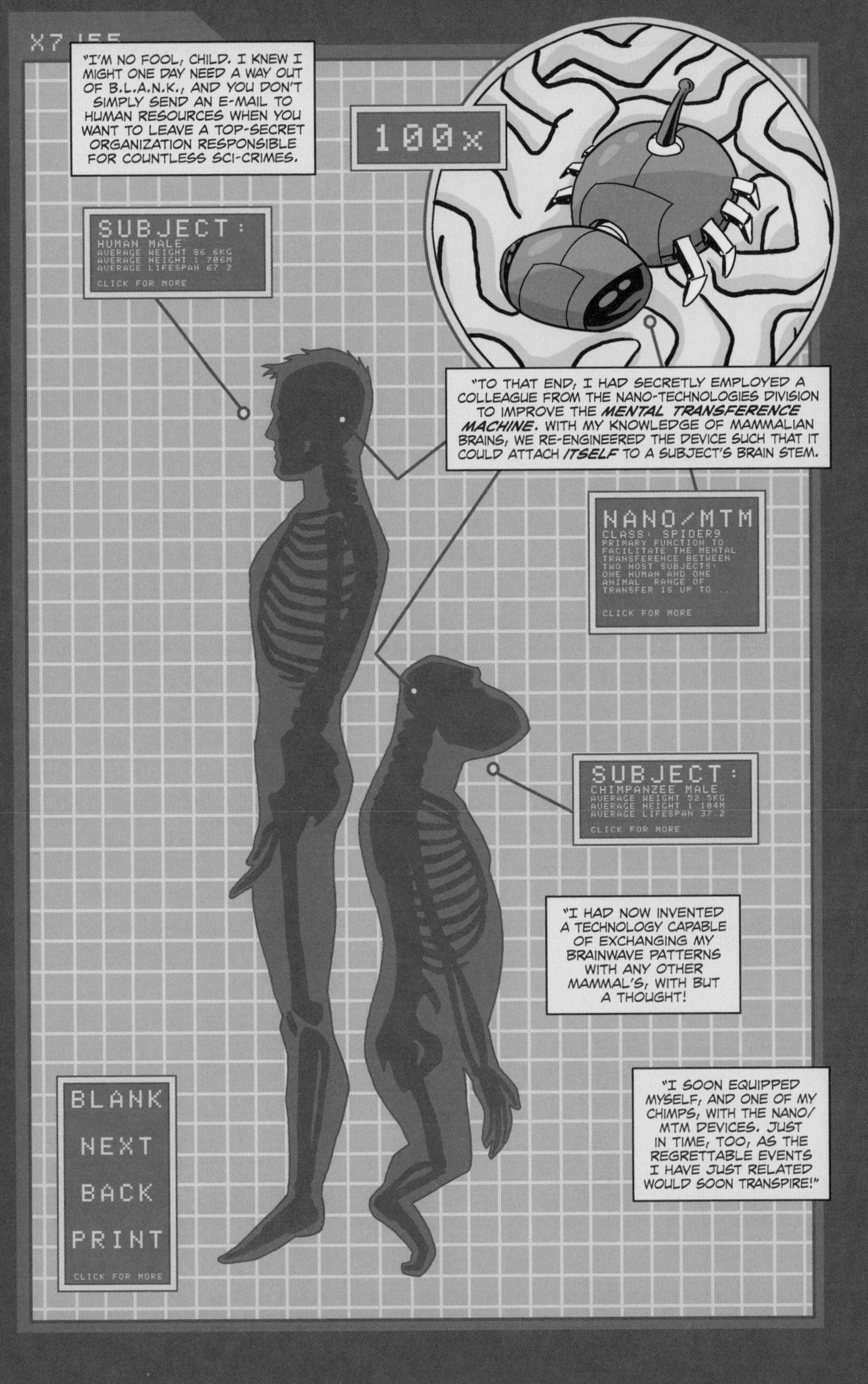
X7
"I'M NO FOOL, CHILD. I KNEW I MIGHT ONE DAY NEED A WAY OUT OF B.L.A.N.K., AND YOU DON'T SIMPLY SEND AN E-MAIL TO HUMAN RESOURCES WHEN YOU WANT TO LEAVE A TOP-SECRET ORGANIZATION RESPONSIBLE FOR COUNTLESS SCI-CRIMES.
100x
SUBJECT:
HUMAN MALE
AVERAGE WEIGHT 86.6KG
AVERAGE HEIGHT 1.706M
AVERAGE LIFESPAN 67.2
CLICK FOR MORE
"TO THAT END, I HAD SECRETLY EMPLOYED A COLLEAGUE FROM THE NANO-TECHNOLOGIES DIVISION TO IMPROVE THE *MENTAL TRANSFERENCE MACHINE*. WITH MY KNOWLEDGE OF MAMMALIAN BRAINS, WE RE-ENGINEERED THE DEVICE SUCH THAT IT COULD ATTACH *ITSELF* TO A SUBJECT'S BRAIN STEM.
NANO/MTM
CLASS: SPIDER9
PRIMARY FUNCTION TO FACILITATE THE MENTAL TRANSFERENCE BETWEEN TWO HOST SUBJECTS: ONE HUMAN AND ONE ANIMAL. RANGE OF TRANSFER IS UP TO...
CLICK FOR MORE
SUBJECT:
CHIMPANZEE MALE
AVERAGE WEIGHT 52.5KG
AVERAGE HEIGHT 1.104M
AVERAGE LIFESPAN 37.2
CLICK FOR MORE
"I HAD NOW INVENTED A TECHNOLOGY CAPABLE OF EXCHANGING MY BRAINWAVE PATTERNS WITH ANY OTHER MAMMAL'S, WITH BUT A THOUGHT!
BLANK
NEXT
BACK
PRINT
CLICK FOR MORE
"I SOON EQUIPPED MYSELF, AND ONE OF MY CHIMPS, WITH THE NANO/MTM DEVICES. JUST IN TIME, TOO, AS THE REGRETTABLE EVENTS I HAVE JUST RELATED WOULD SOON TRANSPIRE!"

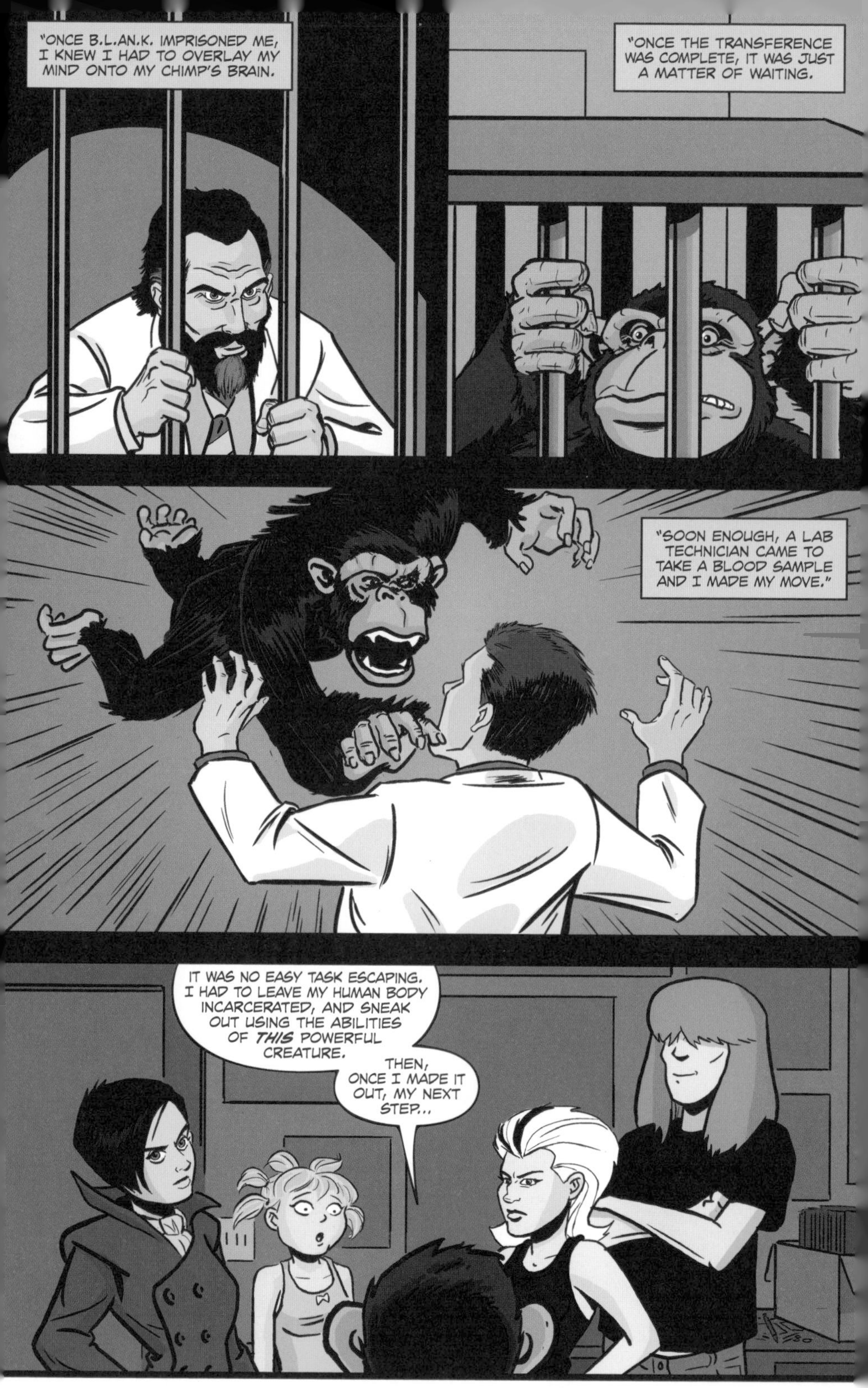
"ONCE B.L.AN.K. IMPRISONED ME, I KNEW I HAD TO OVERLAY MY MIND ONTO MY CHIMP'S BRAIN.
"ONCE THE TRANSFERENCE WAS COMPLETE, IT WAS JUST A MATTER OF WAITING.
"SOON ENOUGH, A LAB TECHNICIAN CAME TO TAKE A BLOOD SAMPLE AND I MADE MY MOVE."
IT WAS NO EASY TASK ESCAPING. I HAD TO LEAVE MY HUMAN BODY INCARCERATED, AND SNEAK OUT USING THE ABILITIES OF *THIS* POWERFUL CREATURE.
THEN, ONCE I MADE IT OUT, MY NEXT STEP...

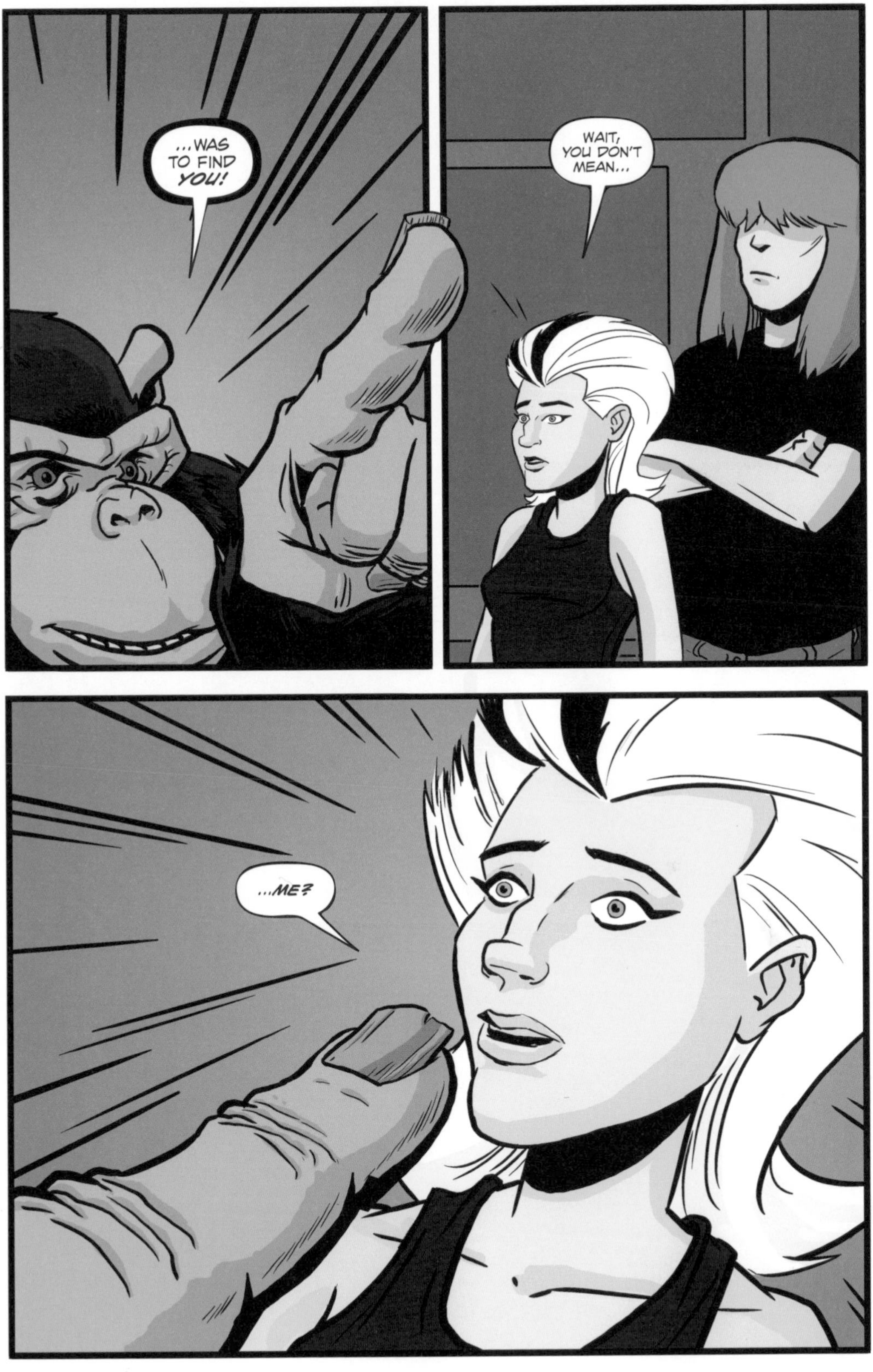
...WAS TO FIND *YOU!*
WAIT, YOU DON'T MEAN...
...*ME?*

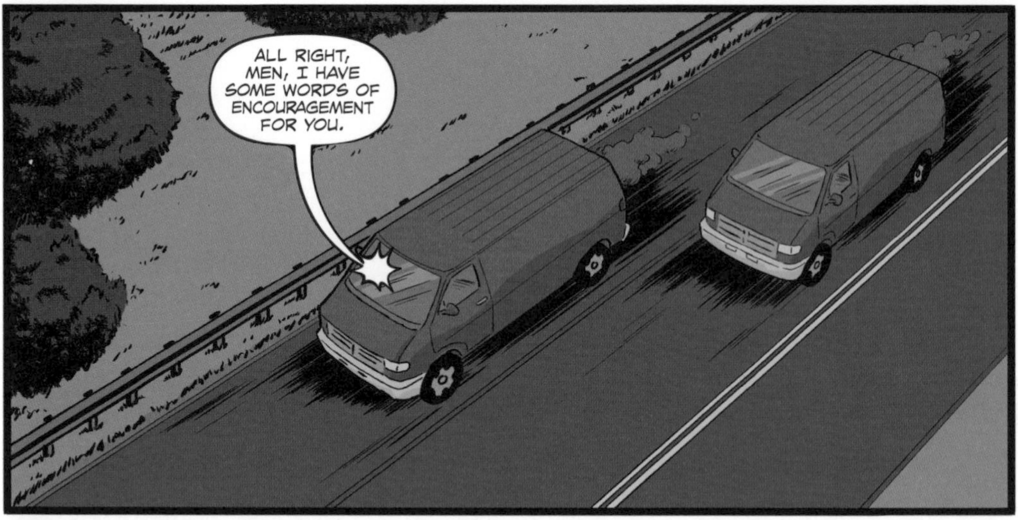
ALL RIGHT, MEN, I HAVE SOME WORDS OF ENCOURAGEMENT FOR YOU.

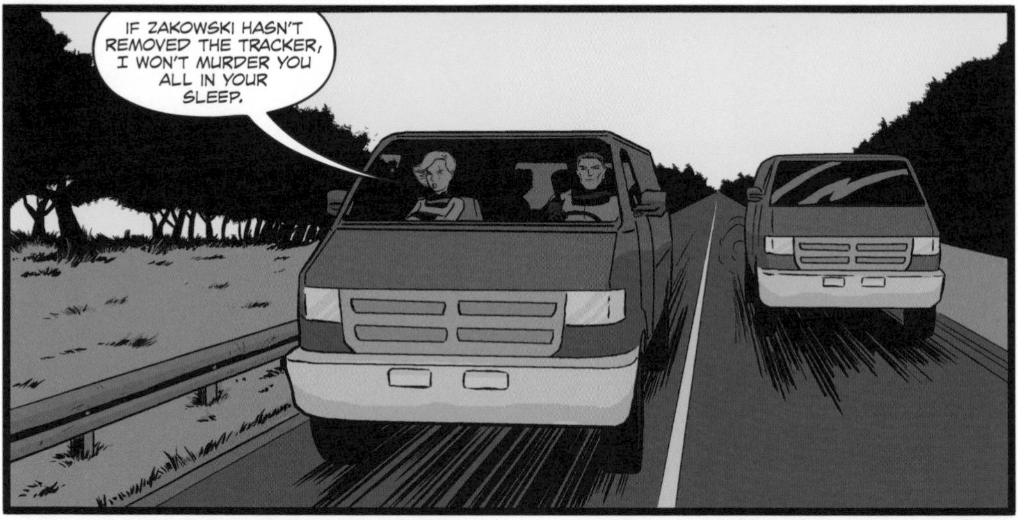
IF ZAKOWSKI HASN'T REMOVED THE TRACKER, I WON'T MURDER YOU ALL IN YOUR SLEEP.

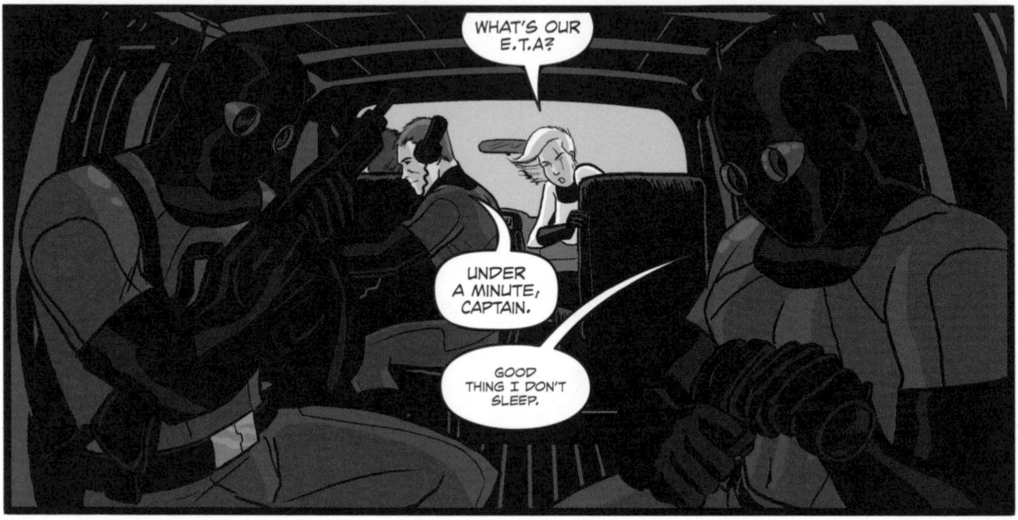
WHAT'S OUR E.T.A?
UNDER A MINUTE, CAPTAIN.
GOOD THING I DON'T SLEEP.

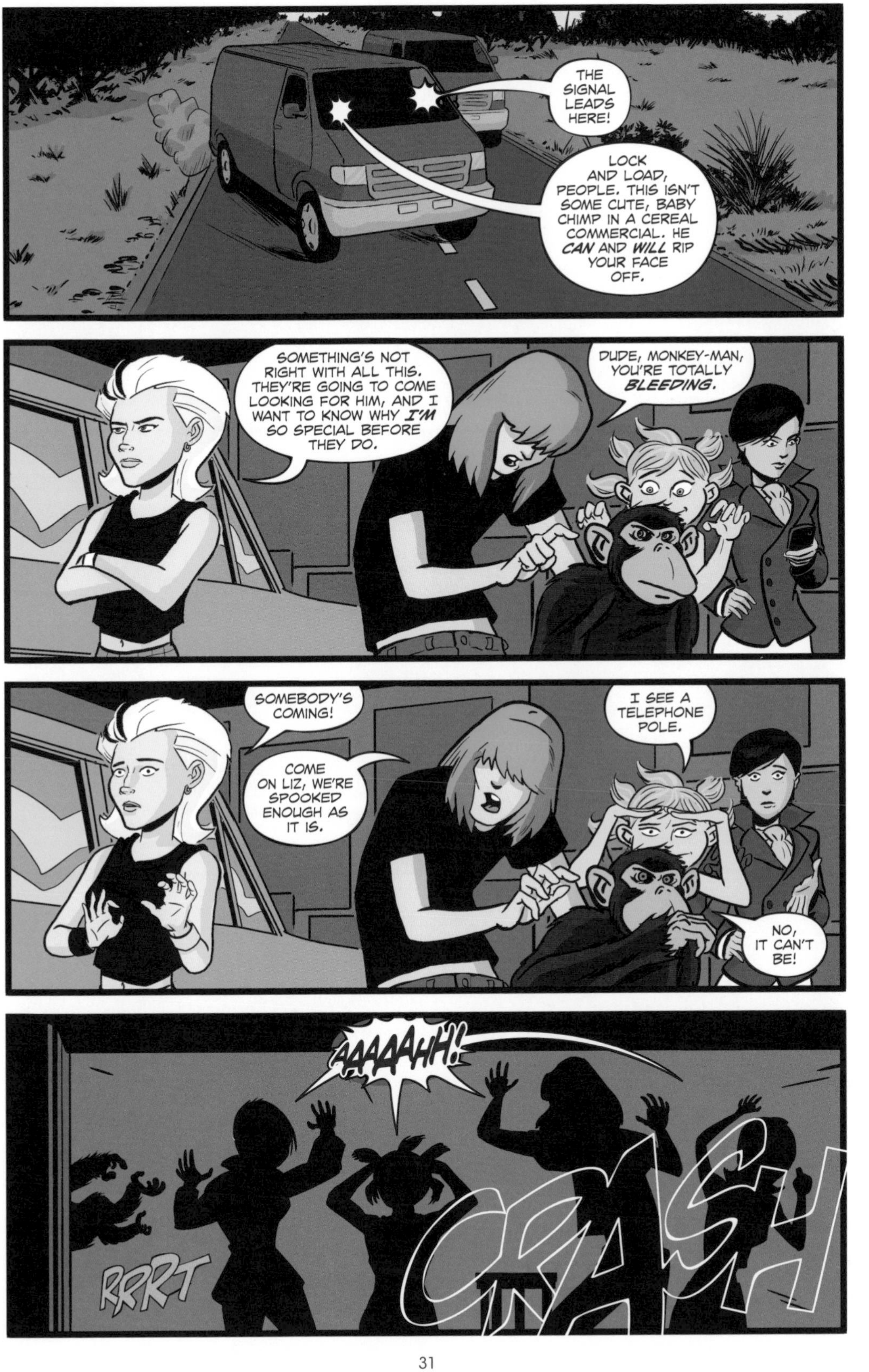
THE SIGNAL LEADS HERE!
LOCK AND LOAD, PEOPLE. THIS ISN'T SOME CUTE, BABY CHIMP IN A CEREAL COMMERCIAL. HE CAN AND WILL RIP YOUR FACE OFF.
SOMETHING'S NOT RIGHT WITH ALL THIS. THEY'RE GOING TO COME LOOKING FOR HIM, AND I WANT TO KNOW WHY I'M SO SPECIAL BEFORE THEY DO.
DUDE, MONKEY-MAN, YOU'RE TOTALLY BLEEDING.
SOMEBODY'S COMING!
COME ON LIZ, WE'RE SPOOKED ENOUGH AS IT IS.
I SEE A TELEPHONE POLE.
NO, IT CAN'T BE!
AAAAAHH!
RRRT
CRASH

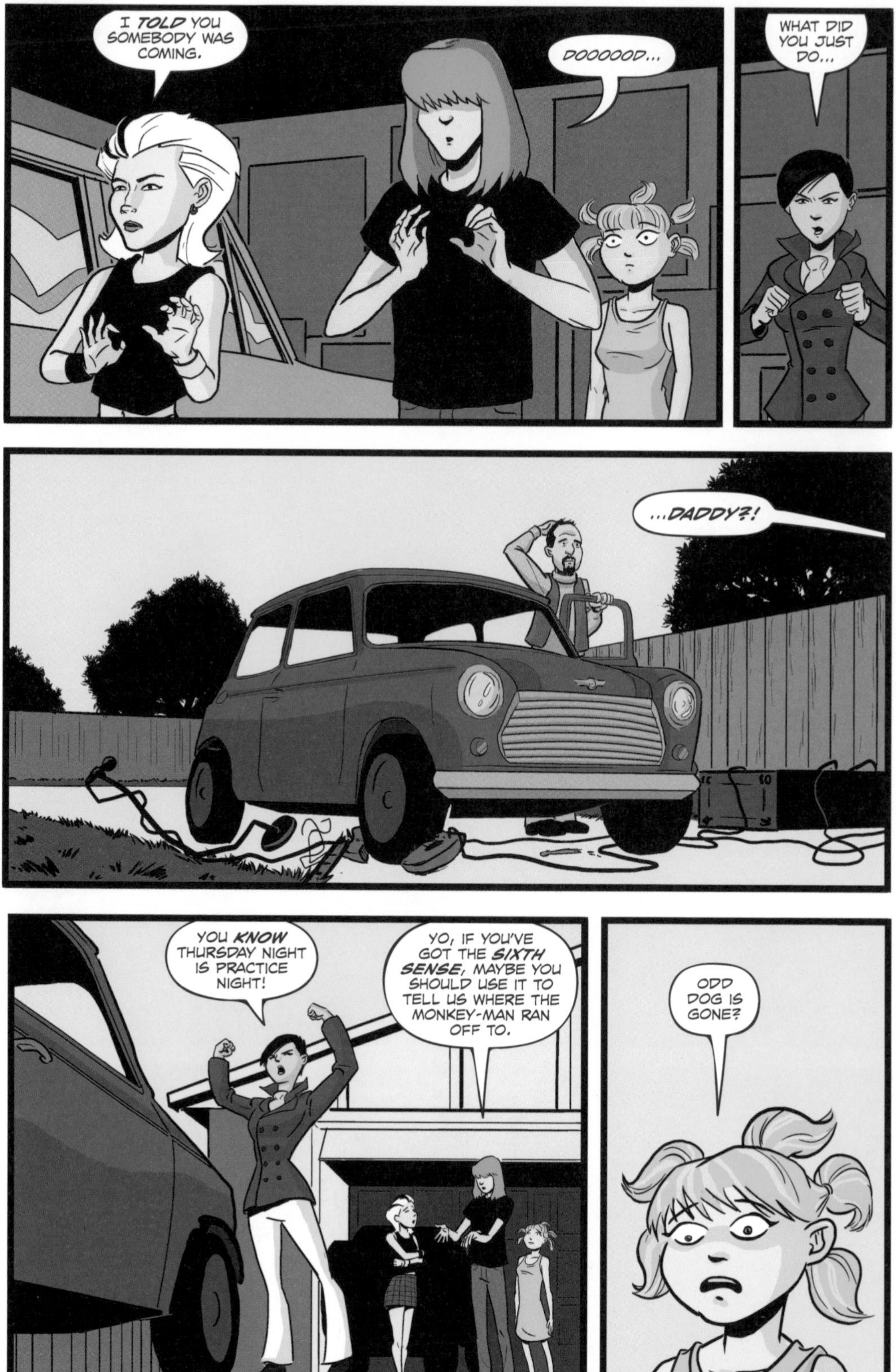
I TOLD YOU SOMEBODY WAS COMING.
DOOOOOD...
WHAT DID YOU JUST DO...
...DADDY?!
YOU KNOW THURSDAY NIGHT IS PRACTICE NIGHT!
YO, IF YOU'VE GOT THE SIXTH SENSE, MAYBE YOU SHOULD USE IT TO TELL US WHERE THE MONKEY-MAN RAN OFF TO.
ODD DOG IS GONE?

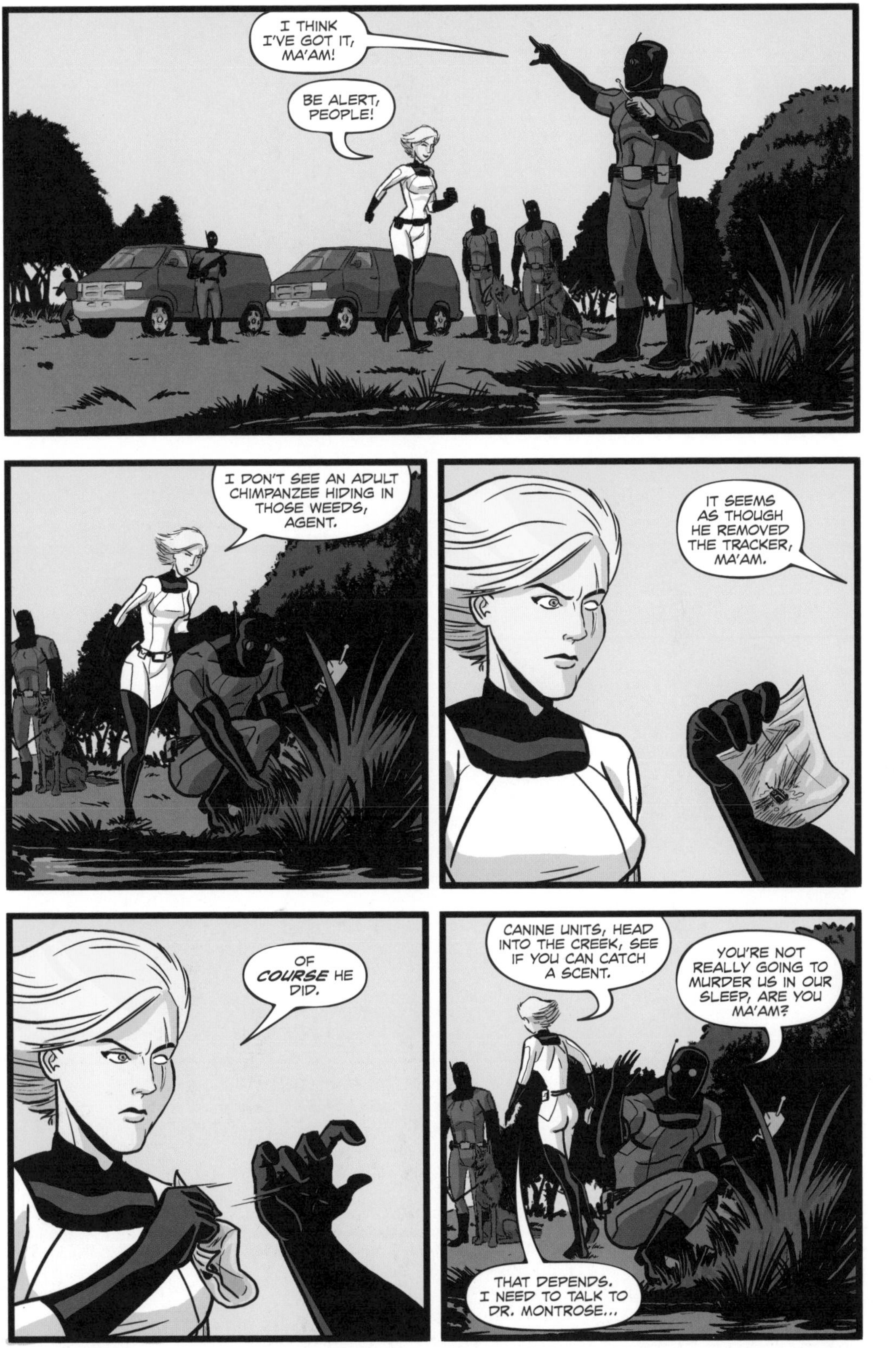
I THINK I'VE GOT IT, MA'AM!
BE ALERT, PEOPLE!
I DON'T SEE AN ADULT CHIMPANZEE HIDING IN THOSE WEEDS, AGENT.
IT SEEMS AS THOUGH HE REMOVED THE TRACKER, MA'AM.
OF *COURSE* HE DID.
CANINE UNITS, HEAD INTO THE CREEK, SEE IF YOU CAN CATCH A SCENT.
YOU'RE NOT REALLY GOING TO MURDER US IN OUR SLEEP, ARE YOU MA'AM?
THAT DEPENDS. I NEED TO TALK TO DR. MONTROSE...

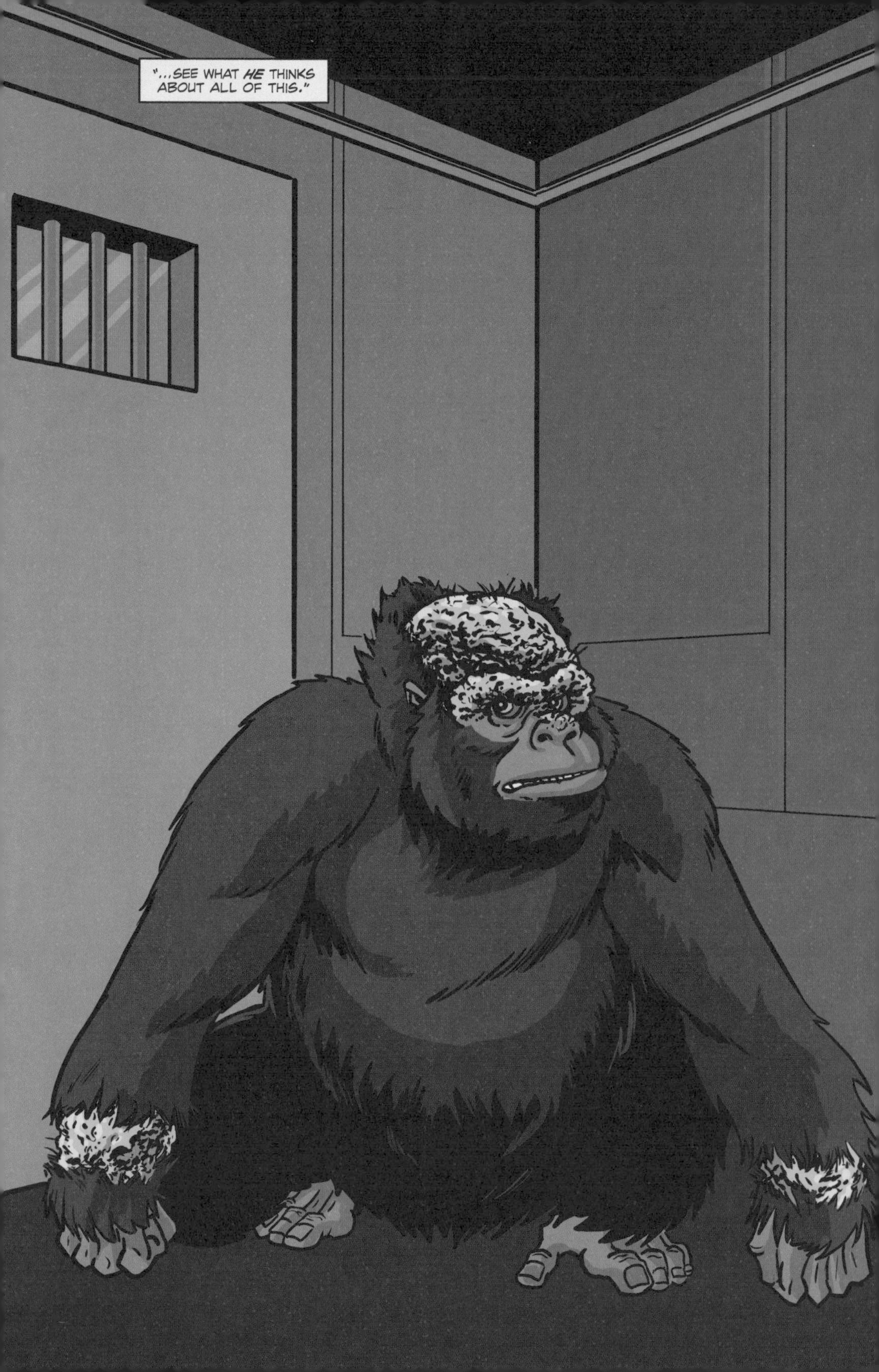
"...SEE WHAT HE THINKS ABOUT ALL OF THIS."

FRIDAY, 9:55 A.M.

BRRRRIINNNG

I'M A LITTLE WORRIED, GUYS. NONE OF THOSE JOCK TURDS WERE IN FIRST PERIOD.

MAYBE THEY'RE AFRAID TO SHOW THEIR NOW DISFIGURED FACES 'ROUND THESE PARTS.

IT'LL ALL BE *FINE.* THOSE GUYS GOT WHAT THEY DESERVED, AND *EVERYBODY* KNOWS IT.

VINES

I'M *TELLING YOU*, WE'RE GOING TO GET CALLED INTO DEAN ODEN'S OFFICE ANY MINUTE NOW. BESIDES, YOU *REALLY* HURT JOEY, MOD.

THEY WERE ON *MY* PROPERTY! IN TEXAS YOU CAN PRACTICALLY DO WHATEVER YOU WANT TO TRESPASSERS.

YEAH, LIZ. IT'S LIKE, *THE LAW.* WE'RE *TOTALLY* COOL.

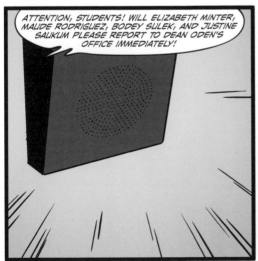

ATTENTION, STUDENTS! WILL ELIZABETH MINTER, MAUDE RODRIGUEZ, BODEY SULEK, AND JUSTINE SAUKUM PLEASE REPORT TO DEAN ODEN'S OFFICE IMMEDIATELY!

ALRIGHTY THEN. NOBODY MENTION THE TALKING CHIMP.

I'M GETTING A LITTLE SICK OF YOU ALWAYS BEING RIGHT.

35

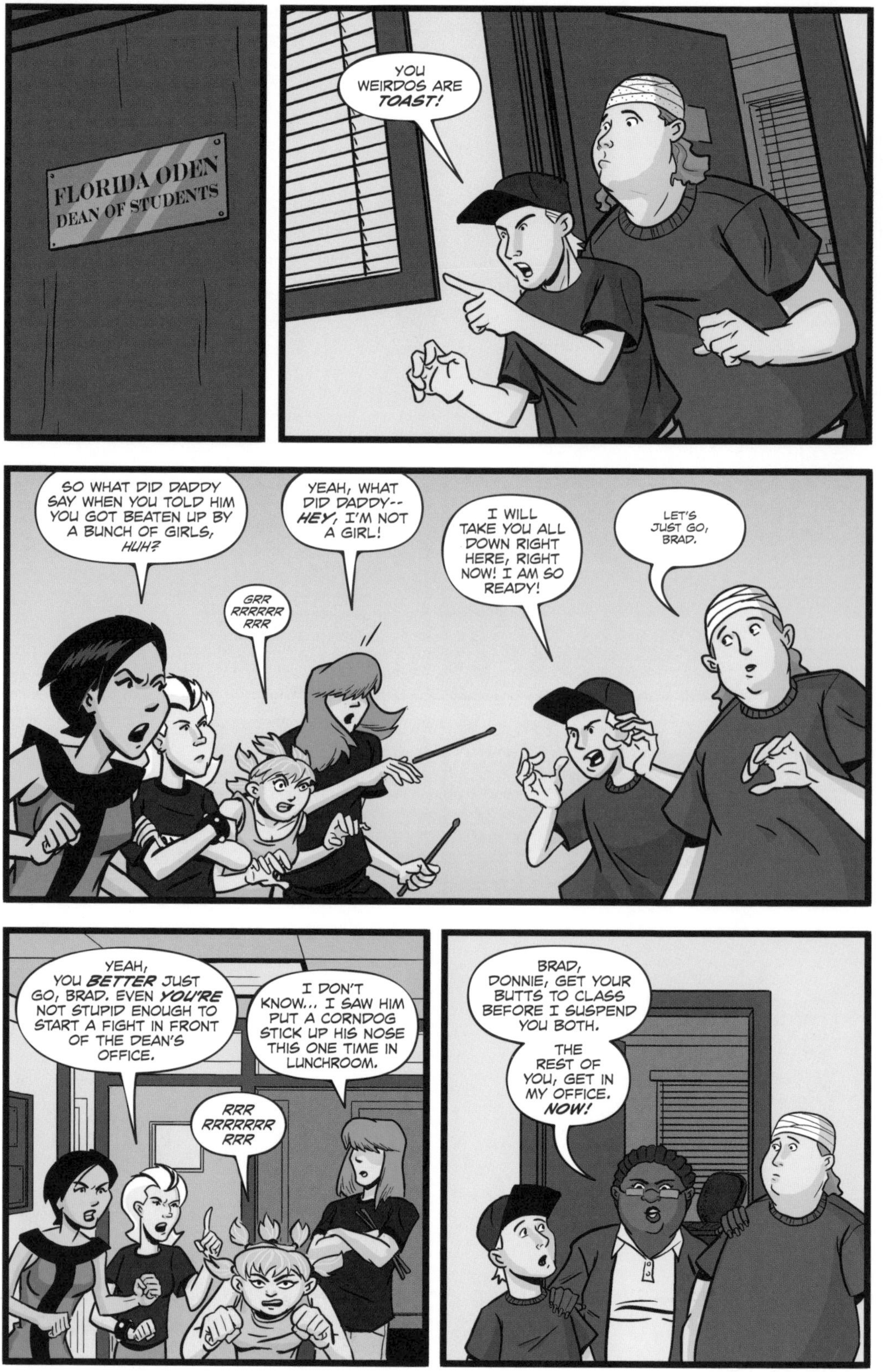
FLORIDA ODEN
DEAN OF STUDENTS
YOU WEIRDOS ARE TOAST!
SO WHAT DID DADDY SAY WHEN YOU TOLD HIM YOU GOT BEATEN UP BY A BUNCH OF GIRLS, HUH?
GRR RRRRRR RRR
YEAH, WHAT DID DADDY-- HEY, I'M NOT A GIRL!
I WILL TAKE YOU ALL DOWN RIGHT HERE, RIGHT NOW! I AM SO READY!
LET'S JUST GO, BRAD.
YEAH, YOU BETTER JUST GO, BRAD. EVEN YOU'RE NOT STUPID ENOUGH TO START A FIGHT IN FRONT OF THE DEAN'S OFFICE.
I DON'T KNOW... I SAW HIM PUT A CORNDOG STICK UP HIS NOSE THIS ONE TIME IN LUNCHROOM.
RRR RRRRRRR RRR
BRAD, DONNIE, GET YOUR BUTTS TO CLASS BEFORE I SUSPEND YOU BOTH.
THE REST OF YOU, GET IN MY OFFICE. NOW!

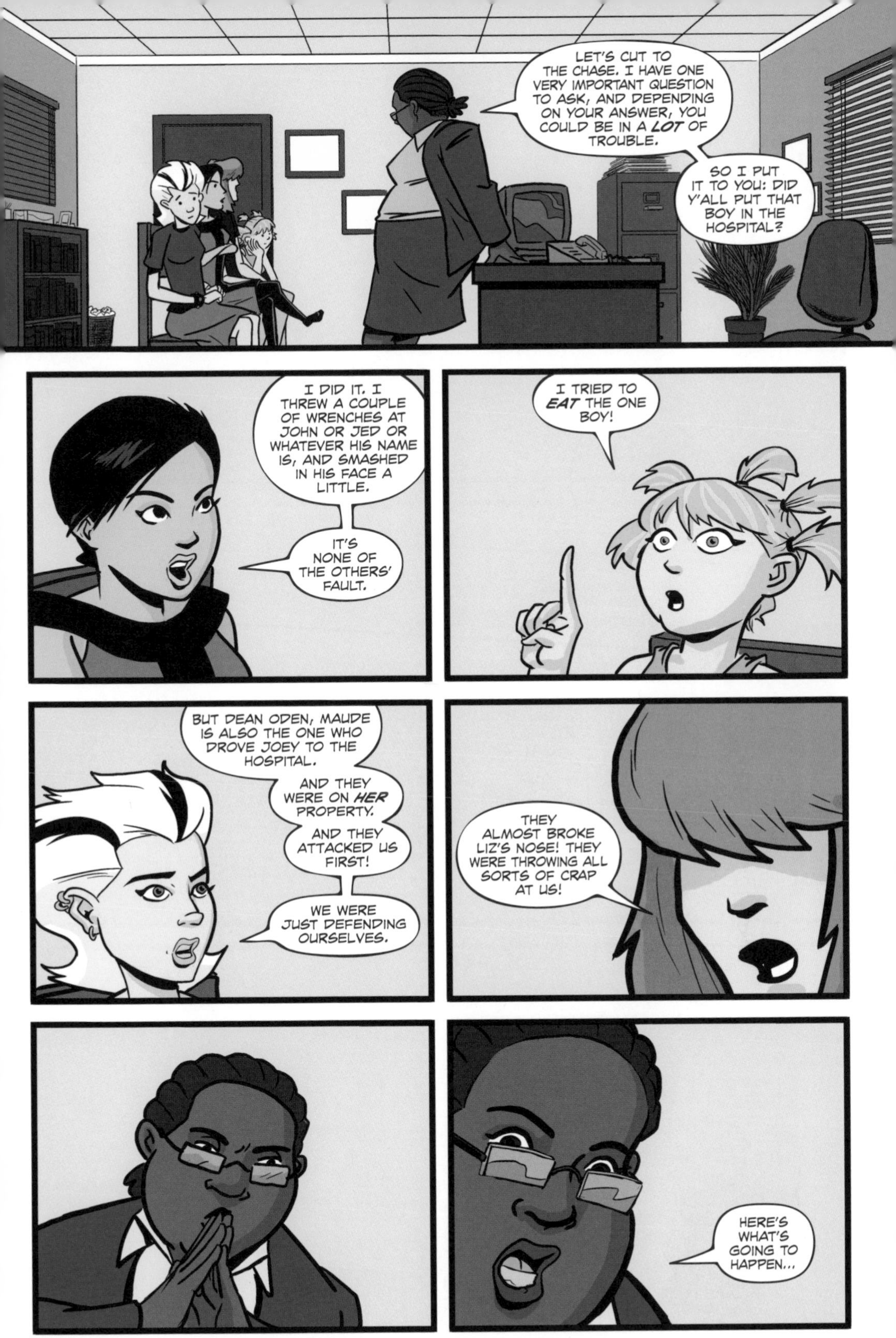
LET'S CUT TO THE CHASE. I HAVE ONE VERY IMPORTANT QUESTION TO ASK, AND DEPENDING ON YOUR ANSWER, YOU COULD BE IN A *LOT* OF TROUBLE.
SO I PUT IT TO YOU: DID Y'ALL PUT THAT BOY IN THE HOSPITAL?
I DID IT. I THREW A COUPLE OF WRENCHES AT JOHN OR JED OR WHATEVER HIS NAME IS, AND SMASHED IN HIS FACE A LITTLE.
IT'S NONE OF THE OTHERS' FAULT.
I TRIED TO *EAT* THE ONE BOY!
BUT DEAN ODEN, MAUDE IS ALSO THE ONE WHO DROVE JOEY TO THE HOSPITAL.
AND THEY WERE ON *HER* PROPERTY.
AND THEY ATTACKED US FIRST!
WE WERE JUST DEFENDING OURSELVES.
THEY ALMOST BROKE LIZ'S NOSE! THEY WERE THROWING ALL SORTS OF CRAP AT US!
HERE'S WHAT'S GOING TO HAPPEN...

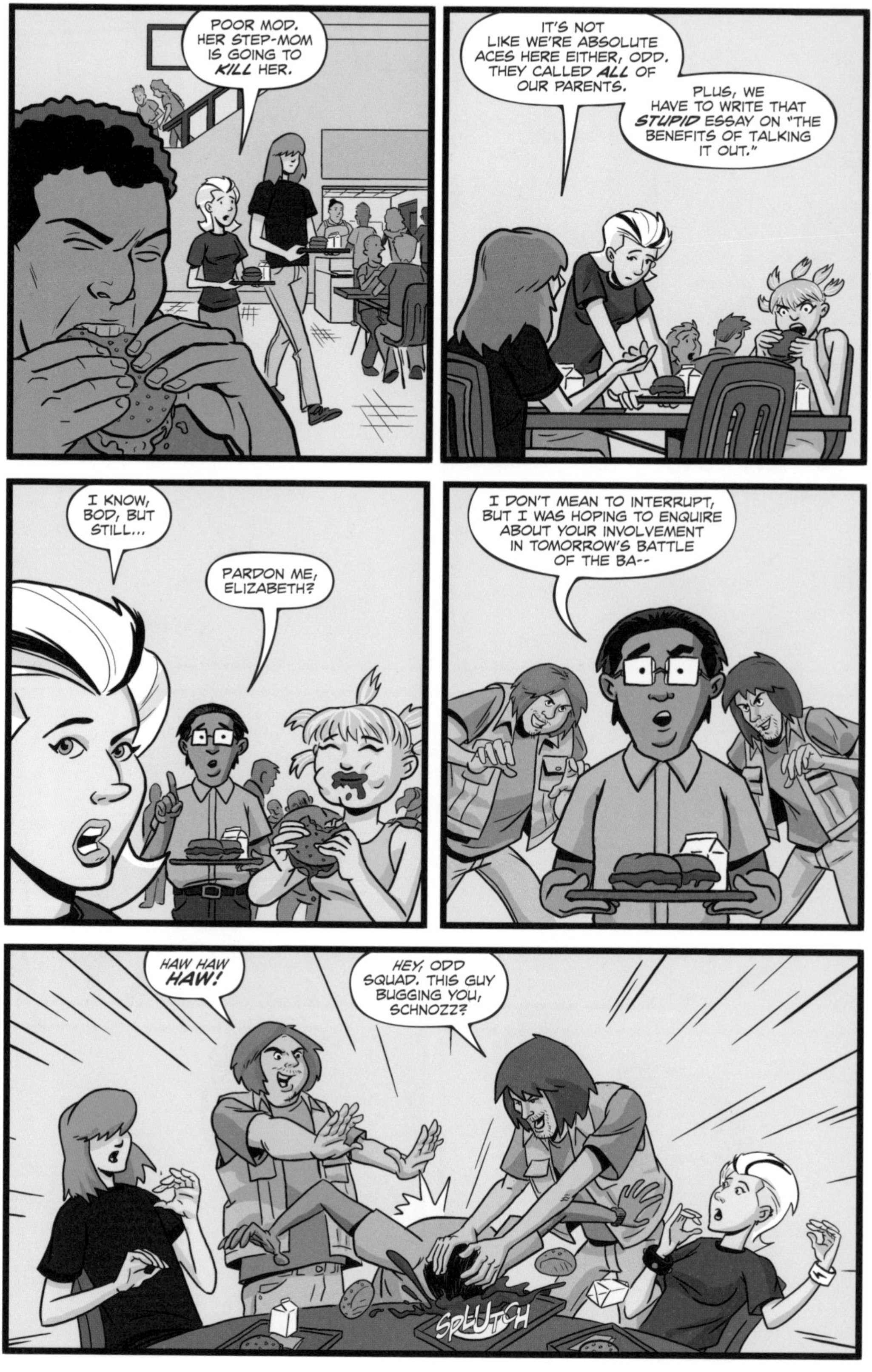
POOR MOD. HER STEP-MOM IS GOING TO *KILL* HER.
IT'S NOT LIKE WE'RE ABSOLUTE ACES HERE EITHER, ODD. THEY CALLED *ALL* OF OUR PARENTS.
PLUS, WE HAVE TO WRITE THAT *STUPID* ESSAY ON "THE BENEFITS OF TALKING IT OUT."
I KNOW, BOD, BUT STILL...
PARDON ME, ELIZABETH?
I DON'T MEAN TO INTERRUPT, BUT I WAS HOPING TO ENQUIRE ABOUT YOUR INVOLVEMENT IN TOMORROW'S BATTLE OF THE BA--
HAW HAW HAW!
HEY, ODD SQUAD. THIS GUY BUGGING YOU, SCHNOZZ?
SPLUTCH

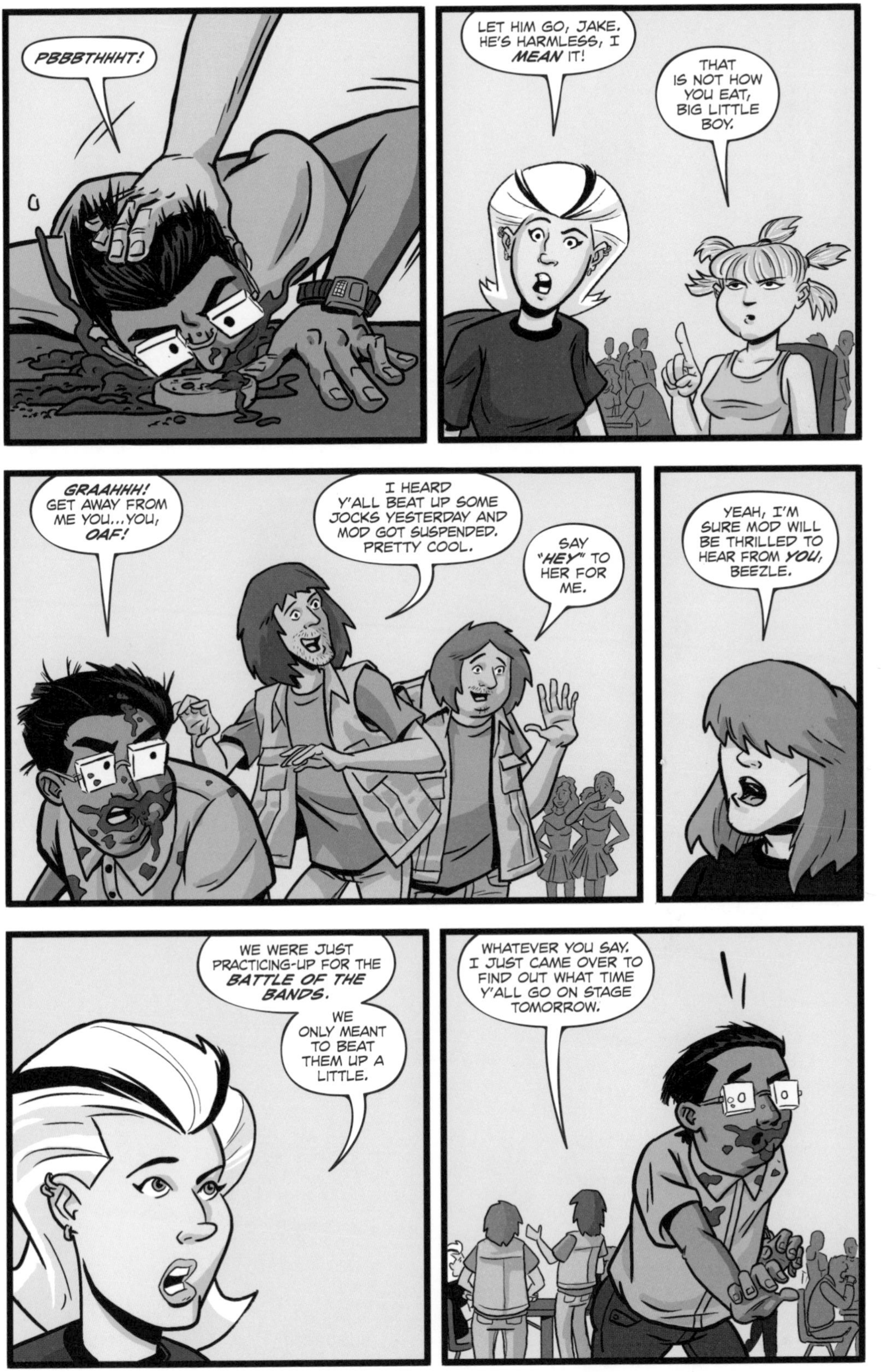
PBBBTHHHT!
LET HIM GO, JAKE. HE'S HARMLESS, I MEAN IT!
THAT IS NOT HOW YOU EAT, BIG LITTLE BOY.
GRAAHHH! GET AWAY FROM ME YOU...YOU, OAF!
I HEARD Y'ALL BEAT UP SOME JOCKS YESTERDAY AND MOD GOT SUSPENDED. PRETTY COOL.
SAY "HEY" TO HER FOR ME.
YEAH, I'M SURE MOD WILL BE THRILLED TO HEAR FROM YOU, BEEZLE.
WE WERE JUST PRACTICING-UP FOR THE BATTLE OF THE BANDS.
WE ONLY MEANT TO BEAT THEM UP A LITTLE.
WHATEVER YOU SAY. I JUST CAME OVER TO FIND OUT WHAT TIME Y'ALL GO ON STAGE TOMORROW.

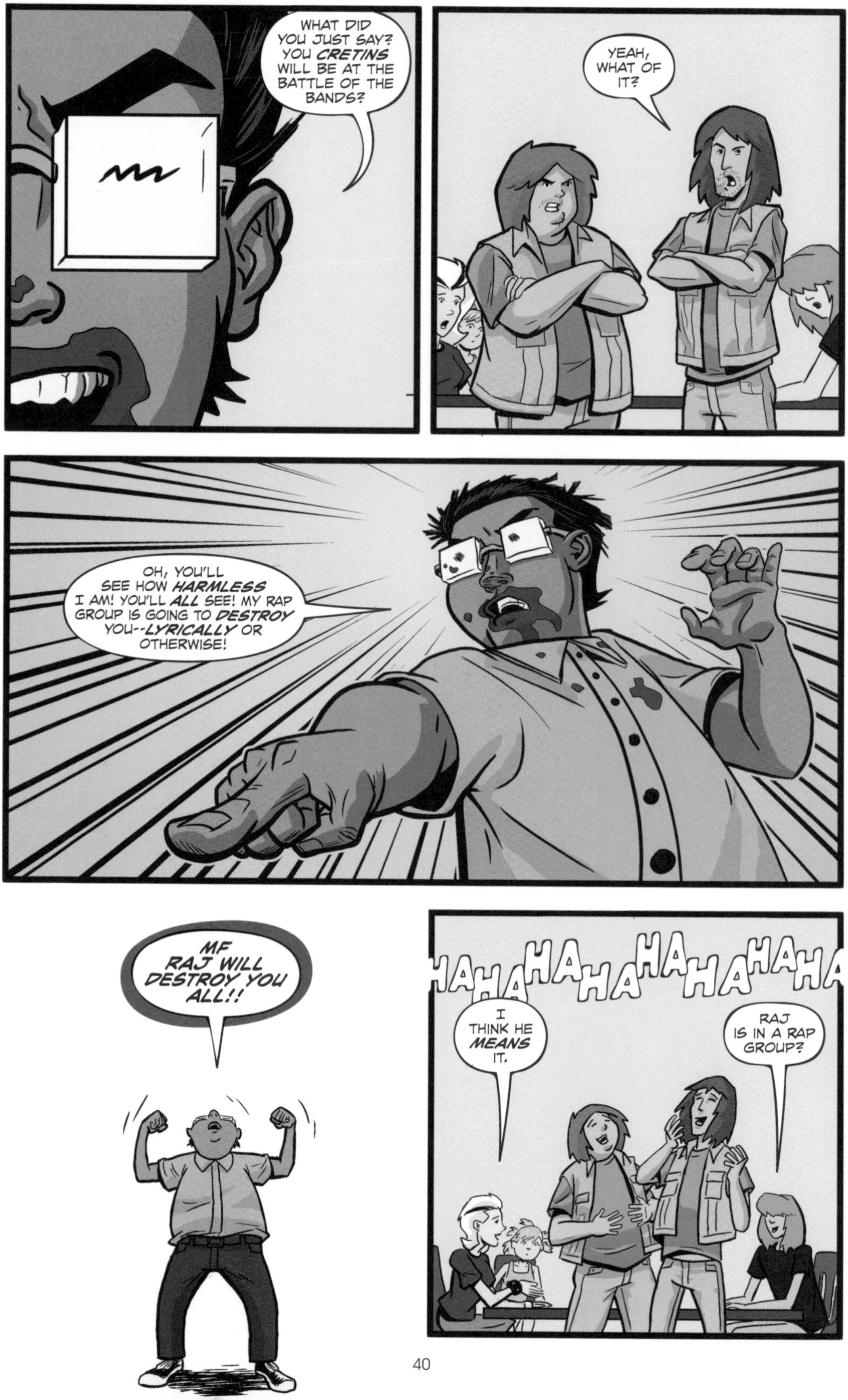
WHAT DID YOU JUST SAY? YOU *CRETINS* WILL BE AT THE BATTLE OF THE BANDS?
YEAH, WHAT OF IT?
OH, YOU'LL SEE HOW *HARMLESS* I AM! YOU'LL *ALL* SEE! MY RAP GROUP IS GOING TO *DESTROY* YOU--*LYRICALLY* OR OTHERWISE!
MF RAJ WILL DESTROY YOU ALL!!
HAHAHAHAHAHAHAHAHAHA
I THINK HE *MEANS* IT.
RAJ IS IN A RAP GROUP?

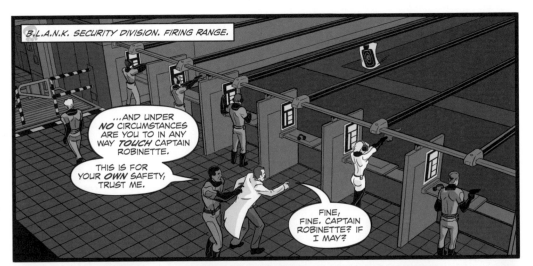

B.L.A.N.K. SECURITY DIVISION. FIRING RANGE.

...AND UNDER *NO* CIRCUMSTANCES ARE YOU TO IN ANY WAY *TOUCH* CAPTAIN ROBINETTE.

THIS IS FOR YOUR *OWN* SAFETY; TRUST ME.

FINE, FINE. CAPTAIN ROBINETTE? IF I MAY?

EXCUSE ME, CAPTAIN...

PAP. PAP. PAP

...I HAVE *URGENT* NEWS!

MS. ROBINETTE, IT'S OF THE *UTMOST* IMPORTANCE THAT YOU LISTEN TO ME!

DR. FILBIN! I TOLD YOU NOT TO--

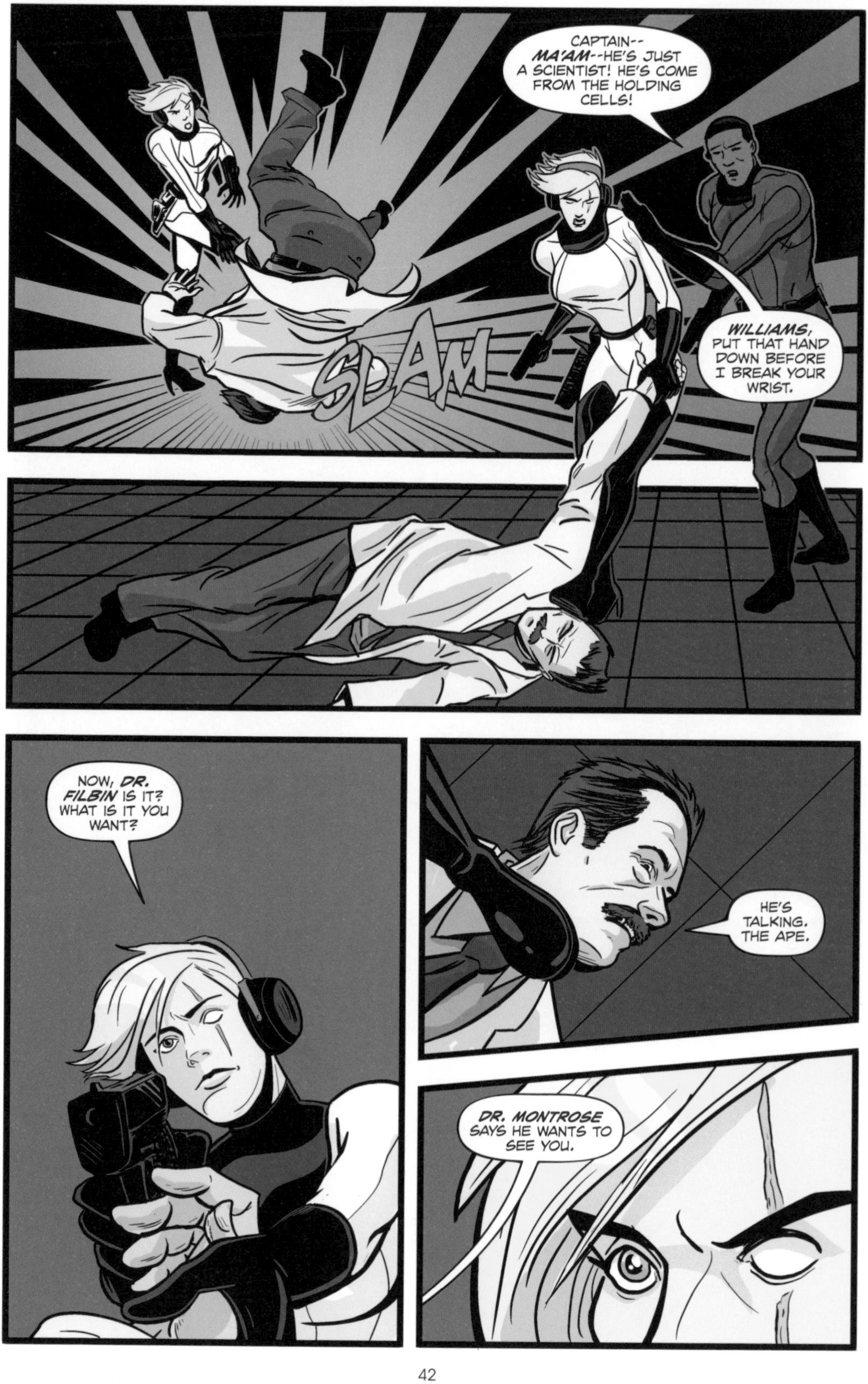
CAPTAIN--
MA'AM--HE'S JUST A SCIENTIST! HE'S COME FROM THE HOLDING CELLS!
SLAM
WILLIAMS, PUT THAT HAND DOWN BEFORE I BREAK YOUR WRIST.
NOW, DR. FILBIN IS IT? WHAT IS IT YOU WANT?
HE'S TALKING. THE APE.
DR. MONTROSE SAYS HE WANTS TO SEE YOU.

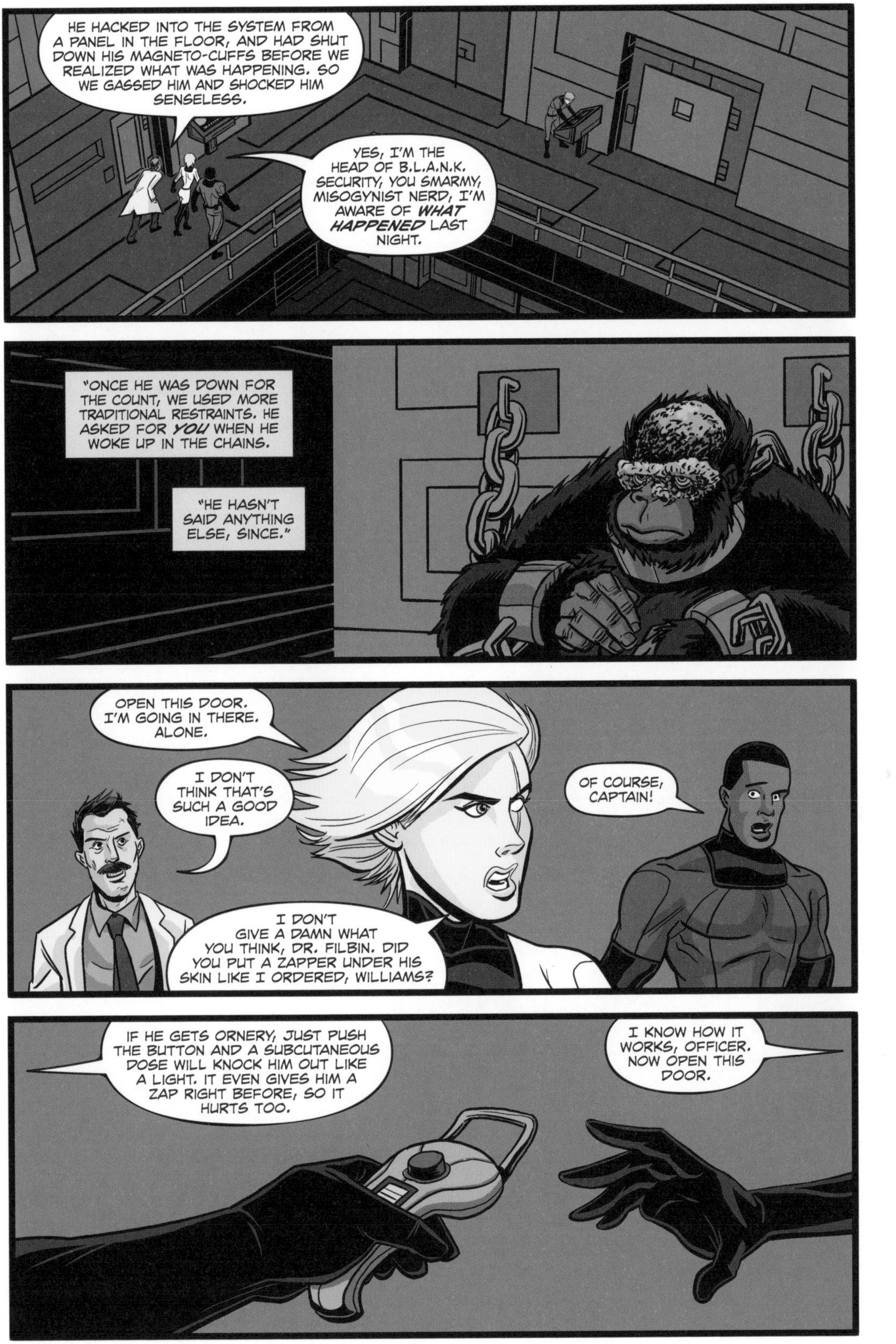
HE HACKED INTO THE SYSTEM FROM A PANEL IN THE FLOOR, AND HAD SHUT DOWN HIS MAGNETO-CUFFS BEFORE WE REALIZED WHAT WAS HAPPENING. SO WE GASSED HIM AND SHOCKED HIM SENSELESS.
YES, I'M THE HEAD OF B.L.A.N.K. SECURITY, YOU SMARMY, MISOGYNIST NERD, I'M AWARE OF WHAT HAPPENED LAST NIGHT.
"ONCE HE WAS DOWN FOR THE COUNT, WE USED MORE TRADITIONAL RESTRAINTS. HE ASKED FOR YOU WHEN HE WOKE UP IN THE CHAINS.
"HE HASN'T SAID ANYTHING ELSE, SINCE."
OPEN THIS DOOR. I'M GOING IN THERE. ALONE.
I DON'T THINK THAT'S SUCH A GOOD IDEA.
OF COURSE, CAPTAIN!
I DON'T GIVE A DAMN WHAT YOU THINK, DR. FILBIN. DID YOU PUT A ZAPPER UNDER HIS SKIN LIKE I ORDERED, WILLIAMS?
IF HE GETS ORNERY, JUST PUSH THE BUTTON AND A SUBCUTANEOUS DOSE WILL KNOCK HIM OUT LIKE A LIGHT. IT EVEN GIVES HIM A ZAP RIGHT BEFORE, SO IT HURTS TOO.
I KNOW HOW IT WORKS, OFFICER. NOW OPEN THIS DOOR.

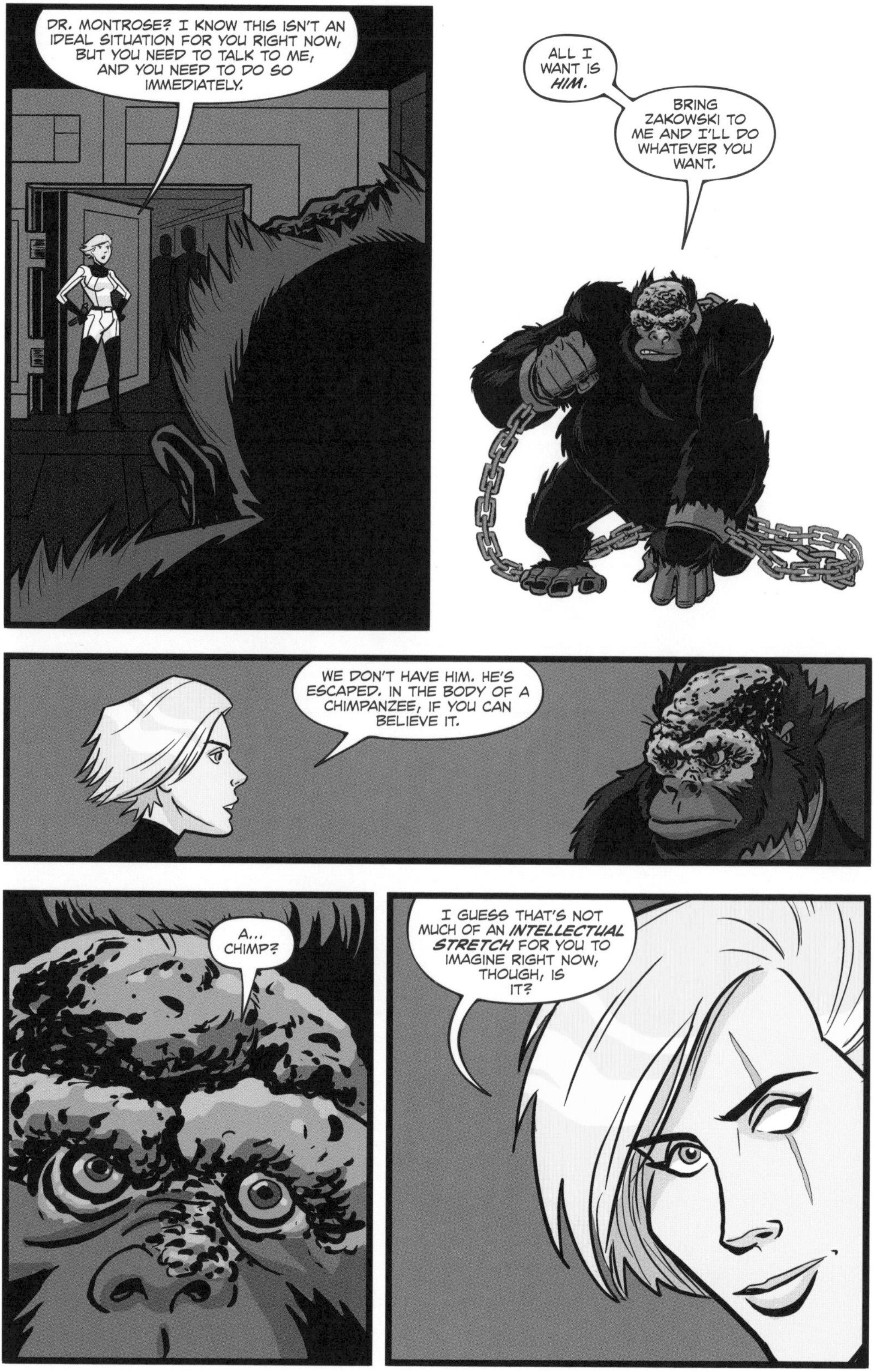
DR. MONTROSE? I KNOW THIS ISN'T AN IDEAL SITUATION FOR YOU RIGHT NOW, BUT YOU NEED TO TALK TO ME, AND YOU NEED TO DO SO IMMEDIATELY.
ALL I WANT IS *HIM.*
BRING ZAKOWSKI TO ME AND I'LL DO WHATEVER YOU WANT.
WE DON'T HAVE HIM. HE'S ESCAPED. IN THE BODY OF A CHIMPANZEE, IF YOU CAN BELIEVE IT.
A... CHIMP?
I GUESS THAT'S NOT MUCH OF AN *INTELLECTUAL STRETCH* FOR YOU TO IMAGINE RIGHT NOW, THOUGH, IS IT?

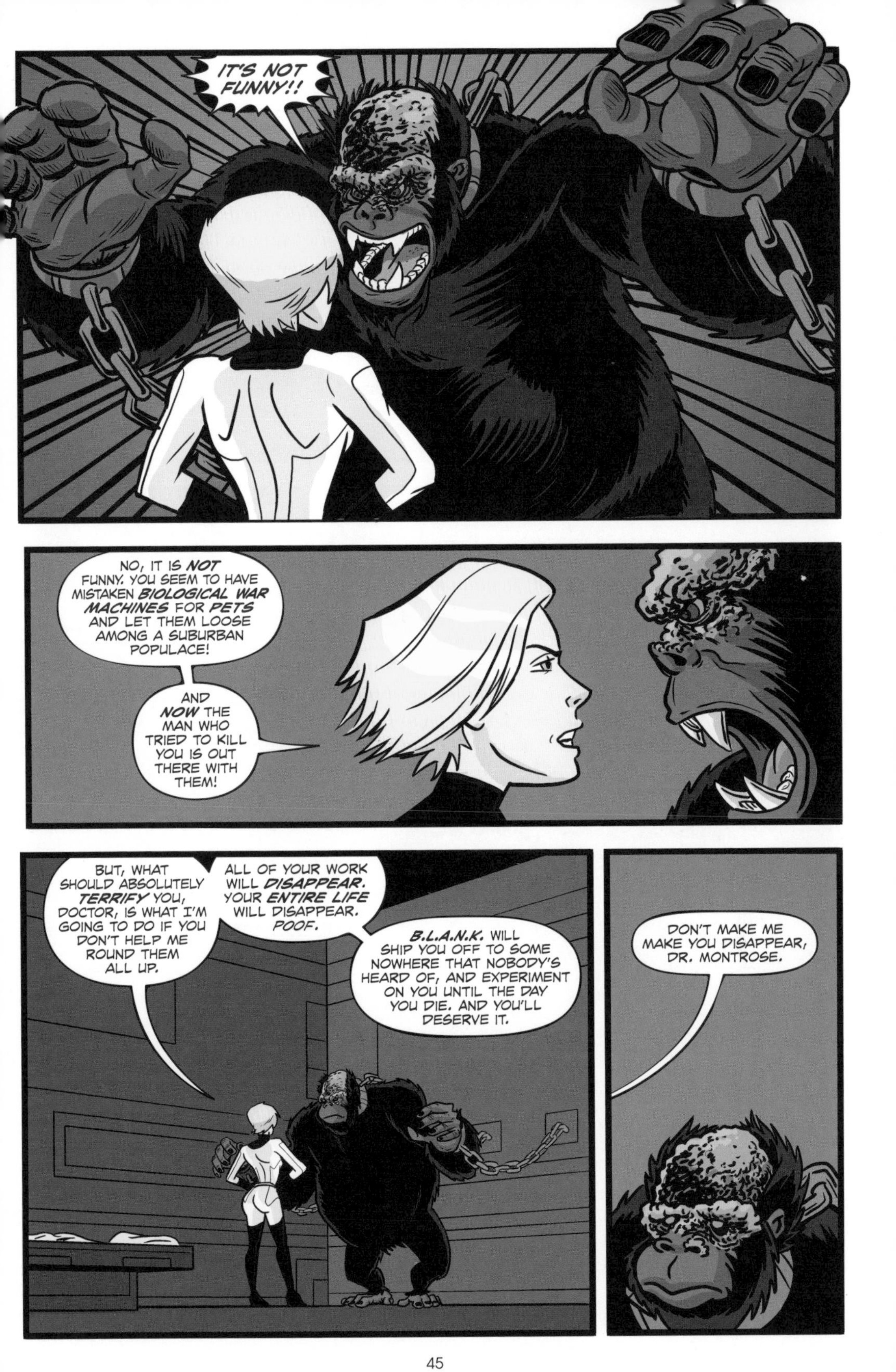
IT'S NOT FUNNY!!
NO, IT IS NOT FUNNY. YOU SEEM TO HAVE MISTAKEN BIOLOGICAL WAR MACHINES FOR PETS AND LET THEM LOOSE AMONG A SUBURBAN POPULACE!
AND NOW THE MAN WHO TRIED TO KILL YOU IS OUT THERE WITH THEM!
BUT, WHAT SHOULD ABSOLUTELY TERRIFY YOU, DOCTOR, IS WHAT I'M GOING TO DO IF YOU DON'T HELP ME ROUND THEM ALL UP.
ALL OF YOUR WORK WILL DISAPPEAR. YOUR ENTIRE LIFE WILL DISAPPEAR. POOF.
B.L.A.N.K. WILL SHIP YOU OFF TO SOME NOWHERE THAT NOBODY'S HEARD OF, AND EXPERIMENT ON YOU UNTIL THE DAY YOU DIE. AND YOU'LL DESERVE IT.
DON'T MAKE ME MAKE YOU DISAPPEAR, DR. MONTROSE.

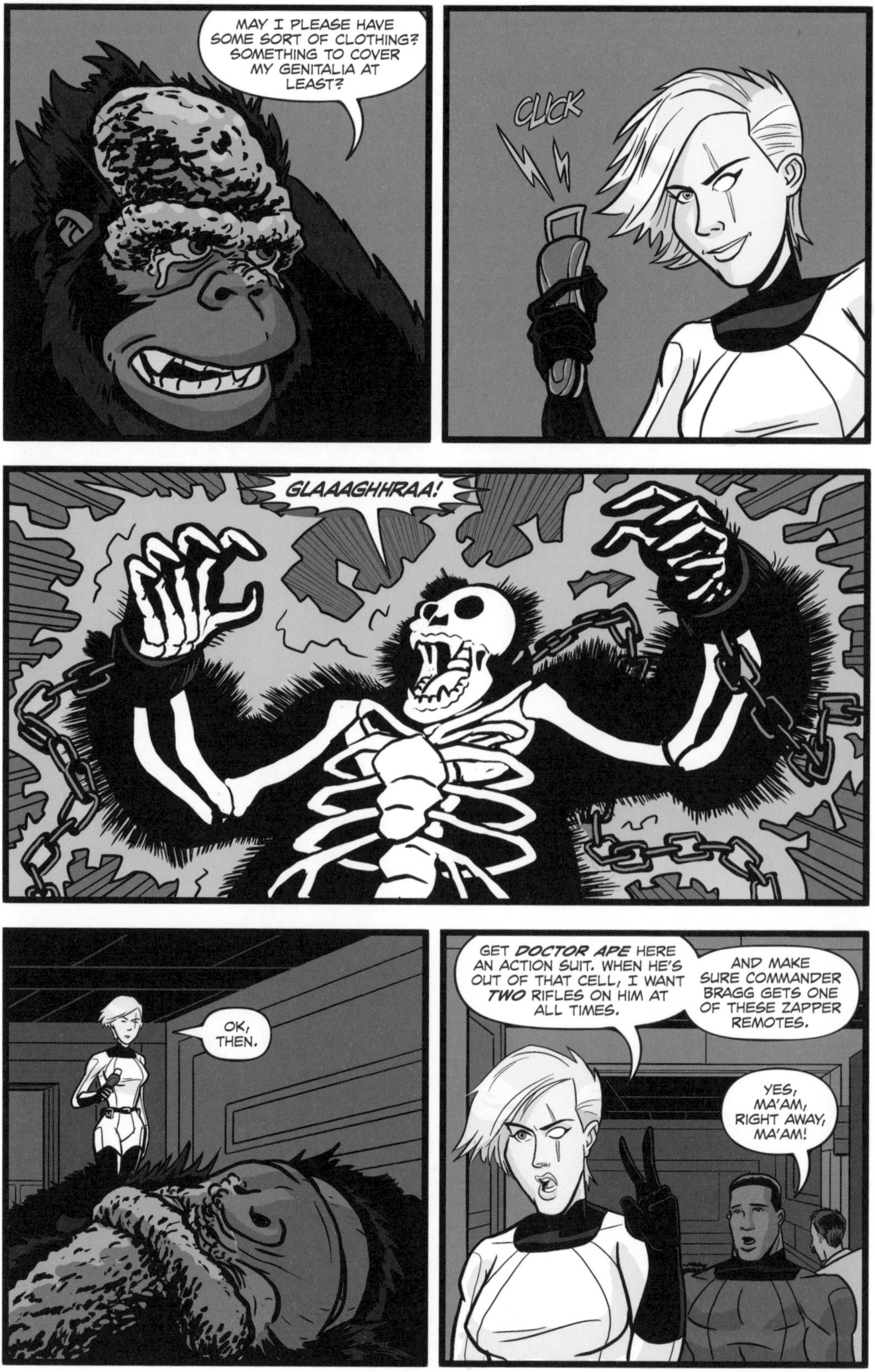
MAY I PLEASE HAVE SOME SORT OF CLOTHING? SOMETHING TO COVER MY GENITALIA AT LEAST?
CLICK
GLAAAGHHRAA!
OK, THEN.
GET DOCTOR APE HERE AN ACTION SUIT. WHEN HE'S OUT OF THAT CELL, I WANT TWO RIFLES ON HIM AT ALL TIMES.
AND MAKE SURE COMMANDER BRAGG GETS ONE OF THESE ZAPPER REMOTES.
YES, MA'AM, RIGHT AWAY, MA'AM!

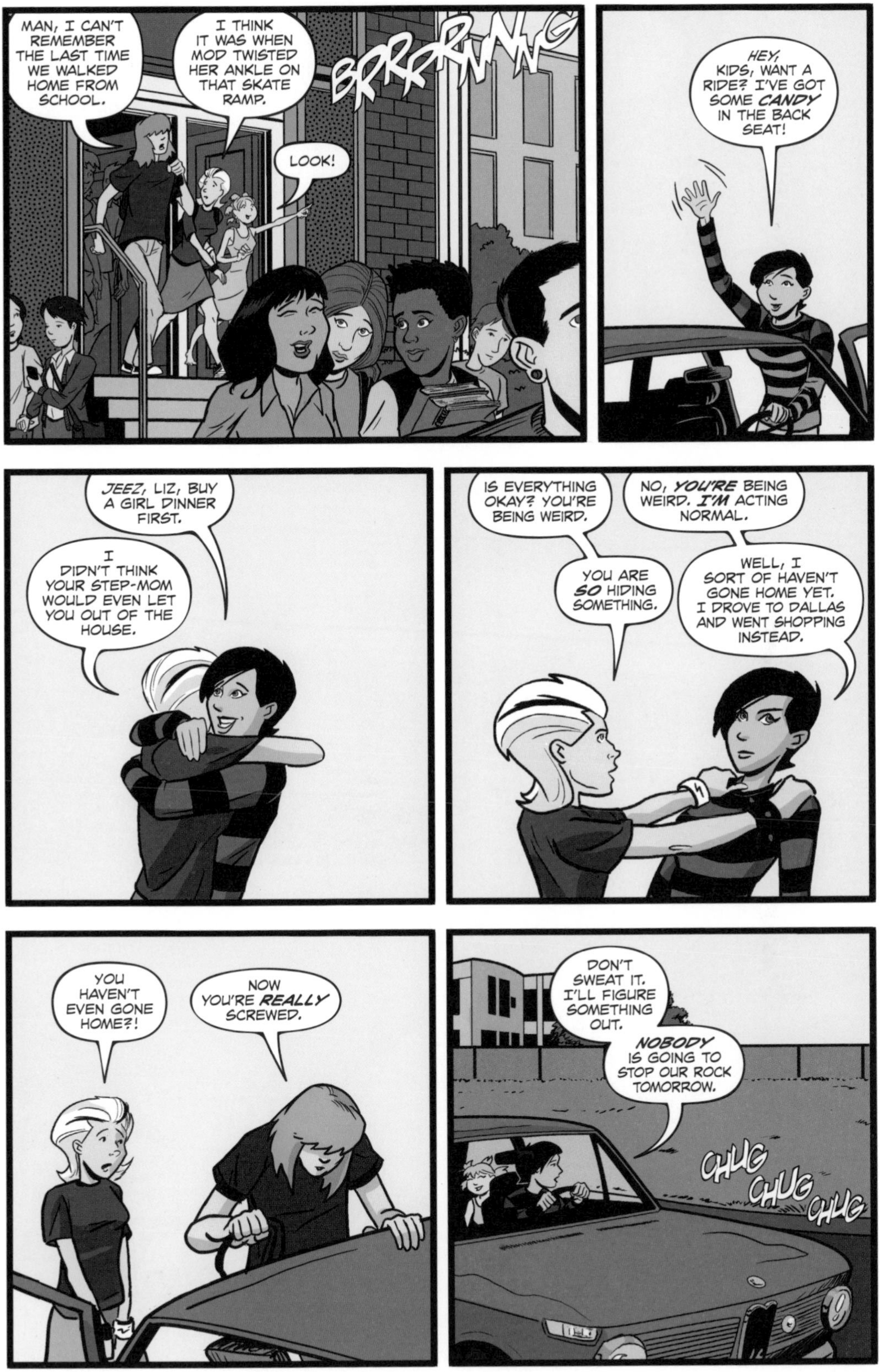
MAN, I CAN'T REMEMBER THE LAST TIME WE WALKED HOME FROM SCHOOL.
I THINK IT WAS WHEN MOD TWISTED HER ANKLE ON THAT SKATE RAMP.
BRRRRNNNG
LOOK!
HEY, KIDS, WANT A RIDE? I'VE GOT SOME CANDY IN THE BACK SEAT!
JEEZ, LIZ, BUY A GIRL DINNER FIRST.
I DIDN'T THINK YOUR STEP-MOM WOULD EVEN LET YOU OUT OF THE HOUSE.
IS EVERYTHING OKAY? YOU'RE BEING WEIRD.
NO, YOU'RE BEING WEIRD. I'M ACTING NORMAL.
YOU ARE SO HIDING SOMETHING.
WELL, I SORT OF HAVEN'T GONE HOME YET. I DROVE TO DALLAS AND WENT SHOPPING INSTEAD.
YOU HAVEN'T EVEN GONE HOME?!
NOW YOU'RE REALLY SCREWED.
DON'T SWEAT IT. I'LL FIGURE SOMETHING OUT.
NOBODY IS GOING TO STOP OUR ROCK TOMORROW.
CHUG CHUG CHUG

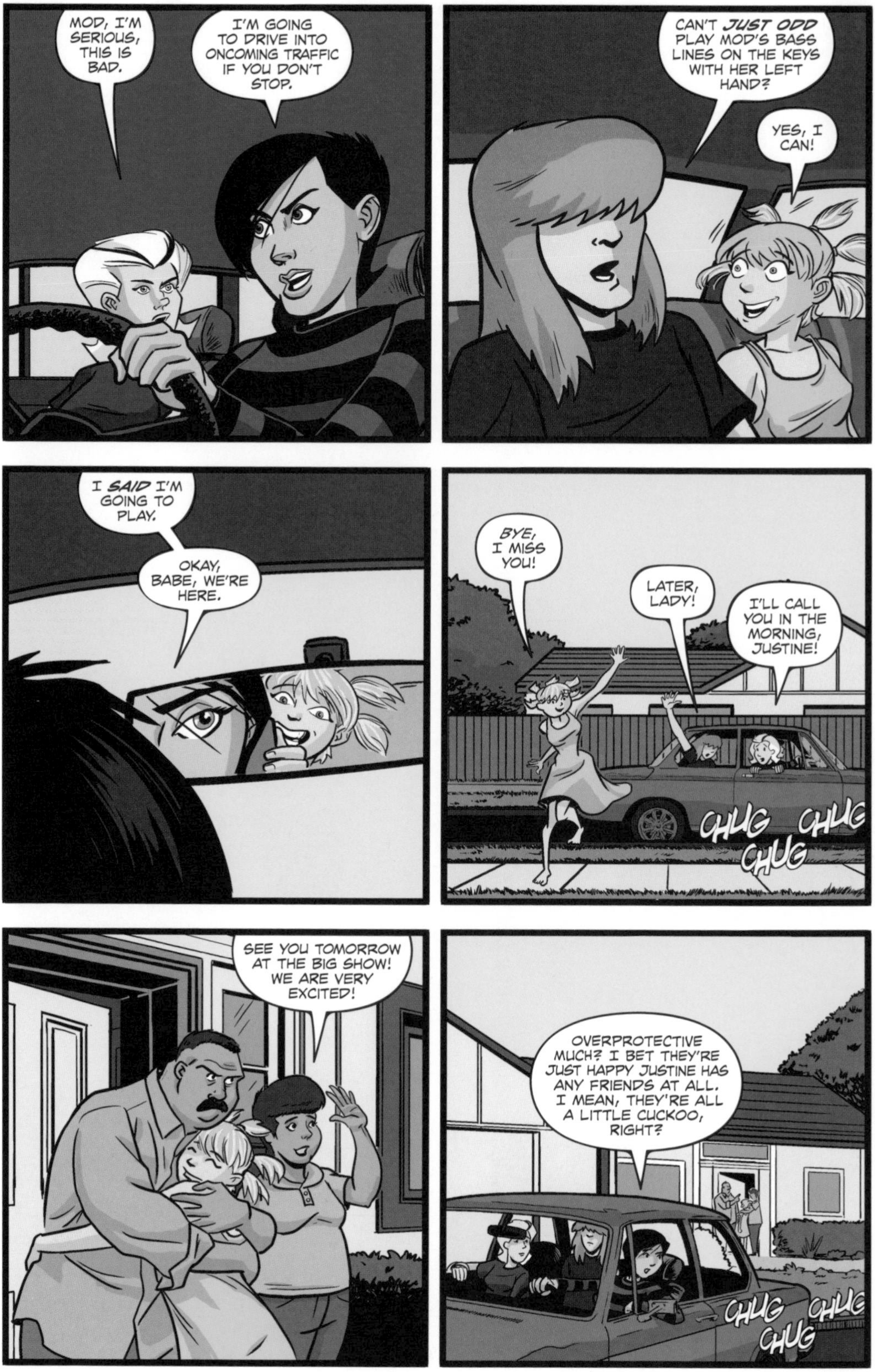
MOD, I'M SERIOUS, THIS IS BAD.
I'M GOING TO DRIVE INTO ONCOMING TRAFFIC IF YOU DON'T STOP.
CAN'T JUST ODD PLAY MOD'S BASS LINES ON THE KEYS WITH HER LEFT HAND?
YES, I CAN!
I SAID I'M GOING TO PLAY.
OKAY, BABE, WE'RE HERE.
BYE, I MISS YOU!
LATER, LADY!
I'LL CALL YOU IN THE MORNING, JUSTINE!
CHUG CHUG CHUG
SEE YOU TOMORROW AT THE BIG SHOW! WE ARE VERY EXCITED!
OVERPROTECTIVE MUCH? I BET THEY'RE JUST HAPPY JUSTINE HAS ANY FRIENDS AT ALL. I MEAN, THEY'RE ALL A LITTLE CUCKOO, RIGHT?
CHUG CHUG CHUG

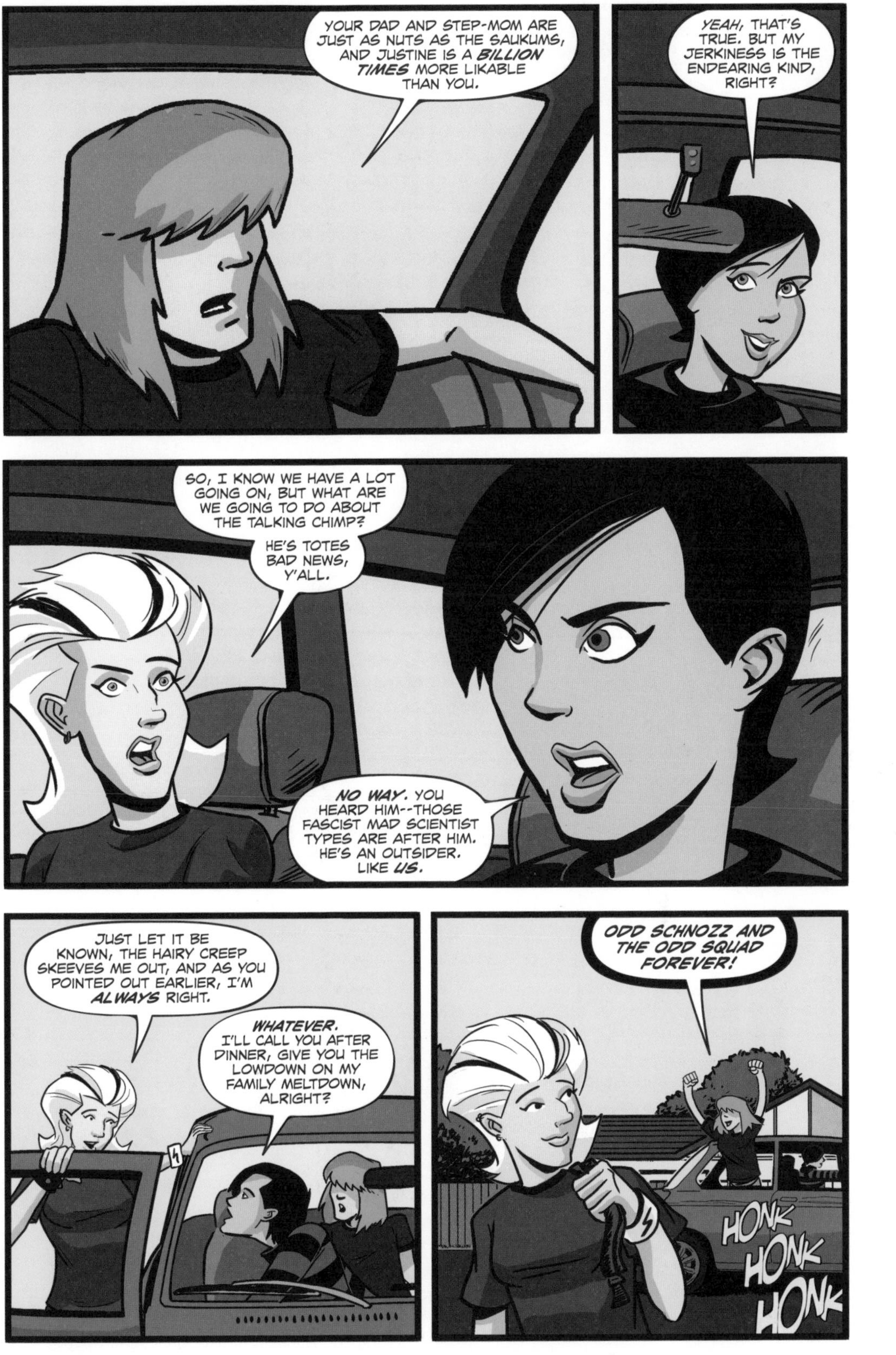
YOUR DAD AND STEP-MOM ARE JUST AS NUTS AS THE SAUKUMS, AND JUSTINE IS A BILLION TIMES MORE LIKABLE THAN YOU.
YEAH, THAT'S TRUE. BUT MY JERKINESS IS THE ENDEARING KIND, RIGHT?
SO, I KNOW WE HAVE A LOT GOING ON, BUT WHAT ARE WE GOING TO DO ABOUT THE TALKING CHIMP?
HE'S TOTES BAD NEWS, Y'ALL.
NO WAY. YOU HEARD HIM--THOSE FASCIST MAD SCIENTIST TYPES ARE AFTER HIM. HE'S AN OUTSIDER. LIKE US.
JUST LET IT BE KNOWN, THE HAIRY CREEP SKEEVES ME OUT, AND AS YOU POINTED OUT EARLIER, I'M ALWAYS RIGHT.
WHATEVER. I'LL CALL YOU AFTER DINNER, GIVE YOU THE LOWDOWN ON MY FAMILY MELTDOWN, ALRIGHT?
ODD SCHNOZZ AND THE ODD SQUAD FOREVER!
HONK
HONK
HONK

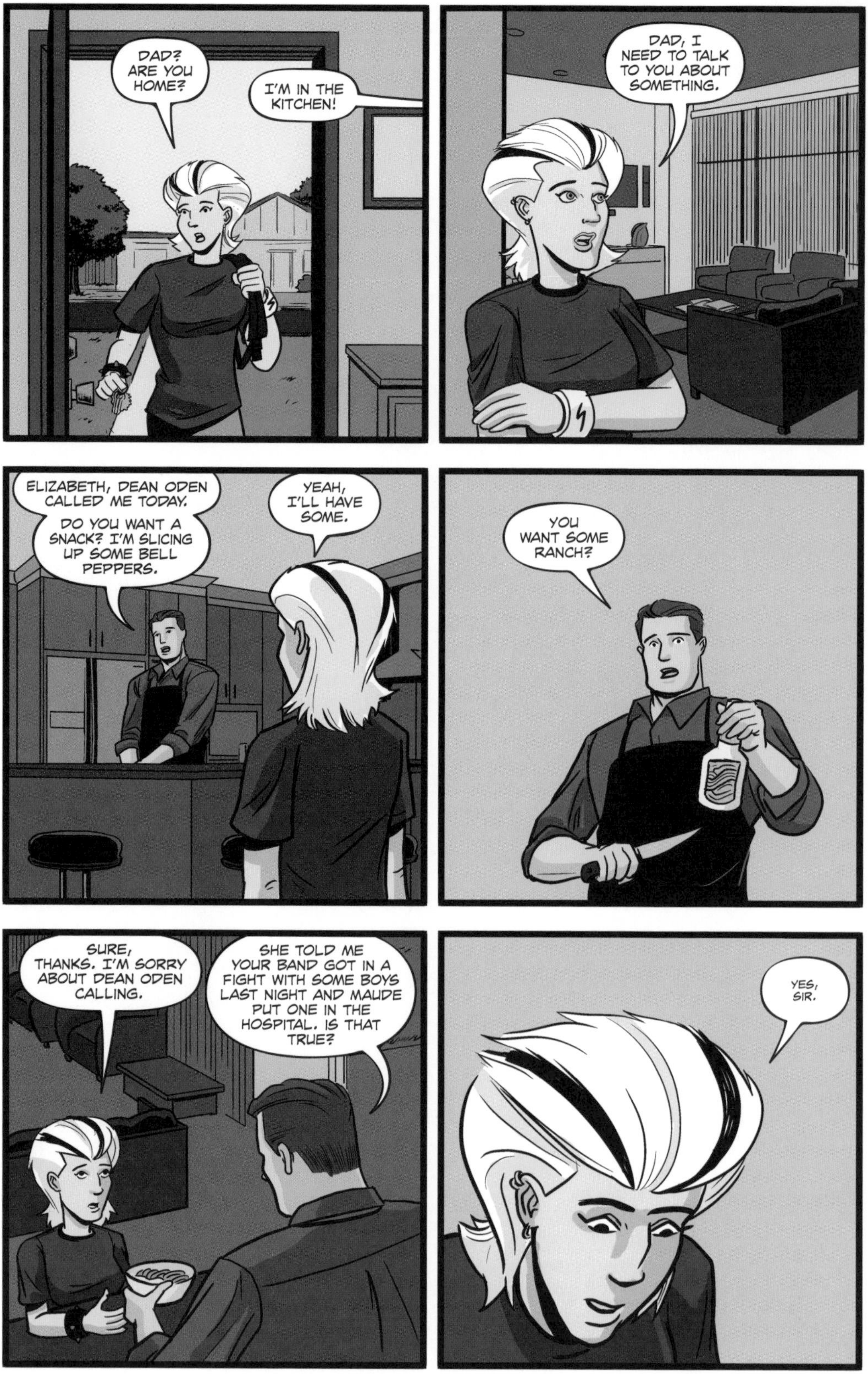
DAD? ARE YOU HOME?
I'M IN THE KITCHEN!
DAD, I NEED TO TALK TO YOU ABOUT SOMETHING.
ELIZABETH, DEAN ODEN CALLED ME TODAY.
DO YOU WANT A SNACK? I'M SLICING UP SOME BELL PEPPERS.
YEAH, I'LL HAVE SOME.
YOU WANT SOME RANCH?
SURE, THANKS. I'M SORRY ABOUT DEAN ODEN CALLING.
SHE TOLD ME YOUR BAND GOT IN A FIGHT WITH SOME BOYS LAST NIGHT AND MAUDE PUT ONE IN THE HOSPITAL. IS THAT TRUE?
YES, SIR.

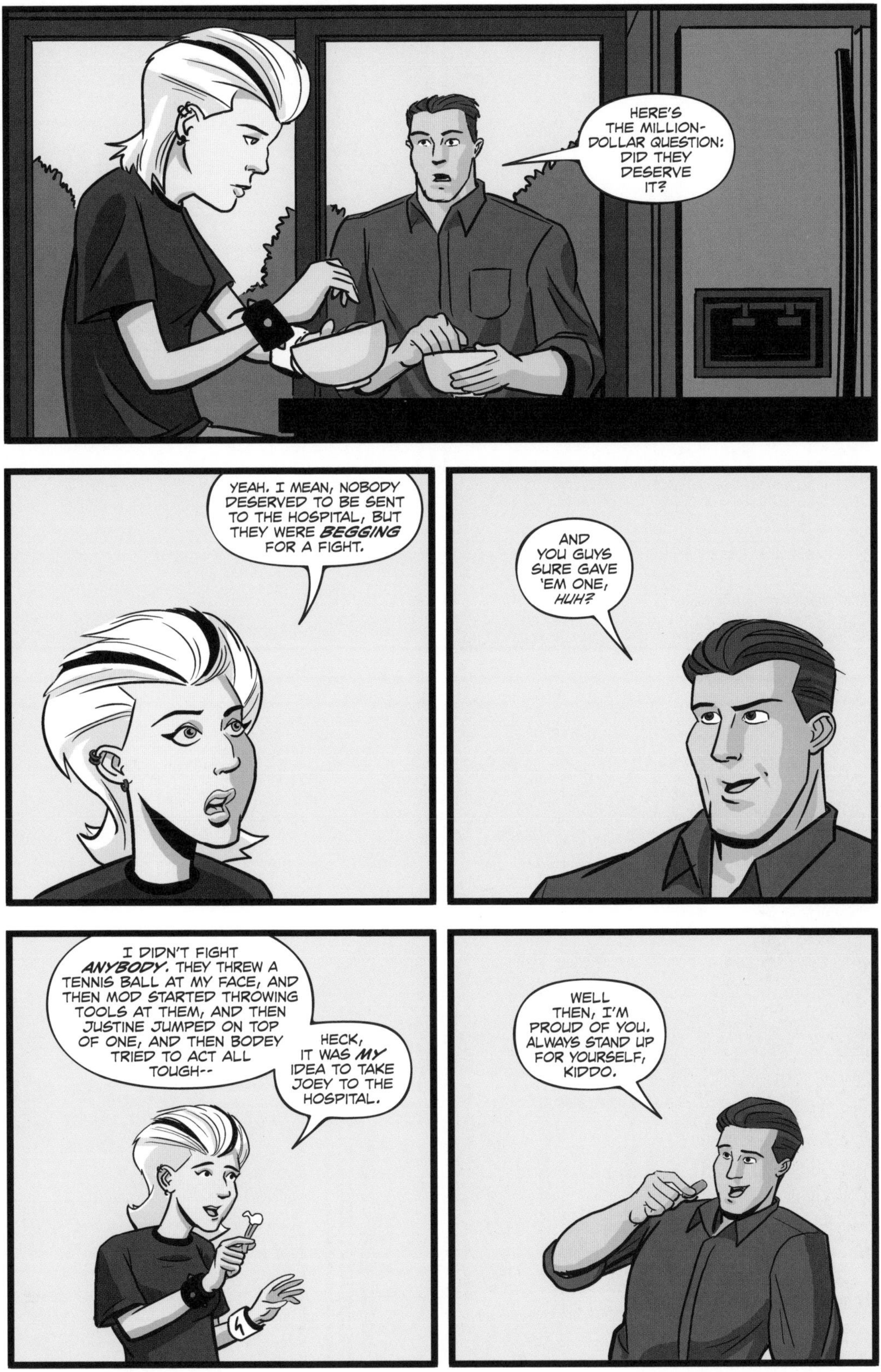
HERE'S THE MILLION-DOLLAR QUESTION: DID THEY DESERVE IT?
YEAH. I MEAN, NOBODY DESERVED TO BE SENT TO THE HOSPITAL, BUT THEY WERE BEGGING FOR A FIGHT.
AND YOU GUYS SURE GAVE 'EM ONE, HUH?
I DIDN'T FIGHT ANYBODY. THEY THREW A TENNIS BALL AT MY FACE, AND THEN MOD STARTED THROWING TOOLS AT THEM, AND THEN JUSTINE JUMPED ON TOP OF ONE, AND THEN BODEY TRIED TO ACT ALL TOUGH--
HECK, IT WAS MY IDEA TO TAKE JOEY TO THE HOSPITAL.
WELL THEN, I'M PROUD OF YOU. ALWAYS STAND UP FOR YOURSELF, KIDDO.

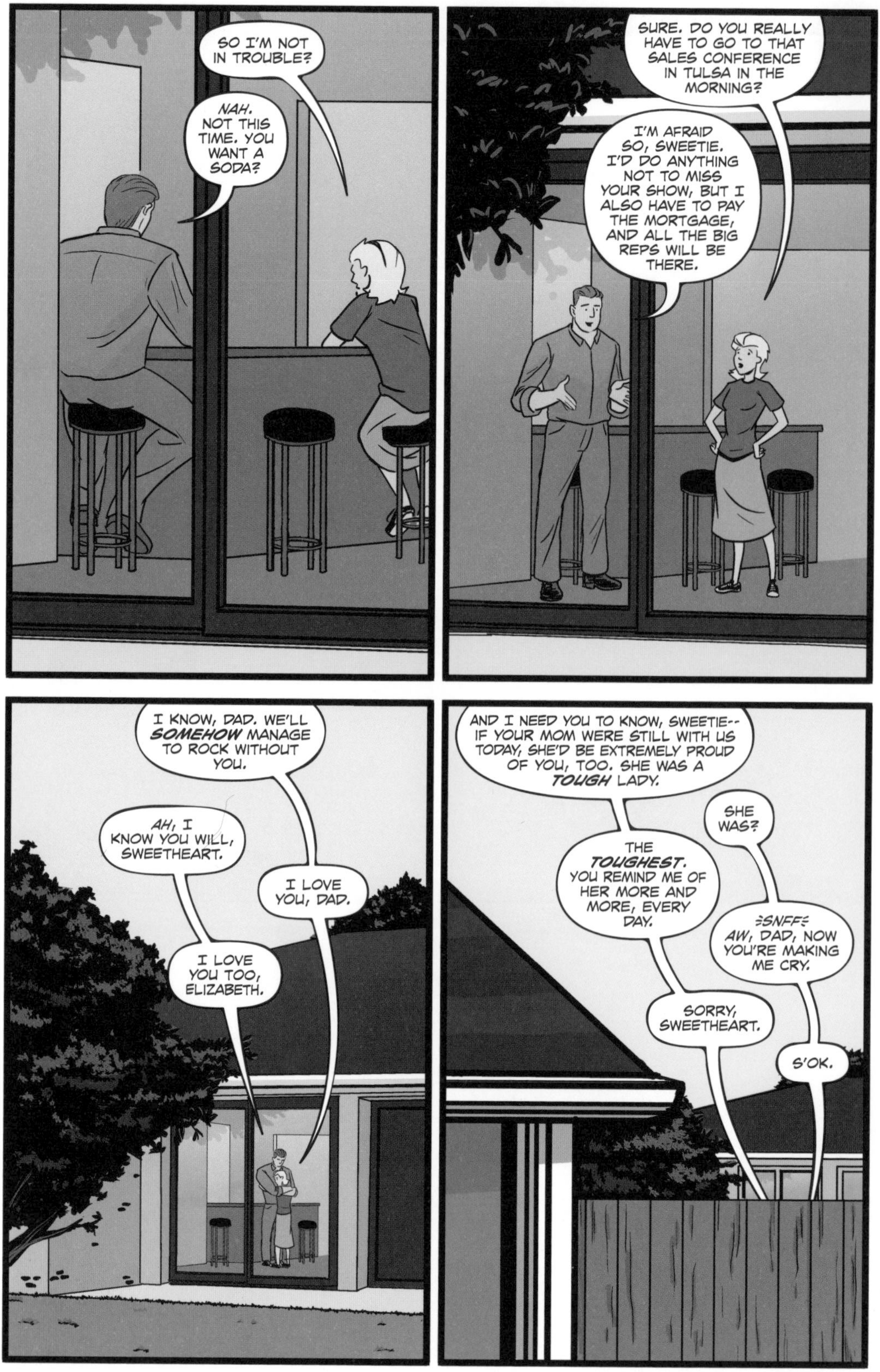
SO I'M NOT IN TROUBLE?
NAH. NOT THIS TIME. YOU WANT A SODA?
SURE. DO YOU REALLY HAVE TO GO TO THAT SALES CONFERENCE IN TULSA IN THE MORNING?
I'M AFRAID SO, SWEETIE. I'D DO ANYTHING NOT TO MISS YOUR SHOW, BUT I ALSO HAVE TO PAY THE MORTGAGE, AND ALL THE BIG REPS WILL BE THERE.
I KNOW, DAD. WE'LL *SOMEHOW* MANAGE TO ROCK WITHOUT YOU.
AH, I KNOW YOU WILL, SWEETHEART.
I LOVE YOU, DAD.
I LOVE YOU TOO, ELIZABETH.
AND I NEED YOU TO KNOW, SWEETIE-- IF YOUR MOM WERE STILL WITH US TODAY, SHE'D BE EXTREMELY PROUD OF YOU, TOO. SHE WAS A *TOUGH* LADY.
SHE WAS?
THE *TOUGHEST*. YOU REMIND ME OF HER MORE AND MORE, EVERY DAY.
SNFF *AW*, DAD, NOW YOU'RE MAKING ME CRY.
SORRY, SWEETHEART.
S'OK.

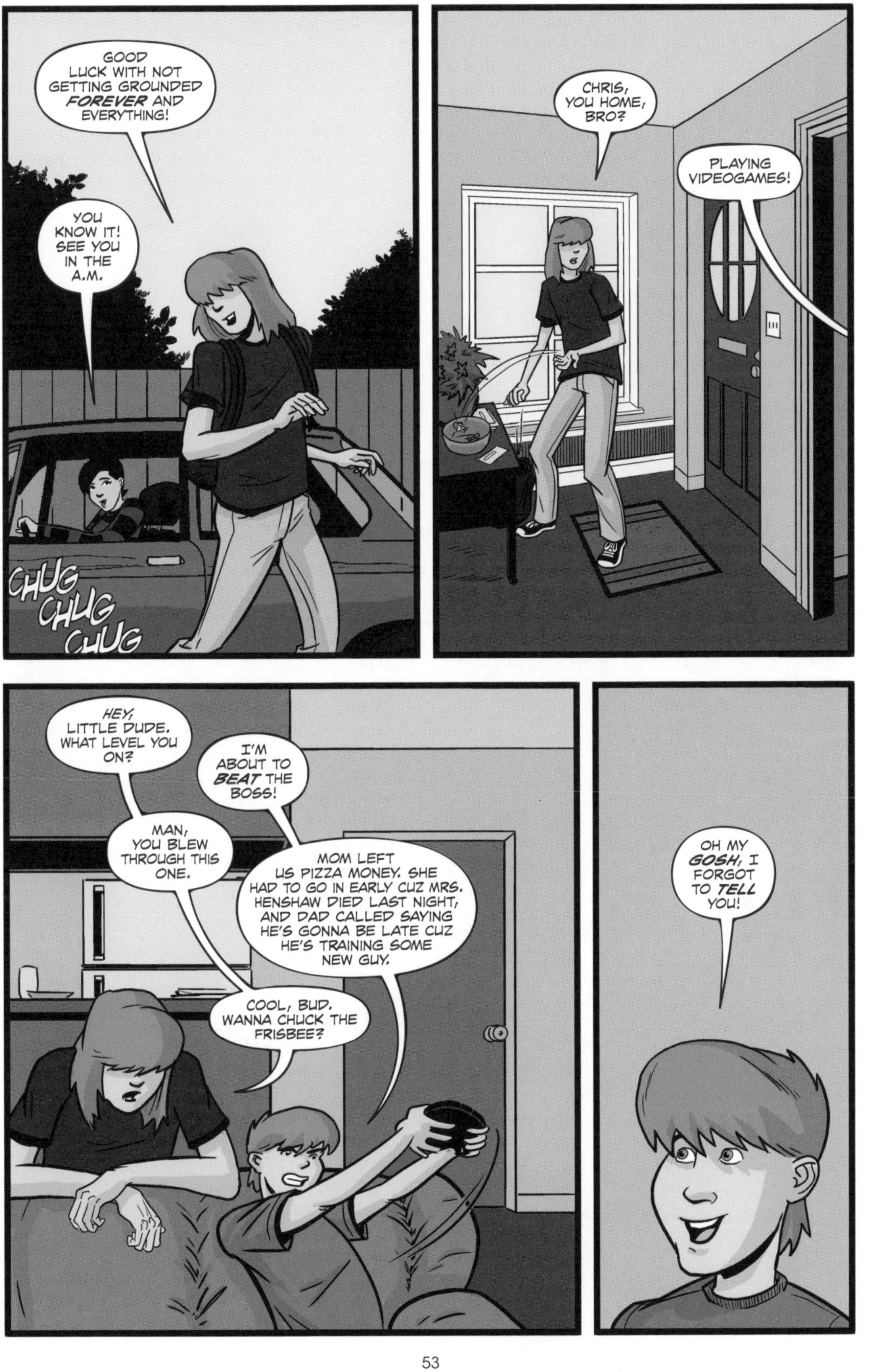
GOOD LUCK WITH NOT GETTING GROUNDED *FOREVER* AND EVERYTHING!
YOU KNOW IT! SEE YOU IN THE A.M.
CHUG CHUG CHUG
CHRIS, YOU HOME, BRO?
PLAYING VIDEOGAMES!
HEY, LITTLE DUDE. WHAT LEVEL YOU ON?
I'M ABOUT TO *BEAT* THE BOSS!
MAN, YOU BLEW THROUGH THIS ONE.
MOM LEFT US PIZZA MONEY. SHE HAD TO GO IN EARLY CUZ MRS. HENSHAW DIED LAST NIGHT, AND DAD CALLED SAYING HE'S GONNA BE LATE CUZ HE'S TRAINING SOME NEW GUY.
COOL, BUD. WANNA CHUCK THE FRISBEE?
OH MY *GOSH,* I FORGOT TO *TELL* YOU!

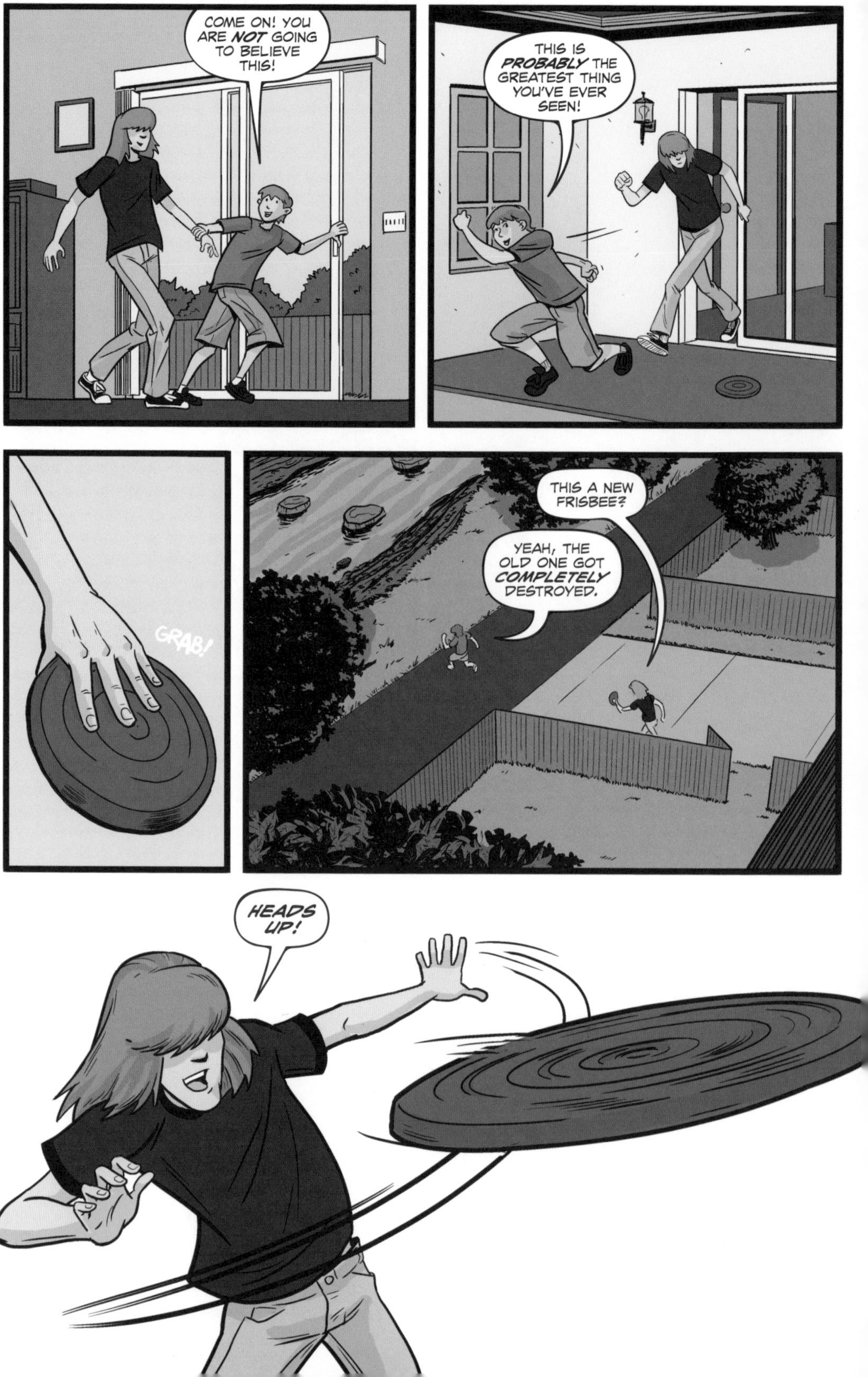
COME ON! YOU ARE *NOT* GOING TO BELIEVE THIS!
THIS IS *PROBABLY* THE GREATEST THING YOU'VE EVER SEEN!
GRAB!
THIS A NEW FRISBEE?
YEAH, THE OLD ONE GOT *COMPLETELY* DESTROYED.
HEADS UP!

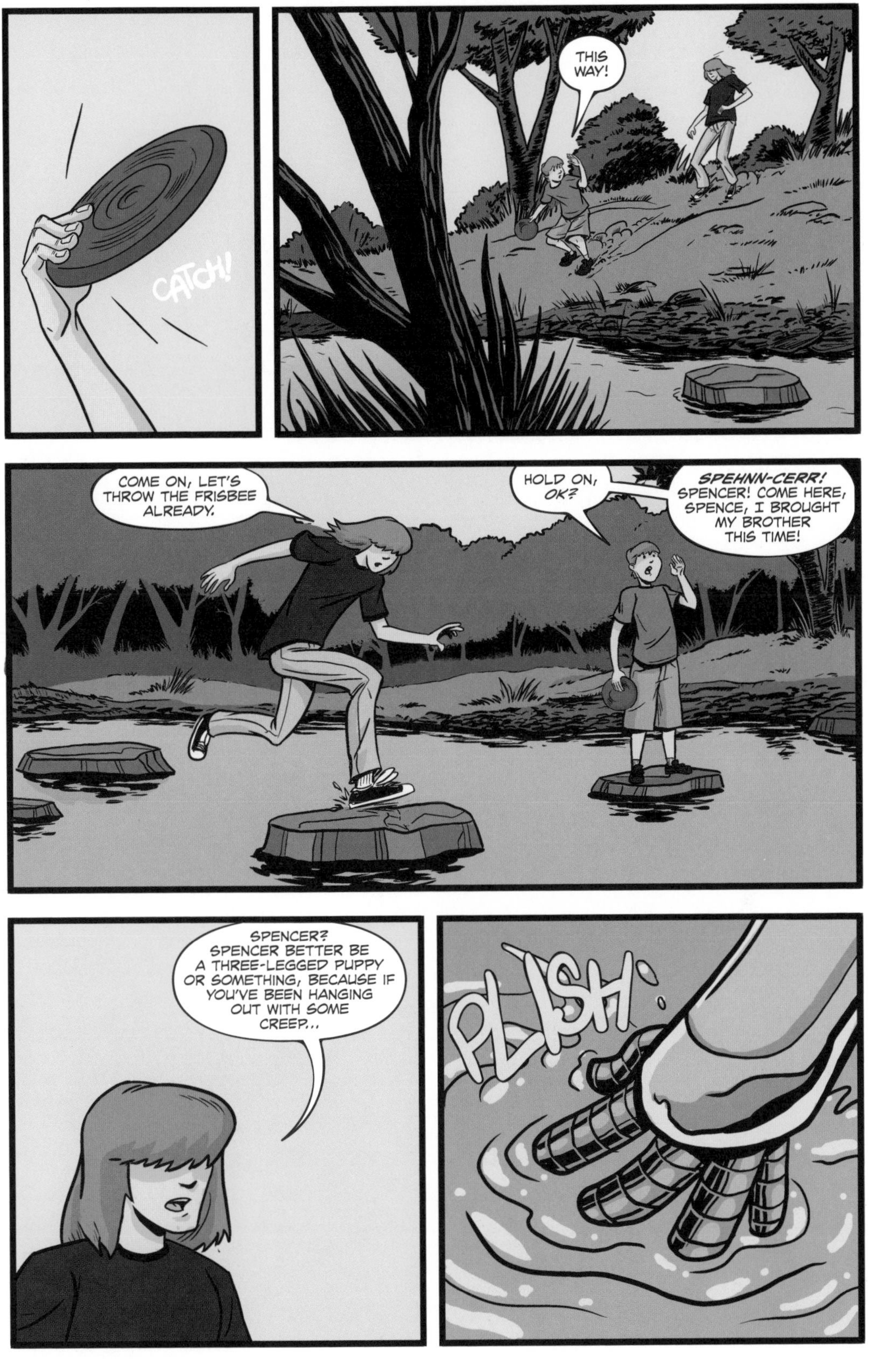
CATCH!
THIS WAY!
COME ON, LET'S THROW THE FRISBEE ALREADY.
HOLD ON, OK?
SPEHNN-CERR! SPENCER! COME HERE, SPENCE, I BROUGHT MY BROTHER THIS TIME!
SPENCER? SPENCER BETTER BE A THREE-LEGGED PUPPY OR SOMETHING, BECAUSE IF YOU'VE BEEN HANGING OUT WITH SOME CREEP...
PLISH

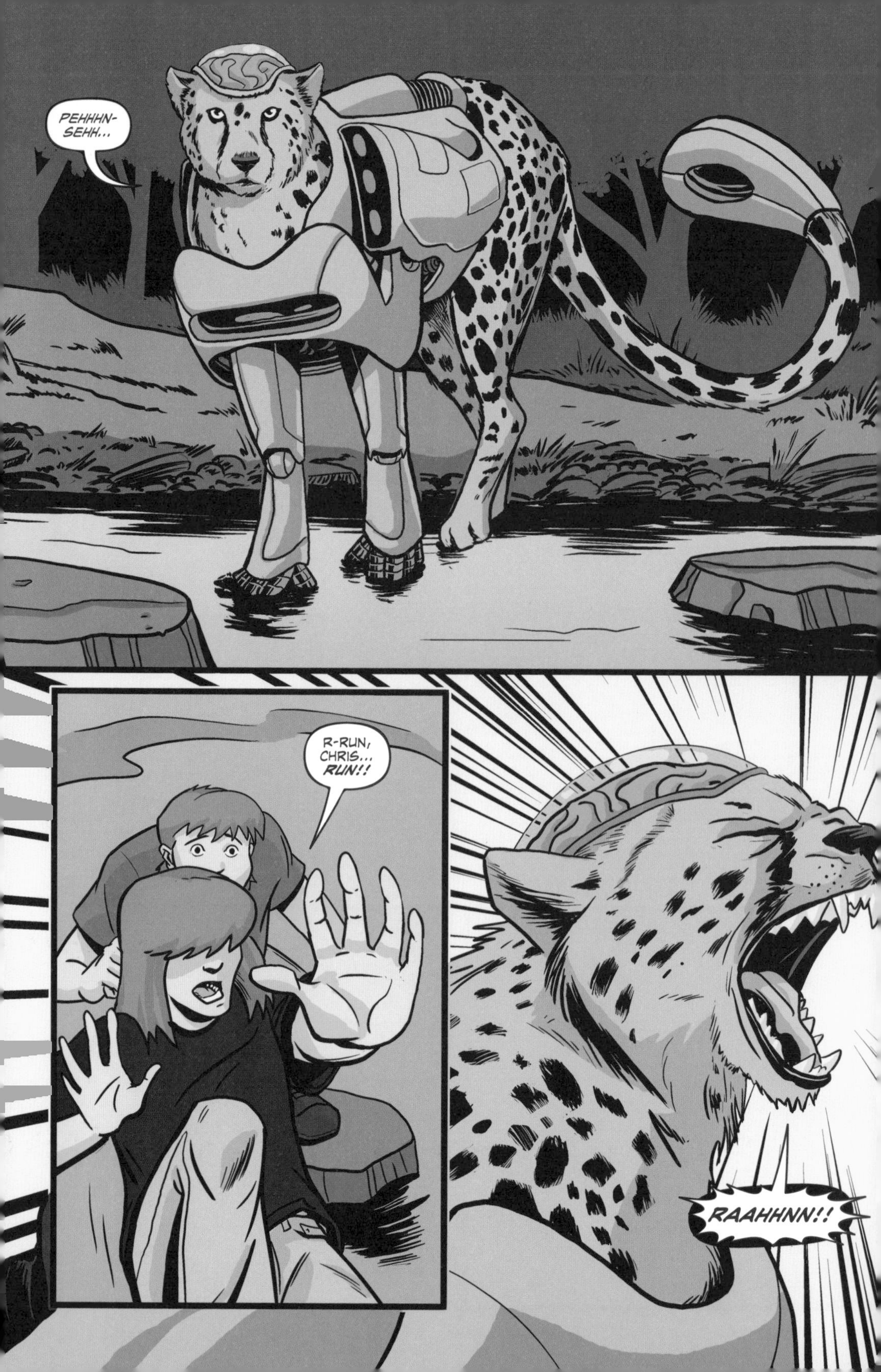
PEHHHN-
SEHH...
R-RUN,
CHRIS...
RUN!!
RAAHHNN!!

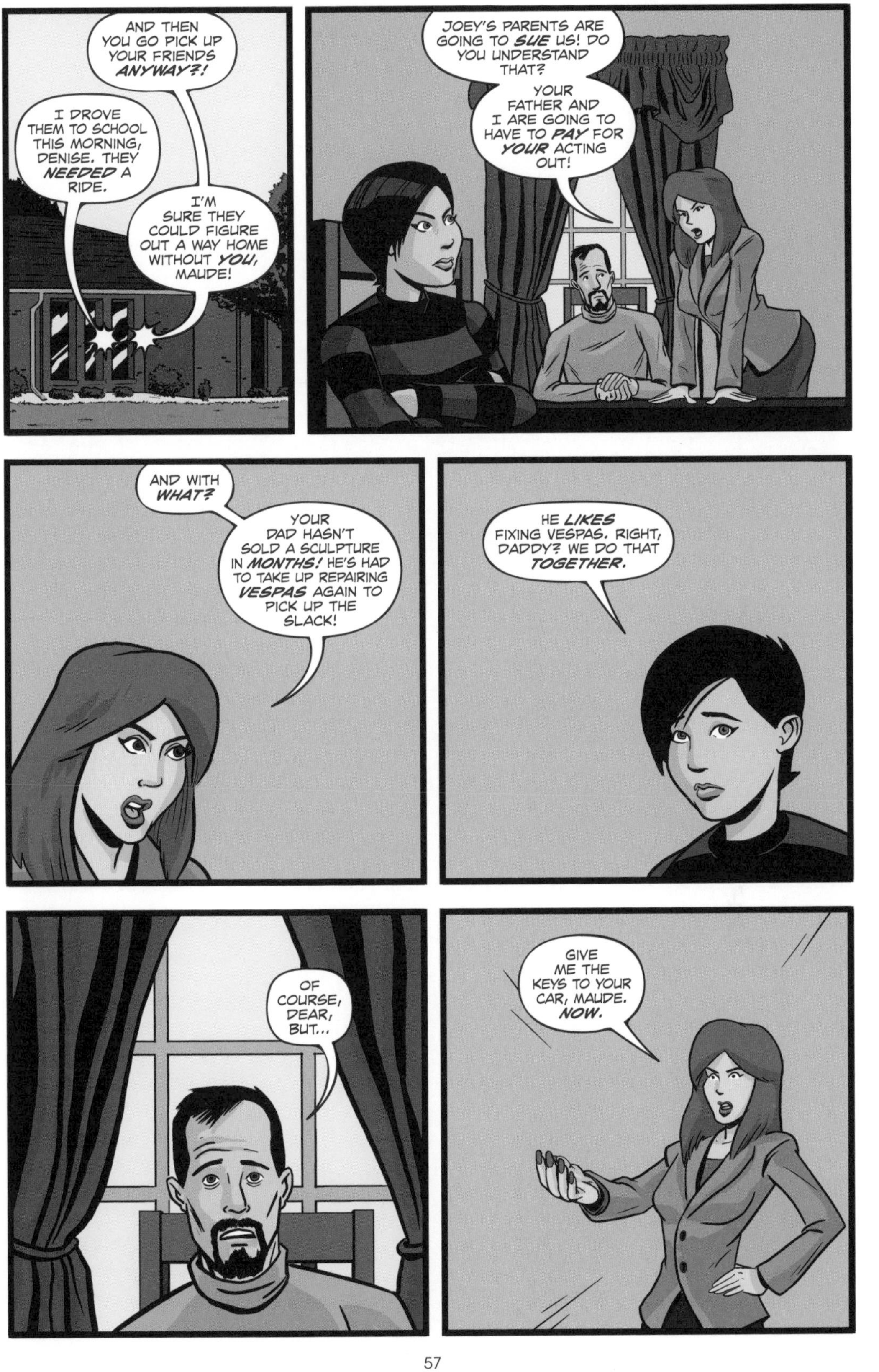
AND THEN YOU GO PICK UP YOUR FRIENDS ANYWAY?!
I DROVE THEM TO SCHOOL THIS MORNING, DENISE. THEY NEEDED A RIDE.
I'M SURE THEY COULD FIGURE OUT A WAY HOME WITHOUT YOU, MAUDE!
JOEY'S PARENTS ARE GOING TO SUE US! DO YOU UNDERSTAND THAT?
YOUR FATHER AND I ARE GOING TO HAVE TO PAY FOR YOUR ACTING OUT!
AND WITH WHAT?
YOUR DAD HASN'T SOLD A SCULPTURE IN MONTHS! HE'S HAD TO TAKE UP REPAIRING VESPAS AGAIN TO PICK UP THE SLACK!
HE LIKES FIXING VESPAS. RIGHT, DADDY? WE DO THAT TOGETHER.
OF COURSE, DEAR, BUT...
GIVE ME THE KEYS TO YOUR CAR, MAUDE. NOW.

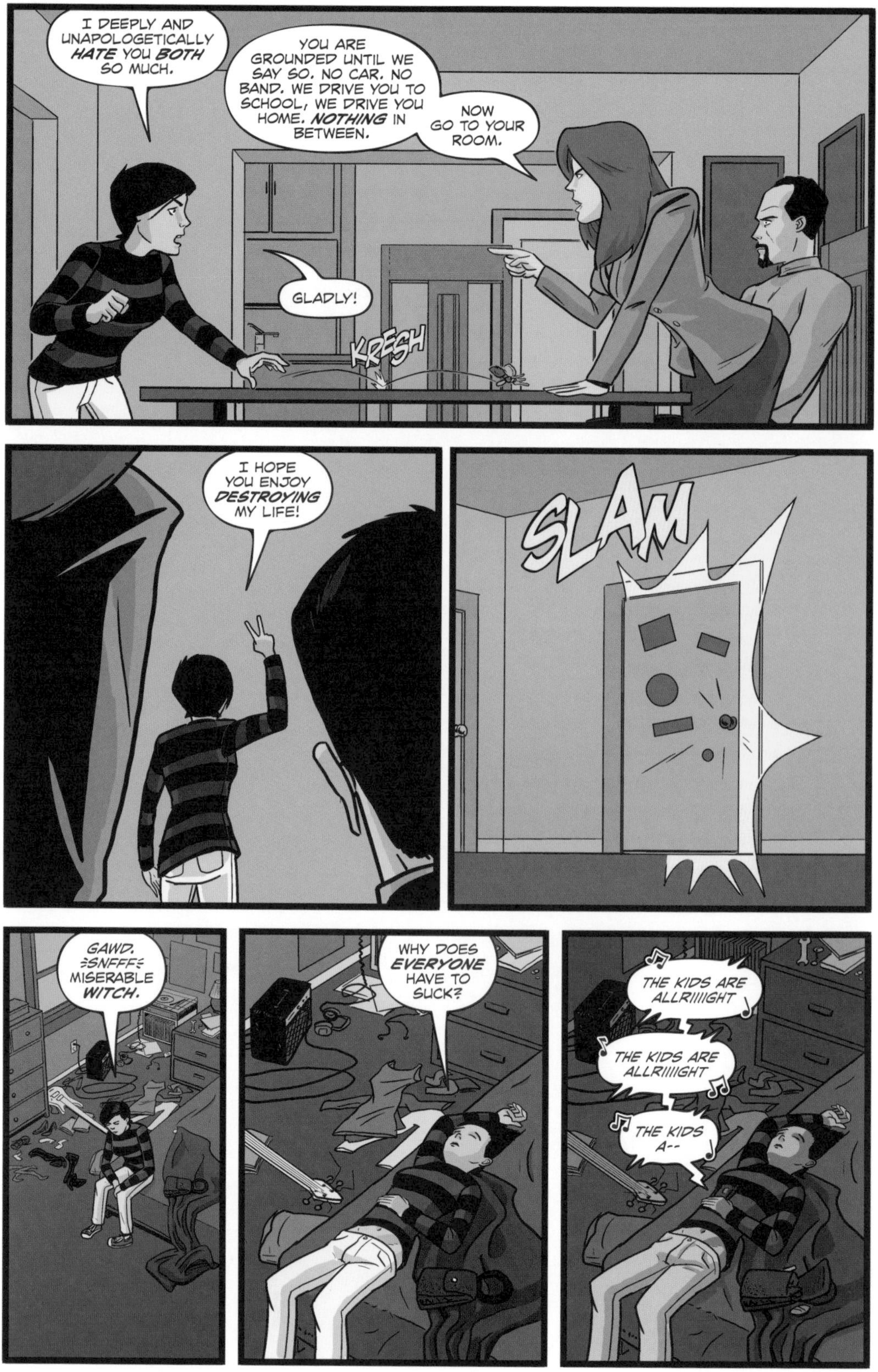
I DEEPLY AND UNAPOLOGETICALLY HATE YOU BOTH SO MUCH.
YOU ARE GROUNDED UNTIL WE SAY SO. NO CAR. NO BAND. WE DRIVE YOU TO SCHOOL, WE DRIVE YOU HOME. NOTHING IN BETWEEN.
NOW GO TO YOUR ROOM.
GLADLY!
KRESH
I HOPE YOU ENJOY DESTROYING MY LIFE!
SLAM
GAWD. SNFFF MISERABLE WITCH.
WHY DOES EVERYONE HAVE TO SUCK?
THE KIDS ARE ALLRIIIIGHT
THE KIDS ARE ALLRIIIIGHT
THE KIDS A--

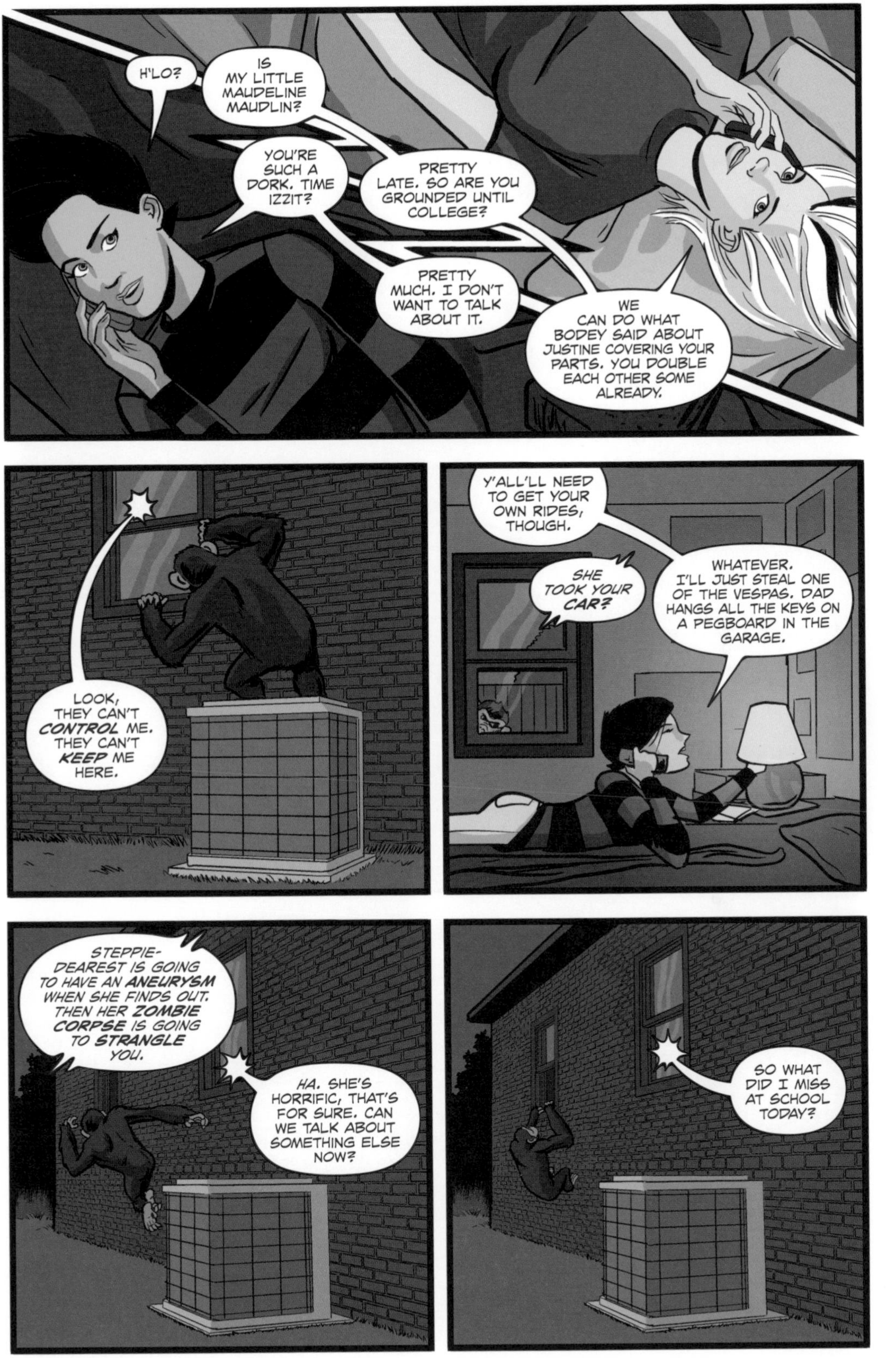
H'LO?
IS MY LITTLE MAUDELINE MAUDLIN?
YOU'RE SUCH A DORK. TIME IZZIT?
PRETTY LATE. SO ARE YOU GROUNDED UNTIL COLLEGE?
PRETTY MUCH. I DON'T WANT TO TALK ABOUT IT.
WE CAN DO WHAT BODEY SAID ABOUT JUSTINE COVERING YOUR PARTS. YOU DOUBLE EACH OTHER SOME ALREADY.
LOOK, THEY CAN'T CONTROL ME. THEY CAN'T KEEP ME HERE.
Y'ALL'LL NEED TO GET YOUR OWN RIDES, THOUGH.
SHE TOOK YOUR CAR?
WHATEVER. I'LL JUST STEAL ONE OF THE VESPAS. DAD HANGS ALL THE KEYS ON A PEGBOARD IN THE GARAGE.
STEPPIE-DEAREST IS GOING TO HAVE AN ANEURYSM WHEN SHE FINDS OUT. THEN HER ZOMBIE CORPSE IS GOING TO STRANGLE YOU.
HA. SHE'S HORRIFIC, THAT'S FOR SURE. CAN WE TALK ABOUT SOMETHING ELSE NOW?
SO WHAT DID I MISS AT SCHOOL TODAY?

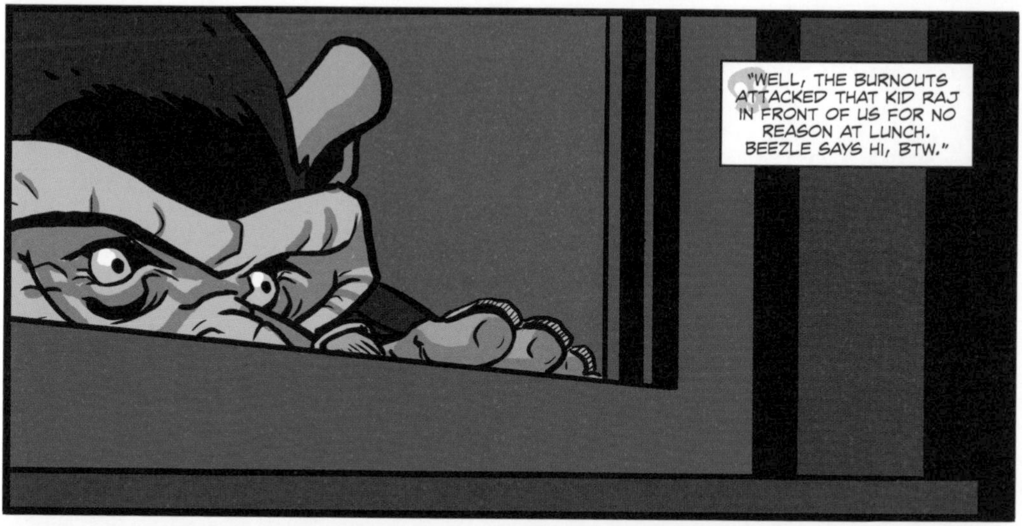
"WELL, THE BURNOUTS ATTACKED THAT KID RAJ IN FRONT OF US FOR NO REASON AT LUNCH. BEEZLE SAYS HI, BTW."

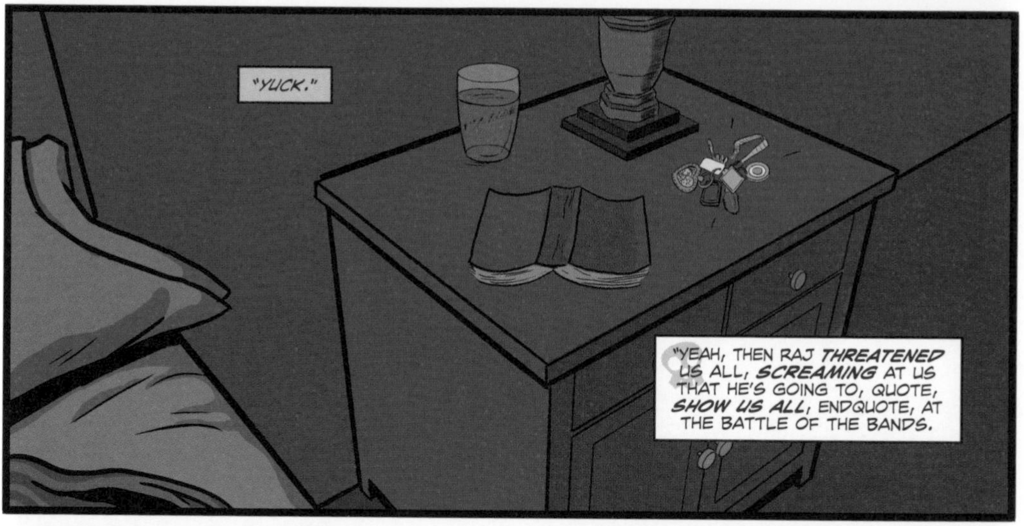
"YUCK."
"YEAH, THEN RAJ THREATENED US ALL, SCREAMING AT US THAT HE'S GOING TO, QUOTE, SHOW US ALL, ENDQUOTE, AT THE BATTLE OF THE BANDS.

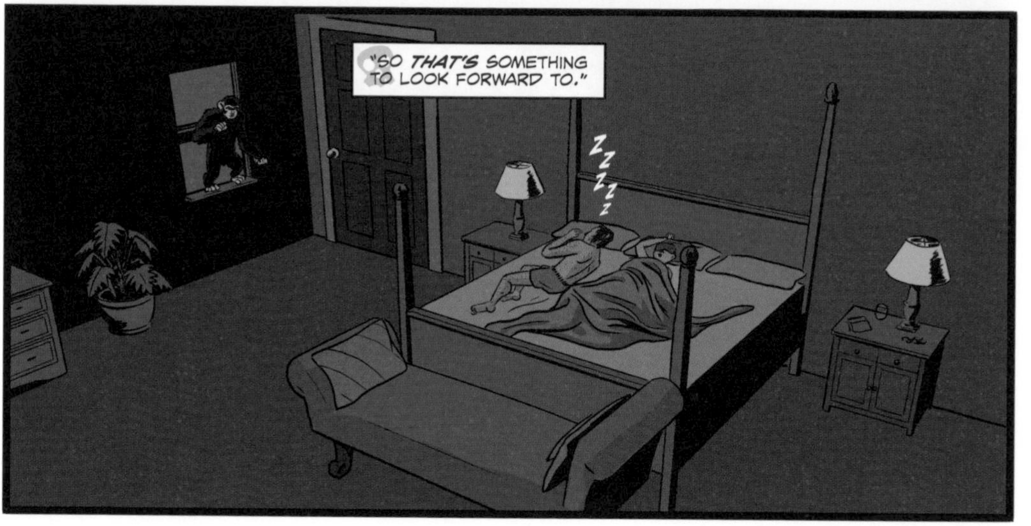
"SO THAT'S SOMETHING TO LOOK FORWARD TO."
ZZZZZ

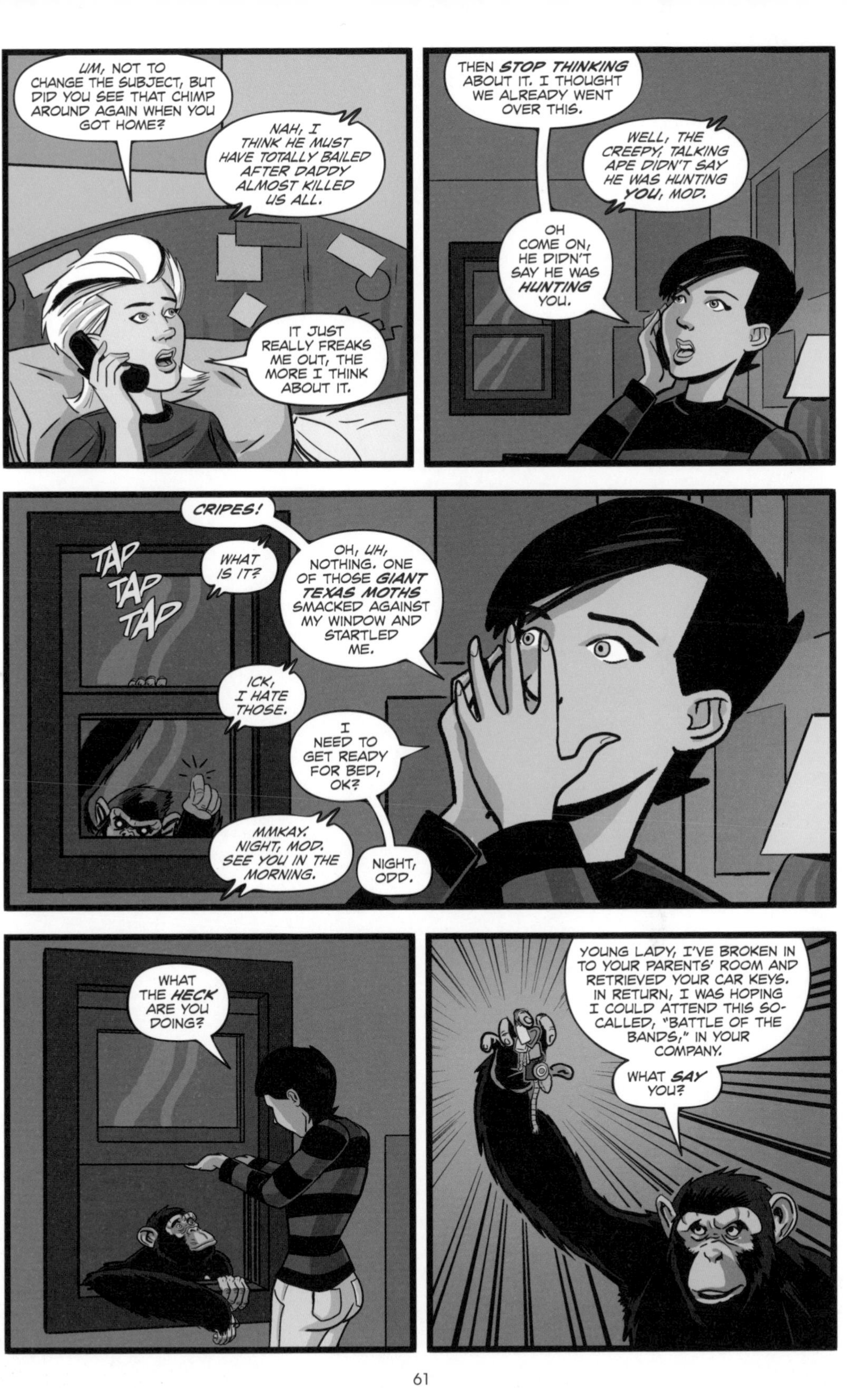
UM, NOT TO CHANGE THE SUBJECT, BUT DID YOU SEE THAT CHIMP AROUND AGAIN WHEN YOU GOT HOME?
NAH, I THINK HE MUST HAVE TOTALLY BAILED AFTER DADDY ALMOST KILLED US ALL.
IT JUST REALLY FREAKS ME OUT, THE MORE I THINK ABOUT IT.
THEN STOP THINKING ABOUT IT. I THOUGHT WE ALREADY WENT OVER THIS.
WELL, THE CREEPY, TALKING APE DIDN'T SAY HE WAS HUNTING YOU, MOD.
OH COME ON, HE DIDN'T SAY HE WAS HUNTING YOU.
TAP TAP TAP
CRIPES!
WHAT IS IT?
OH, UH, NOTHING. ONE OF THOSE GIANT TEXAS MOTHS SMACKED AGAINST MY WINDOW AND STARTLED ME.
ICK, I HATE THOSE.
I NEED TO GET READY FOR BED, OK?
MMKAY. NIGHT, MOD. SEE YOU IN THE MORNING.
NIGHT, ODD.
WHAT THE HECK ARE YOU DOING?
YOUNG LADY, I'VE BROKEN IN TO YOUR PARENTS' ROOM AND RETRIEVED YOUR CAR KEYS. IN RETURN, I WAS HOPING I COULD ATTEND THIS SO-CALLED, "BATTLE OF THE BANDS," IN YOUR COMPANY.
WHAT SAY YOU?

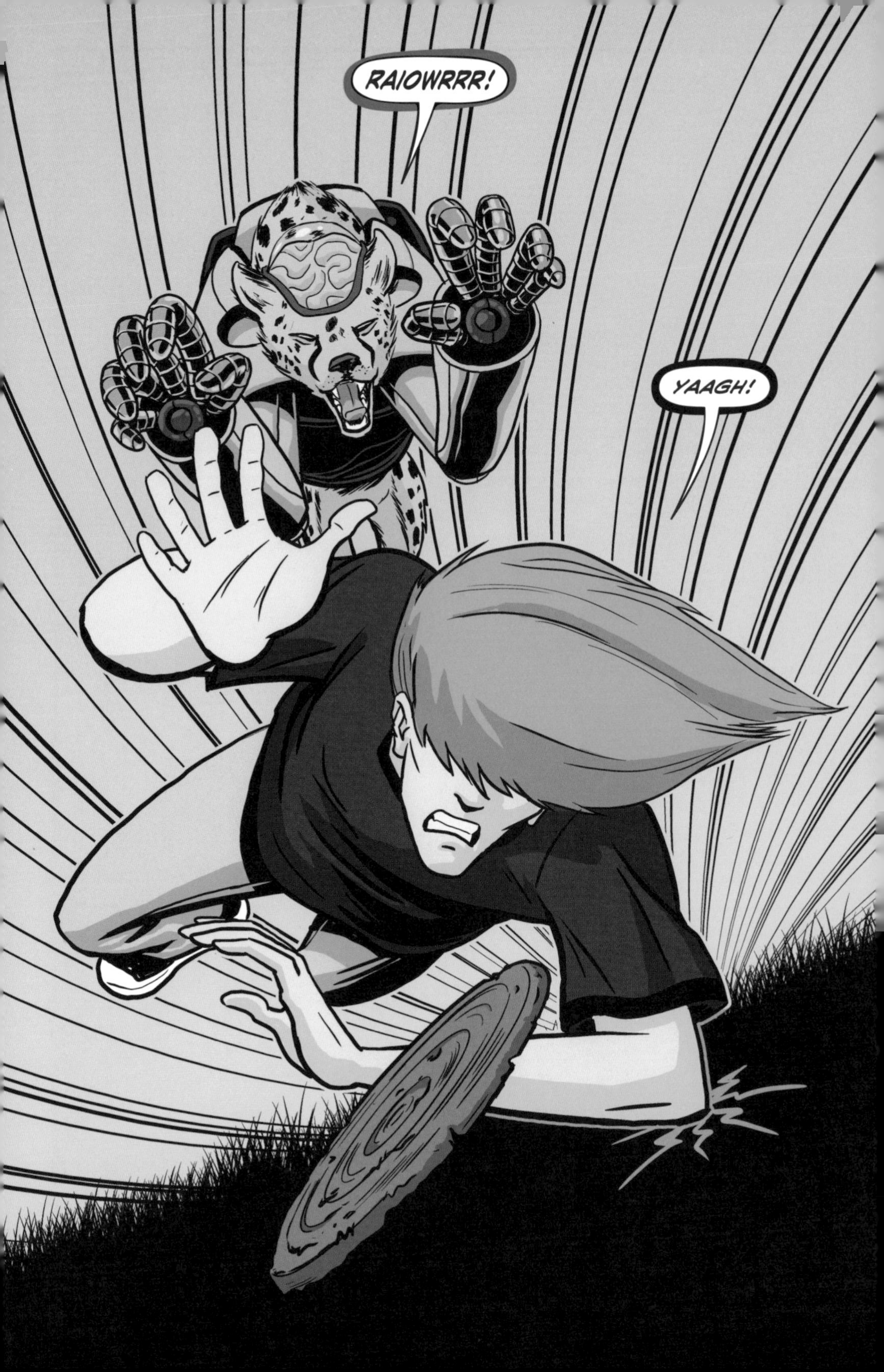
RAIOWRRR!
YAAGH!

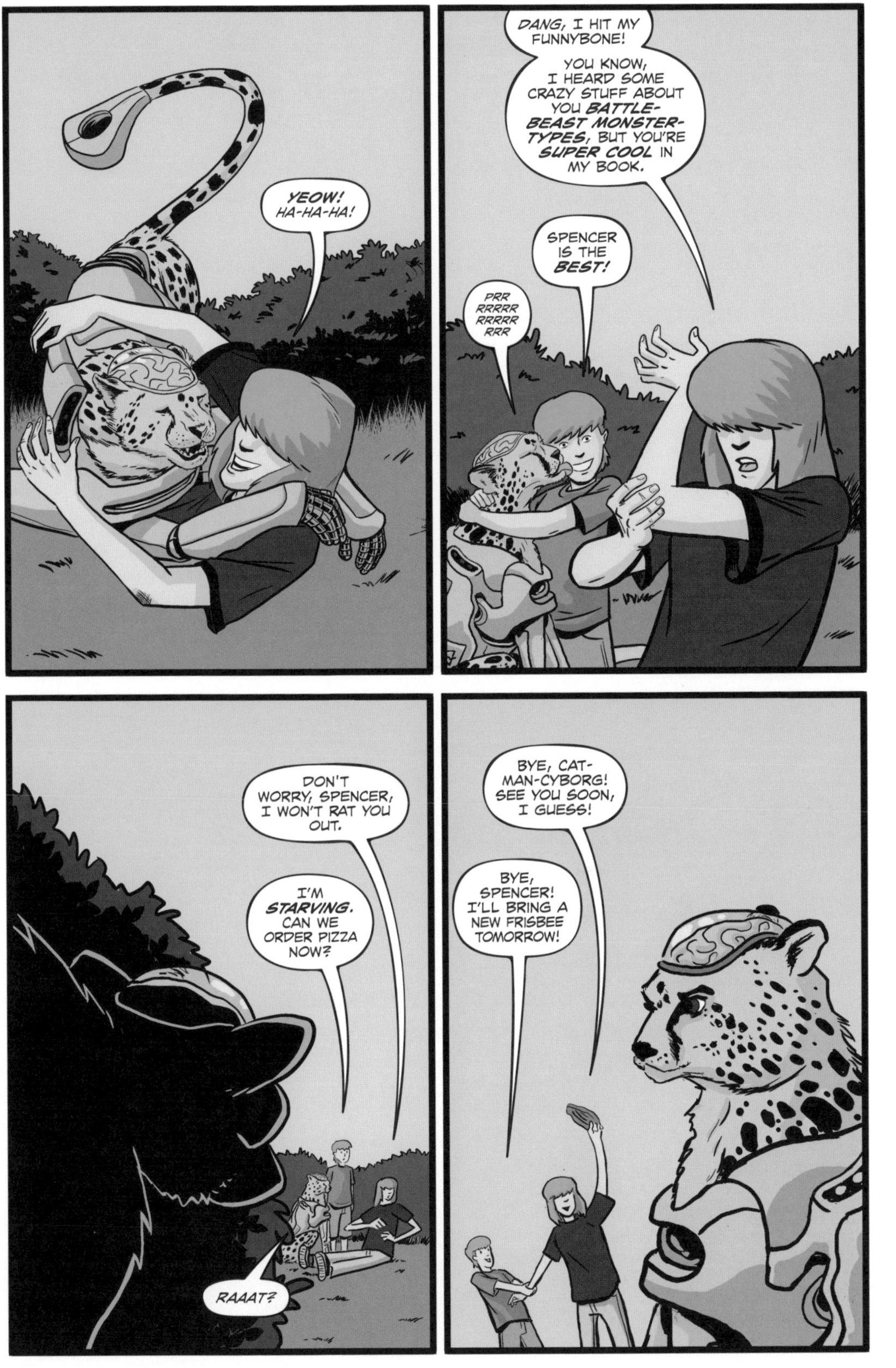
YEOW! HA-HA-HA!
DANG, I HIT MY FUNNYBONE!
YOU KNOW, I HEARD SOME CRAZY STUFF ABOUT YOU BATTLE-BEAST MONSTER-TYPES, BUT YOU'RE SUPER COOL IN MY BOOK.
SPENCER IS THE BEST!
PRR RRRRR RRRRR RRR
DON'T WORRY, SPENCER, I WON'T RAT YOU OUT.
I'M STARVING. CAN WE ORDER PIZZA NOW?
RAAAT?
BYE, CAT-MAN-CYBORG! SEE YOU SOON, I GUESS!
BYE, SPENCER! I'LL BRING A NEW FRISBEE TOMORROW!

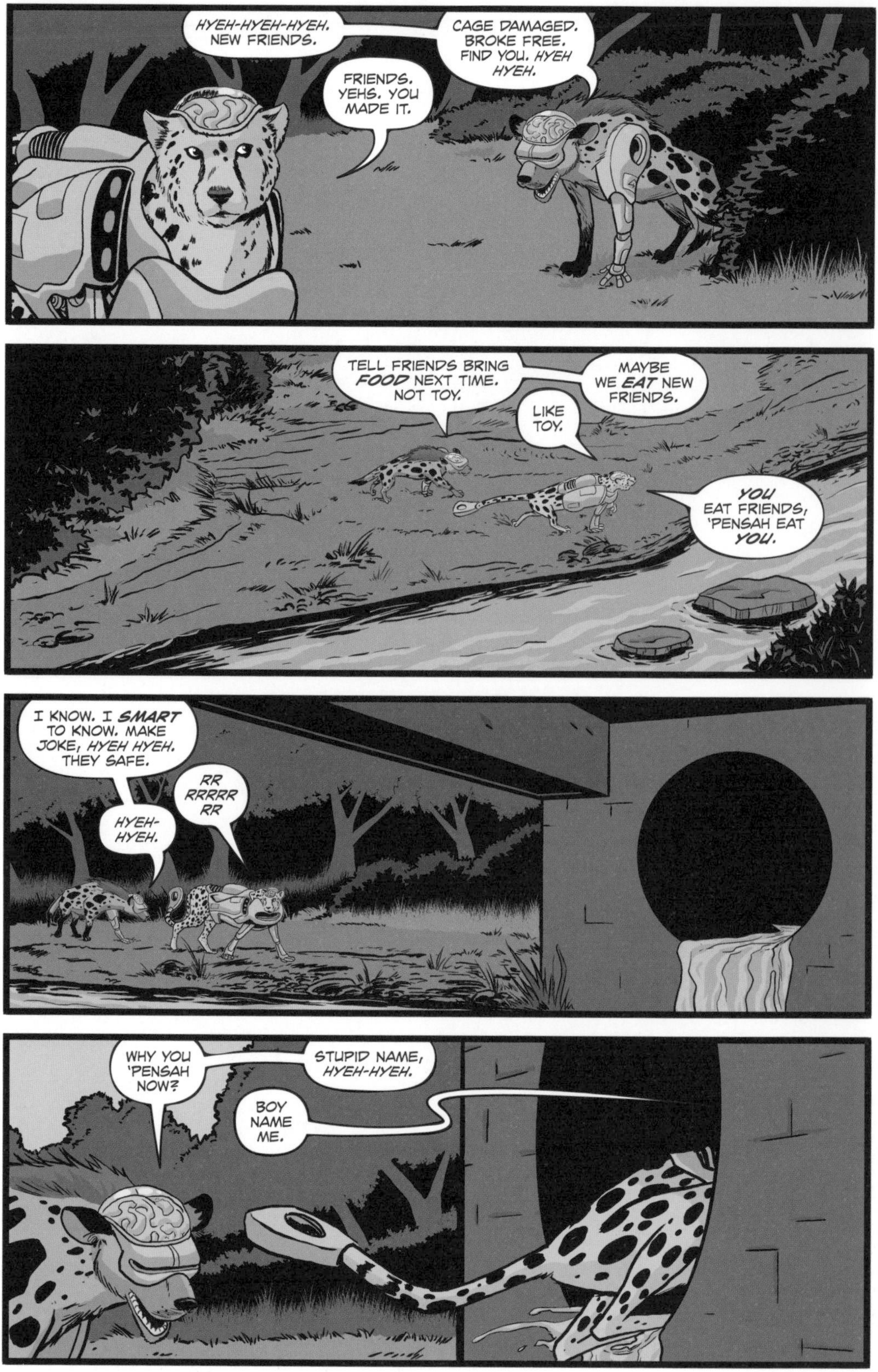
HYEH-HYEH-HYEH. NEW FRIENDS.
FRIENDS. YEHS. YOU MADE IT.
CAGE DAMAGED. BROKE FREE. FIND YOU. HYEH HYEH.
TELL FRIENDS BRING FOOD NEXT TIME. NOT TOY.
MAYBE WE EAT NEW FRIENDS.
LIKE TOY.
YOU EAT FRIENDS, 'PENSAH EAT YOU.
I KNOW. I SMART TO KNOW. MAKE JOKE, HYEH HYEH. THEY SAFE.
HYEH-HYEH.
RR RRRRR RR
WHY YOU 'PENSAH NOW?
STUPID NAME, HYEH-HYEH.
BOY NAME ME.

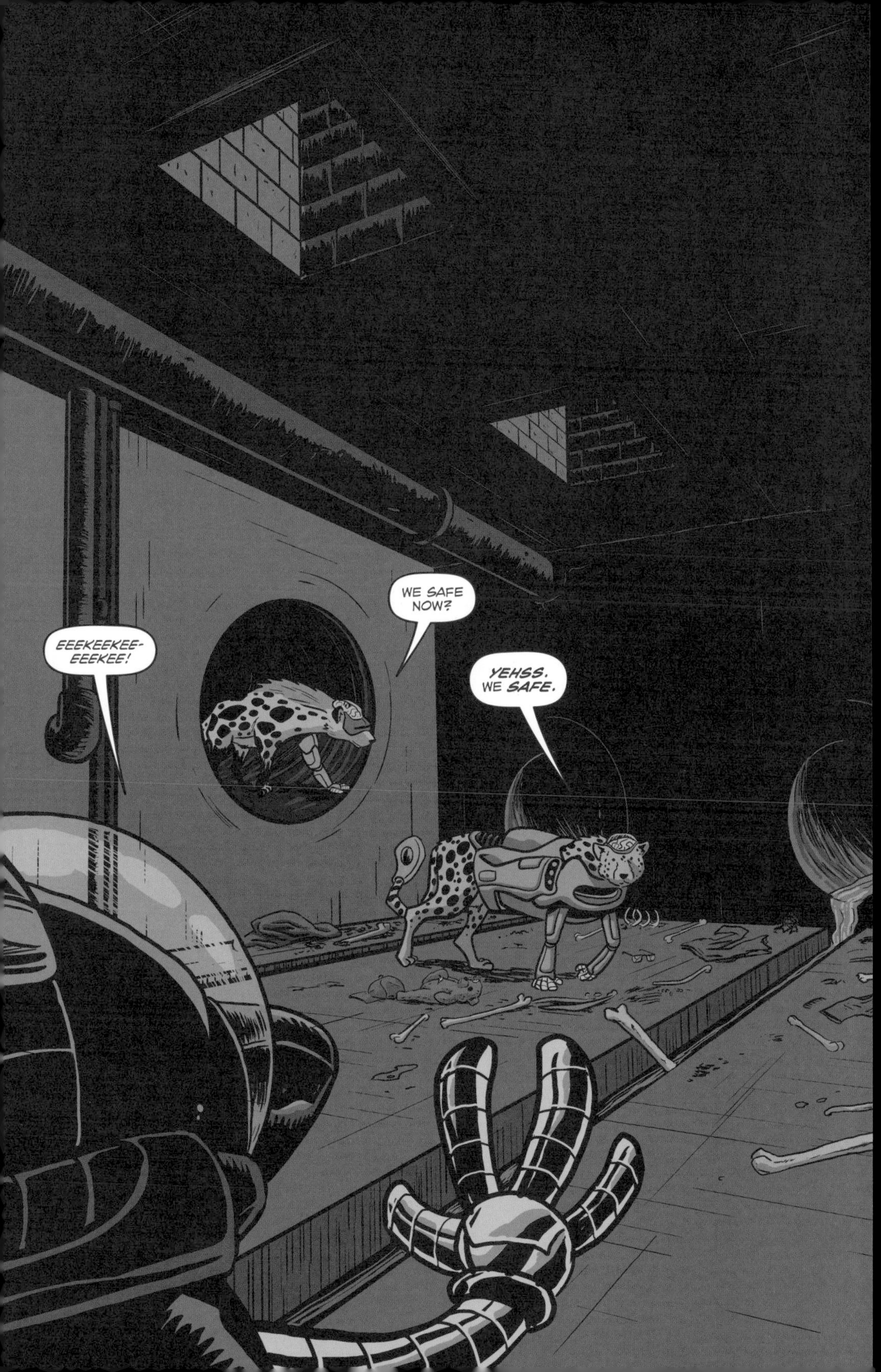
EEEKEEKEE-
EEEKEE!
WE SAFE
NOW?
YEHSS.
WE SAFE.

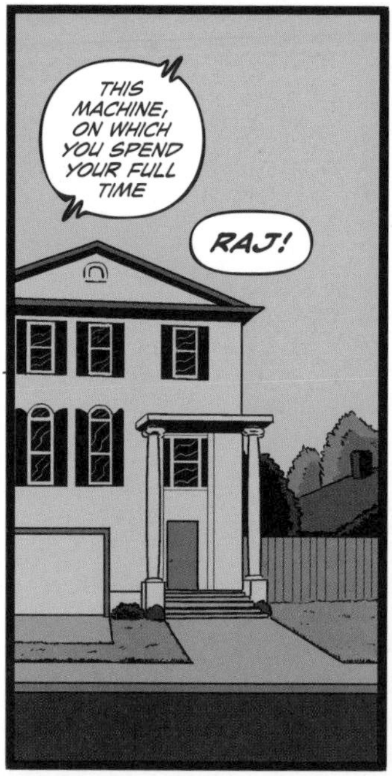
THIS MACHINE, ON WHICH YOU SPEND YOUR FULL TIME
RAJ!

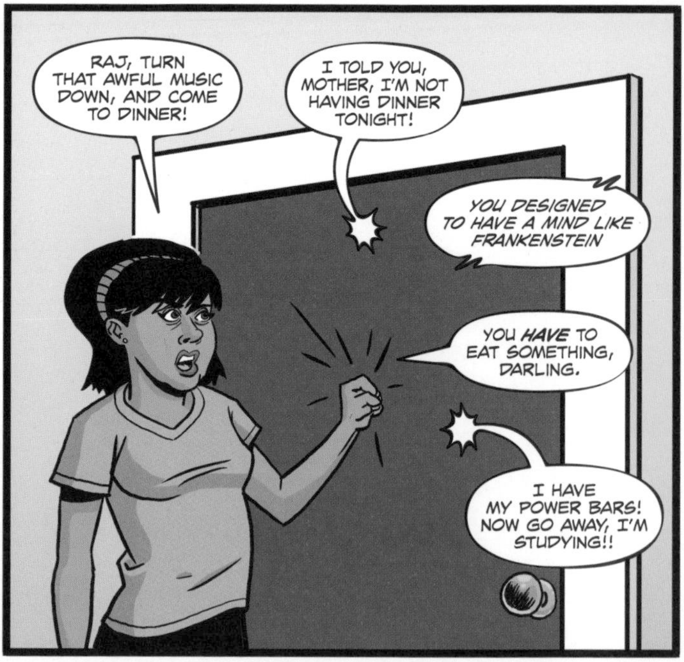
RAJ, TURN THAT AWFUL MUSIC DOWN, AND COME TO DINNER!
I TOLD YOU, MOTHER, I'M NOT HAVING DINNER TONIGHT!
YOU DESIGNED TO HAVE A MIND LIKE FRANKENSTEIN
YOU HAVE TO EAT SOMETHING, DARLING.
I HAVE MY POWER BARS! NOW GO AWAY, I'M STUDYING!!

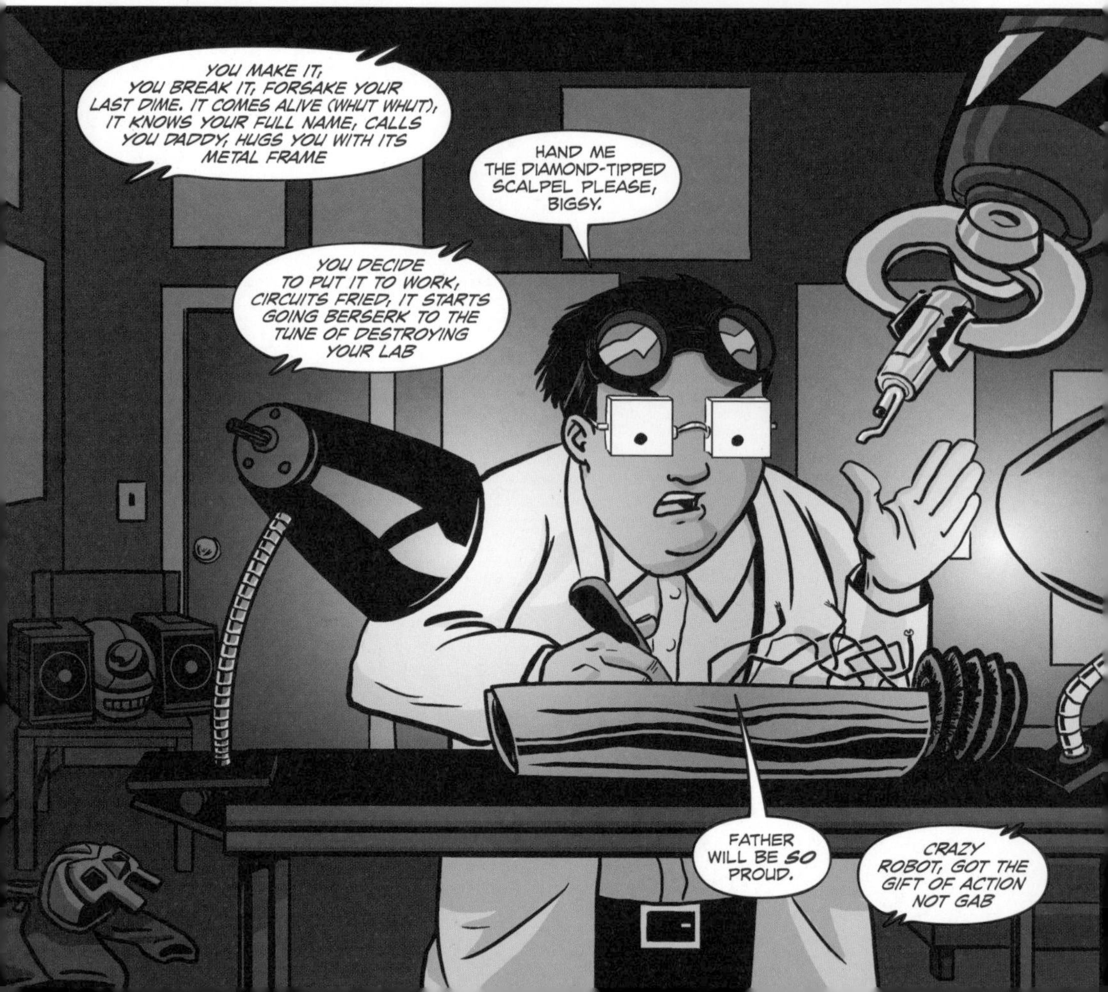
YOU MAKE IT, YOU BREAK IT, FORSAKE YOUR LAST DIME. IT COMES ALIVE (WHUT WHUT), IT KNOWS YOUR FULL NAME, CALLS YOU DADDY, HUGS YOU WITH ITS METAL FRAME
HAND ME THE DIAMOND-TIPPED SCALPEL PLEASE, BIGSY.
YOU DECIDE TO PUT IT TO WORK, CIRCUITS FRIED, IT STARTS GOING BERSERK TO THE TUNE OF DESTROYING YOUR LAB
FATHER WILL BE SO PROUD.
CRAZY ROBOT, GOT THE GIFT OF ACTION NOT GAB

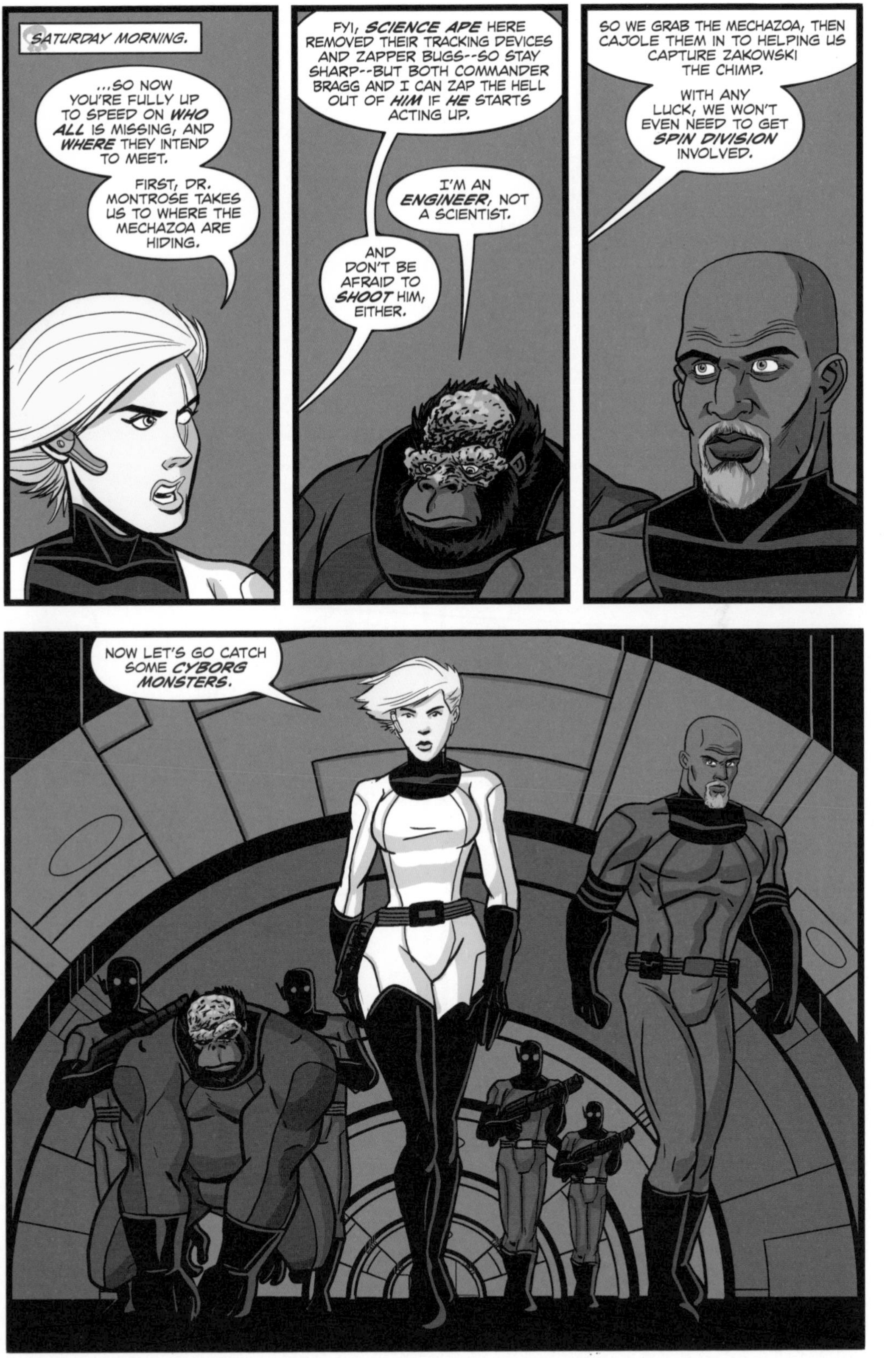
SATURDAY MORNING.
...SO NOW YOU'RE FULLY UP TO SPEED ON WHO ALL IS MISSING, AND WHERE THEY INTEND TO MEET.
FIRST, DR. MONTROSE TAKES US TO WHERE THE MECHAZOA ARE HIDING.
FYI, SCIENCE APE HERE REMOVED THEIR TRACKING DEVICES AND ZAPPER BUGS--SO STAY SHARP--BUT BOTH COMMANDER BRAGG AND I CAN ZAP THE HELL OUT OF HIM IF HE STARTS ACTING UP.
AND DON'T BE AFRAID TO SHOOT HIM, EITHER.
I'M AN ENGINEER, NOT A SCIENTIST.
SO WE GRAB THE MECHAZOA, THEN CAJOLE THEM IN TO HELPING US CAPTURE ZAKOWSKI THE CHIMP.
WITH ANY LUCK, WE WON'T EVEN NEED TO GET SPIN DIVISION INVOLVED.
NOW LET'S GO CATCH SOME CYBORG MONSTERS.

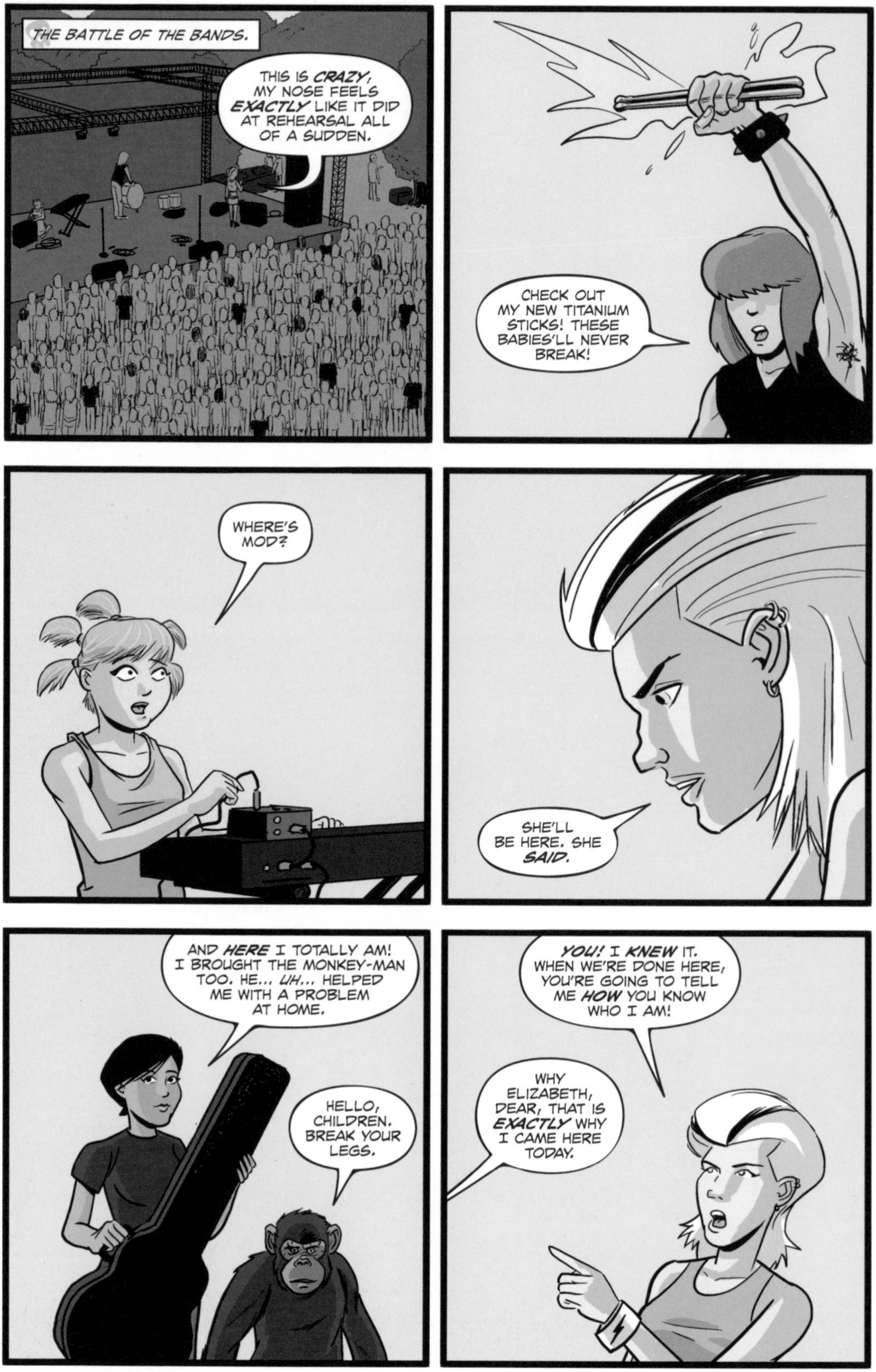
THE BATTLE OF THE BANDS.
THIS IS CRAZY, MY NOSE FEELS EXACTLY LIKE IT DID AT REHEARSAL ALL OF A SUDDEN.
CHECK OUT MY NEW TITANIUM STICKS! THESE BABIES'LL NEVER BREAK!
WHERE'S MOD?
SHE'LL BE HERE. SHE SAID.
AND HERE I TOTALLY AM! I BROUGHT THE MONKEY-MAN TOO. HE... UH... HELPED ME WITH A PROBLEM AT HOME.
HELLO, CHILDREN. BREAK YOUR LEGS.
YOU! I KNEW IT. WHEN WE'RE DONE HERE, YOU'RE GOING TO TELL ME HOW YOU KNOW WHO I AM!
WHY ELIZABETH, DEAR, THAT IS EXACTLY WHY I CAME HERE TODAY.

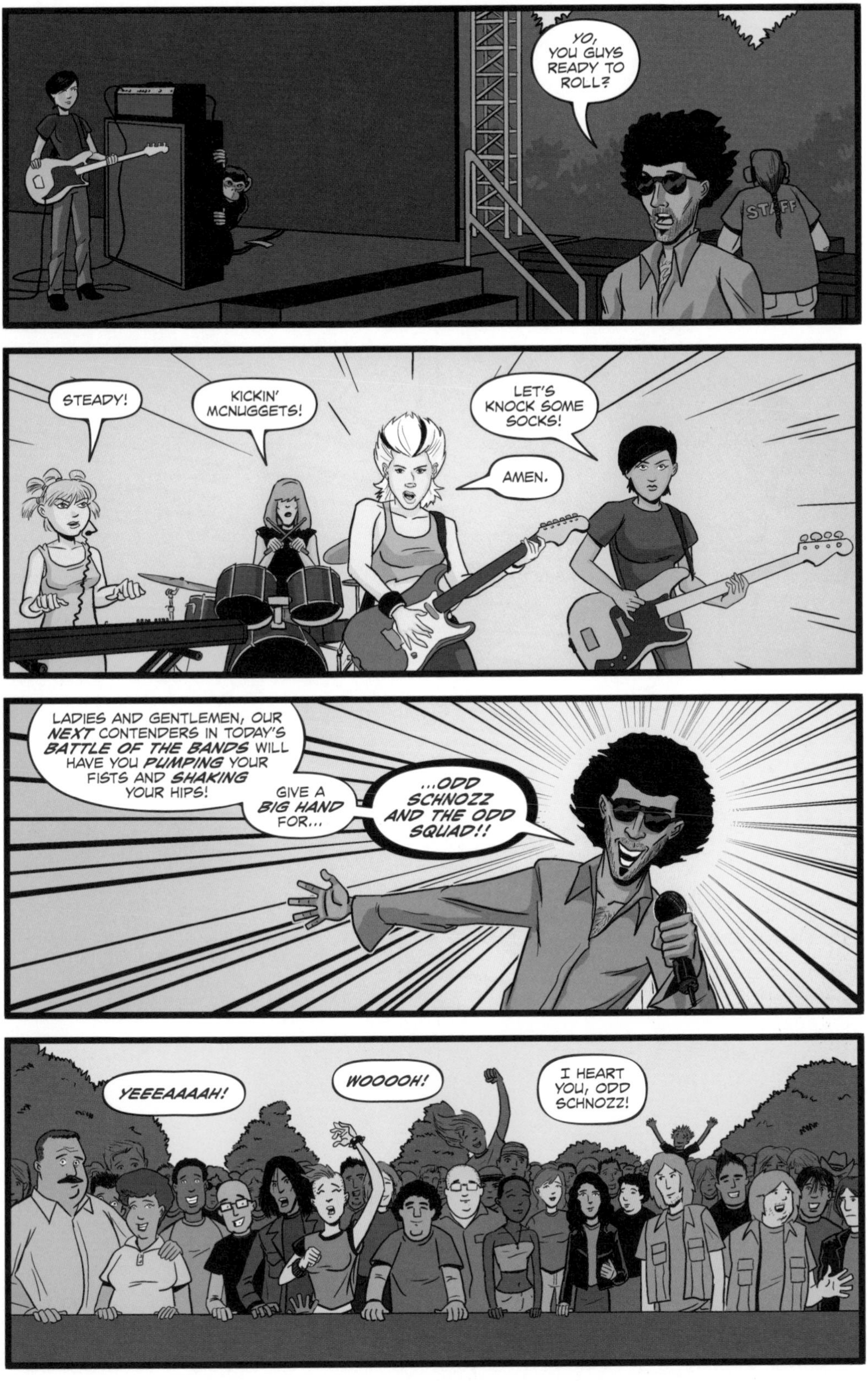
YO, YOU GUYS READY TO ROLL?
STAFF
STEADY!
KICKIN' MCNUGGETS!
LET'S KNOCK SOME SOCKS!
AMEN.
LADIES AND GENTLEMEN, OUR NEXT CONTENDERS IN TODAY'S BATTLE OF THE BANDS WILL HAVE YOU PUMPING YOUR FISTS AND SHAKING YOUR HIPS!
GIVE A BIG HAND FOR...
...ODD SCHNOZZ AND THE ODD SQUAD!!
YEEEAAAAH!
WOOOOH!
I HEART YOU, ODD SCHNOZZ!

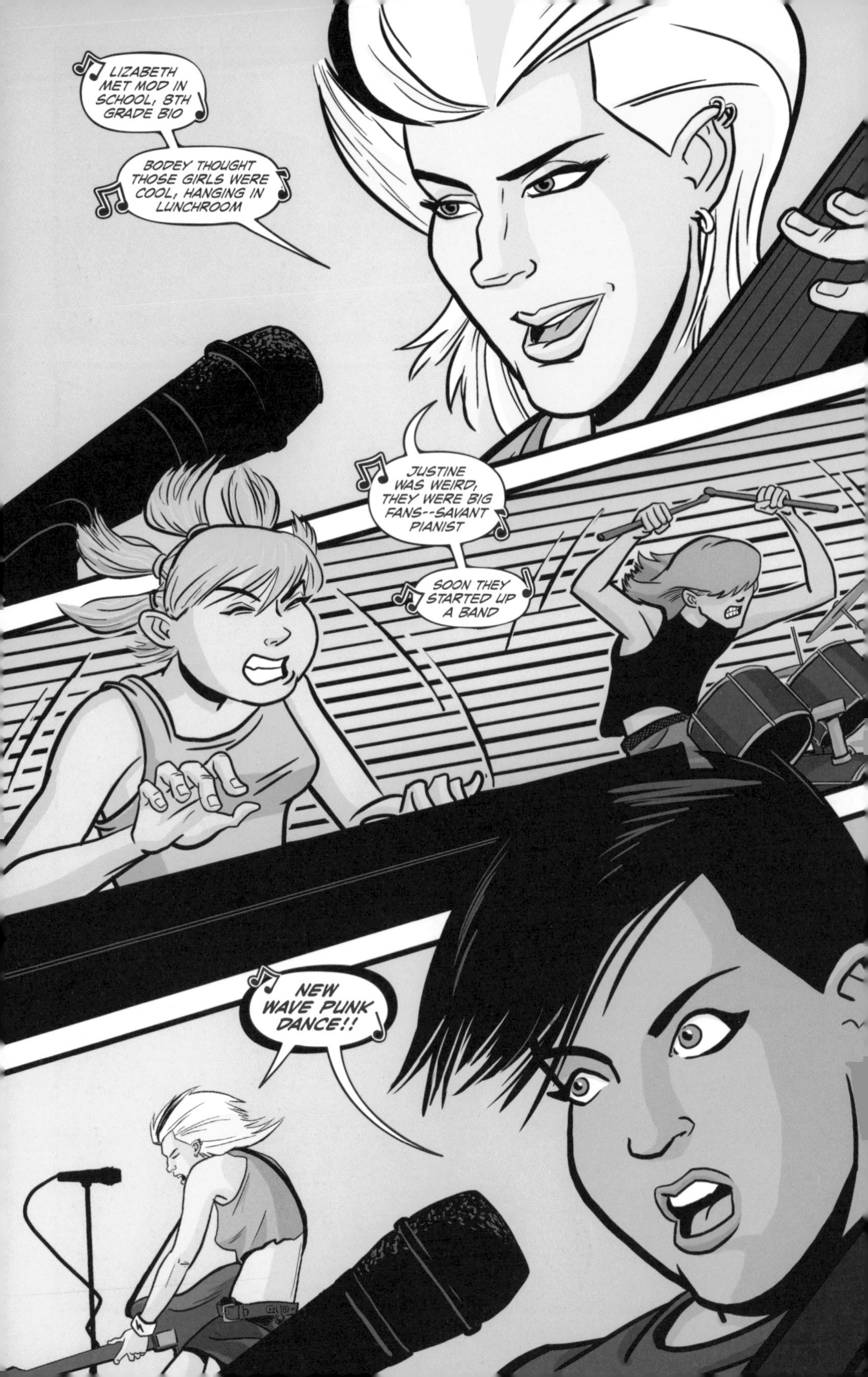
LIZABETH MET MOD IN SCHOOL, 8TH GRADE BIO
BODEY THOUGHT THOSE GIRLS WERE COOL, HANGING IN LUNCHROOM
JUSTINE WAS WEIRD, THEY WERE BIG FANS--SAVANT PIANIST
SOON THEY STARTED UP A BAND
NEW WAVE PUNK DANCE!!

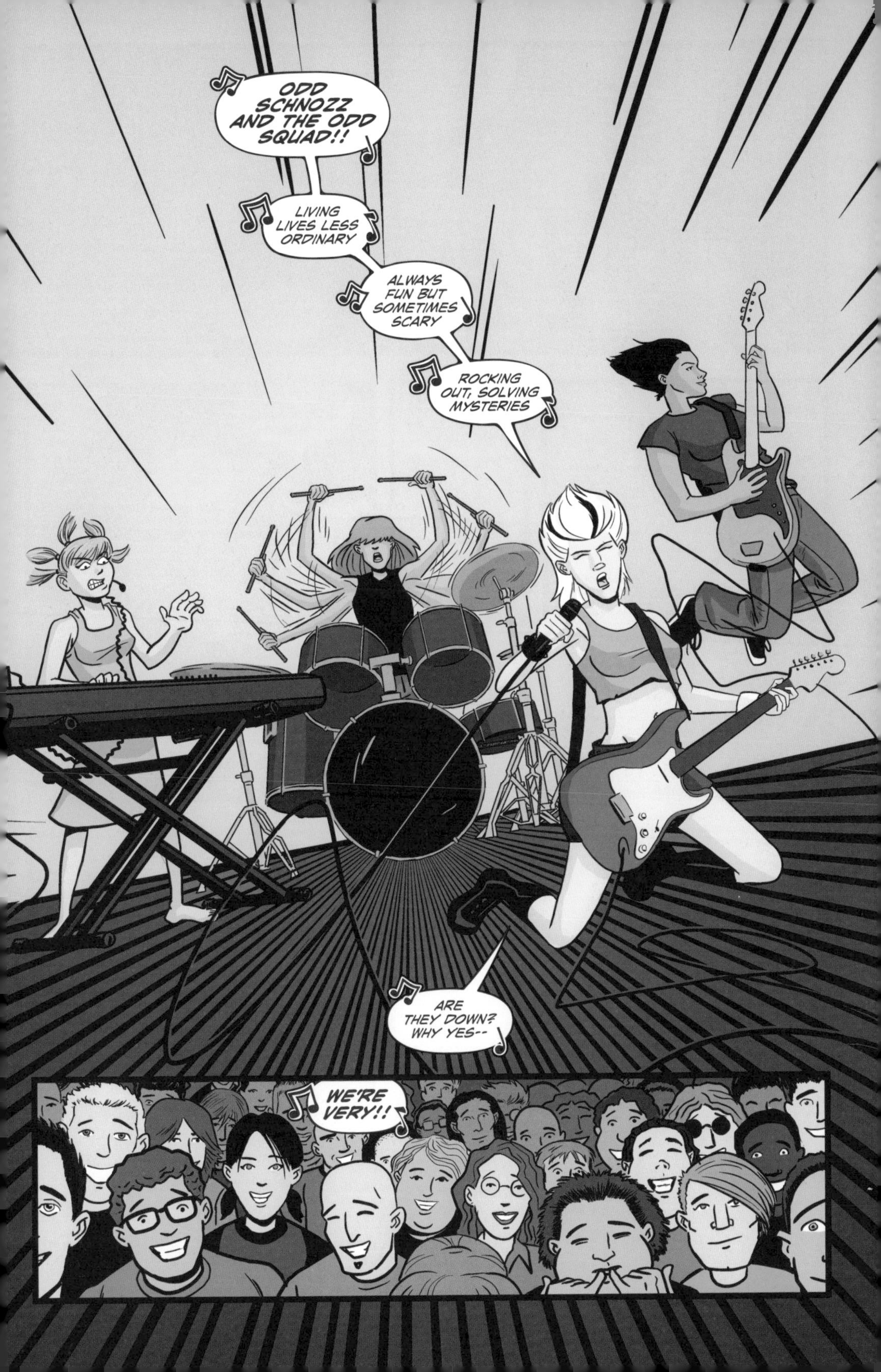
ODD SCHNOZZ AND THE ODD SQUAD!!
LIVING LIVES LESS ORDINARY
ALWAYS FUN BUT SOMETIMES SCARY
ROCKING OUT, SOLVING MYSTERIES
ARE THEY DOWN? WHY YES--
WE'RE VERY!!

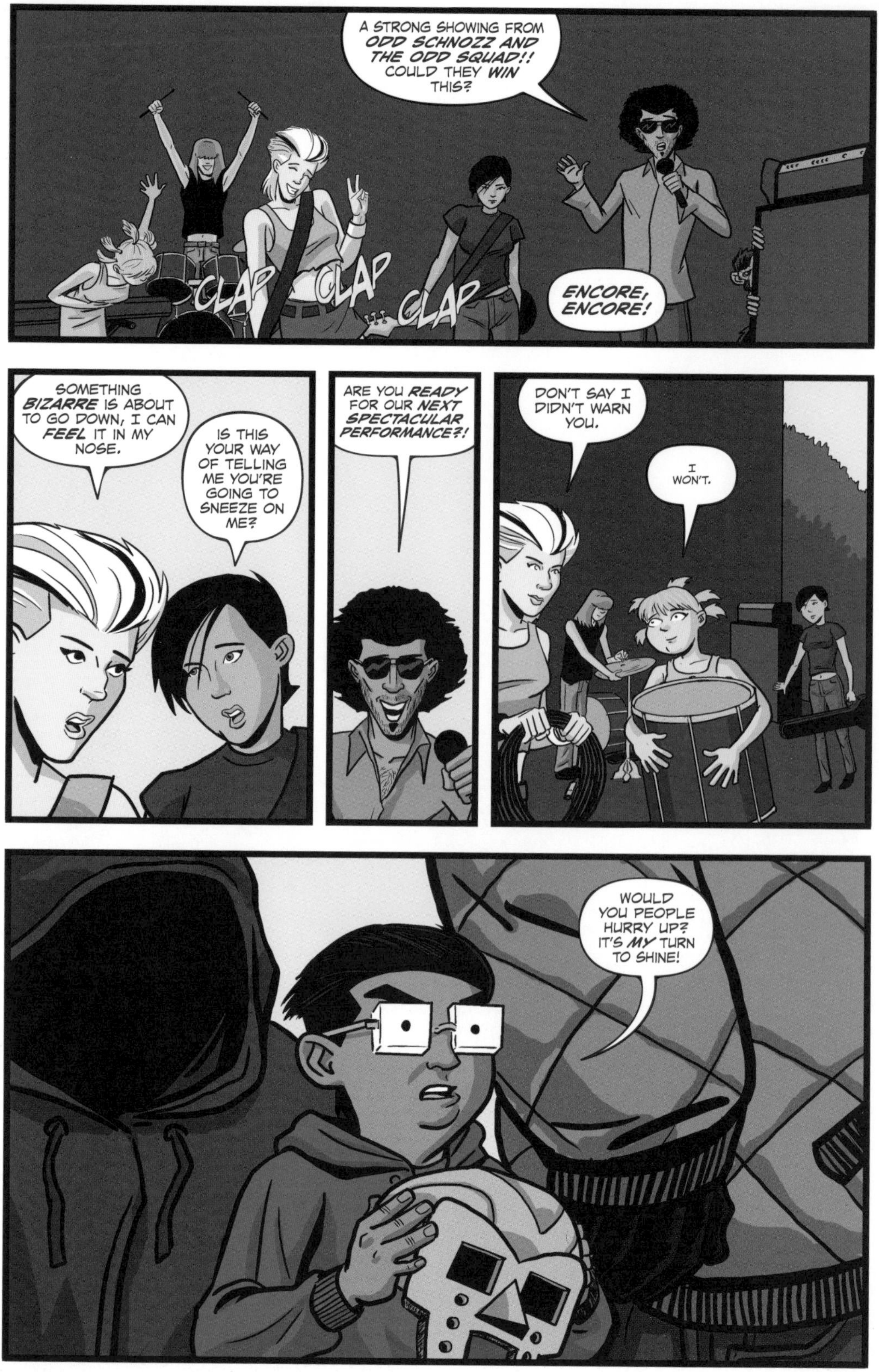
A STRONG SHOWING FROM ODD SCHNOZZ AND THE ODD SQUAD!! COULD THEY WIN THIS?
CLAP CLAP CLAP
ENCORE, ENCORE!
SOMETHING BIZARRE IS ABOUT TO GO DOWN, I CAN FEEL IT IN MY NOSE.
IS THIS YOUR WAY OF TELLING ME YOU'RE GOING TO SNEEZE ON ME?
ARE YOU READY FOR OUR NEXT SPECTACULAR PERFORMANCE?!
DON'T SAY I DIDN'T WARN YOU.
I WON'T.
WOULD YOU PEOPLE HURRY UP? IT'S MY TURN TO SHINE!

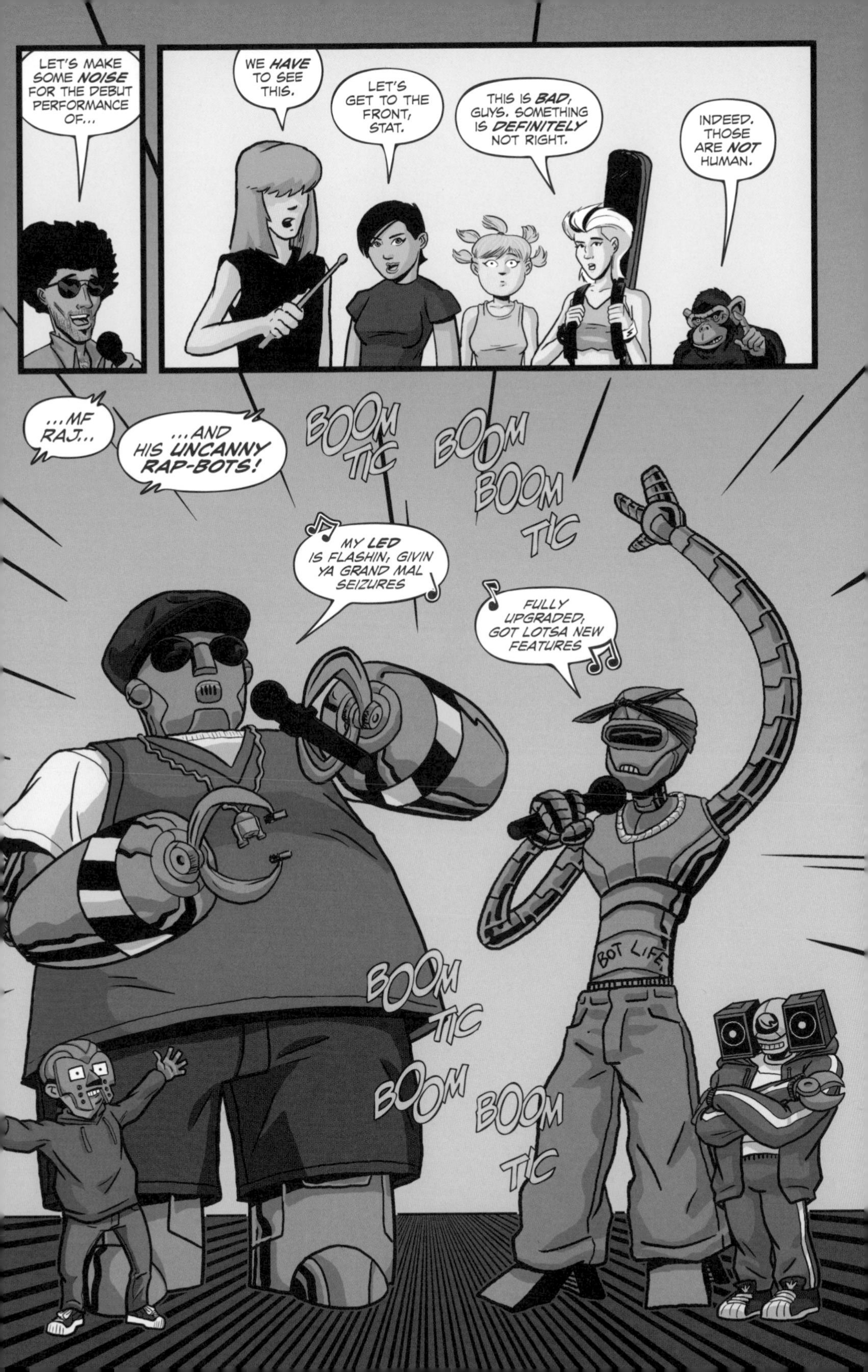

LET'S MAKE SOME NOISE FOR THE DEBUT PERFORMANCE OF...
WE HAVE TO SEE THIS.
LET'S GET TO THE FRONT, STAT.
THIS IS BAD, GUYS. SOMETHING IS DEFINITELY NOT RIGHT.
INDEED. THOSE ARE NOT HUMAN.
...MF RAJ...
...AND HIS UNCANNY RAP-BOTS!
BOOM TIC
BOOM BOOM TIC
MY LED IS FLASHIN, GIVIN YA GRAND MAL SEIZURES
FULLY UPGRADED, GOT LOTSA NEW FEATURES
BOT LIFE
BOOM TIC
BOOM BOOM TIC

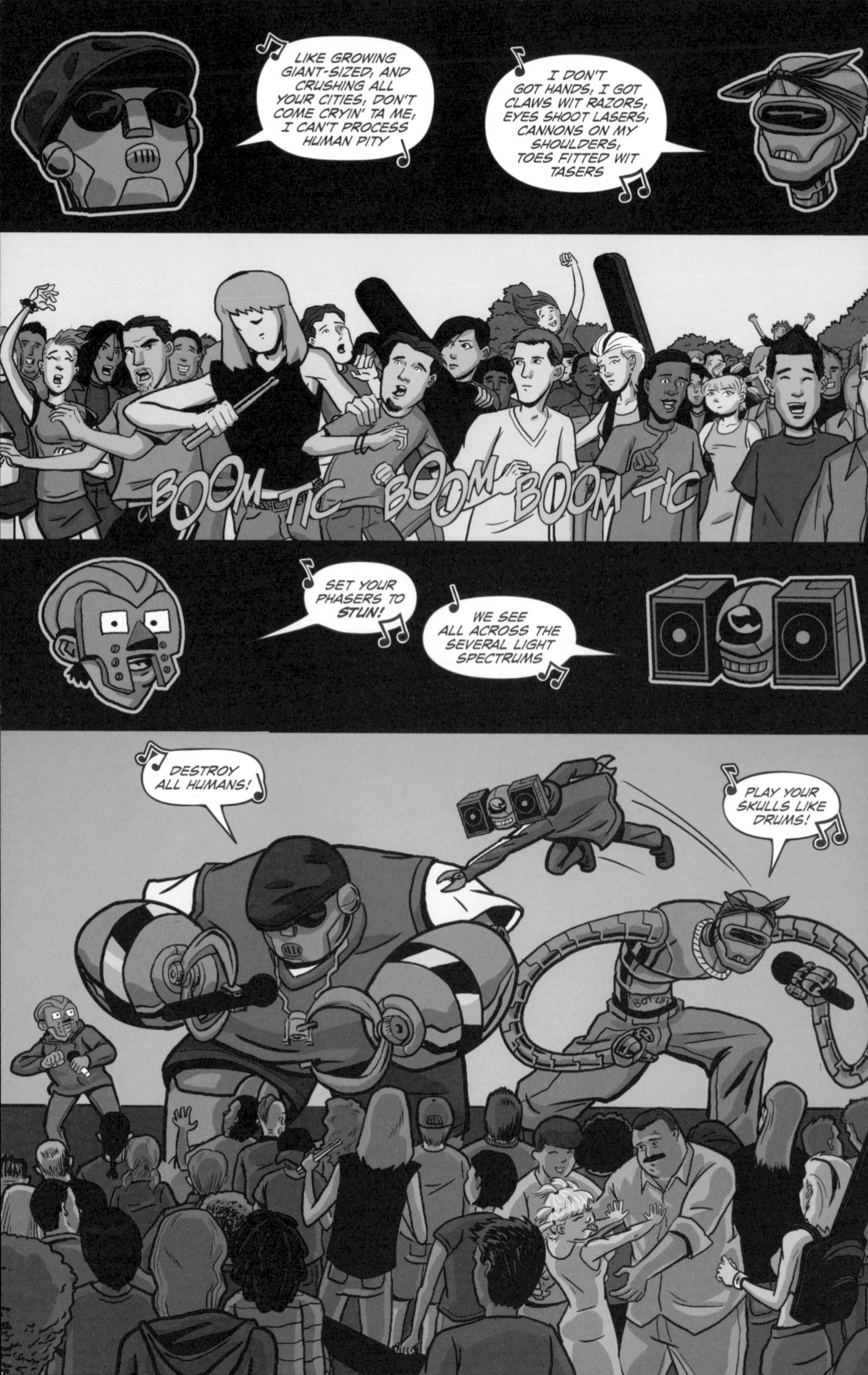
LIKE GROWING GIANT-SIZED, AND CRUSHING ALL YOUR CITIES; DON'T COME CRYIN' TA ME; I CAN'T PROCESS HUMAN PITY
I DON'T GOT HANDS, I GOT CLAWS WIT RAZORS, EYES SHOOT LASERS, CANNONS ON MY SHOULDERS, TOES FITTED WIT TASERS
BOOM TIC BOOM BOOM TIC
SET YOUR PHASERS TO STUN!
WE SEE ALL ACROSS THE SEVERAL LIGHT SPECTRUMS
DESTROY ALL HUMANS!
PLAY YOUR SKULLS LIKE DRUMS!

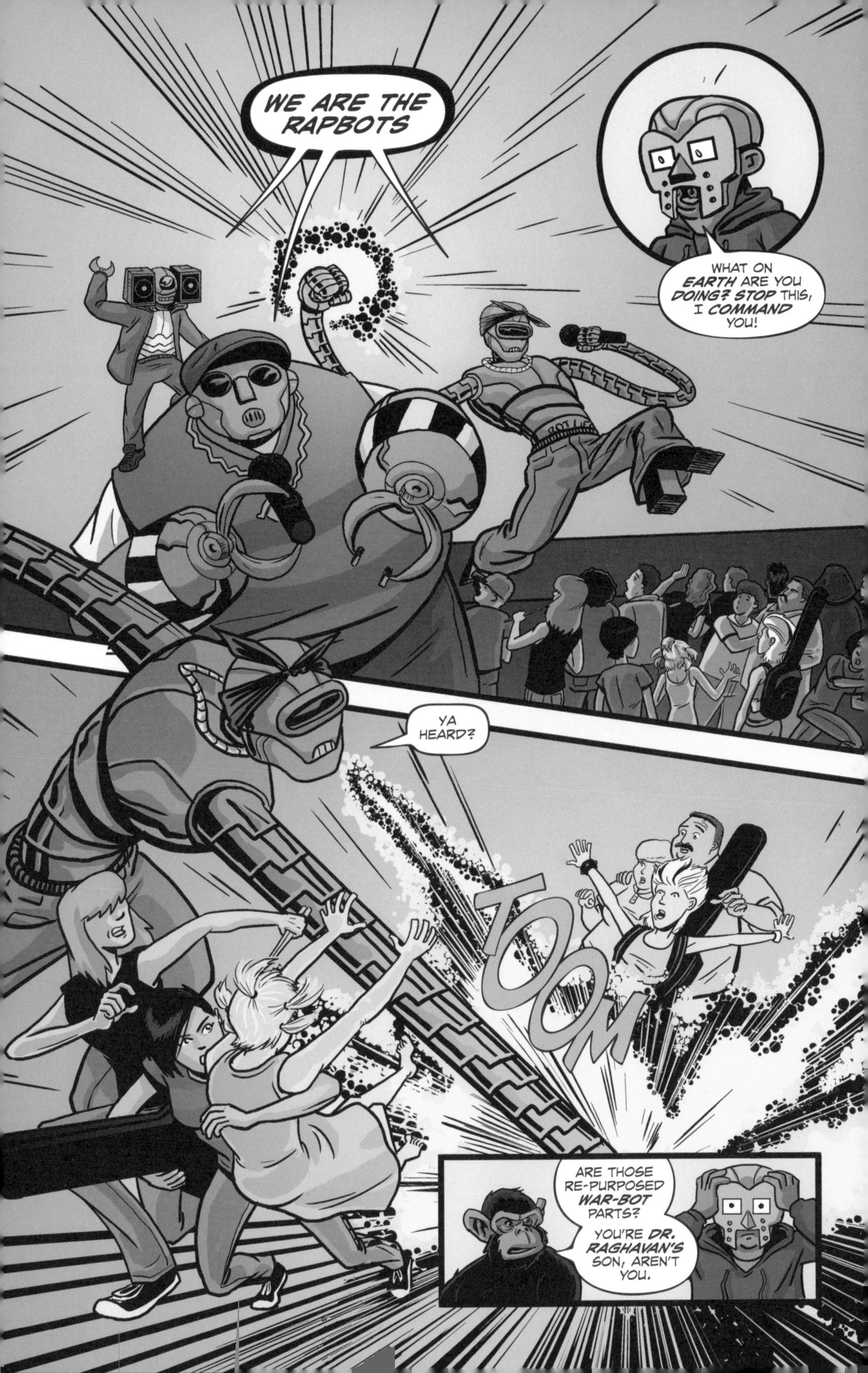
WE ARE THE RAPBOTS
WHAT ON EARTH ARE YOU DOING? STOP THIS, I COMMAND YOU!
YA HEARD?
KOOM
ARE THOSE RE-PURPOSED WAR-BOT PARTS?
YOU'RE DR. RAGHAVAN'S SON, AREN'T YOU.

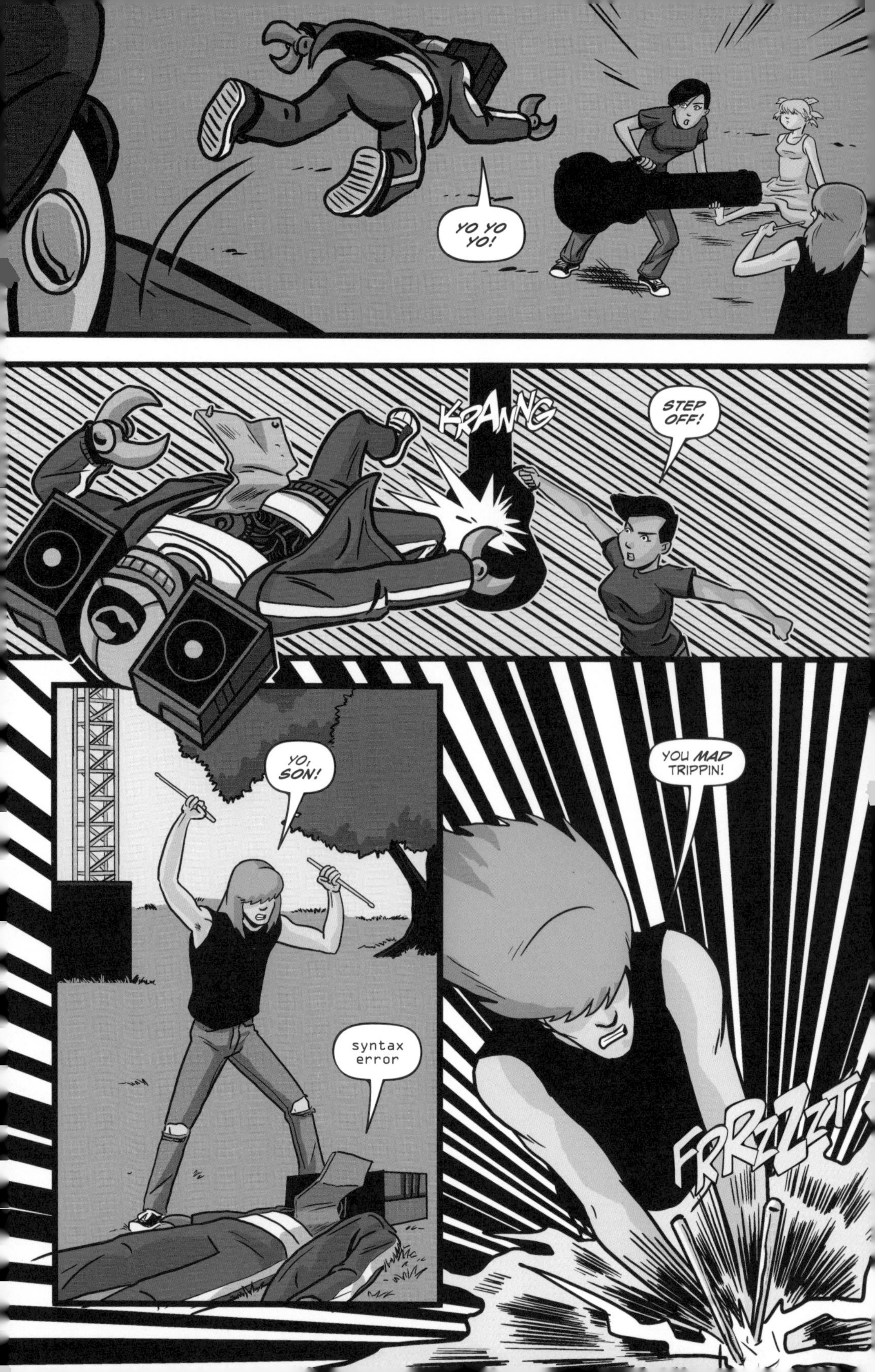
YO YO YO!
KRANNG
STEP OFF!
YO, SON!
syntax error
YOU MAD TRIPPIN!
FRRZZZT

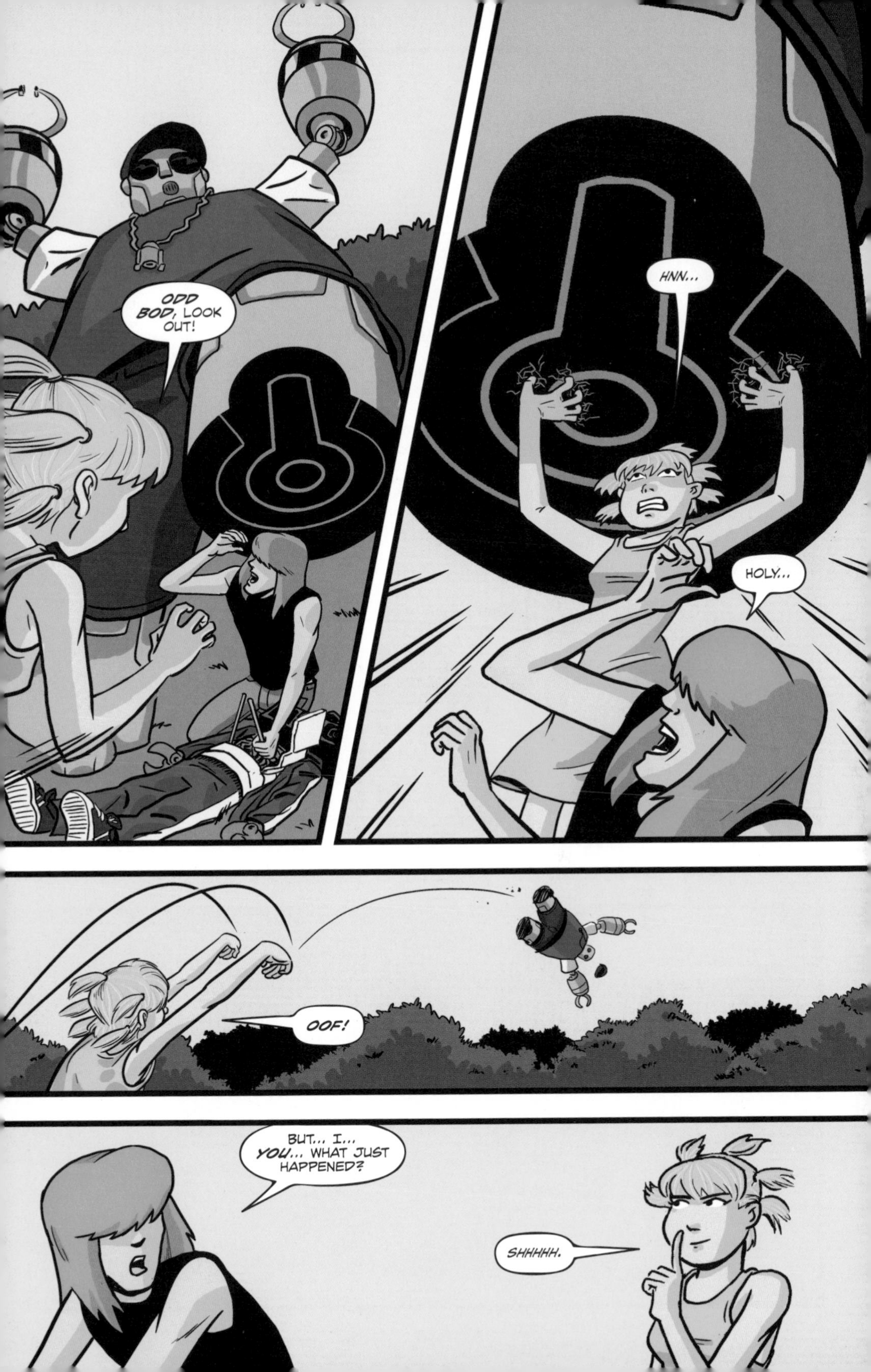
ODD BOD, LOOK OUT!
HNN...
HOLY...
OOF!
BUT... I... YOU... WHAT JUST HAPPENED?
SHHHHH.

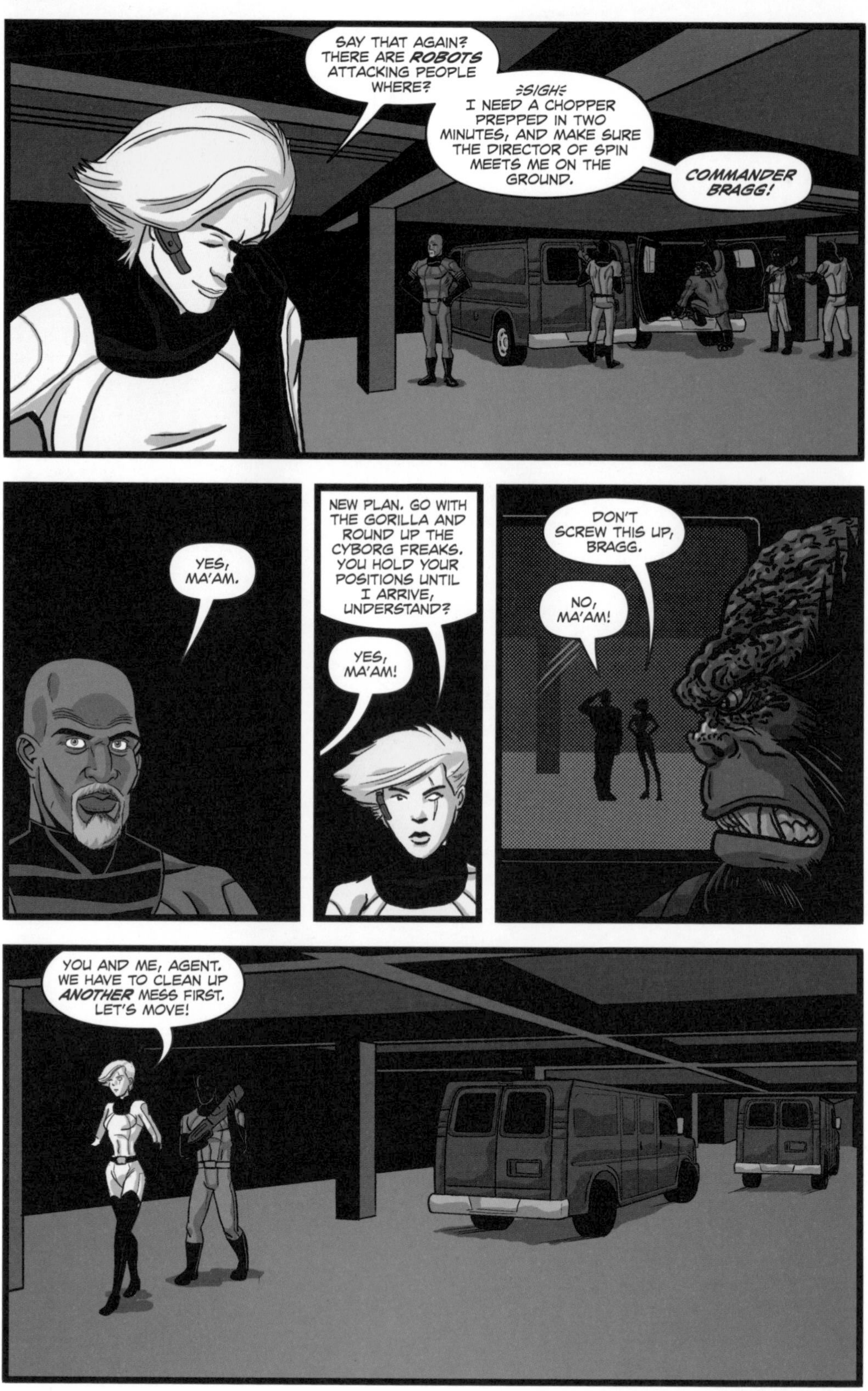
SAY THAT AGAIN? THERE ARE *ROBOTS* ATTACKING PEOPLE WHERE?
SIGH I NEED A CHOPPER PREPPED IN TWO MINUTES, AND MAKE SURE THE DIRECTOR OF SPIN MEETS ME ON THE GROUND.
COMMANDER BRAGG!
YES, MA'AM.
NEW PLAN. GO WITH THE GORILLA AND ROUND UP THE CYBORG FREAKS. YOU HOLD YOUR POSITIONS UNTIL I ARRIVE, UNDERSTAND?
YES, MA'AM!
DON'T SCREW THIS UP, BRAGG.
NO, MA'AM!
YOU AND ME, AGENT. WE HAVE TO CLEAN UP *ANOTHER* MESS FIRST. LET'S MOVE!

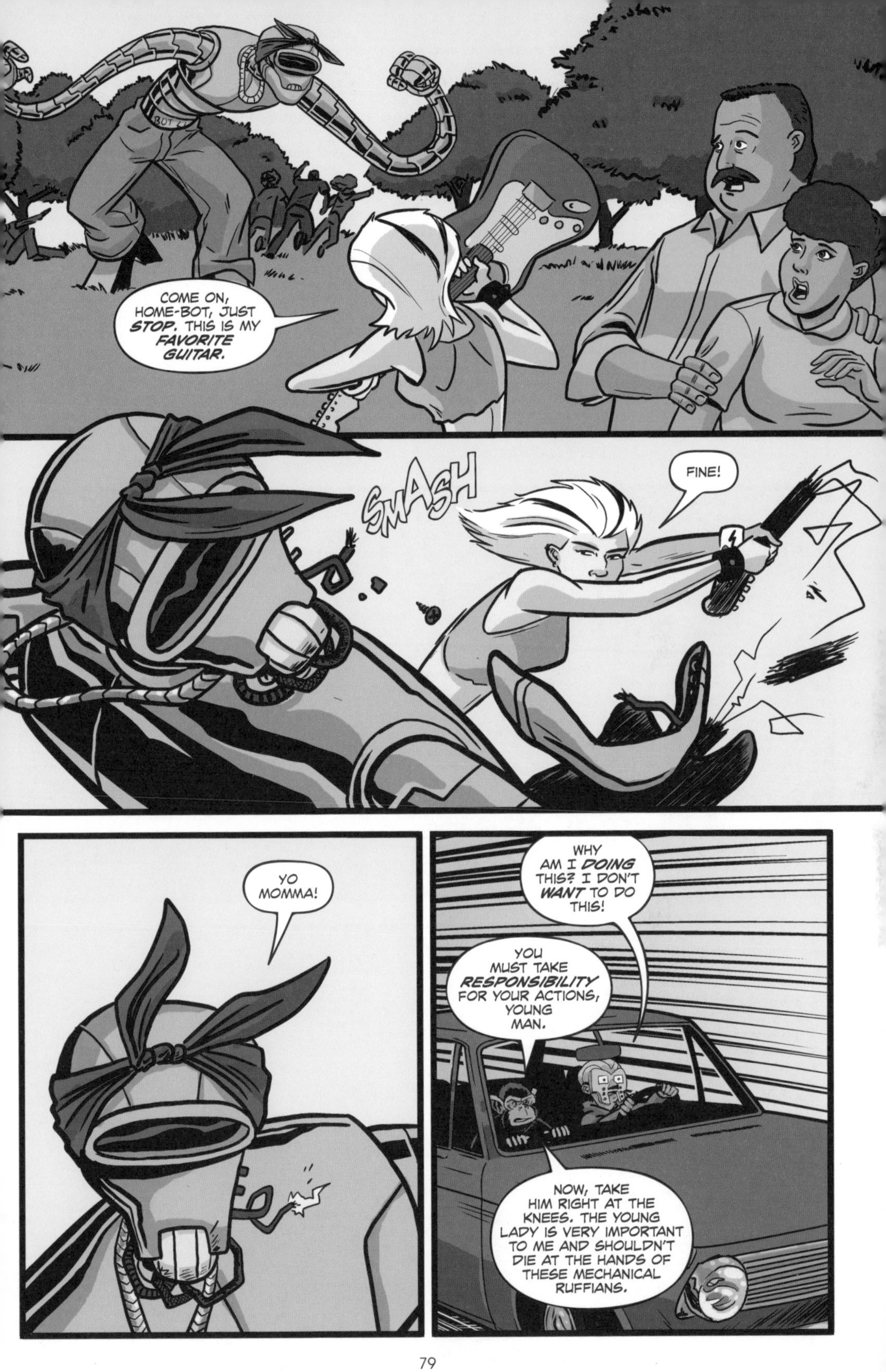

COME ON, HOME-BOT, JUST STOP. THIS IS MY FAVORITE GUITAR.
SMASH
FINE!
YO MOMMA!
WHY AM I DOING THIS? I DON'T WANT TO DO THIS!
YOU MUST TAKE RESPONSIBILITY FOR YOUR ACTIONS, YOUNG MAN.
NOW, TAKE HIM RIGHT AT THE KNEES. THE YOUNG LADY IS VERY IMPORTANT TO ME AND SHOULDN'T DIE AT THE HANDS OF THESE MECHANICAL RUFFIANS.

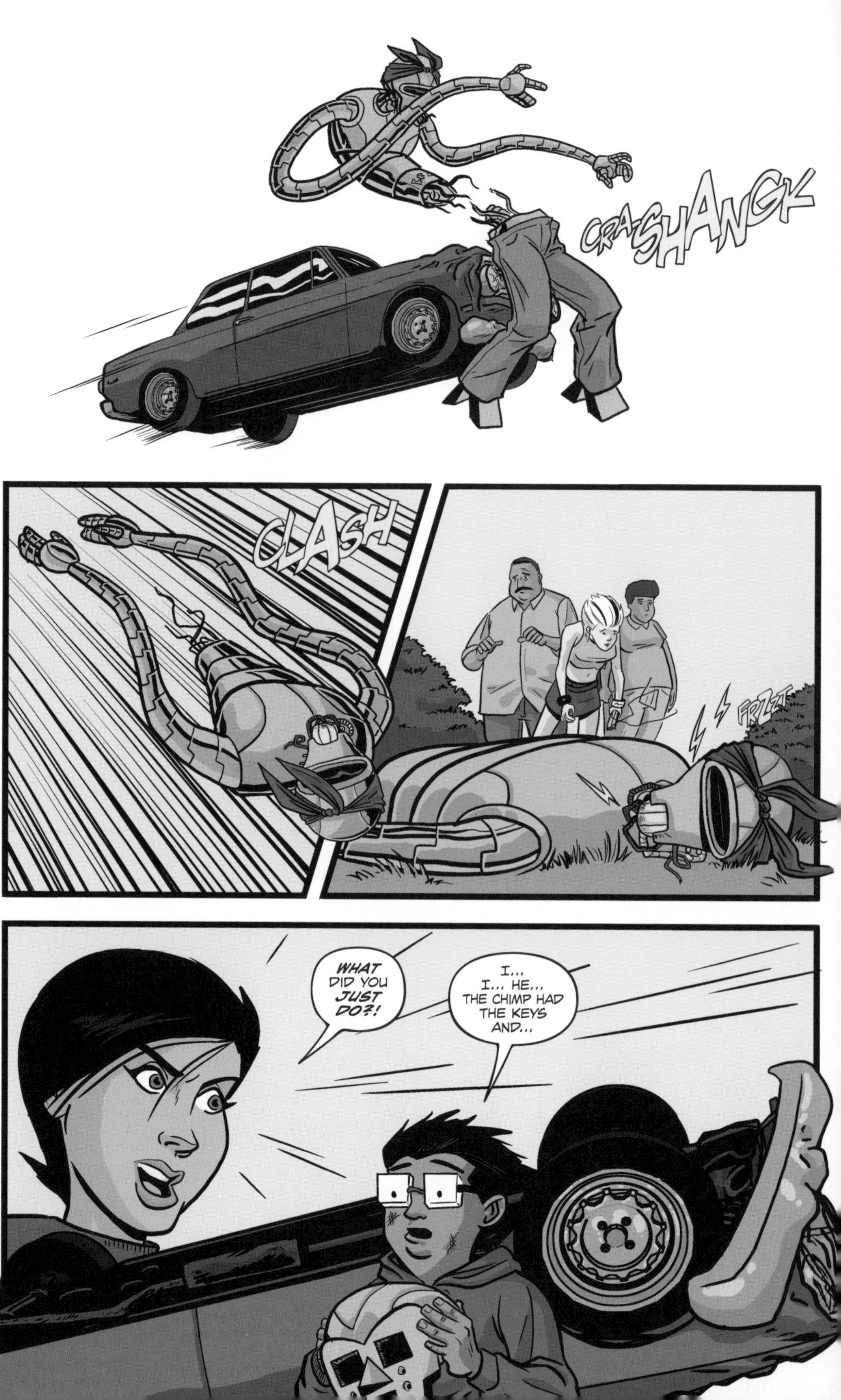
CRA-SHANGK
CLASH
FRZZT
WHAT DID YOU JUST DO?!
I... I... HE... THE CHIMP HAD THE KEYS AND...

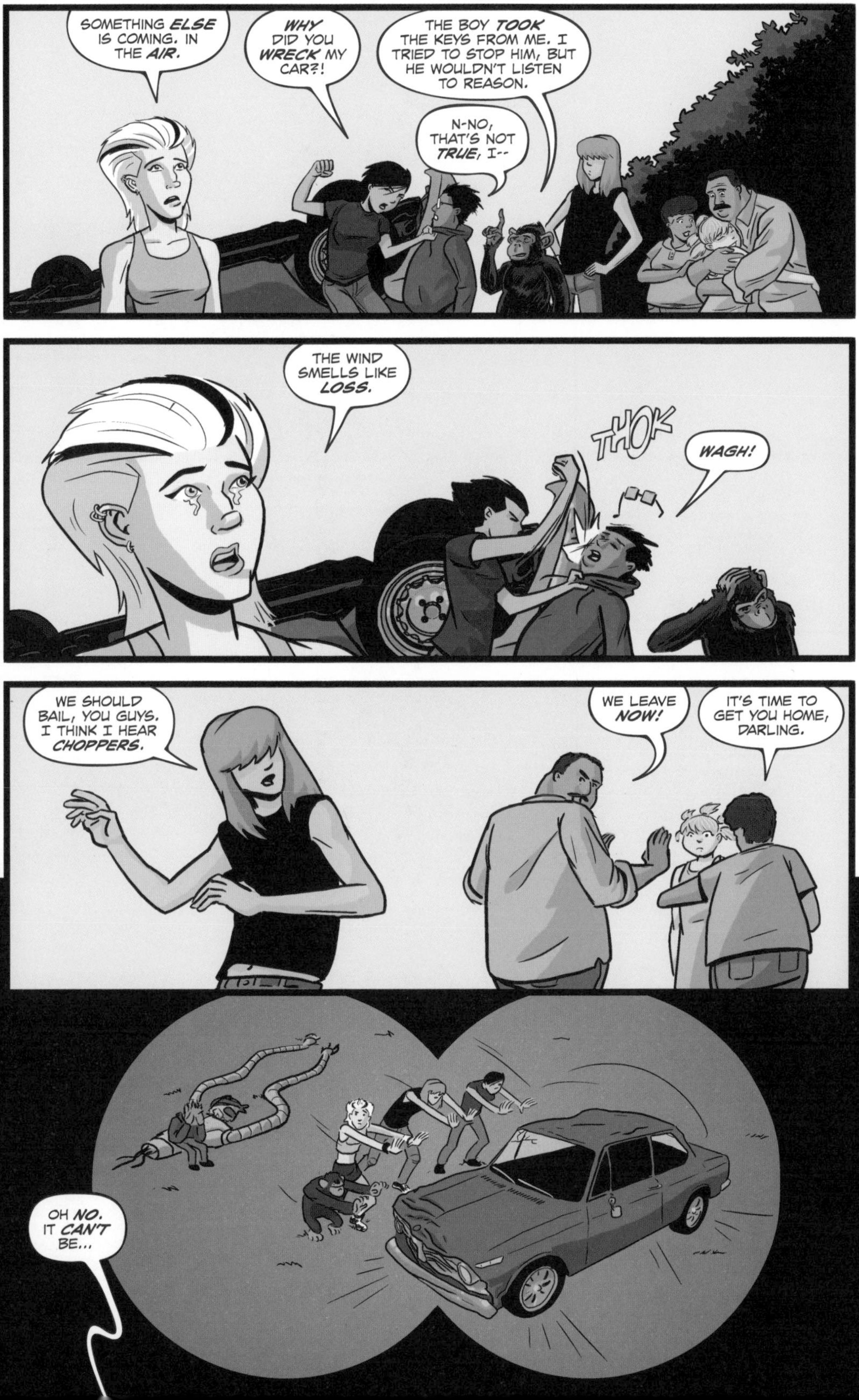
SOMETHING ELSE IS COMING. IN THE AIR.
WHY DID YOU WRECK MY CAR?!
THE BOY TOOK THE KEYS FROM ME. I TRIED TO STOP HIM, BUT HE WOULDN'T LISTEN TO REASON.
N-NO, THAT'S NOT TRUE; I--
THE WIND SMELLS LIKE LOSS.
THOK
WAGH!
WE SHOULD BAIL, YOU GUYS. I THINK I HEAR CHOPPERS.
WE LEAVE NOW!
IT'S TIME TO GET YOU HOME, DARLING.
OH NO. IT CAN'T BE...

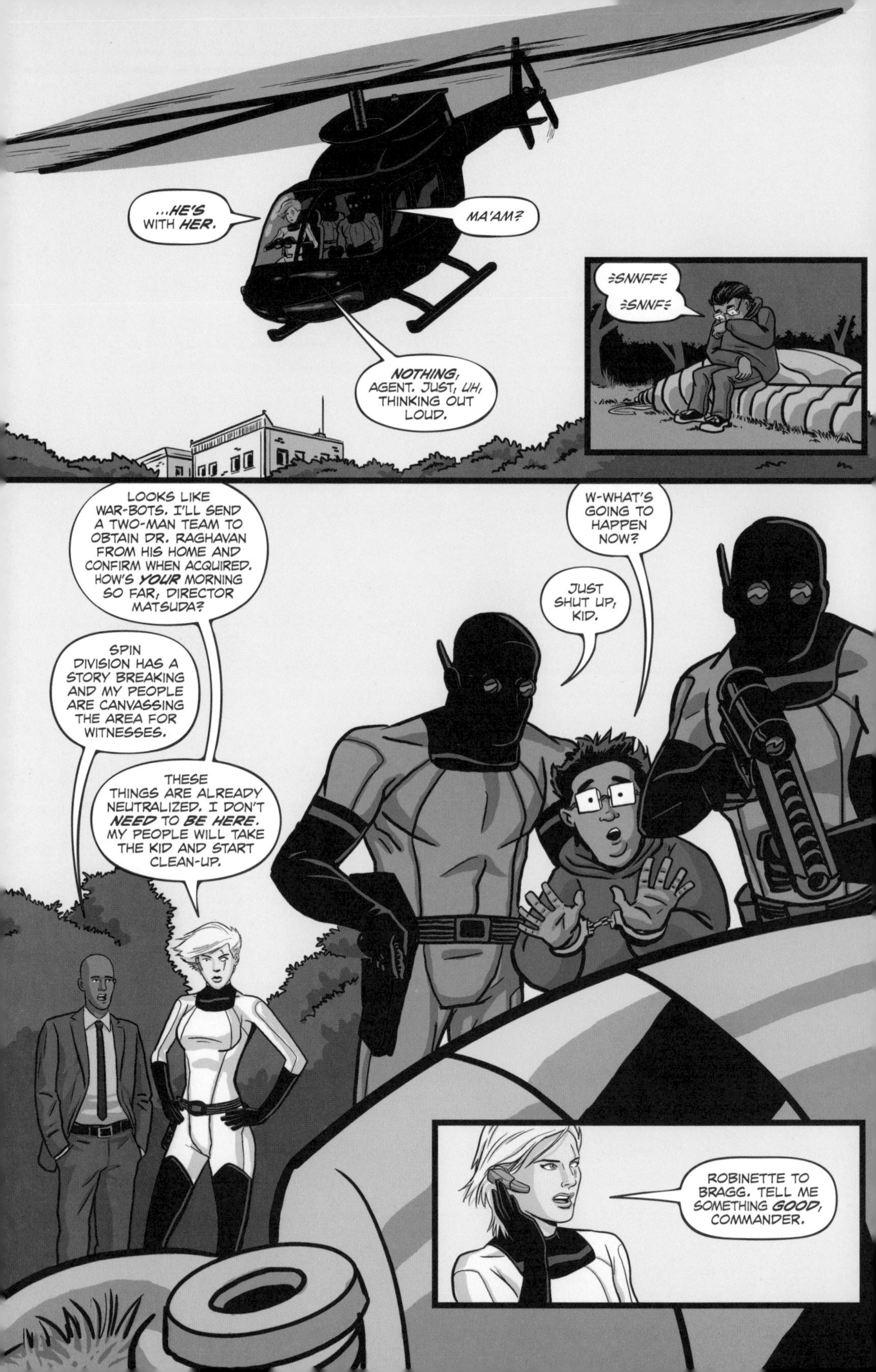
...HE'S WITH HER.
MA'AM?
NOTHING, AGENT. JUST, UH, THINKING OUT LOUD.
SNNFF
SNNF
LOOKS LIKE WAR-BOTS. I'LL SEND A TWO-MAN TEAM TO OBTAIN DR. RAGHAVAN FROM HIS HOME AND CONFIRM WHEN ACQUIRED. HOW'S YOUR MORNING SO FAR, DIRECTOR MATSUDA?
SPIN DIVISION HAS A STORY BREAKING AND MY PEOPLE ARE CANVASSING THE AREA FOR WITNESSES.
THESE THINGS ARE ALREADY NEUTRALIZED. I DON'T NEED TO BE HERE. MY PEOPLE WILL TAKE THE KID AND START CLEAN-UP.
W-WHAT'S GOING TO HAPPEN NOW?
JUST SHUT UP, KID.
ROBINETTE TO BRAGG. TELL ME SOMETHING GOOD, COMMANDER.

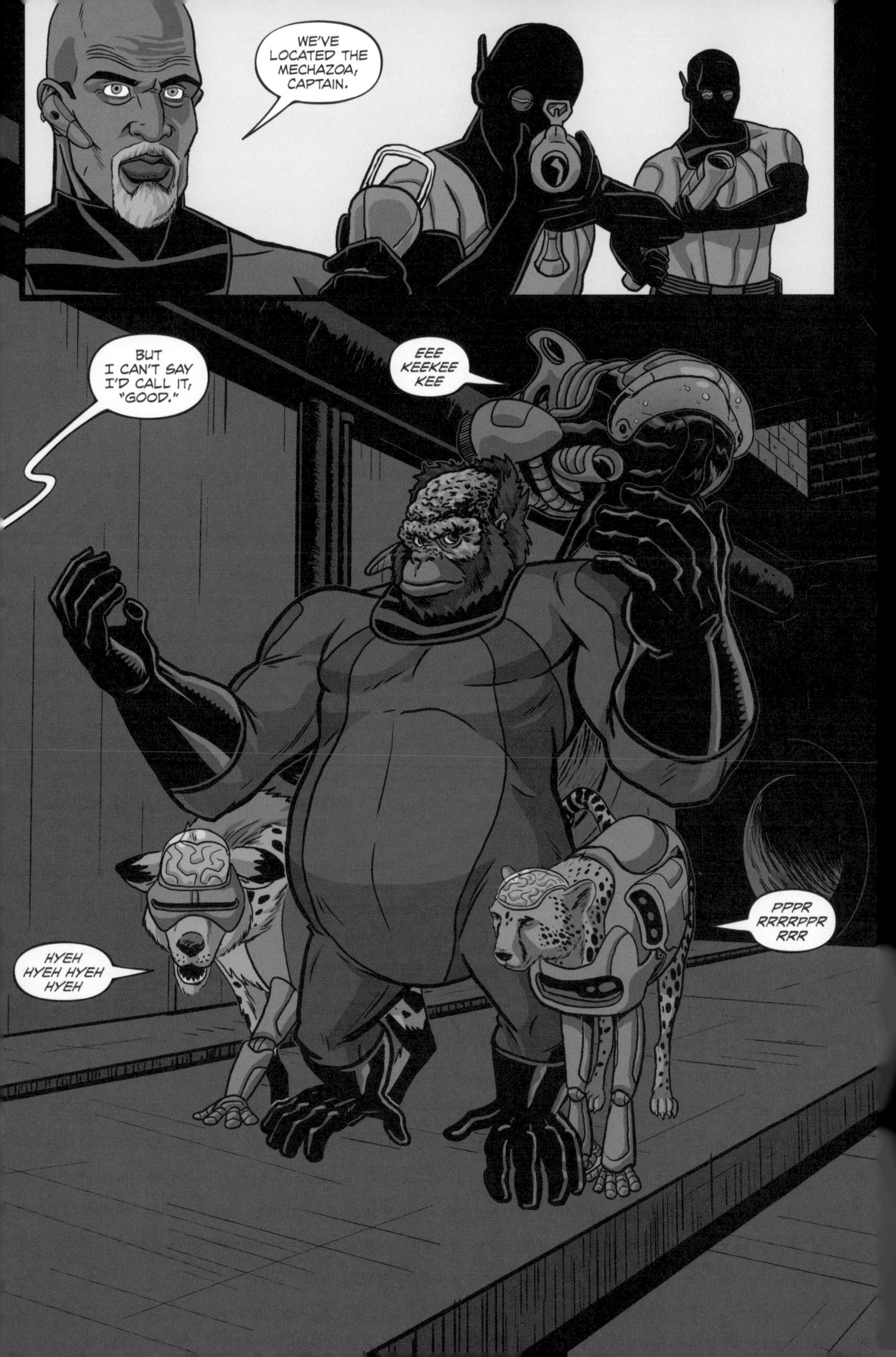
WE'VE LOCATED THE MECHAZOA, CAPTAIN.
BUT I CAN'T SAY I'D CALL IT, "GOOD."
EEE KEEKEE KEE
HYEH HYEH HYEH HYEH
PPPR RRRRPPR RRR

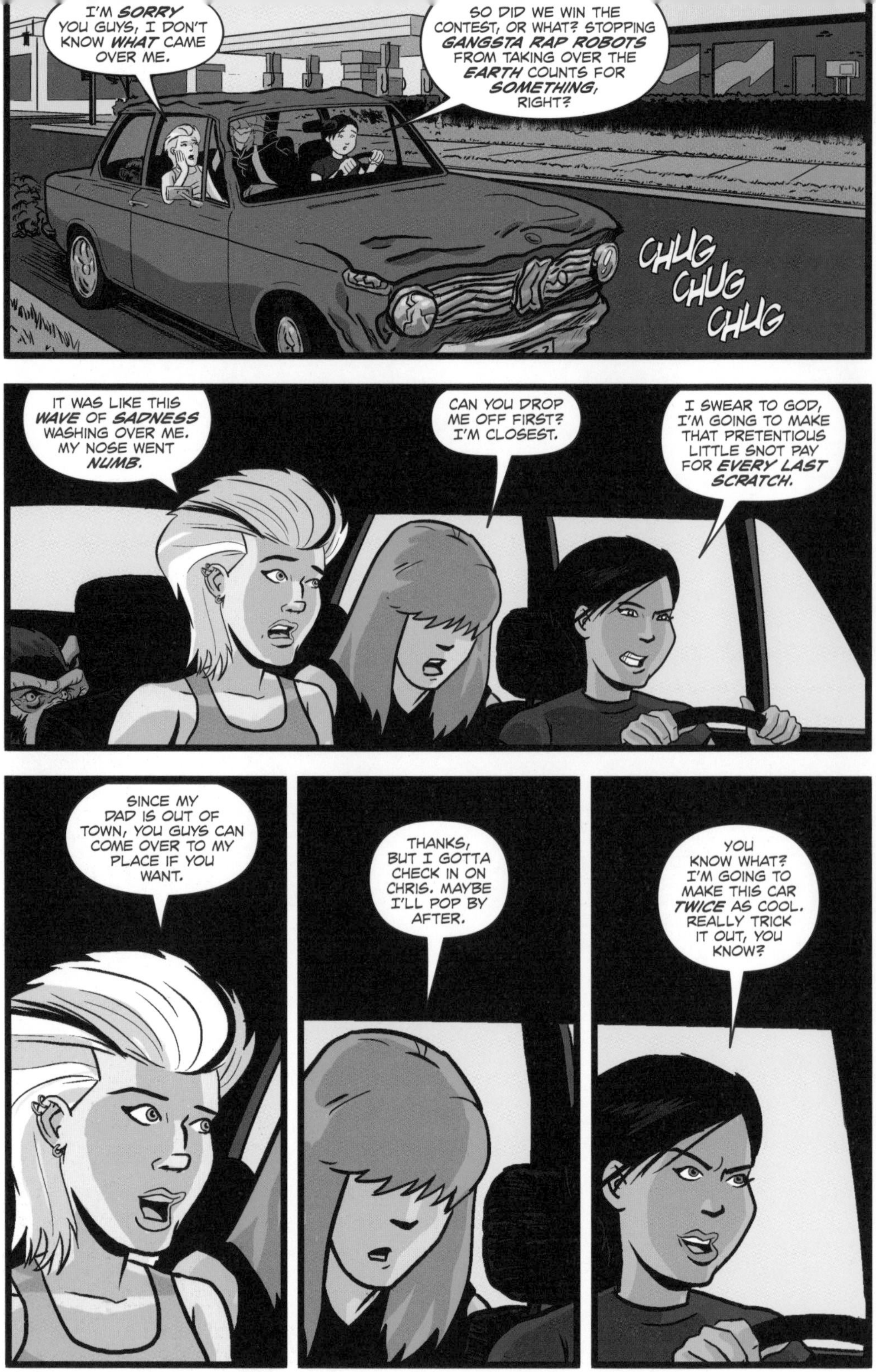
I'M SORRY YOU GUYS, I DON'T KNOW WHAT CAME OVER ME.
SO DID WE WIN THE CONTEST, OR WHAT? STOPPING GANGSTA RAP ROBOTS FROM TAKING OVER THE EARTH COUNTS FOR SOMETHING, RIGHT?
CHUG CHUG CHUG
IT WAS LIKE THIS WAVE OF SADNESS WASHING OVER ME. MY NOSE WENT NUMB.
CAN YOU DROP ME OFF FIRST? I'M CLOSEST.
I SWEAR TO GOD, I'M GOING TO MAKE THAT PRETENTIOUS LITTLE SNOT PAY FOR EVERY LAST SCRATCH.
SINCE MY DAD IS OUT OF TOWN, YOU GUYS CAN COME OVER TO MY PLACE IF YOU WANT.
THANKS, BUT I GOTTA CHECK IN ON CHRIS. MAYBE I'LL POP BY AFTER.
YOU KNOW WHAT? I'M GOING TO MAKE THIS CAR TWICE AS COOL. REALLY TRICK IT OUT, YOU KNOW?

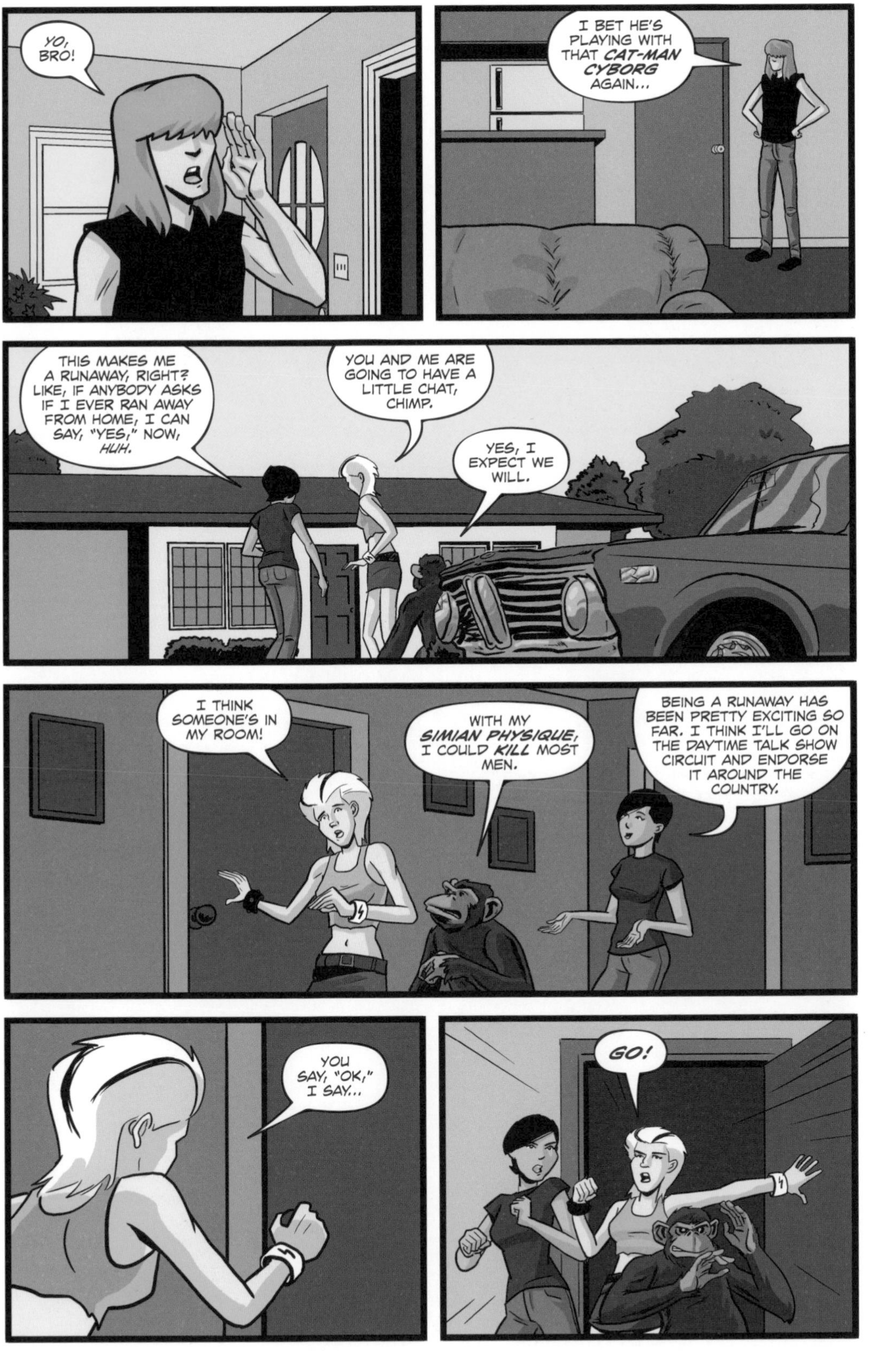
YO, BRO!
I BET HE'S PLAYING WITH THAT CAT-MAN CYBORG AGAIN...
THIS MAKES ME A RUNAWAY, RIGHT? LIKE, IF ANYBODY ASKS IF I EVER RAN AWAY FROM HOME, I CAN SAY, "YES," NOW, HUH.
YOU AND ME ARE GOING TO HAVE A LITTLE CHAT, CHIMP.
YES, I EXPECT WE WILL.
I THINK SOMEONE'S IN MY ROOM!
WITH MY SIMIAN PHYSIQUE, I COULD KILL MOST MEN.
BEING A RUNAWAY HAS BEEN PRETTY EXCITING SO FAR. I THINK I'LL GO ON THE DAYTIME TALK SHOW CIRCUIT AND ENDORSE IT AROUND THE COUNTRY.
YOU SAY, "OK," I SAY...
GO!

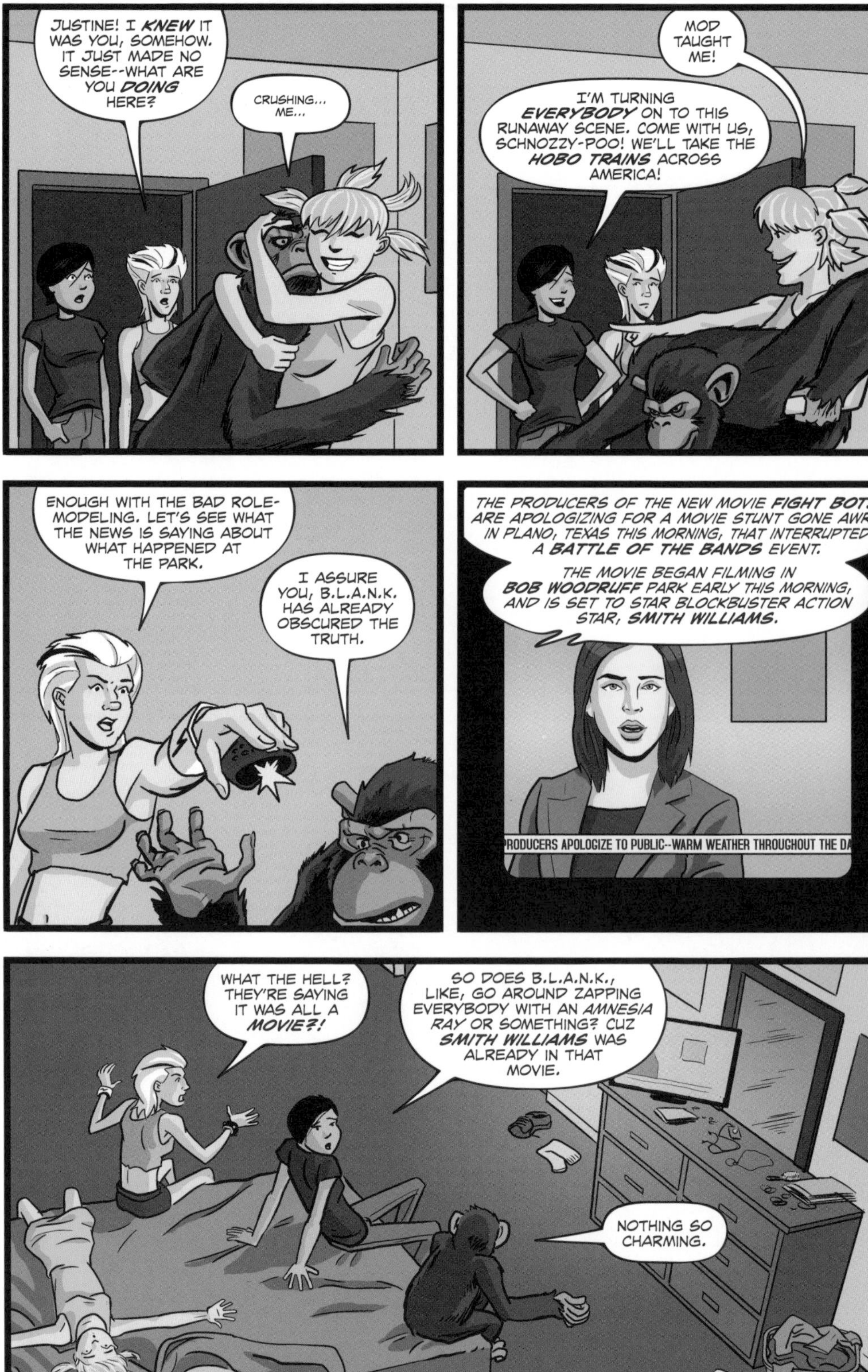
JUSTINE! I *KNEW* IT WAS YOU, SOMEHOW. IT JUST MADE NO SENSE--WHAT ARE YOU *DOING* HERE?
CRUSHING... ME...
MOD TAUGHT ME!
I'M TURNING *EVERYBODY* ON TO THIS RUNAWAY SCENE. COME WITH US, SCHNOZZY-POO! WE'LL TAKE THE *HOBO TRAINS* ACROSS AMERICA!
ENOUGH WITH THE BAD ROLE-MODELING. LET'S SEE WHAT THE NEWS IS SAYING ABOUT WHAT HAPPENED AT THE PARK.
I ASSURE YOU, B.L.A.N.K. HAS ALREADY OBSCURED THE TRUTH.
*THE PRODUCERS OF THE NEW MOVIE **FIGHT BOTS** ARE APOLOGIZING FOR A MOVIE STUNT GONE AWRY IN PLANO, TEXAS THIS MORNING, THAT INTERRUPTED A **BATTLE OF THE BANDS** EVENT.*
*THE MOVIE BEGAN FILMING IN **BOB WOODRUFF** PARK EARLY THIS MORNING, AND IS SET TO STAR BLOCKBUSTER ACTION STAR, **SMITH WILLIAMS**.*
RODUCERS APOLOGIZE TO PUBLIC--WARM WEATHER THROUGHOUT THE DA
WHAT THE HELL? THEY'RE SAYING IT WAS ALL A ***MOVIE?!***
SO DOES B.L.A.N.K., LIKE, GO AROUND ZAPPING EVERYBODY WITH AN *AMNESIA RAY* OR SOMETHING? CUZ ***SMITH WILLIAMS*** WAS ALREADY IN THAT MOVIE.
NOTHING SO CHARMING.

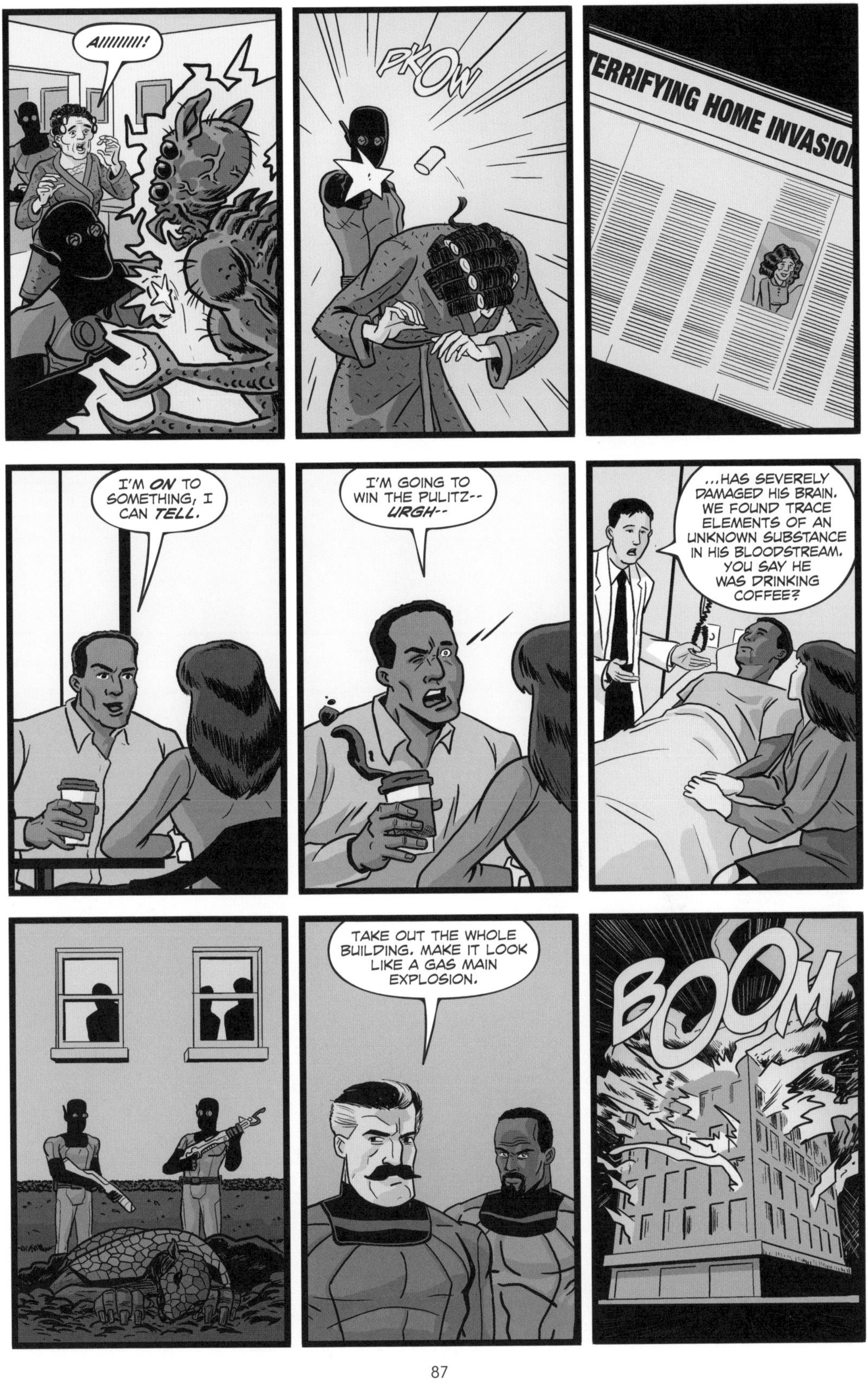
AIIIIIIII!
PKOW
TERRIFYING HOME INVASION
I'M ON TO SOMETHING, I CAN TELL.
I'M GOING TO WIN THE PULITZ-- URGH--
...HAS SEVERELY DAMAGED HIS BRAIN. WE FOUND TRACE ELEMENTS OF AN UNKNOWN SUBSTANCE IN HIS BLOODSTREAM. YOU SAY HE WAS DRINKING COFFEE?
TAKE OUT THE WHOLE BUILDING. MAKE IT LOOK LIKE A GAS MAIN EXPLOSION.
BOOM

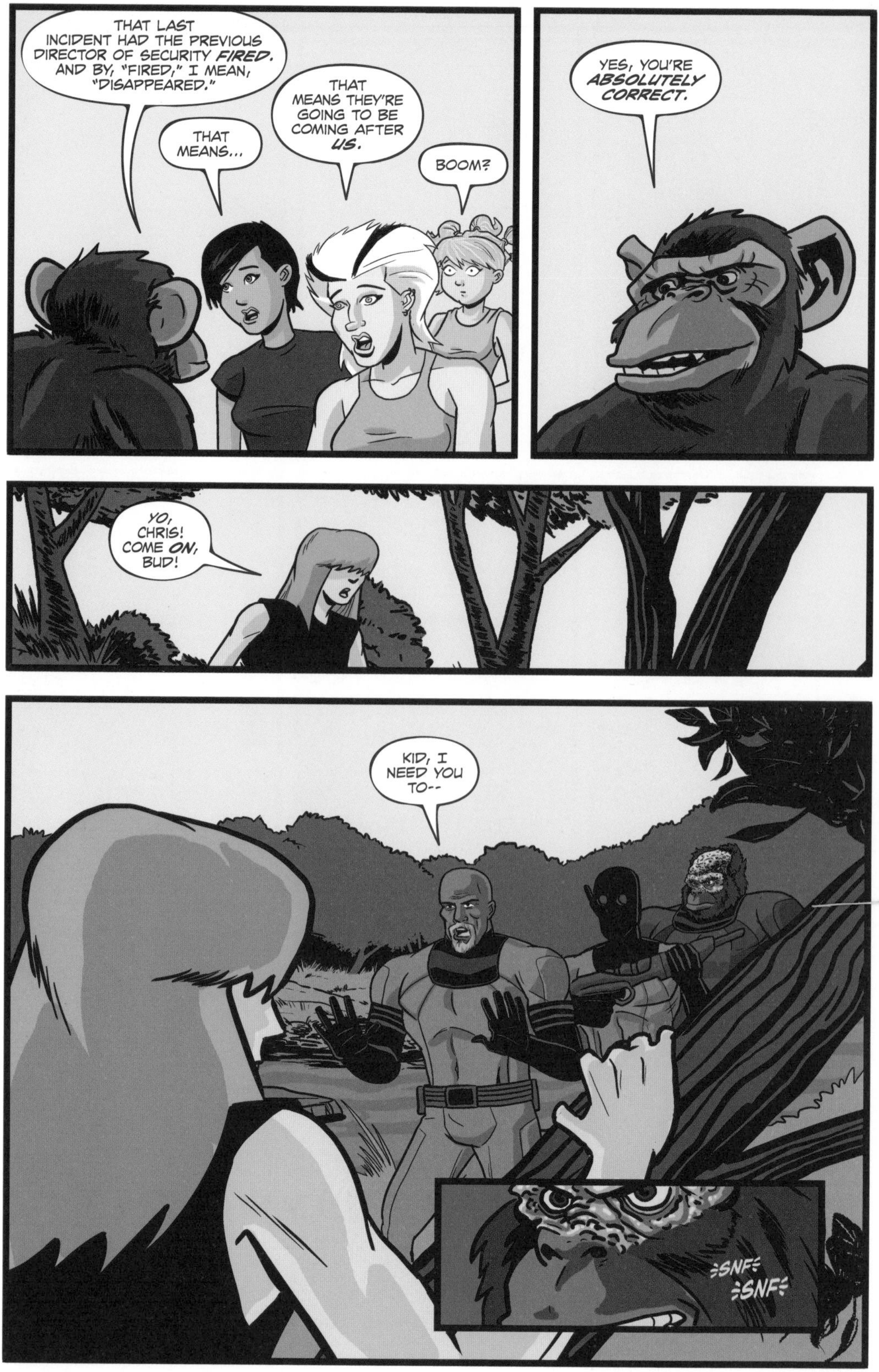
THAT LAST INCIDENT HAD THE PREVIOUS DIRECTOR OF SECURITY *FIRED.* AND BY, "FIRED," I MEAN, "DISAPPEARED."
THAT MEANS...
THAT MEANS THEY'RE GOING TO BE COMING AFTER *US.*
BOOM?
YES, YOU'RE *ABSOLUTELY CORRECT.*
YO, CHRIS! COME *ON,* BUD!
KID, I NEED YOU TO--
SNF
SNF

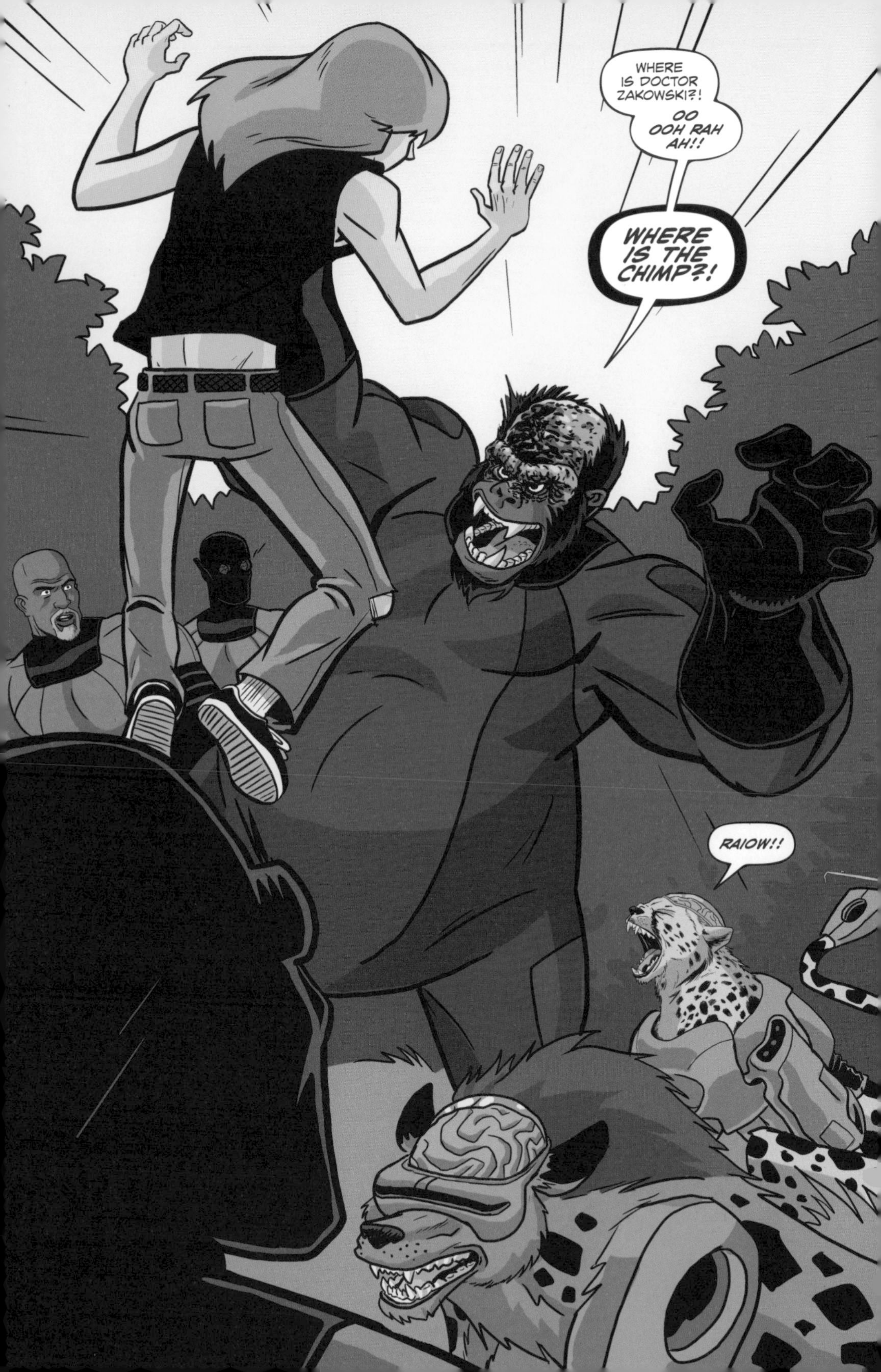
WHERE IS DOCTOR ZAKOWSKI?!
OO OOH RAH AH!!
WHERE IS THE CHIMP?!
RAIOW!!

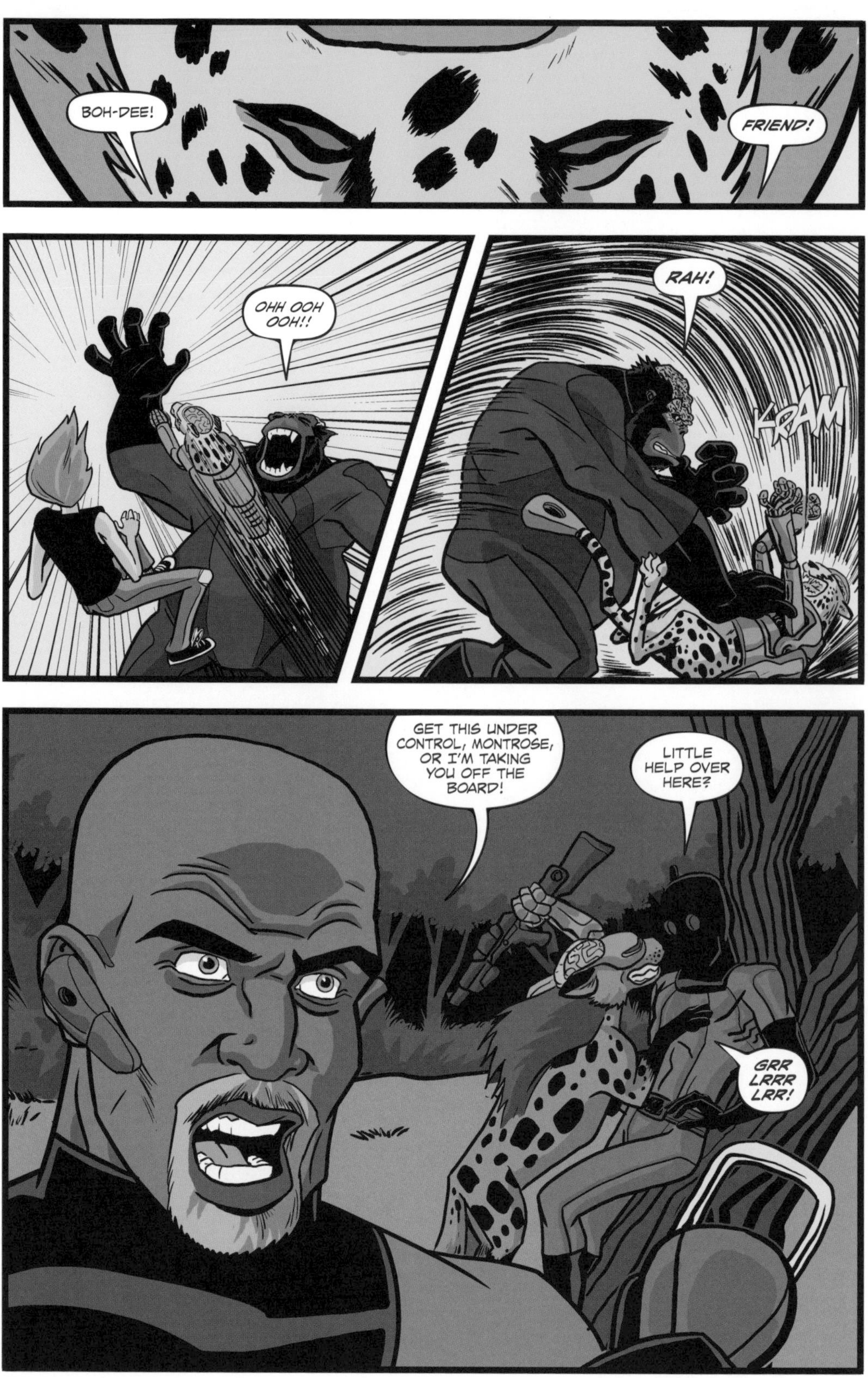
BOH-DEE!
FRIEND!
OHH OOH OOH!!
RAH!
KRAM
GET THIS UNDER CONTROL, MONTROSE, OR I'M TAKING YOU OFF THE BOARD!
LITTLE HELP OVER HERE?
GRR LRRR LRR!

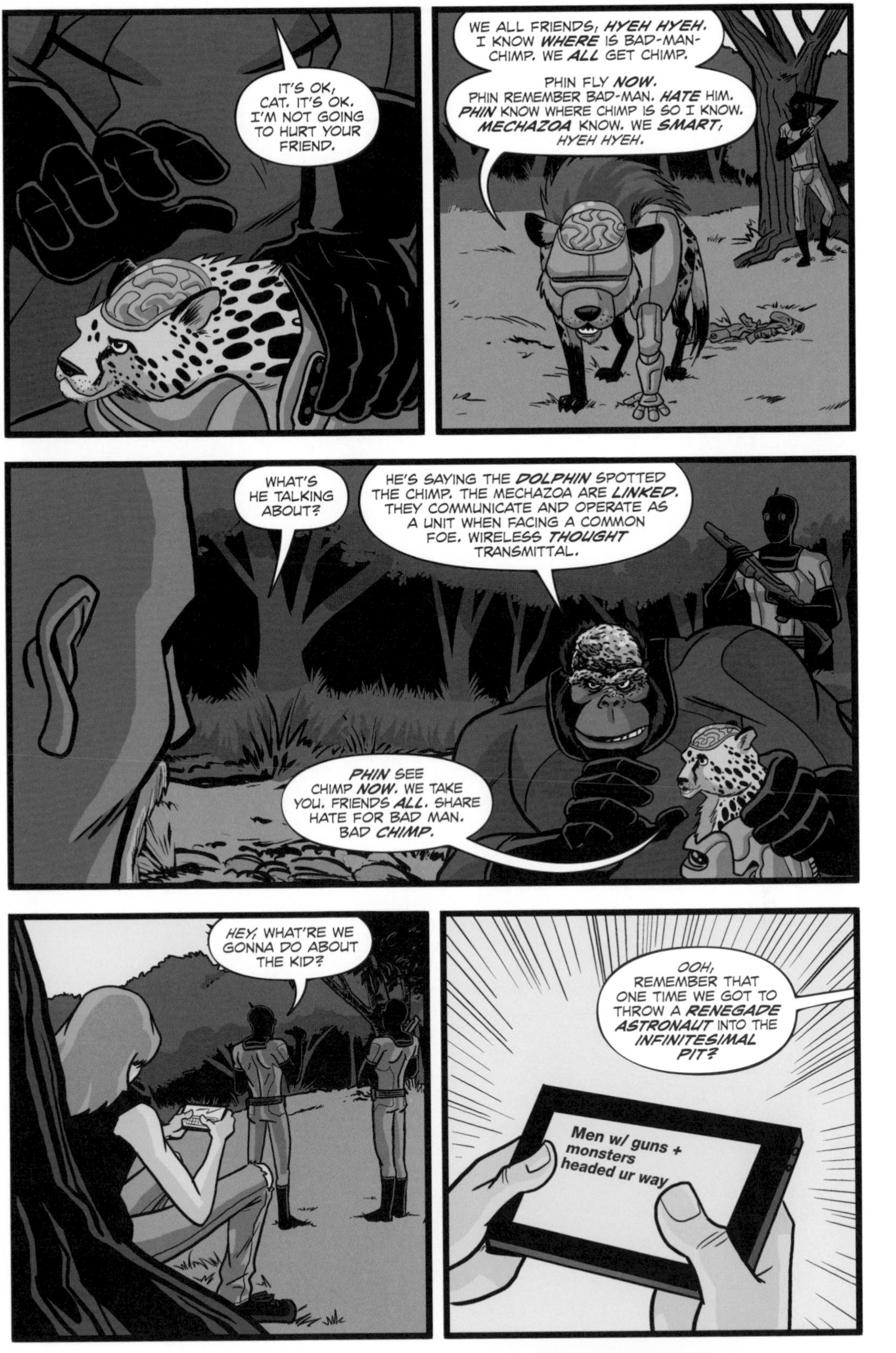
IT'S OK, CAT. IT'S OK. I'M NOT GOING TO HURT YOUR FRIEND.
WE ALL FRIENDS, HYEH HYEH. I KNOW WHERE IS BAD-MAN-CHIMP. WE ALL GET CHIMP.
PHIN FLY NOW. PHIN REMEMBER BAD-MAN. HATE HIM. PHIN KNOW WHERE CHIMP IS SO I KNOW. MECHAZOA KNOW. WE SMART, HYEH HYEH.
WHAT'S HE TALKING ABOUT?
HE'S SAYING THE DOLPHIN SPOTTED THE CHIMP. THE MECHAZOA ARE LINKED. THEY COMMUNICATE AND OPERATE AS A UNIT WHEN FACING A COMMON FOE. WIRELESS THOUGHT TRANSMITTAL.
PHIN SEE CHIMP NOW. WE TAKE YOU. FRIENDS ALL. SHARE HATE FOR BAD MAN. BAD CHIMP.
HEY, WHAT'RE WE GONNA DO ABOUT THE KID?
OOH, REMEMBER THAT ONE TIME WE GOT TO THROW A RENEGADE ASTRONAUT INTO THE INFINITESIMAL PIT?
Men w/ guns + monsters headed ur way

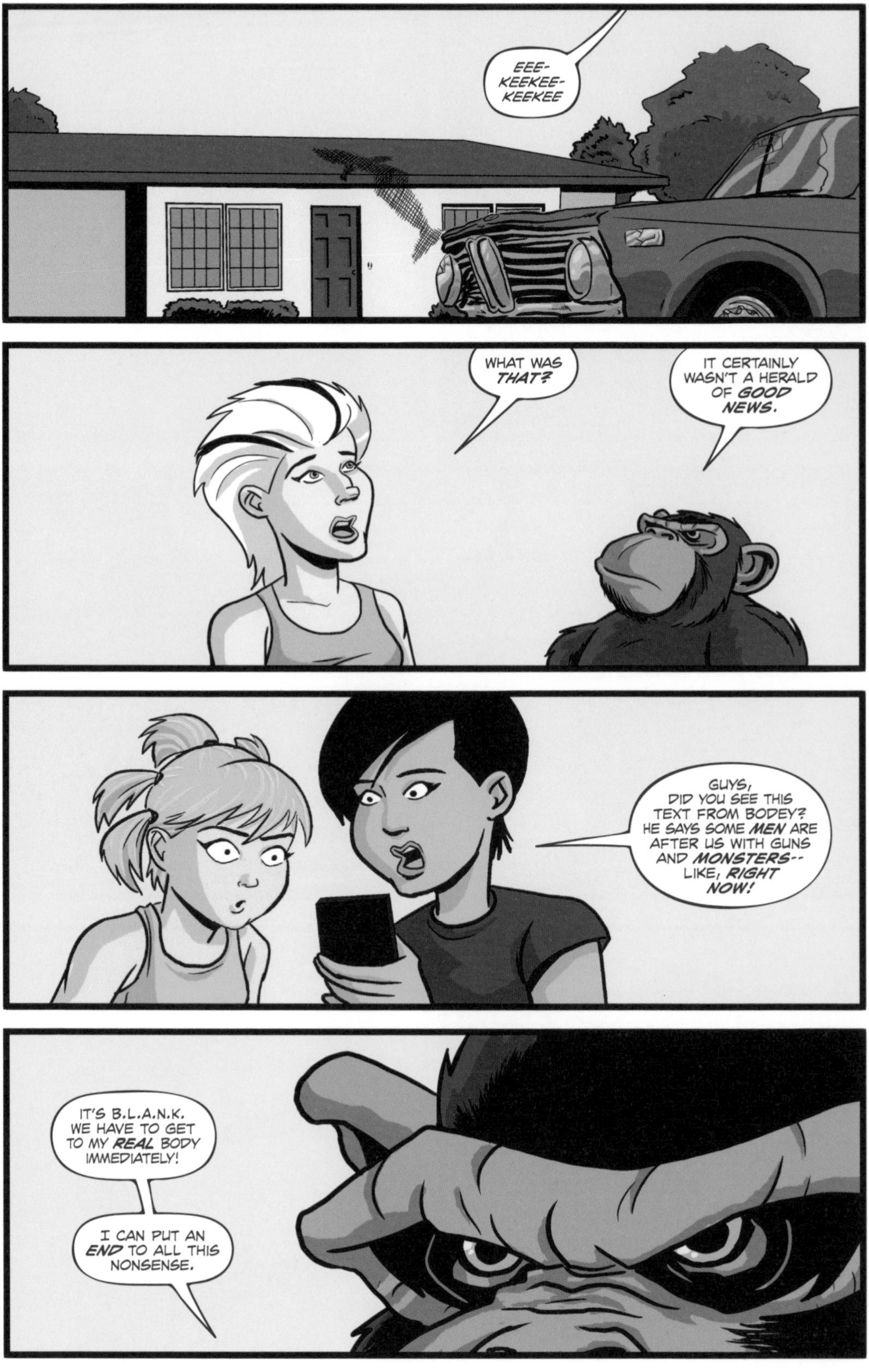
EEE-KEEKEE-KEEKEE
WHAT WAS *THAT?*
IT CERTAINLY WASN'T A HERALD OF *GOOD NEWS.*
GUYS, DID YOU SEE THIS TEXT FROM BODEY? HE SAYS SOME *MEN* ARE AFTER US WITH GUNS AND *MONSTERS*-- LIKE, *RIGHT NOW!*
IT'S B.L.A.N.K. WE HAVE TO GET TO MY *REAL* BODY IMMEDIATELY!
I CAN PUT AN *END* TO ALL THIS NONSENSE.

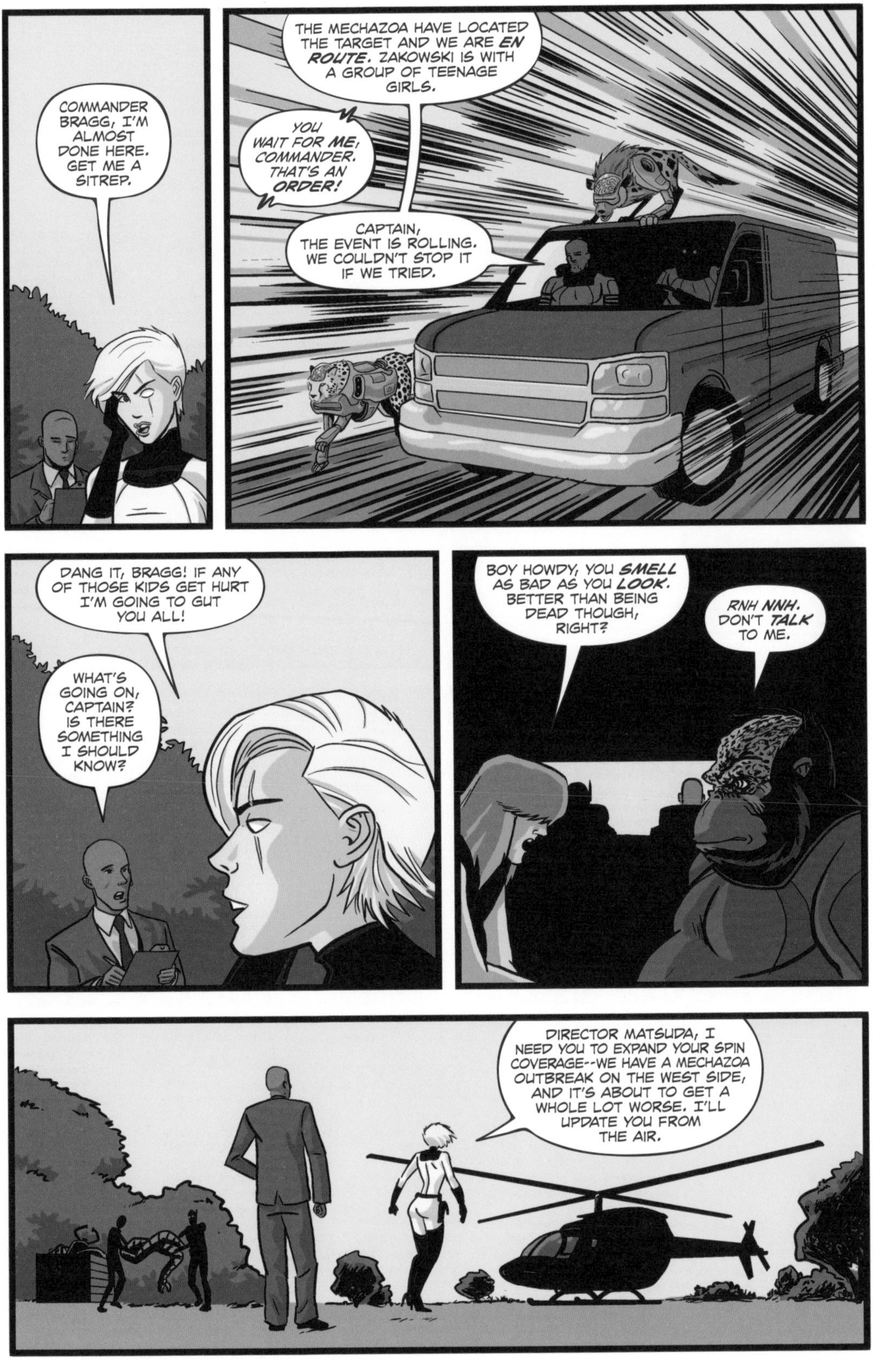
COMMANDER BRAGG, I'M ALMOST DONE HERE. GET ME A SITREP.
THE MECHAZOA HAVE LOCATED THE TARGET AND WE ARE EN ROUTE. ZAKOWSKI IS WITH A GROUP OF TEENAGE GIRLS.
YOU WAIT FOR ME, COMMANDER. THAT'S AN ORDER!
CAPTAIN, THE EVENT IS ROLLING. WE COULDN'T STOP IT IF WE TRIED.
DANG IT, BRAGG! IF ANY OF THOSE KIDS GET HURT I'M GOING TO GUT YOU ALL!
WHAT'S GOING ON, CAPTAIN? IS THERE SOMETHING I SHOULD KNOW?
BOY HOWDY, YOU SMELL AS BAD AS YOU LOOK. BETTER THAN BEING DEAD THOUGH, RIGHT?
RNH NNH. DON'T TALK TO ME.
DIRECTOR MATSUDA, I NEED YOU TO EXPAND YOUR SPIN COVERAGE--WE HAVE A MECHAZOA OUTBREAK ON THE WEST SIDE, AND IT'S ABOUT TO GET A WHOLE LOT WORSE. I'LL UPDATE YOU FROM THE AIR.

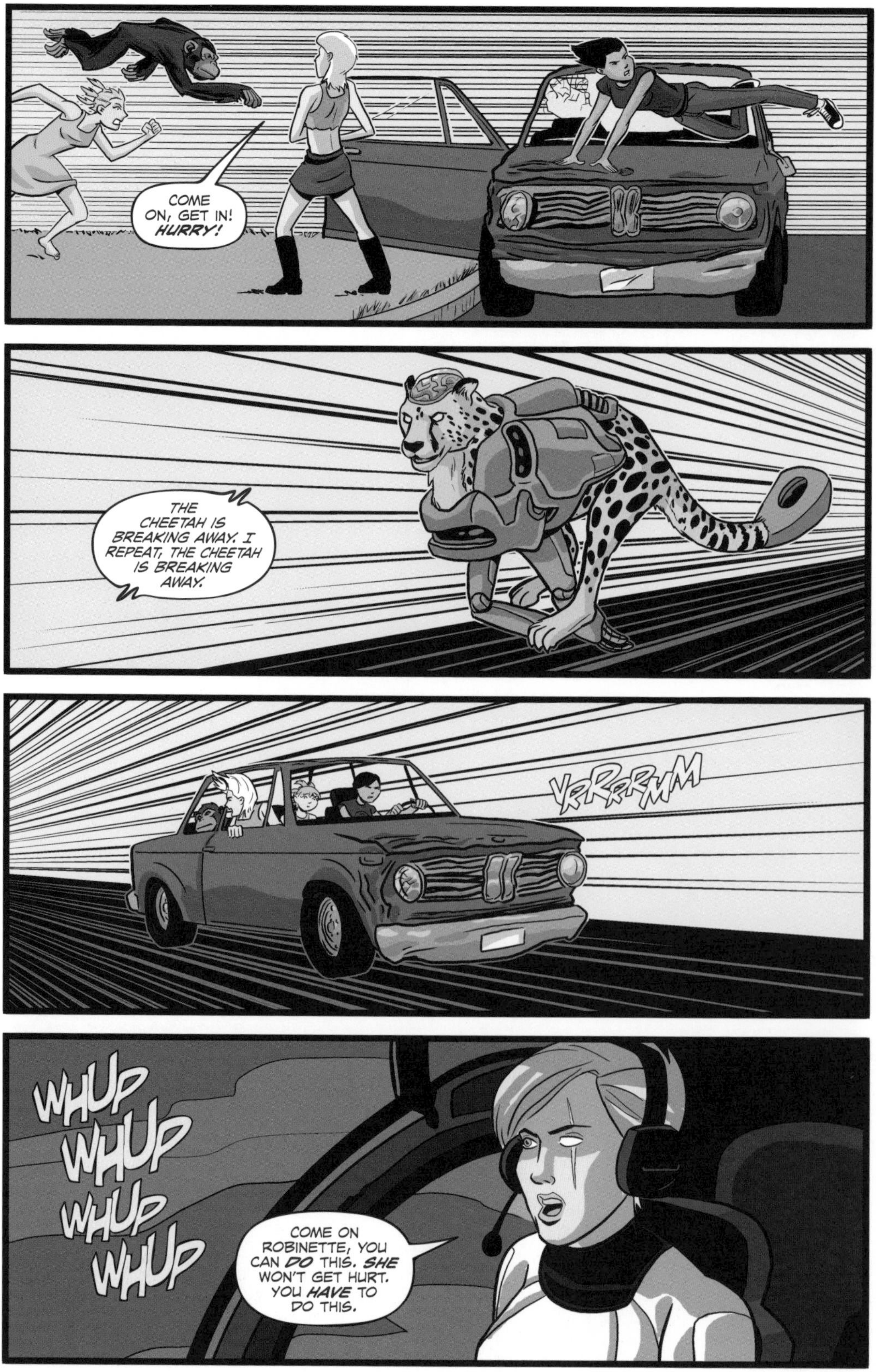
COME ON, GET IN! HURRY!
THE CHEETAH IS BREAKING AWAY. I REPEAT, THE CHEETAH IS BREAKING AWAY.
VRRRRMM
WHUP WHUP WHUP WHUP
COME ON ROBINETTE, YOU CAN DO THIS. SHE WON'T GET HURT. YOU HAVE TO DO THIS.

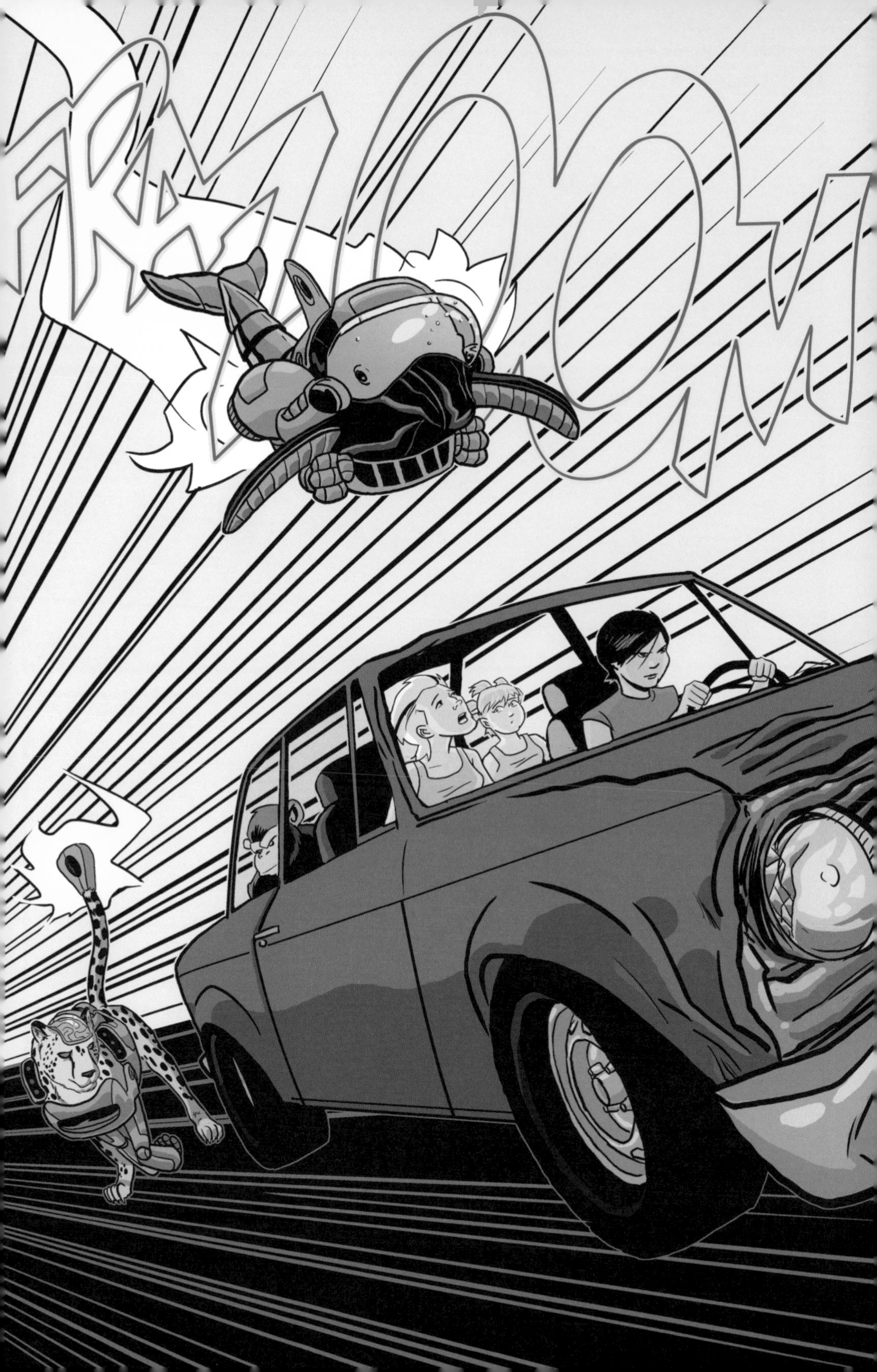

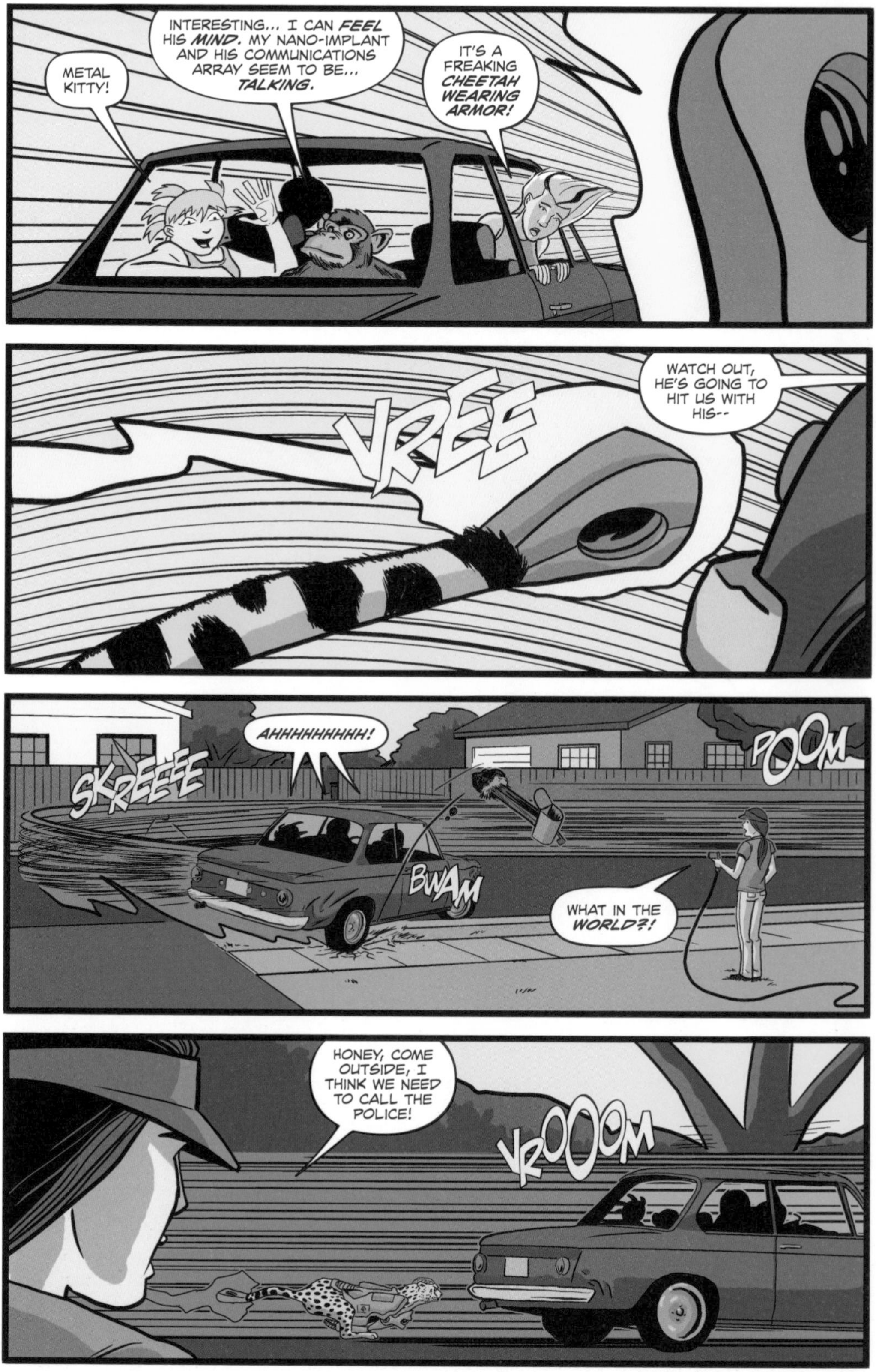
METAL KITTY!
INTERESTING... I CAN FEEL HIS MIND. MY NANO-IMPLANT AND HIS COMMUNICATIONS ARRAY SEEM TO BE... TALKING.
IT'S A FREAKING CHEETAH WEARING ARMOR!
WATCH OUT, HE'S GOING TO HIT US WITH HIS--
VREE
AHHHHHHHHH!
SKREEEEE
POOM
BWAM
WHAT IN THE WORLD?!
HONEY, COME OUTSIDE, I THINK WE NEED TO CALL THE POLICE!
VROOOM

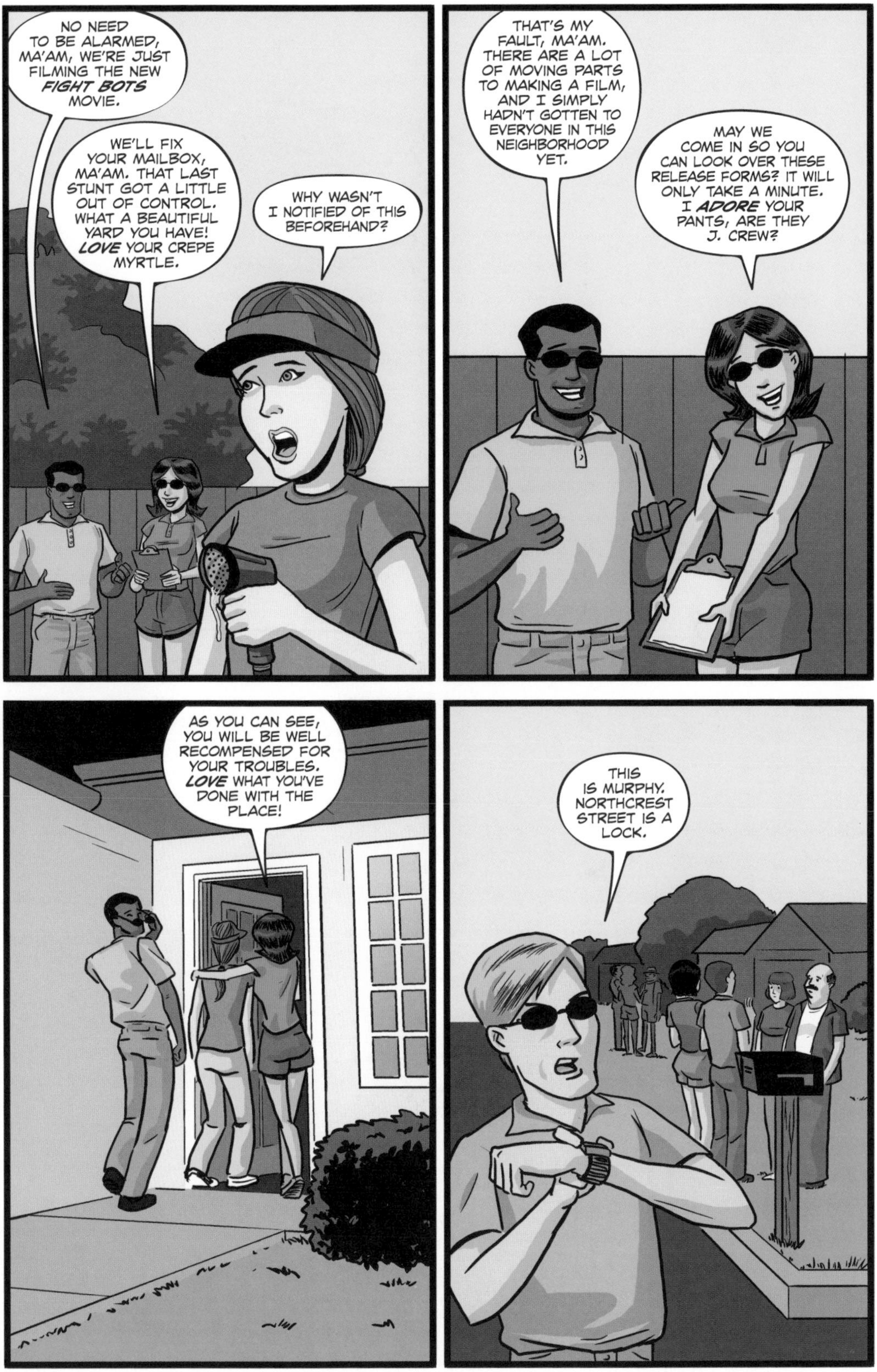
NO NEED TO BE ALARMED, MA'AM, WE'RE JUST FILMING THE NEW *FIGHT BOTS* MOVIE.
WE'LL FIX YOUR MAILBOX, MA'AM. THAT LAST STUNT GOT A LITTLE OUT OF CONTROL. WHAT A BEAUTIFUL YARD YOU HAVE! *LOVE* YOUR CREPE MYRTLE.
WHY WASN'T I NOTIFIED OF THIS BEFOREHAND?
THAT'S MY FAULT, MA'AM. THERE ARE A LOT OF MOVING PARTS TO MAKING A FILM, AND I SIMPLY HADN'T GOTTEN TO EVERYONE IN THIS NEIGHBORHOOD YET.
MAY WE COME IN SO YOU CAN LOOK OVER THESE RELEASE FORMS? IT WILL ONLY TAKE A MINUTE. I *ADORE* YOUR PANTS, ARE THEY J. CREW?
AS YOU CAN SEE, YOU WILL BE WELL RECOMPENSED FOR YOUR TROUBLES. *LOVE* WHAT YOU'VE DONE WITH THE PLACE!
THIS IS MURPHY. NORTHCREST STREET IS A LOCK.

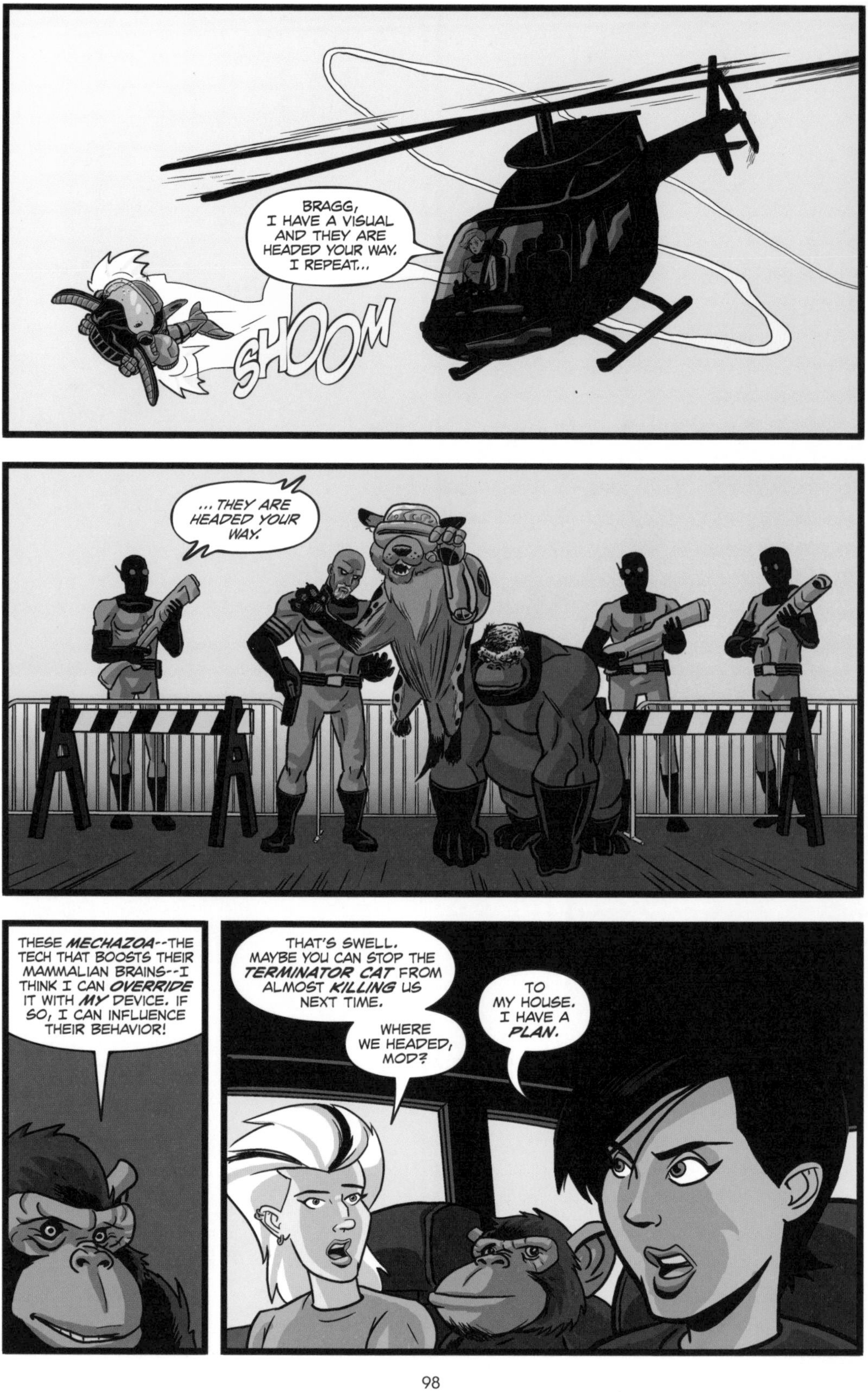
BRAGG, I HAVE A VISUAL AND THEY ARE HEADED YOUR WAY. I REPEAT...
SHOOM
...THEY ARE HEADED YOUR WAY.
THESE MECHAZOA--THE TECH THAT BOOSTS THEIR MAMMALIAN BRAINS--I THINK I CAN OVERRIDE IT WITH MY DEVICE. IF SO, I CAN INFLUENCE THEIR BEHAVIOR!
THAT'S SWELL. MAYBE YOU CAN STOP THE TERMINATOR CAT FROM ALMOST KILLING US NEXT TIME.
WHERE WE HEADED, MOD?
TO MY HOUSE. I HAVE A PLAN.

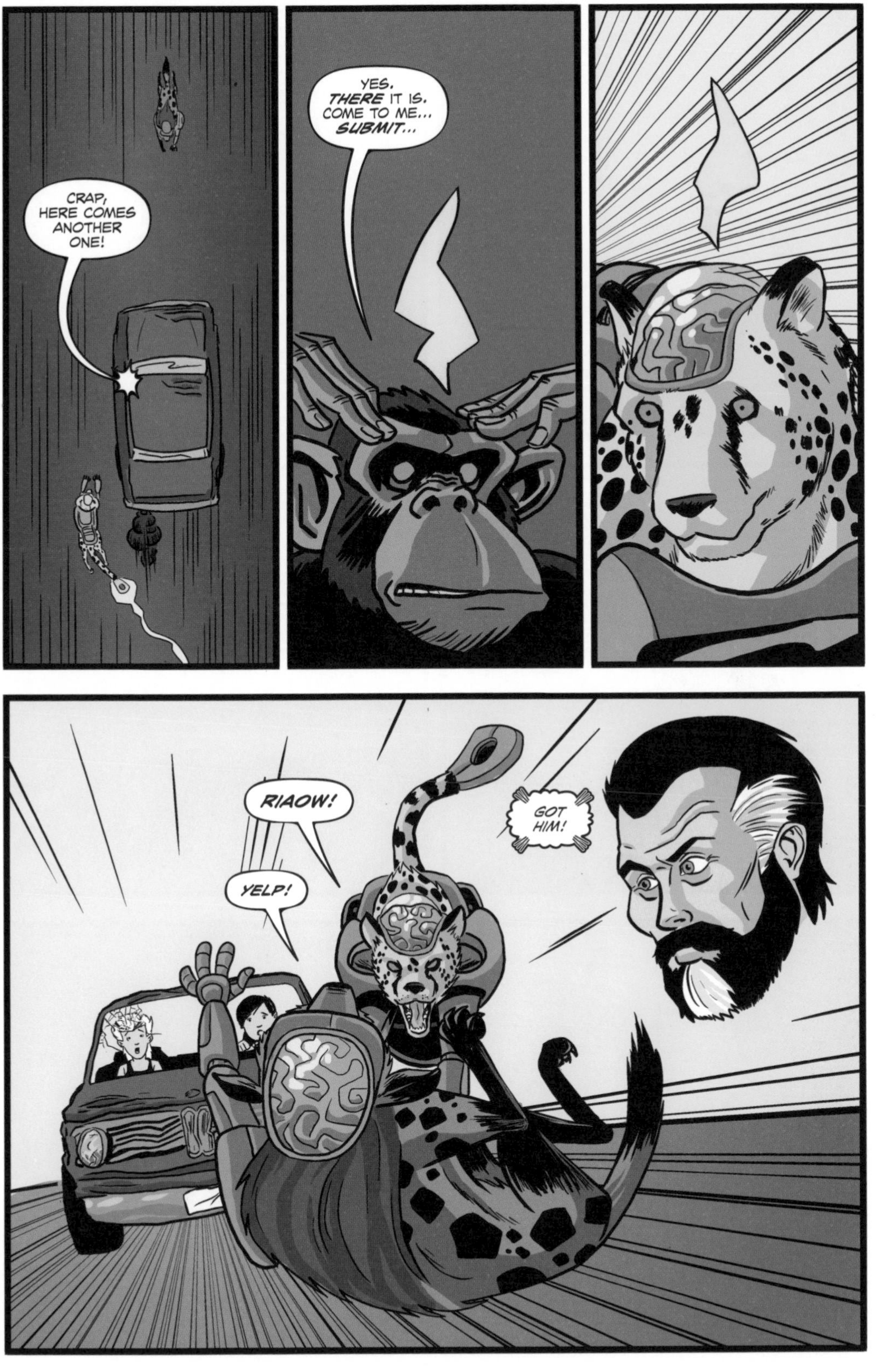
CRAP, HERE COMES ANOTHER ONE!
YES. *THERE* IT IS. COME TO ME... *SUBMIT*...
RIAOW!
YELP!
GOT HIM!

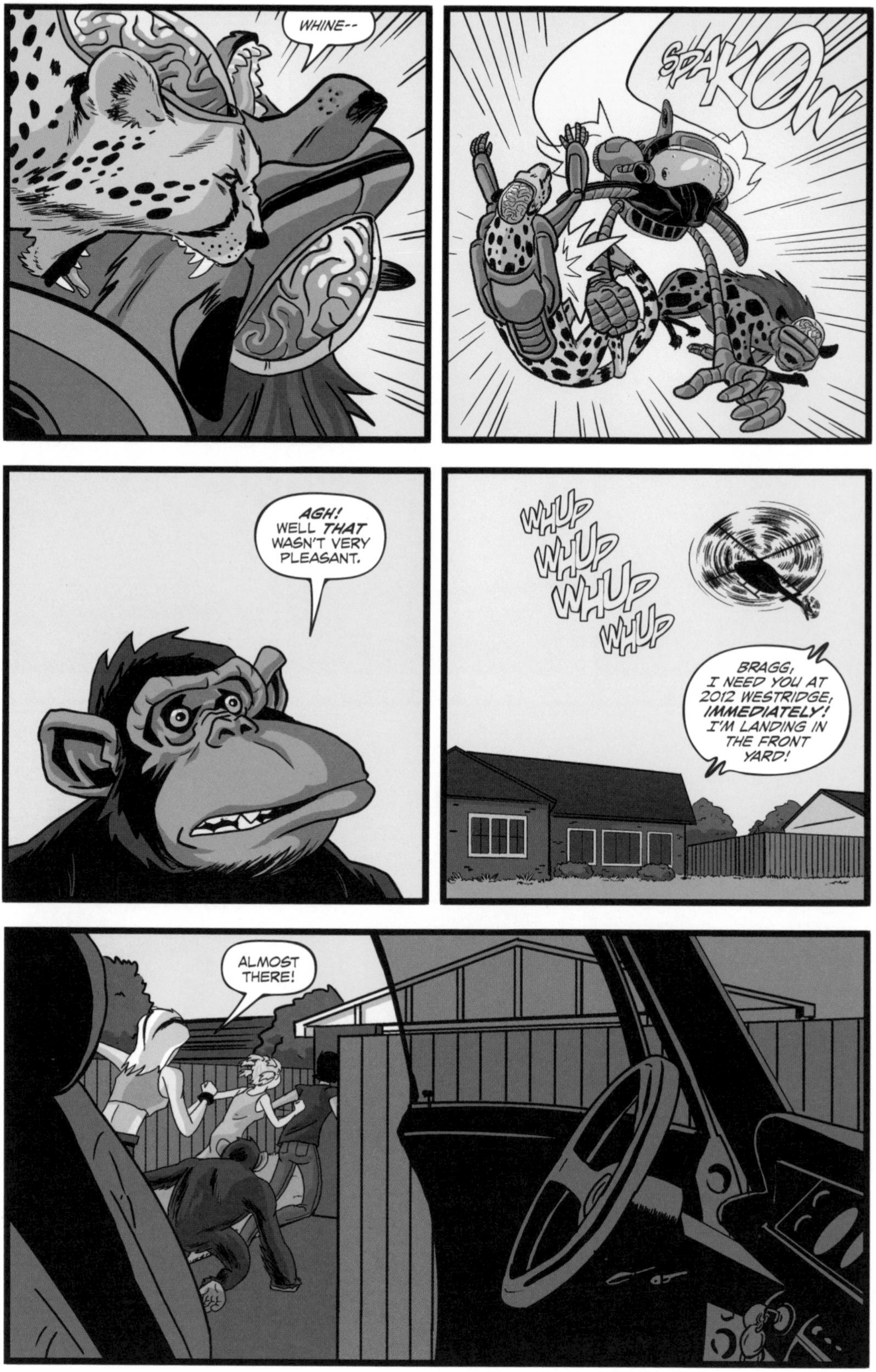
WHINE--
SPAKOW
AGH! WELL THAT WASN'T VERY PLEASANT.
WHUP WHUP WHUP WHUP
BRAGG, I NEED YOU AT 2012 WESTRIDGE; IMMEDIATELY! I'M LANDING IN THE FRONT YARD!
ALMOST THERE!

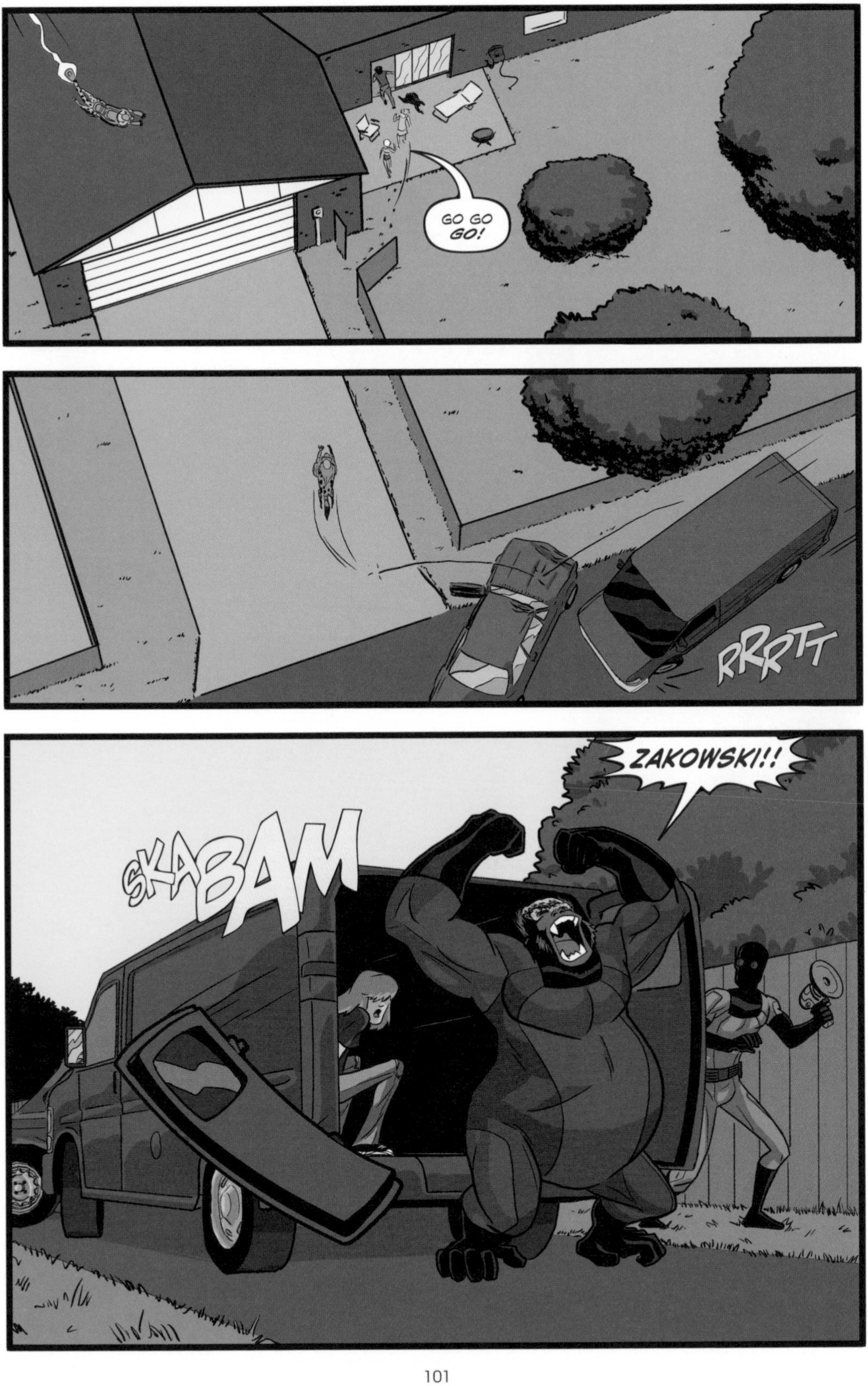
GO GO GO!
RRRTT
ZAKOWSKI!!
SKABAM

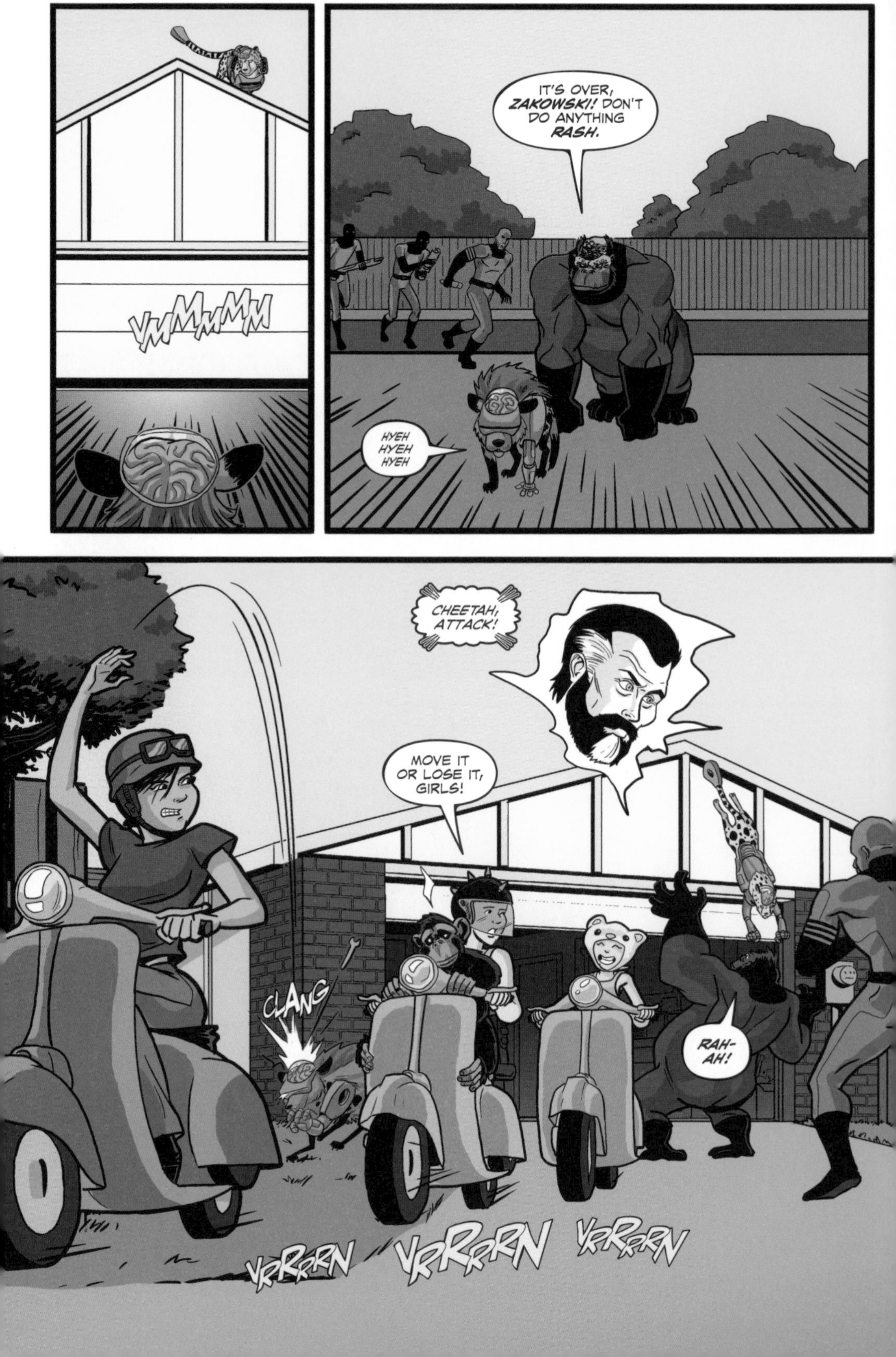
VMMMMM
IT'S OVER, ZAKOWSKI! DON'T DO ANYTHING RASH.
HYEH HYEH HYEH
CHEETAH, ATTACK!
MOVE IT OR LOSE IT, GIRLS!
CLANG
RAH-AH!
VRRRRN
VRRRRN
VRRRRN

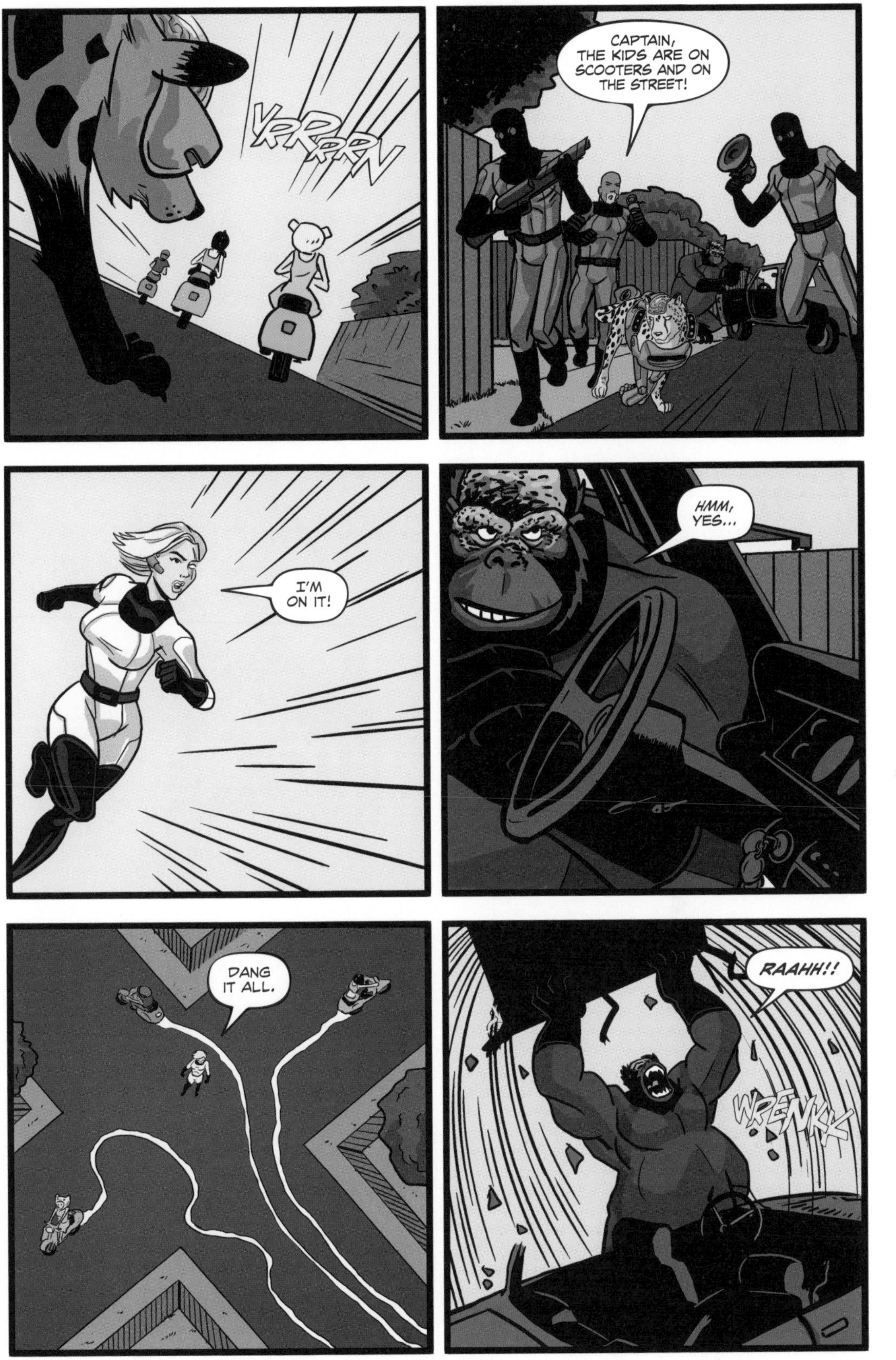
VRRRRRN
CAPTAIN, THE KIDS ARE ON SCOOTERS AND ON THE STREET!
I'M ON IT!
HMM, YES...
DANG IT ALL.
RAAHH!!
WRENKK

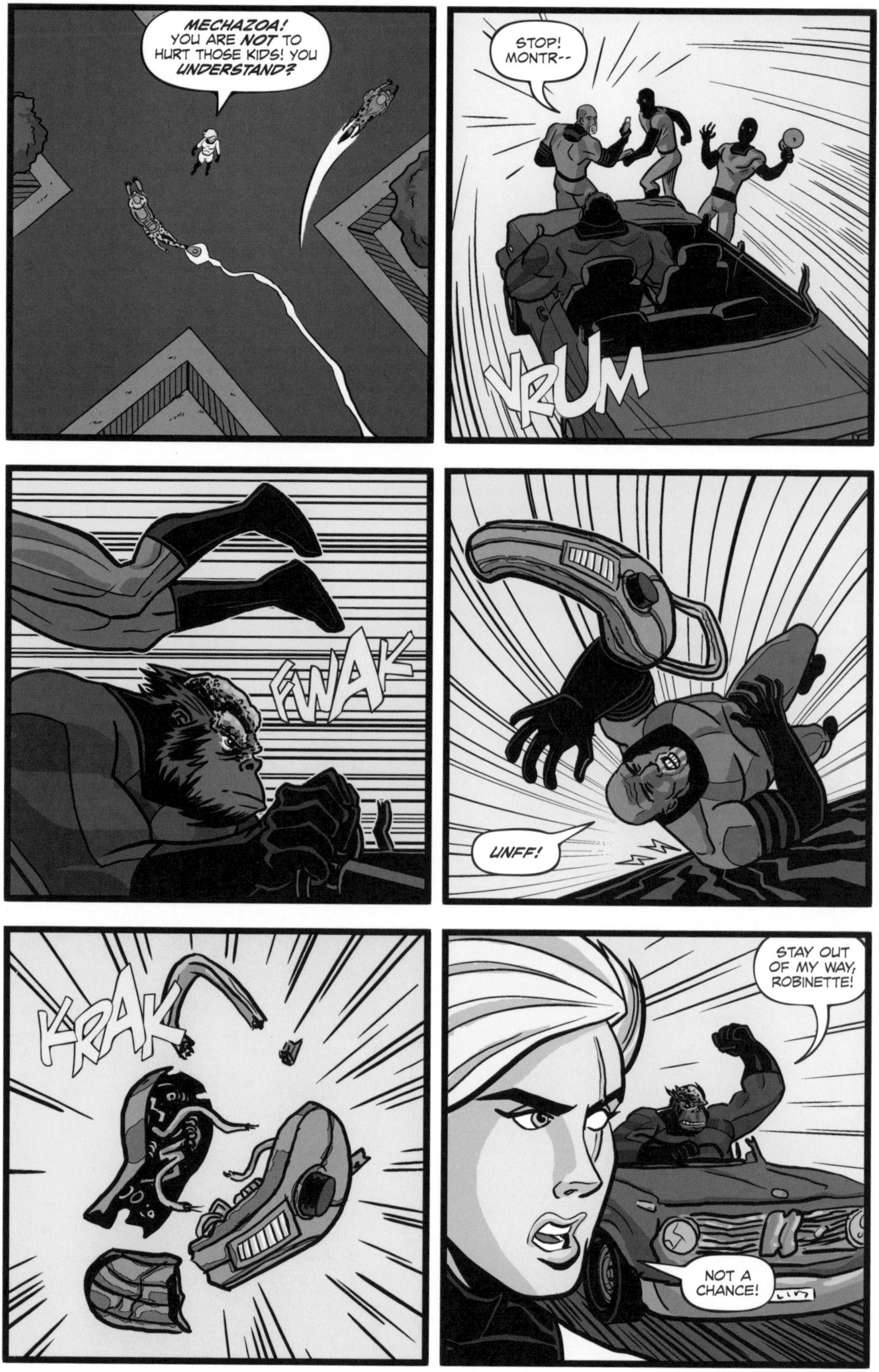
MECHAZOA! YOU ARE NOT TO HURT THOSE KIDS! YOU UNDERSTAND?
STOP! MONTR--
VRUM
FWAK
UNFF!
KRAK
STAY OUT OF MY WAY, ROBINETTE!
NOT A CHANCE!

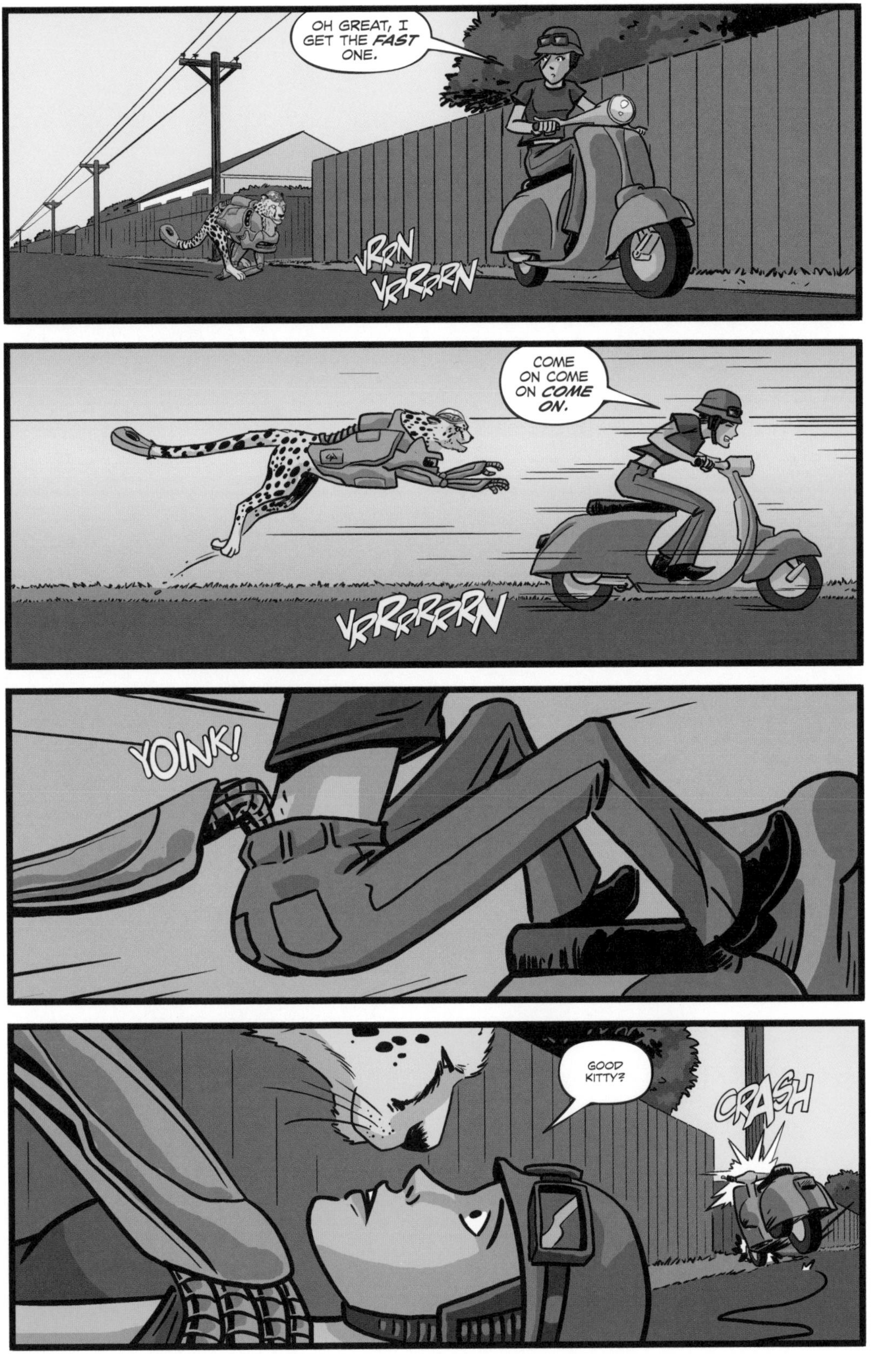
OH GREAT, I GET THE FAST ONE.
VRRN VRRRRN
COME ON COME ON COME ON.
VRRRRRRN
YOINK!
GOOD KITTY?
CRASH

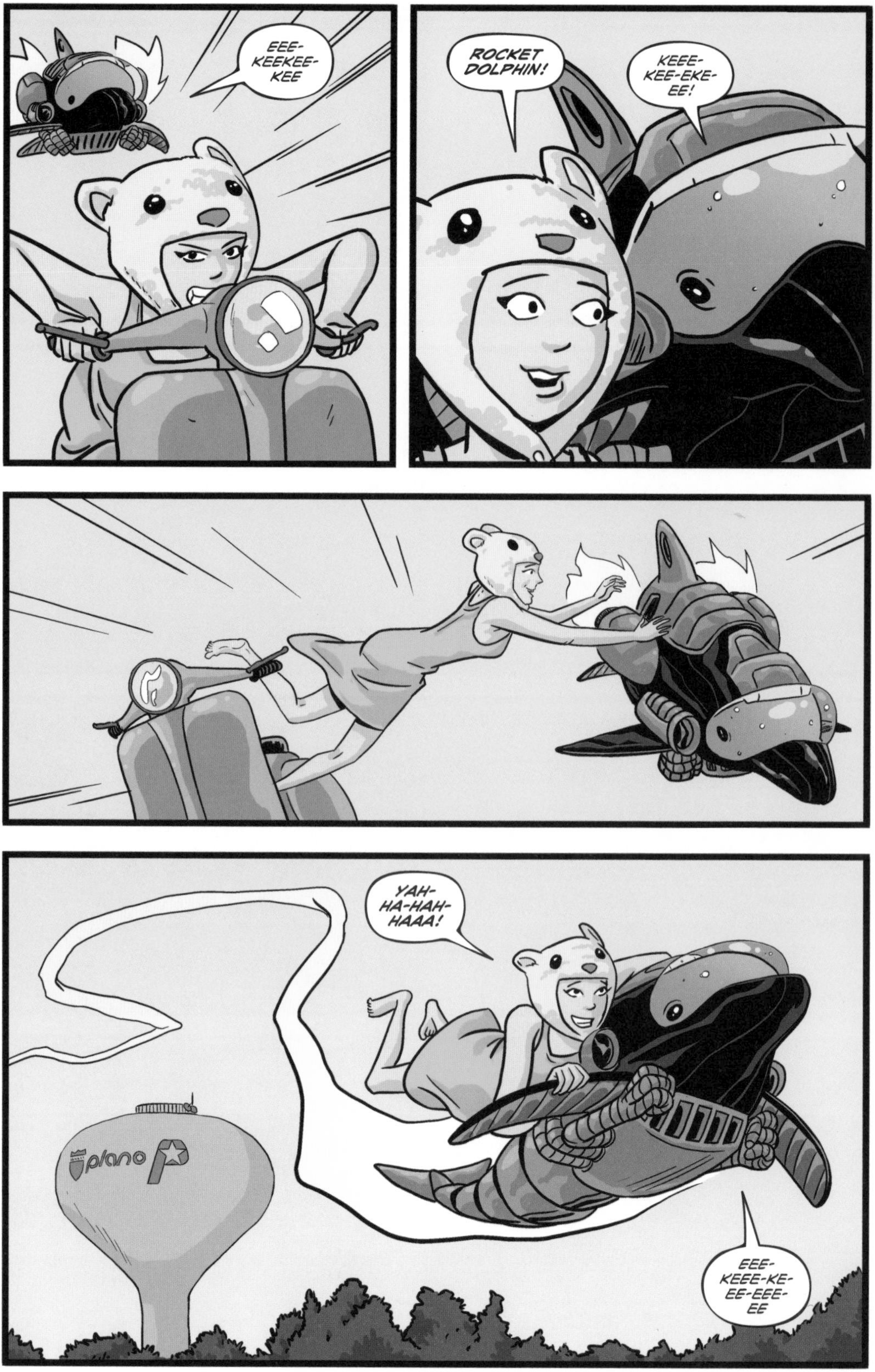
EEE-KEEKEE-KEE
ROCKET DOLPHIN!
KEEE-KEE-EKE-EE!
YAH-HA-HAH-HAAA!
plano
EEE-KEEE-KE-EE-EEE-EE

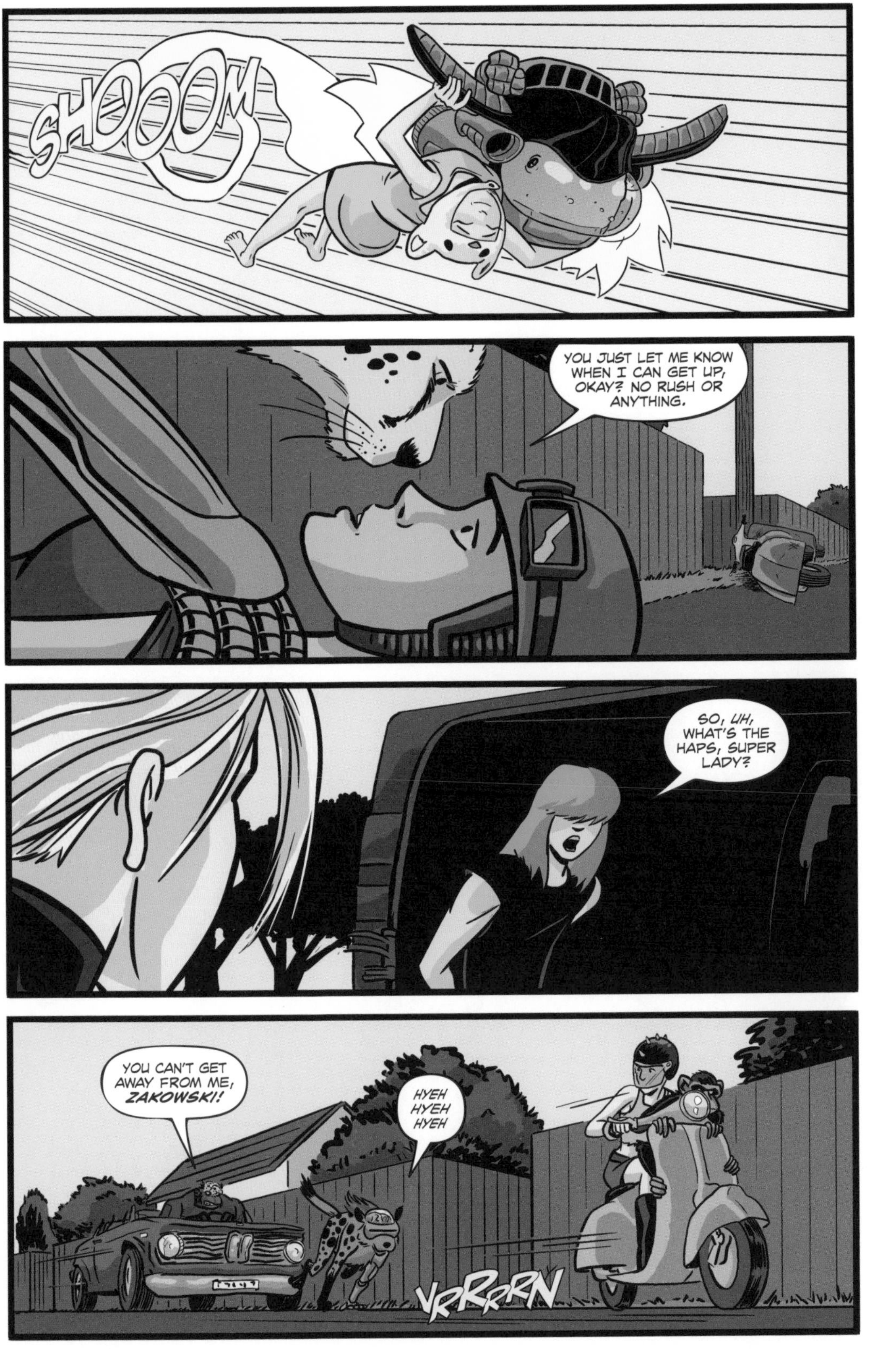
SHOOOM
YOU JUST LET ME KNOW WHEN I CAN GET UP, OKAY? NO RUSH OR ANYTHING.
SO, UH, WHAT'S THE HAPS, SUPER LADY?
YOU CAN'T GET AWAY FROM ME, ZAKOWSKI!
HYEH HYEH HYEH
VRRRRN

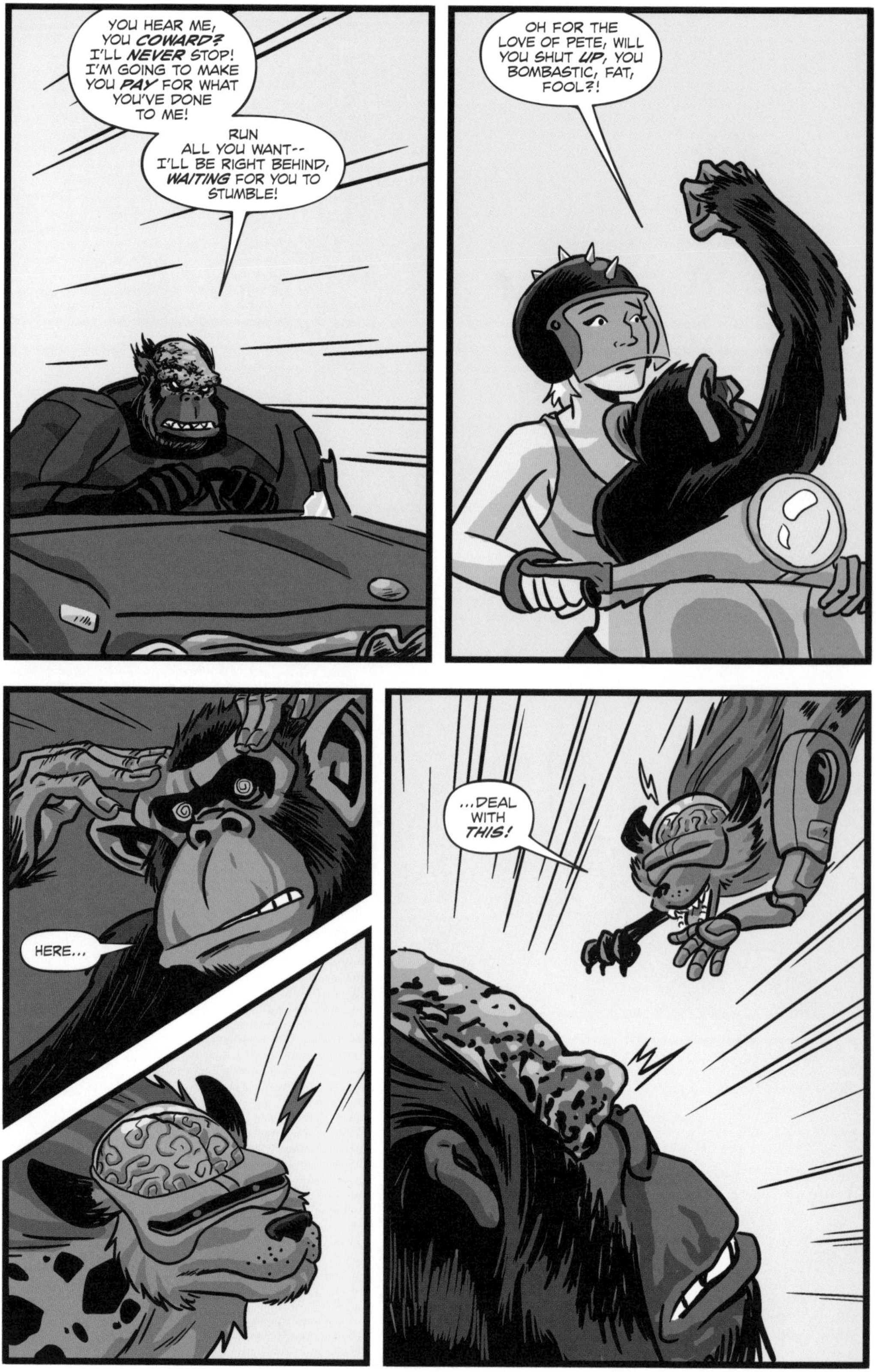
YOU HEAR ME, YOU COWARD? I'LL NEVER STOP! I'M GOING TO MAKE YOU PAY FOR WHAT YOU'VE DONE TO ME!
RUN ALL YOU WANT-- I'LL BE RIGHT BEHIND, WAITING FOR YOU TO STUMBLE!
OH FOR THE LOVE OF PETE, WILL YOU SHUT UP, YOU BOMBASTIC, FAT, FOOL?!
HERE...
...DEAL WITH THIS!

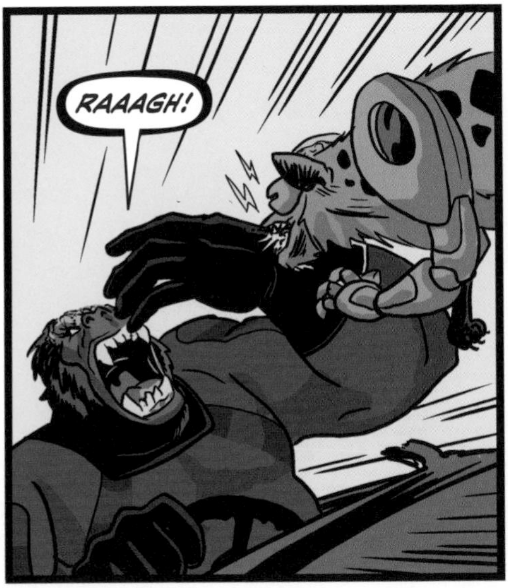
RAAAGH!

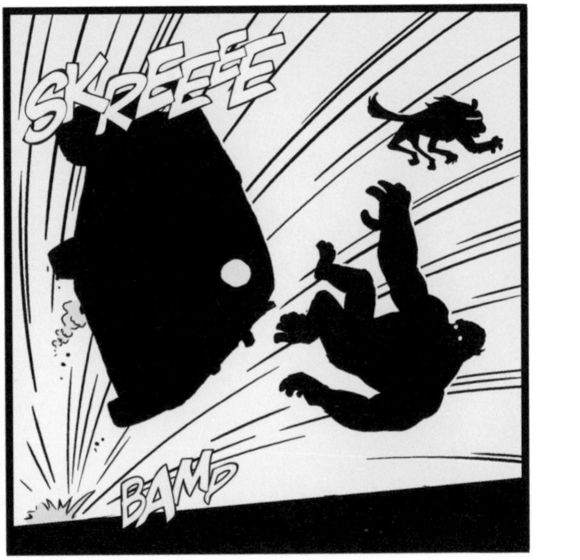
SKREEEE
BAMP

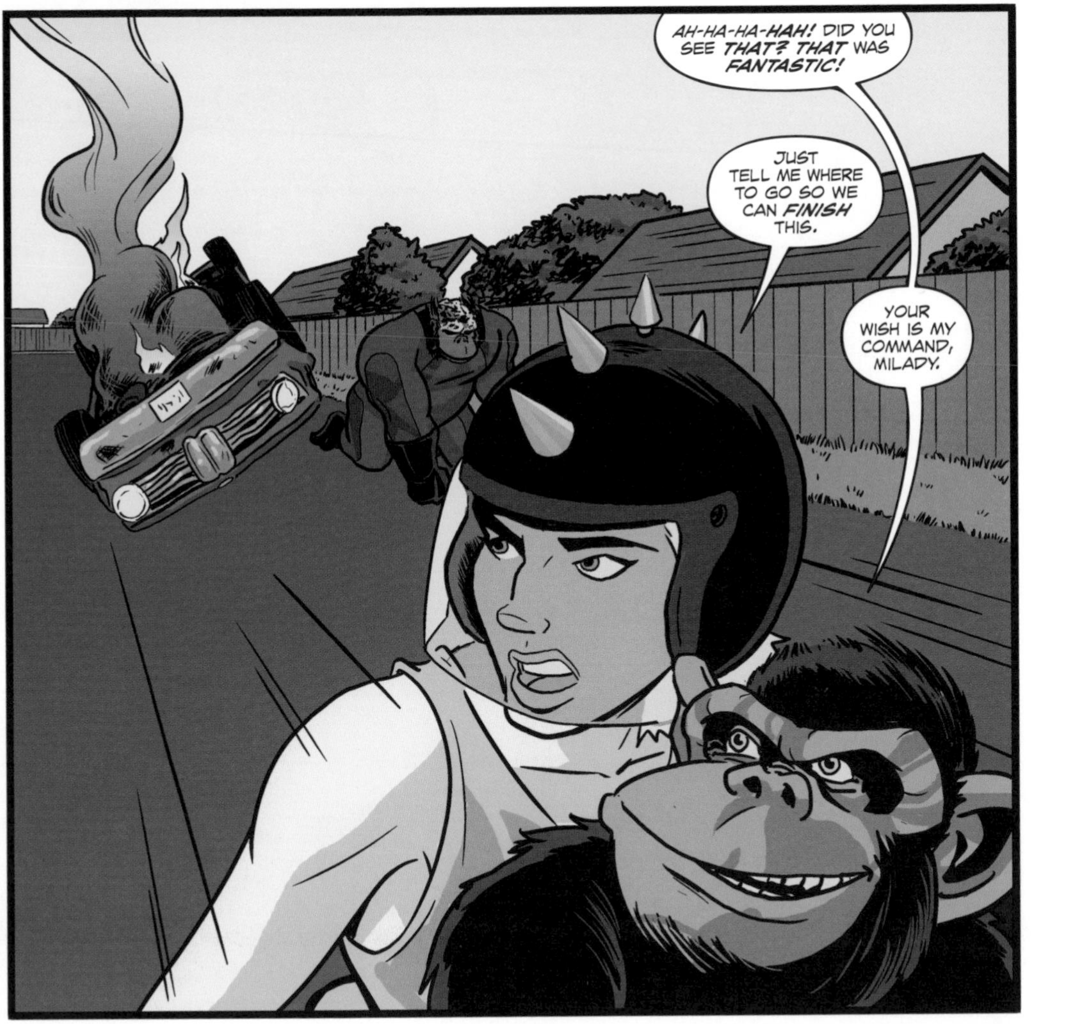
AH-HA-HA-HAH! DID YOU SEE THAT? THAT WAS FANTASTIC!
JUST TELL ME WHERE TO GO SO WE CAN FINISH THIS.
YOUR WISH IS MY COMMAND, MILADY.

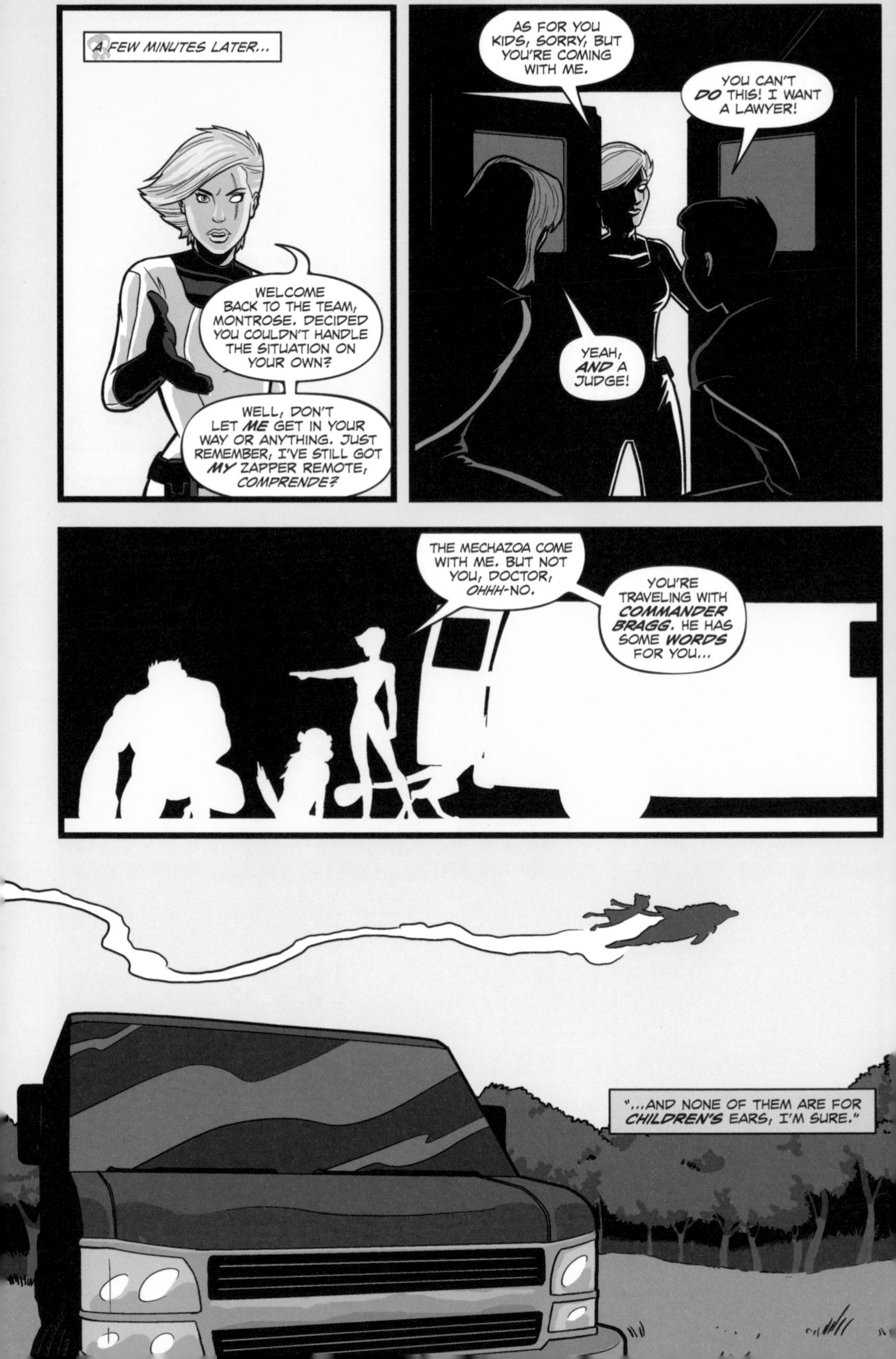
A FEW MINUTES LATER...
WELCOME BACK TO THE TEAM, MONTROSE. DECIDED YOU COULDN'T HANDLE THE SITUATION ON YOUR OWN?
WELL, DON'T LET *ME* GET IN YOUR WAY OR ANYTHING. JUST REMEMBER, I'VE STILL GOT *MY* ZAPPER REMOTE, *COMPRENDE?*
AS FOR YOU KIDS, SORRY, BUT YOU'RE COMING WITH ME.
YOU CAN'T *DO* THIS! I WANT A LAWYER!
YEAH, *AND* A JUDGE!
THE MECHAZOA COME WITH ME. BUT NOT YOU, DOCTOR, *OHHH*-NO.
YOU'RE TRAVELING WITH *COMMANDER BRAGG.* HE HAS SOME *WORDS* FOR YOU...
"...AND NONE OF THEM ARE FOR *CHILDREN'S* EARS, I'M SURE."

KEE-
EEE-KEE-
KEEE
YEEHAW!!
KEE-
EE-EE-
KEE
SHOOM
AGAIN,
AGAIN!!
KEEE-
EEE-KEE-
KEE

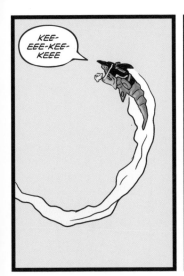

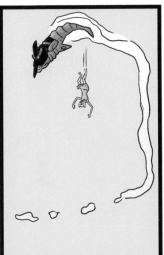

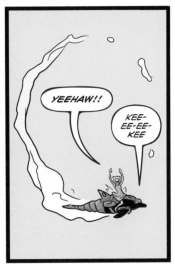

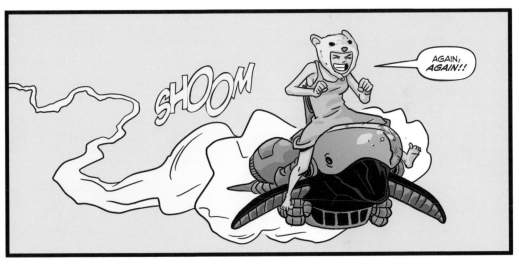

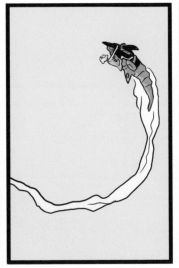

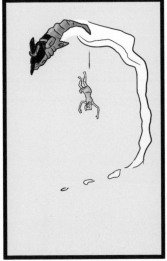

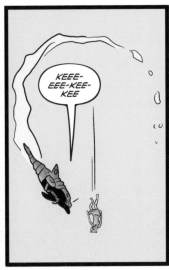

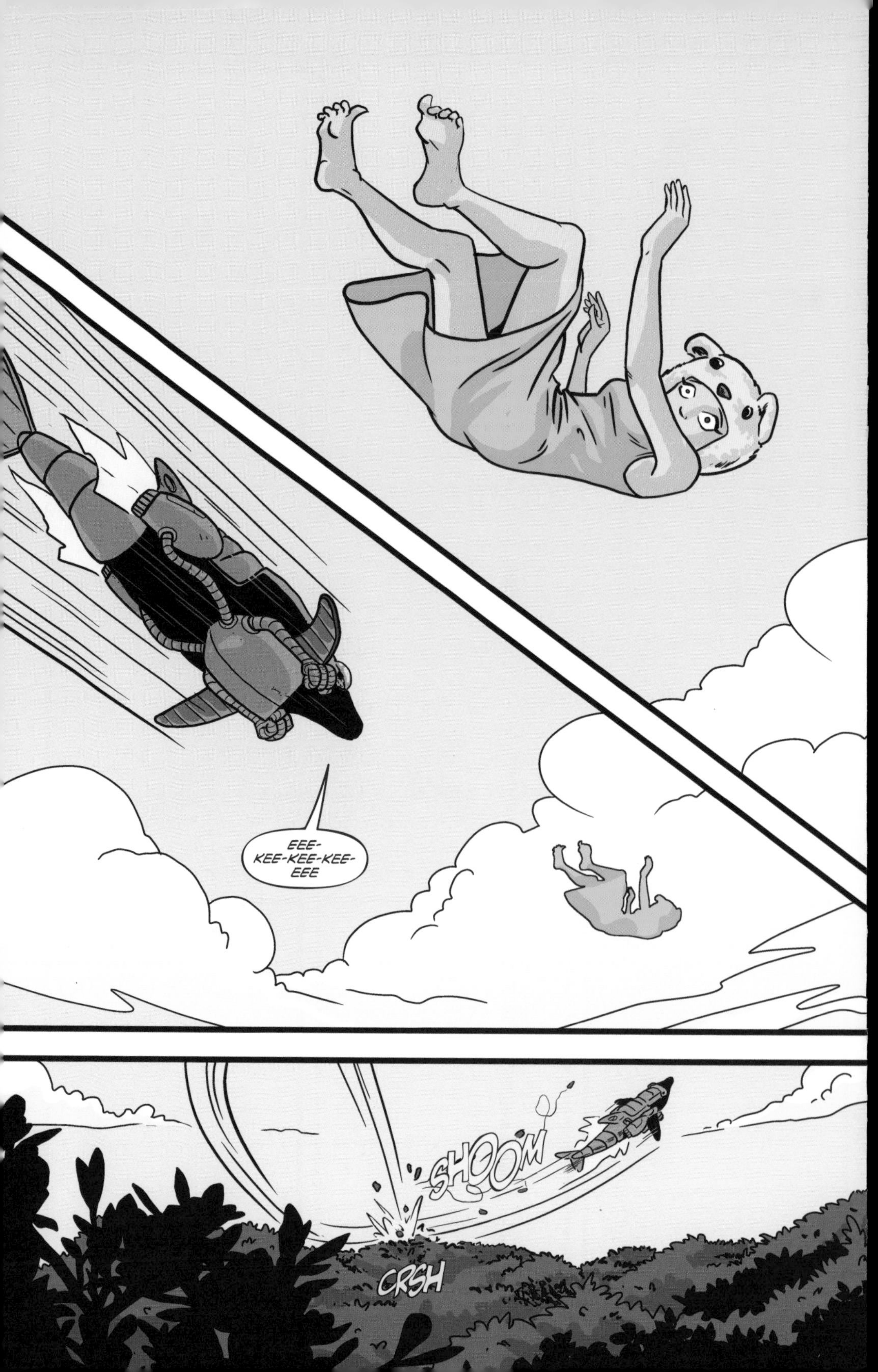
EEE-
KEE-KEE-KEE-
EEE
SHOOM
CRSH

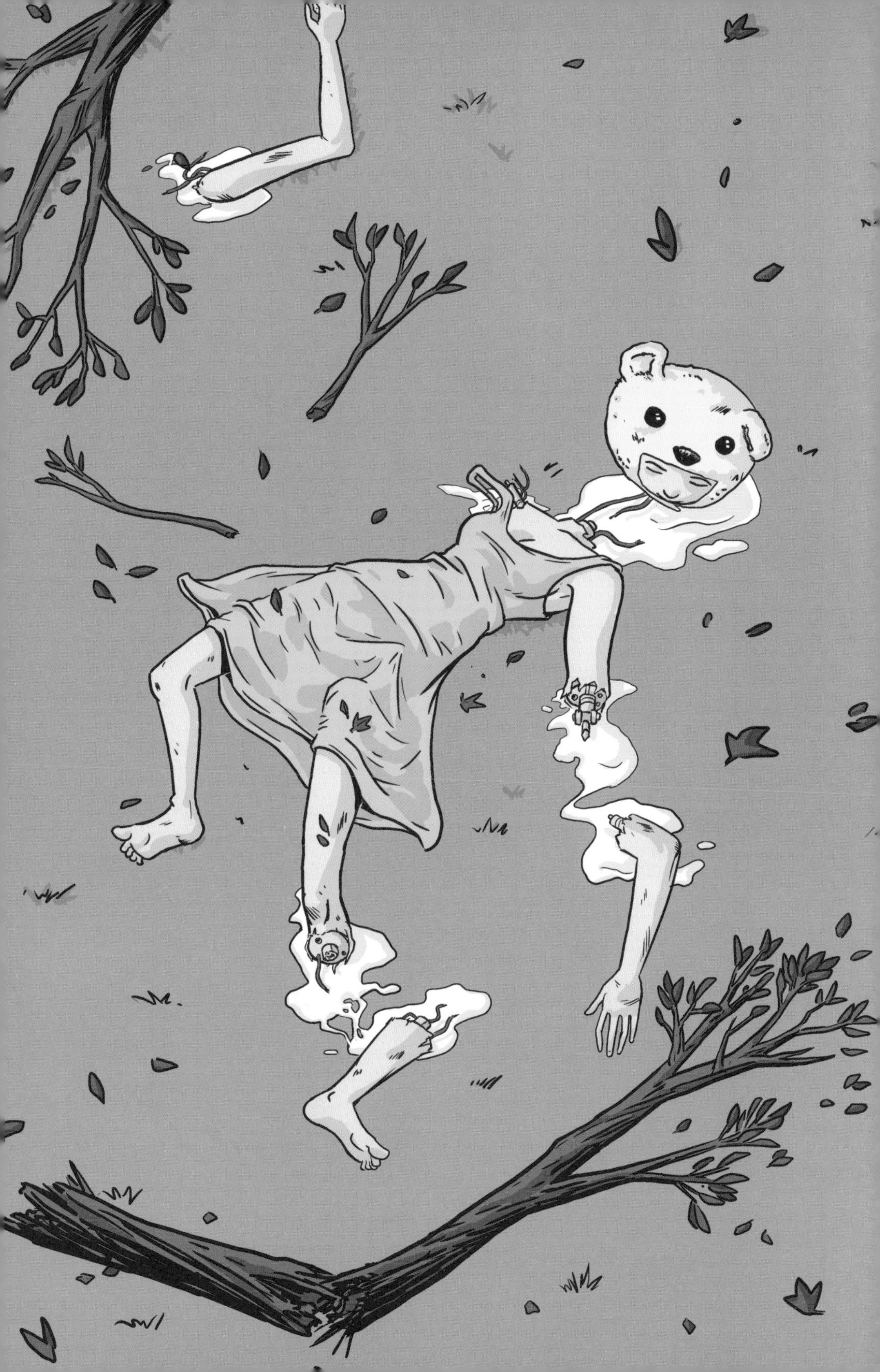

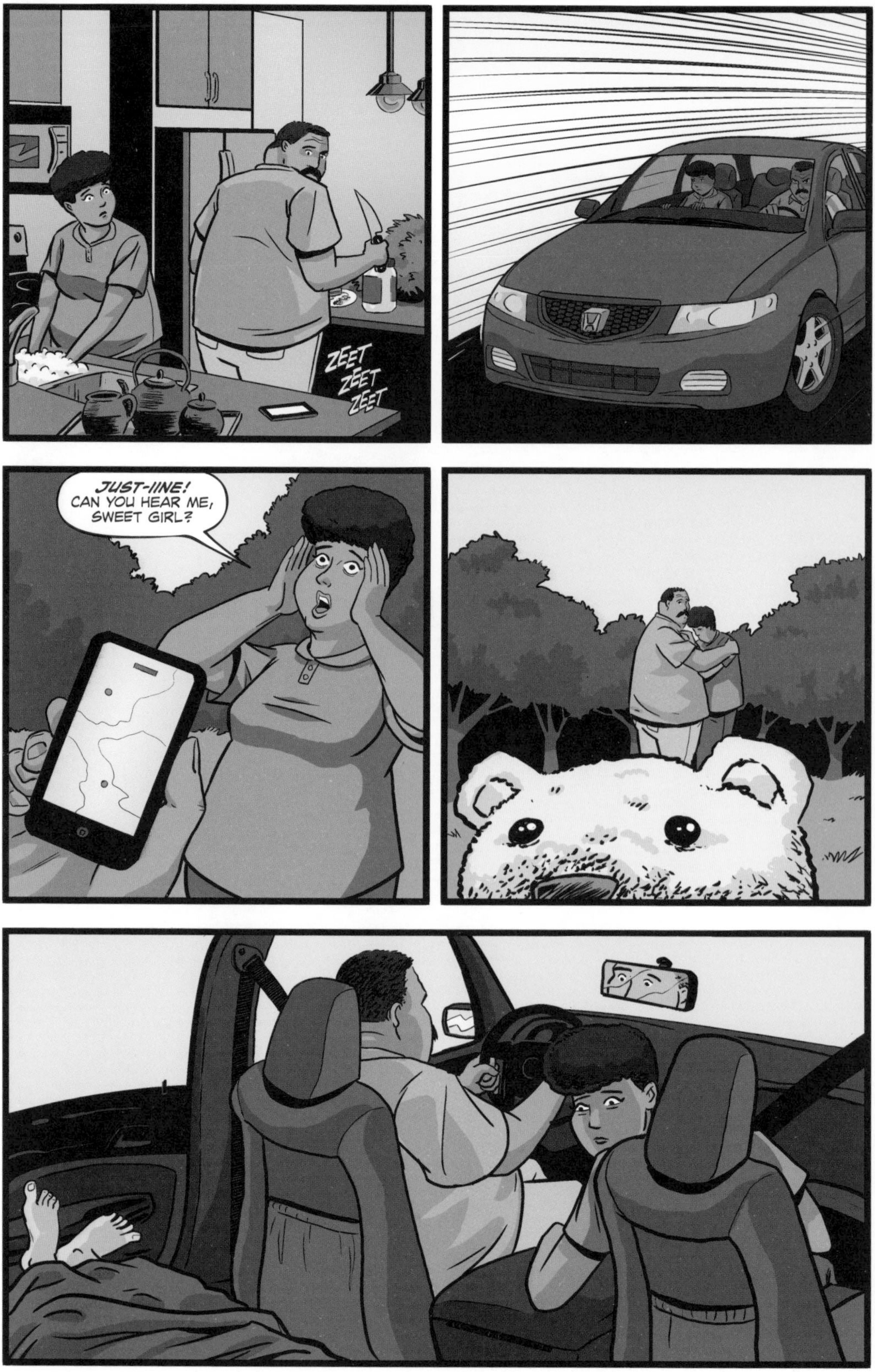
ZEET
ZEET
ZEET
JUST-IINE!
CAN YOU HEAR ME,
SWEET GIRL?

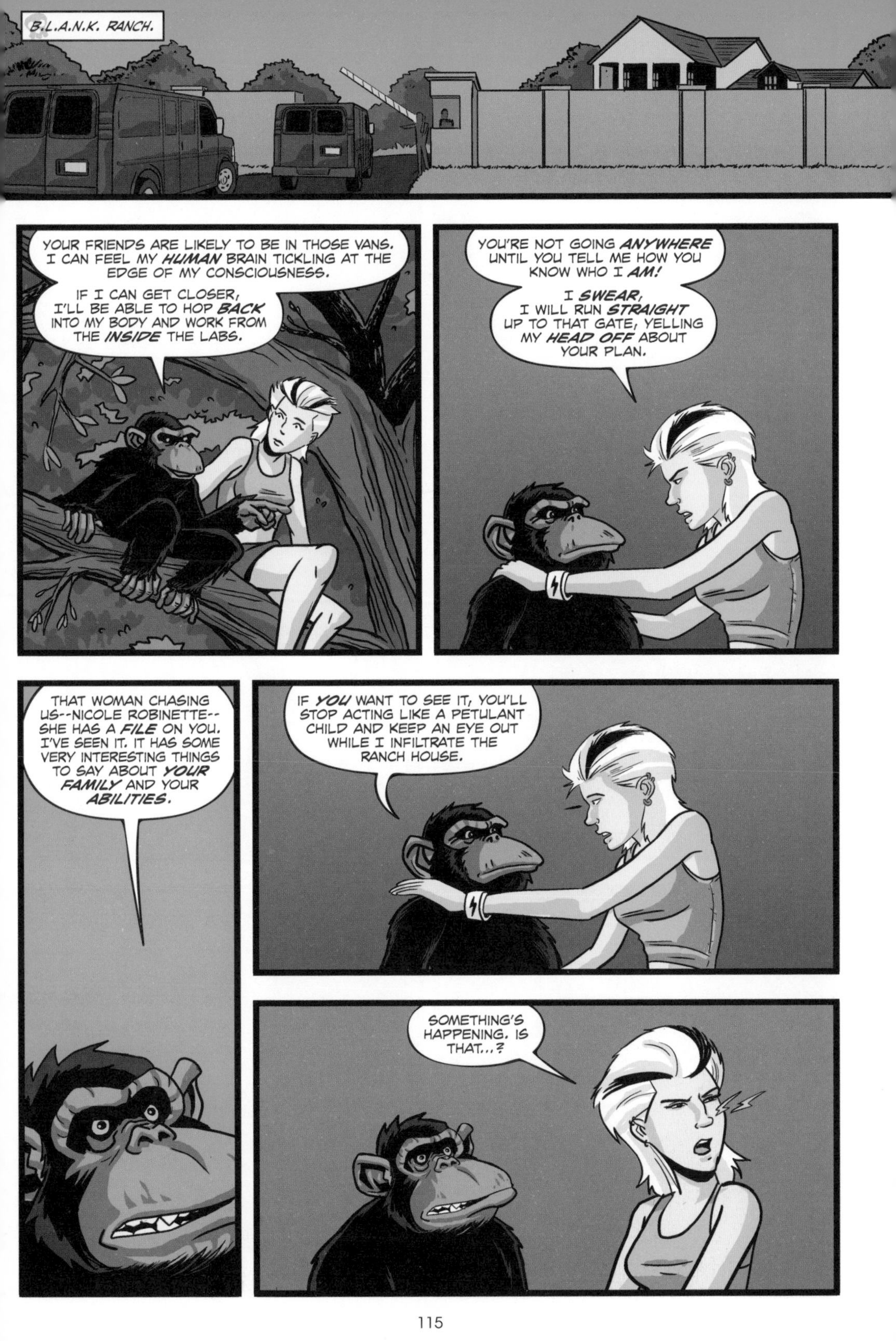

B.L.A.N.K. RANCH.
YOUR FRIENDS ARE LIKELY TO BE IN THOSE VANS. I CAN FEEL MY HUMAN BRAIN TICKLING AT THE EDGE OF MY CONSCIOUSNESS.
IF I CAN GET CLOSER, I'LL BE ABLE TO HOP BACK INTO MY BODY AND WORK FROM THE INSIDE THE LABS.
YOU'RE NOT GOING ANYWHERE UNTIL YOU TELL ME HOW YOU KNOW WHO I AM!
I SWEAR, I WILL RUN STRAIGHT UP TO THAT GATE, YELLING MY HEAD OFF ABOUT YOUR PLAN.
THAT WOMAN CHASING US--NICOLE ROBINETTE--SHE HAS A FILE ON YOU. I'VE SEEN IT. IT HAS SOME VERY INTERESTING THINGS TO SAY ABOUT YOUR FAMILY AND YOUR ABILITIES.
IF YOU WANT TO SEE IT, YOU'LL STOP ACTING LIKE A PETULANT CHILD AND KEEP AN EYE OUT WHILE I INFILTRATE THE RANCH HOUSE.
SOMETHING'S HAPPENING. IS THAT...?

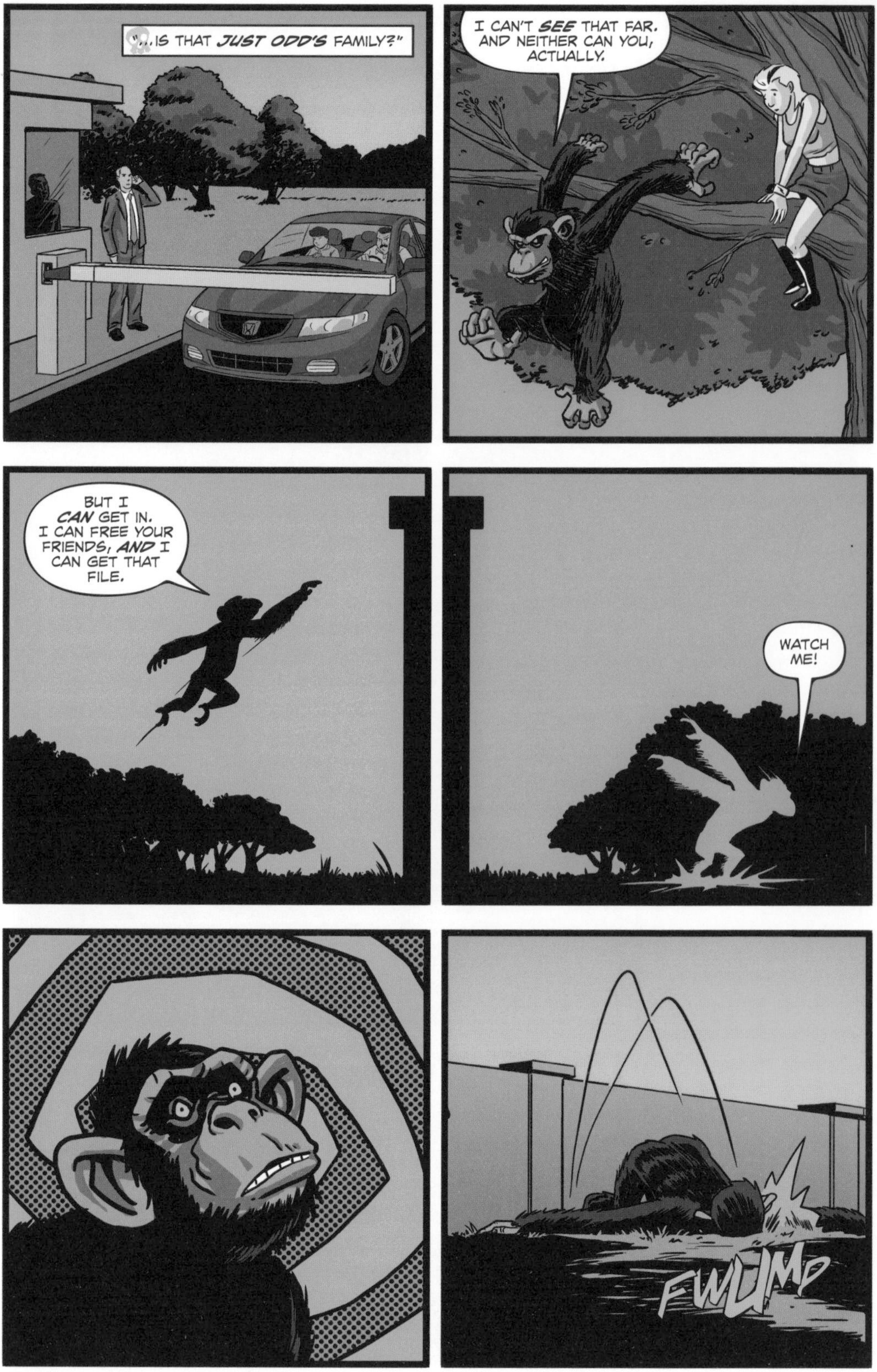
"...IS THAT JUST ODD'S FAMILY?"
I CAN'T SEE THAT FAR. AND NEITHER CAN YOU, ACTUALLY.
BUT I CAN GET IN. I CAN FREE YOUR FRIENDS, AND I CAN GET THAT FILE.
WATCH ME!
FWUMP

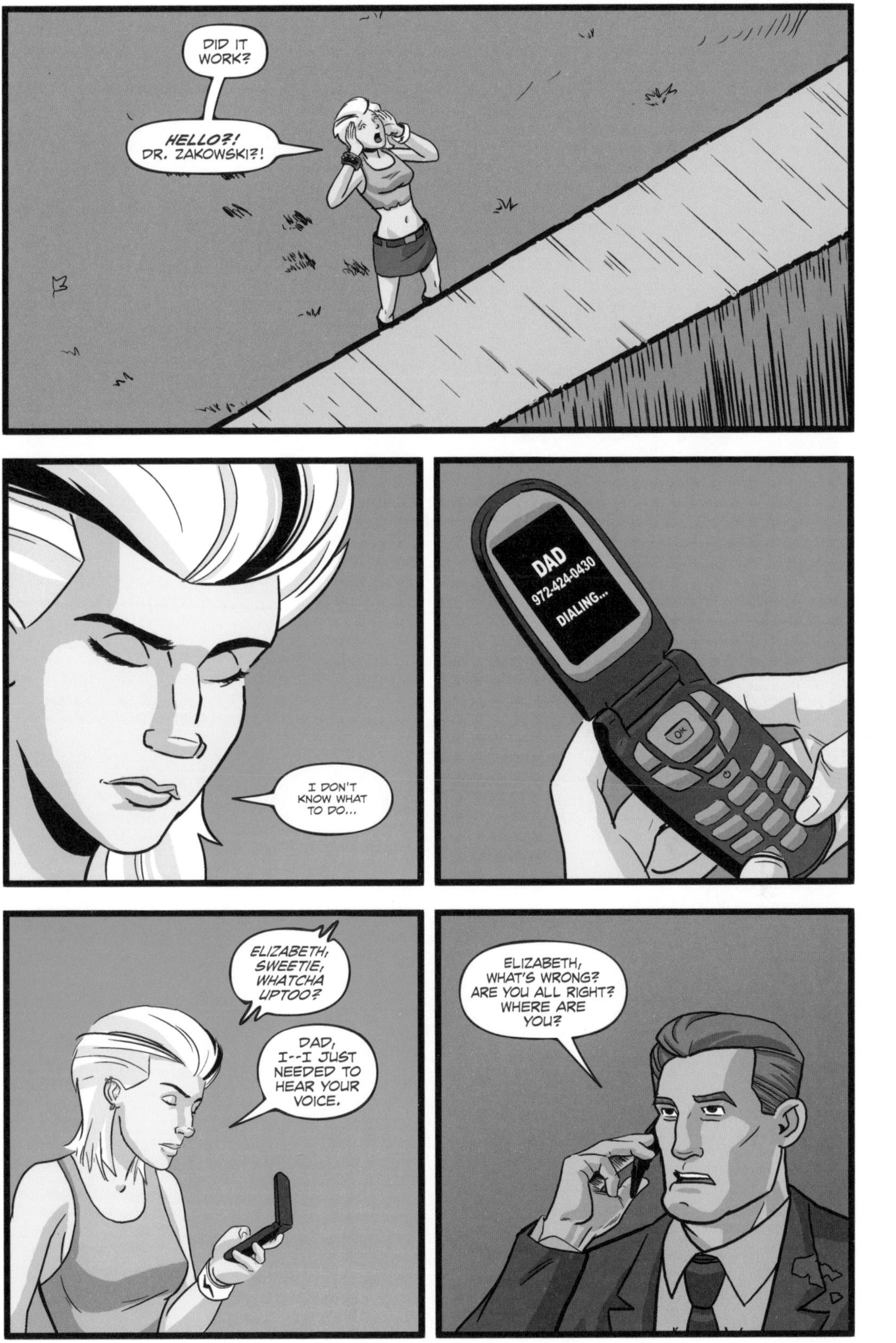
DID IT WORK?
HELLO?! DR. ZAKOWSKI?!
I DON'T KNOW WHAT TO DO...
DAD
972-424-0430
DIALING...
OK
ELIZABETH, SWEETIE, WHATCHA UPTOO?
DAD, I--I JUST NEEDED TO HEAR YOUR VOICE.
ELIZABETH, WHAT'S WRONG? ARE YOU ALL RIGHT? WHERE ARE YOU?

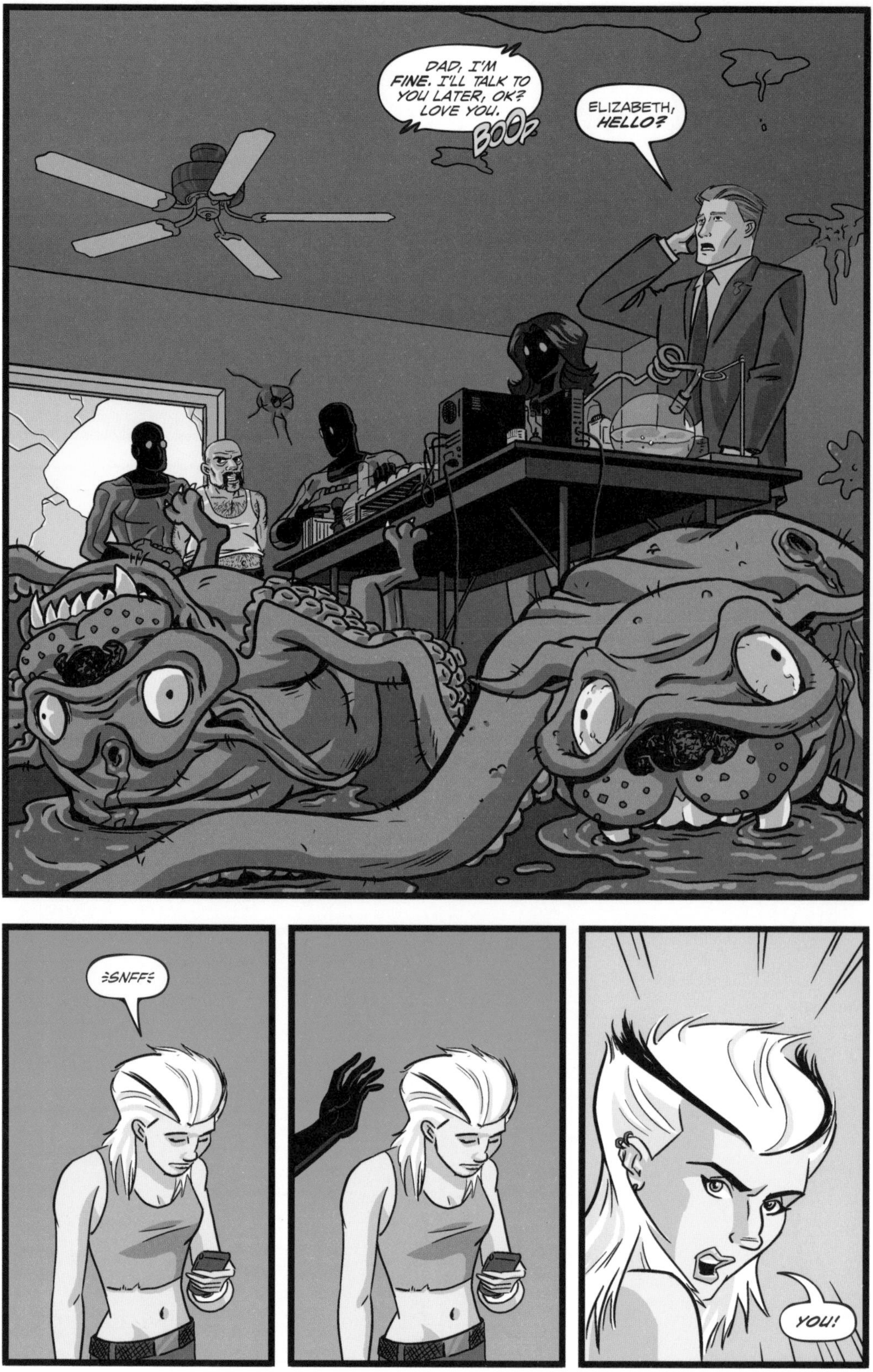
DAD, I'M FINE. I'LL TALK TO YOU LATER, OK? LOVE YOU.
BOOP
ELIZABETH, HELLO?
SNFF
YOU!

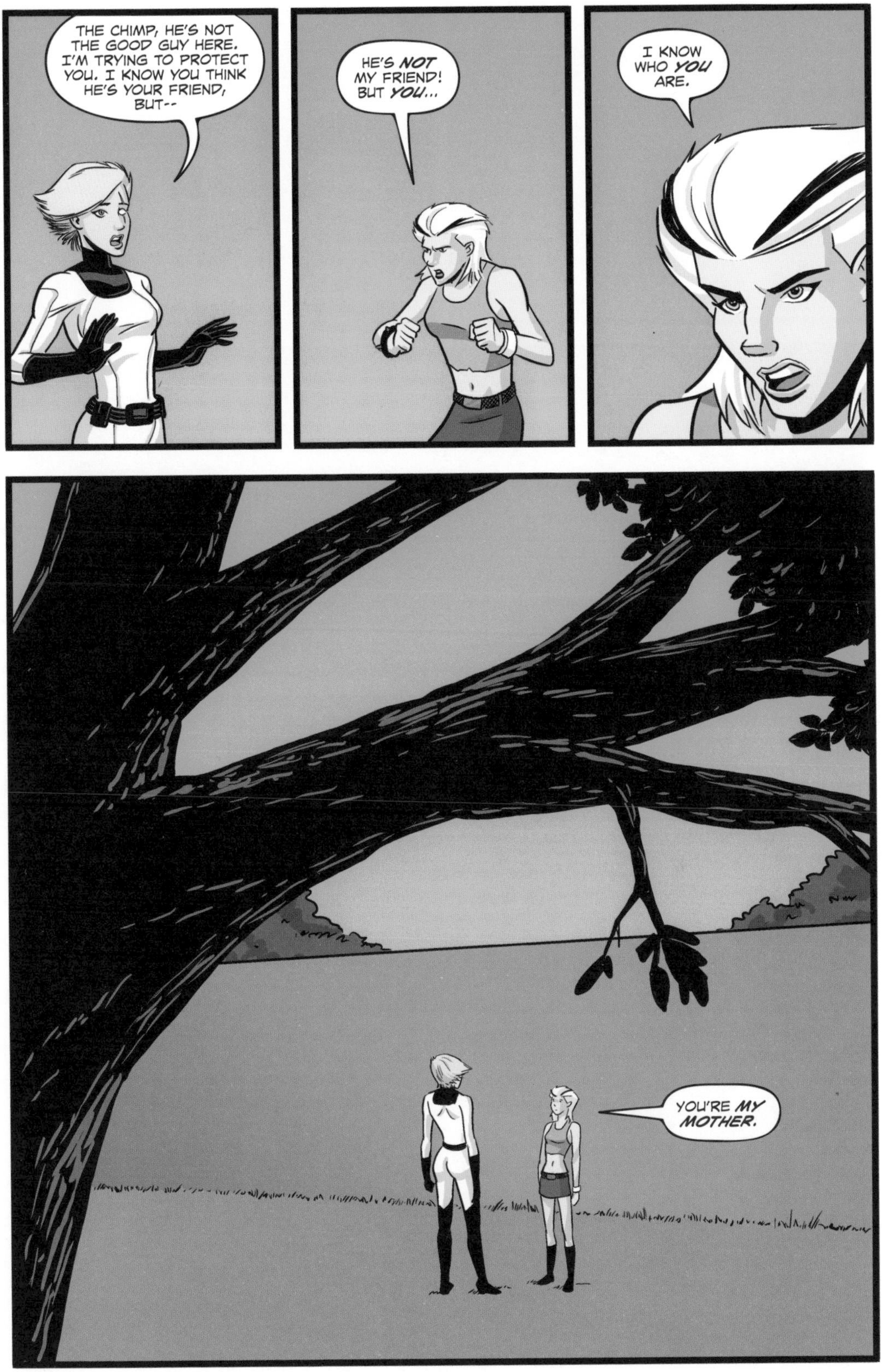
THE CHIMP, HE'S NOT THE GOOD GUY HERE. I'M TRYING TO PROTECT YOU. I KNOW YOU THINK HE'S YOUR FRIEND, BUT--
HE'S NOT MY FRIEND! BUT YOU...
I KNOW WHO YOU ARE.
YOU'RE MY MOTHER.

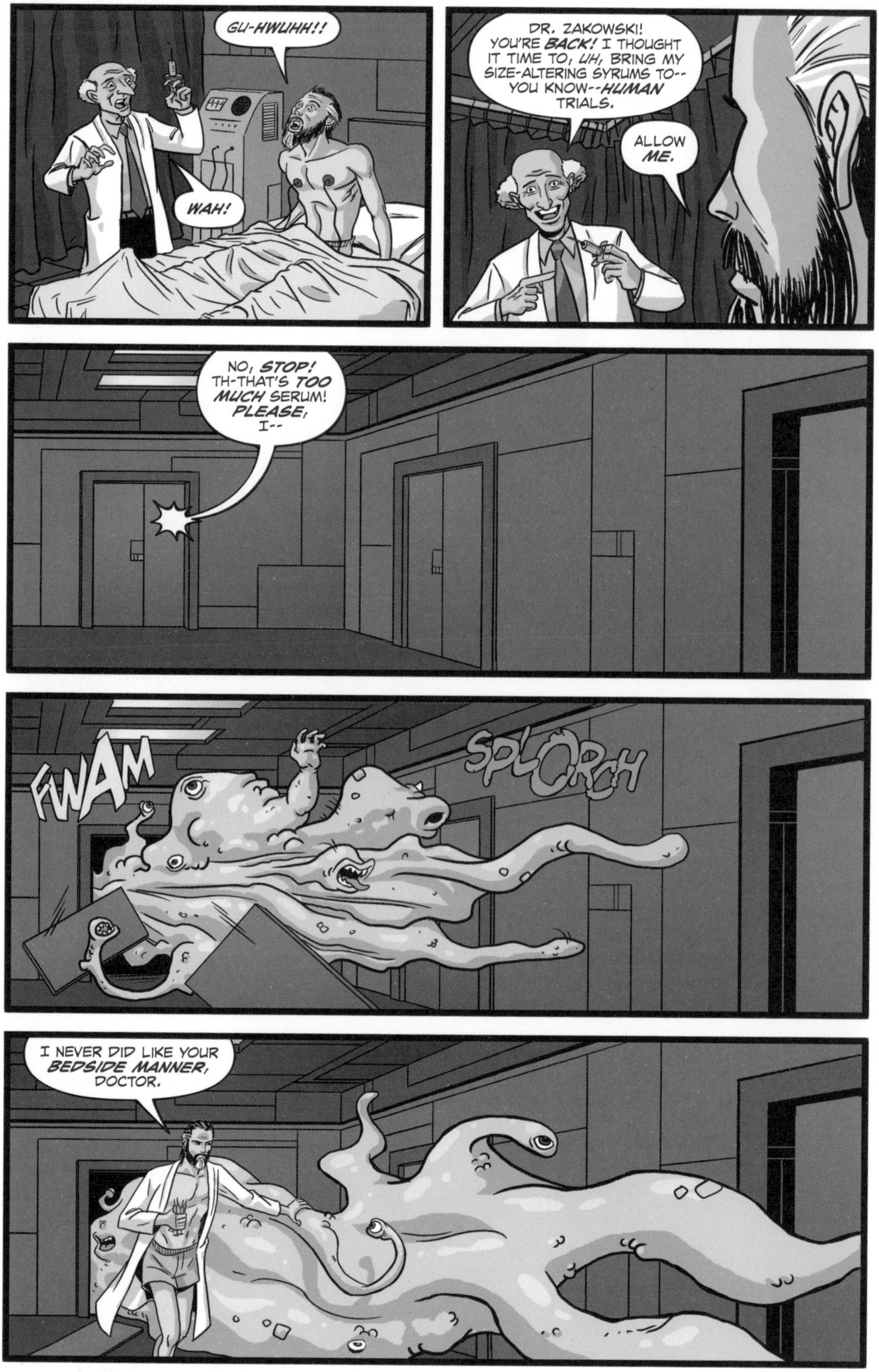
GU-HWUHH!!
WAH!
DR. ZAKOWSKI! YOU'RE BACK! I THOUGHT IT TIME TO, UH, BRING MY SIZE-ALTERING SYRUMS TO-- YOU KNOW--HUMAN TRIALS.
ALLOW ME.
NO, STOP! TH-THAT'S TOO MUCH SERUM! PLEASE, I--
FWAM
SPLORCH
I NEVER DID LIKE YOUR BEDSIDE MANNER, DOCTOR.

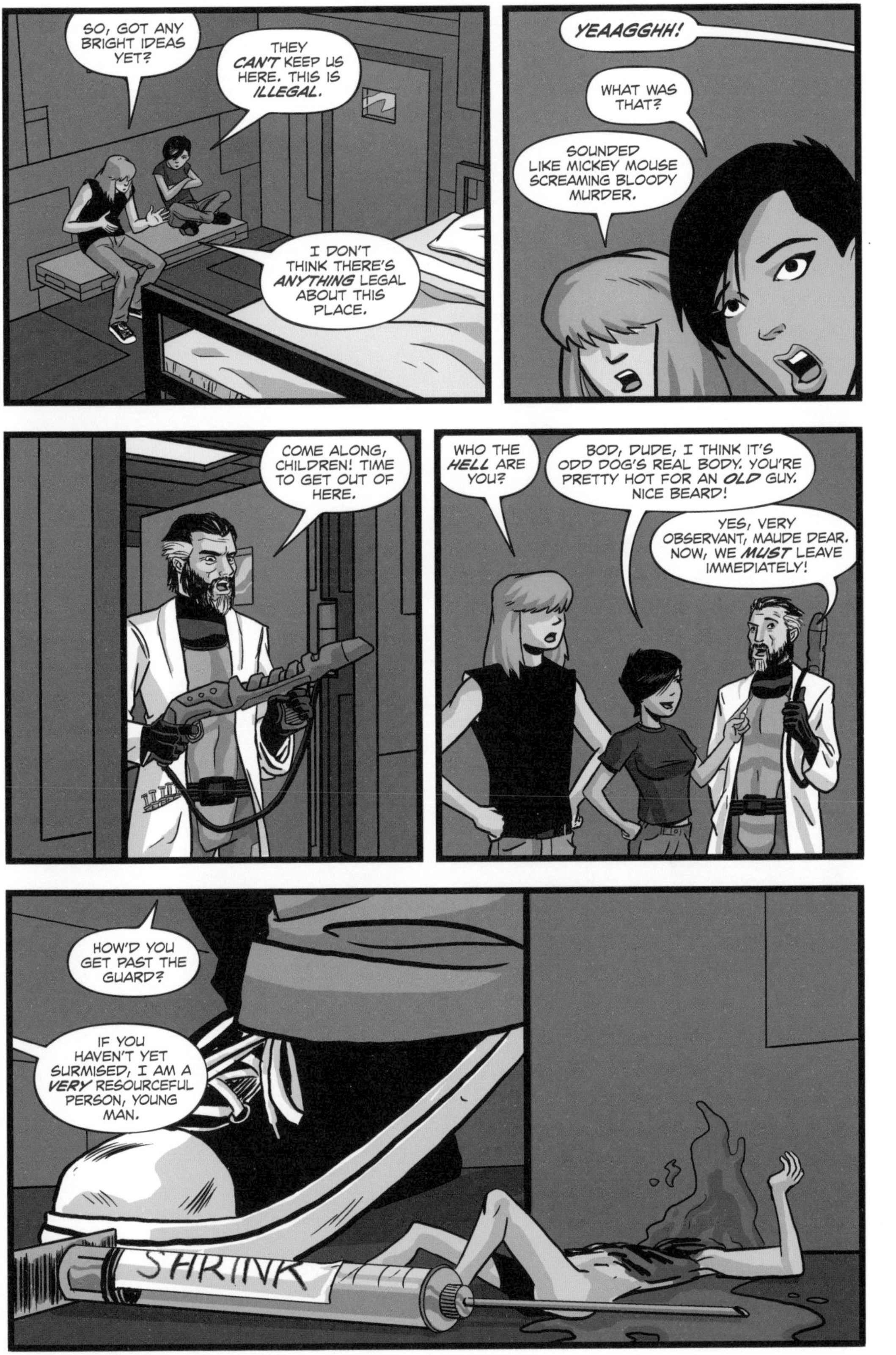
SO, GOT ANY BRIGHT IDEAS YET?
THEY CAN'T KEEP US HERE. THIS IS ILLEGAL.
I DON'T THINK THERE'S ANYTHING LEGAL ABOUT THIS PLACE.
YEAAGGHH!
WHAT WAS THAT?
SOUNDED LIKE MICKEY MOUSE SCREAMING BLOODY MURDER.
COME ALONG, CHILDREN! TIME TO GET OUT OF HERE.
WHO THE HELL ARE YOU?
BOD, DUDE, I THINK IT'S ODD DOG'S REAL BODY. YOU'RE PRETTY HOT FOR AN OLD GUY. NICE BEARD!
YES, VERY OBSERVANT, MAUDE DEAR. NOW, WE MUST LEAVE IMMEDIATELY!
HOW'D YOU GET PAST THE GUARD?
IF YOU HAVEN'T YET SURMISED, I AM A VERY RESOURCEFUL PERSON, YOUNG MAN.
SHRINK

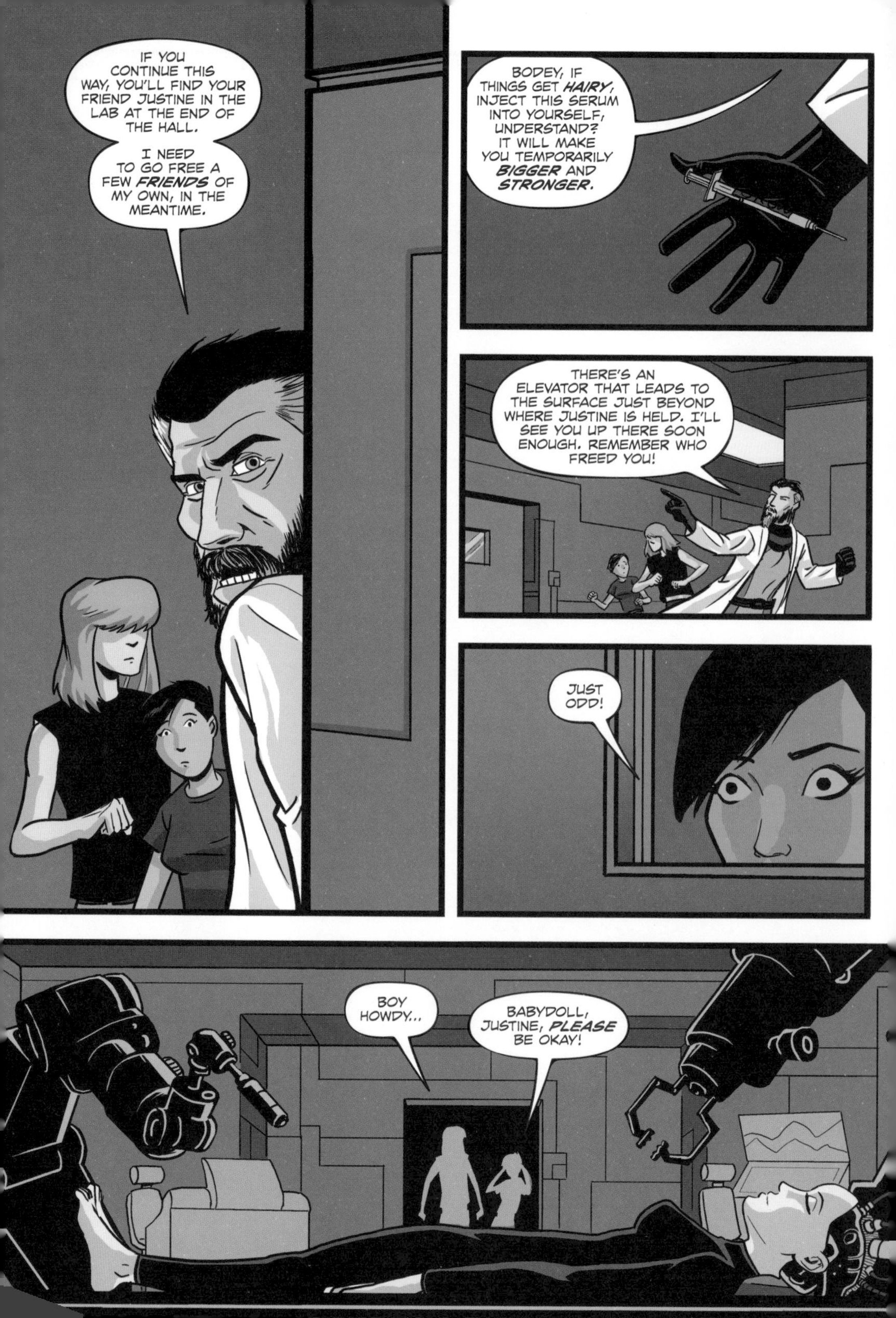
IF YOU CONTINUE THIS WAY, YOU'LL FIND YOUR FRIEND JUSTINE IN THE LAB AT THE END OF THE HALL.
I NEED TO GO FREE A FEW FRIENDS OF MY OWN, IN THE MEANTIME.
BODEY, IF THINGS GET HAIRY, INJECT THIS SERUM INTO YOURSELF, UNDERSTAND? IT WILL MAKE YOU TEMPORARILY BIGGER AND STRONGER.
THERE'S AN ELEVATOR THAT LEADS TO THE SURFACE JUST BEYOND WHERE JUSTINE IS HELD. I'LL SEE YOU UP THERE SOON ENOUGH. REMEMBER WHO FREED YOU!
JUST ODD!
BOY HOWDY...
BABYDOLL, JUSTINE, PLEASE BE OKAY!

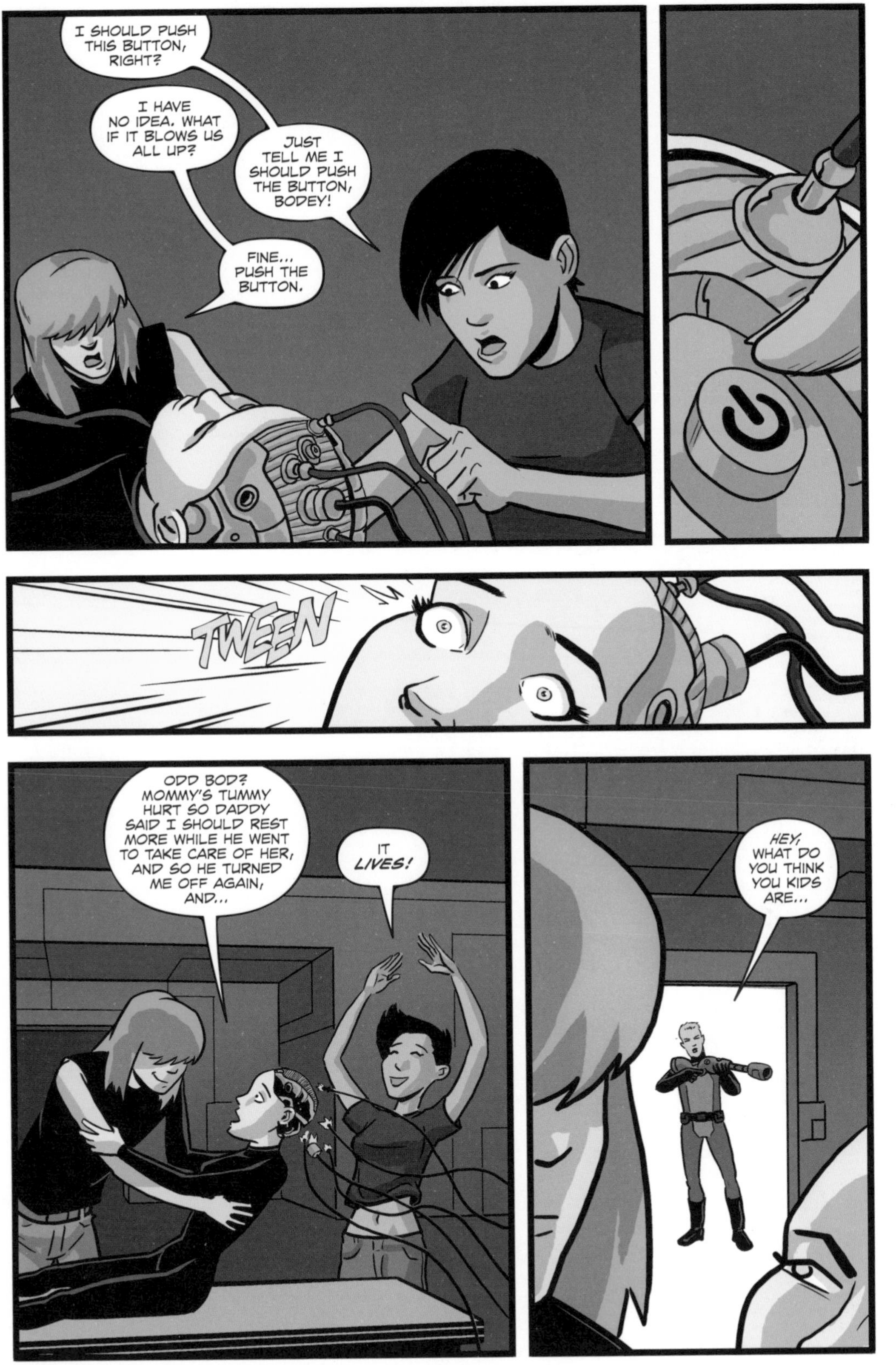
I SHOULD PUSH THIS BUTTON, RIGHT?
I HAVE NO IDEA. WHAT IF IT BLOWS US ALL UP?
JUST TELL ME I SHOULD PUSH THE BUTTON, BODEY!
FINE... PUSH THE BUTTON.
TWEEN
ODD BOD? MOMMY'S TUMMY HURT SO DADDY SAID I SHOULD REST MORE WHILE HE WENT TO TAKE CARE OF HER, AND SO HE TURNED ME OFF AGAIN, AND...
IT *LIVES!*
HEY, WHAT DO YOU THINK YOU KIDS ARE...

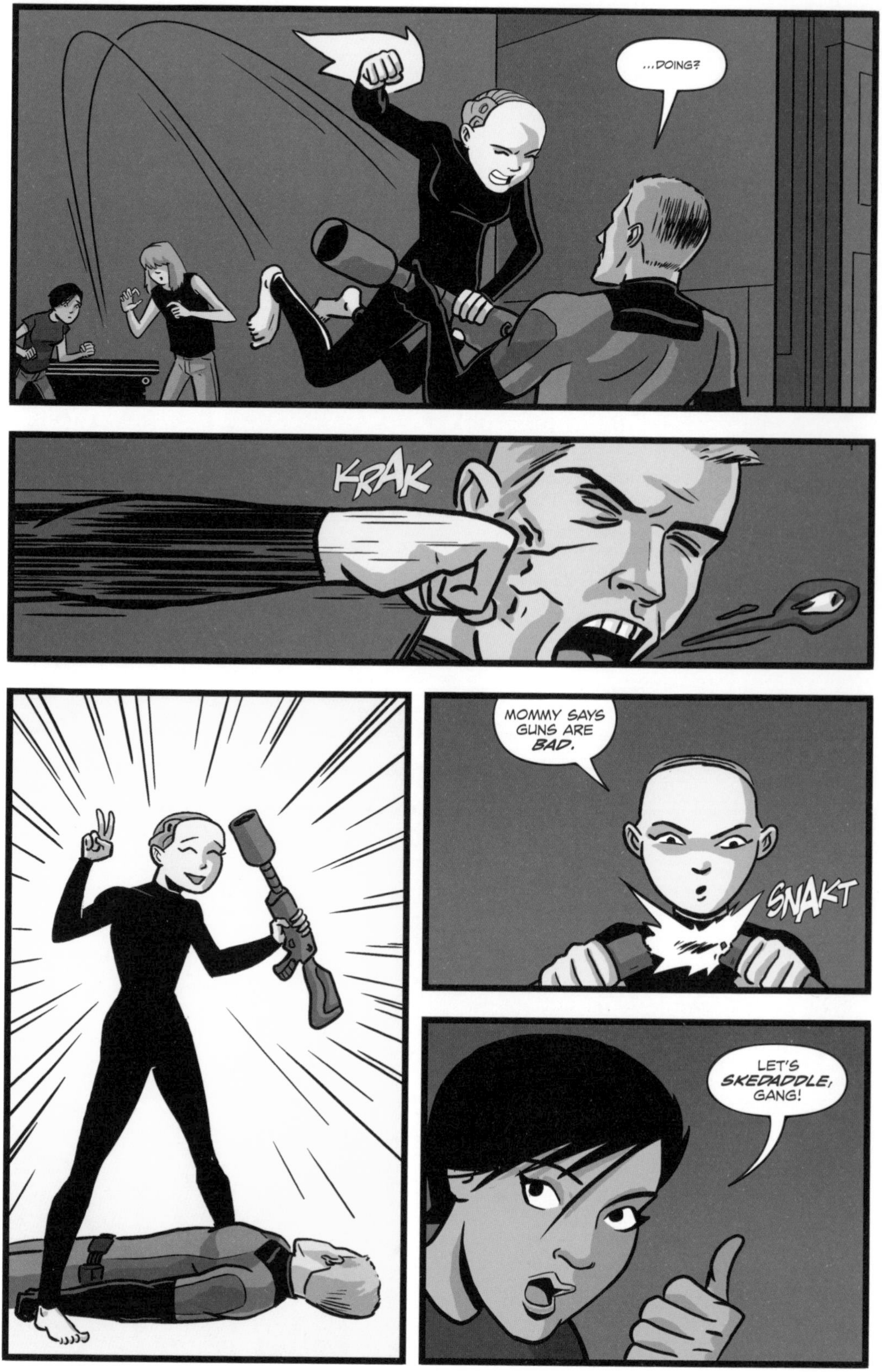
...DOING?
KRAK
MOMMY SAYS GUNS ARE BAD.
SNAKT
LET'S SKEDADDLE, GANG!

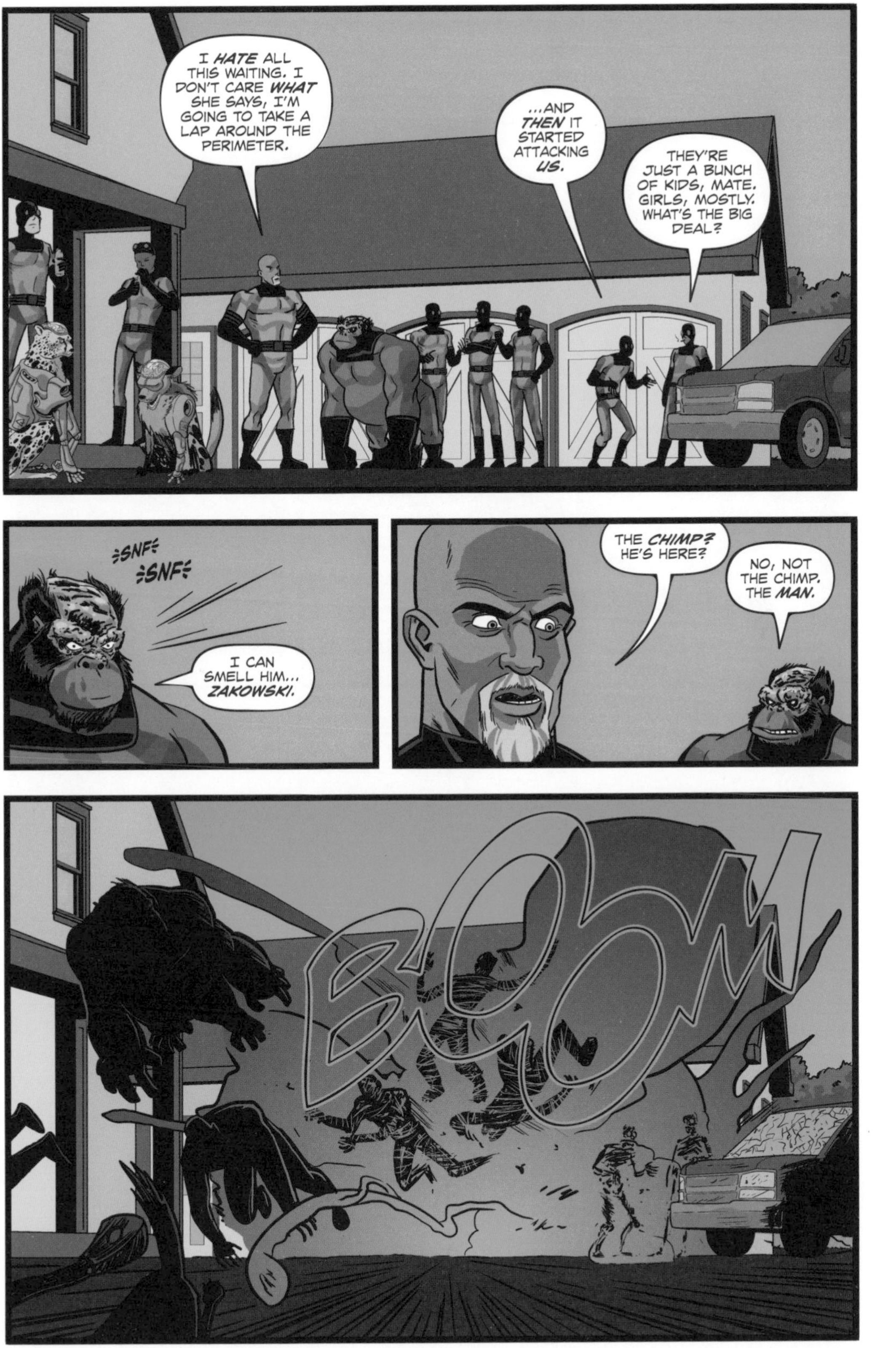
I HATE ALL THIS WAITING. I DON'T CARE WHAT SHE SAYS, I'M GOING TO TAKE A LAP AROUND THE PERIMETER.
...AND THEN IT STARTED ATTACKING US.
THEY'RE JUST A BUNCH OF KIDS, MATE. GIRLS, MOSTLY. WHAT'S THE BIG DEAL?
SNF
SNF
I CAN SMELL HIM... ZAKOWSKI.
THE CHIMP? HE'S HERE?
NO, NOT THE CHIMP. THE MAN.
BOOM

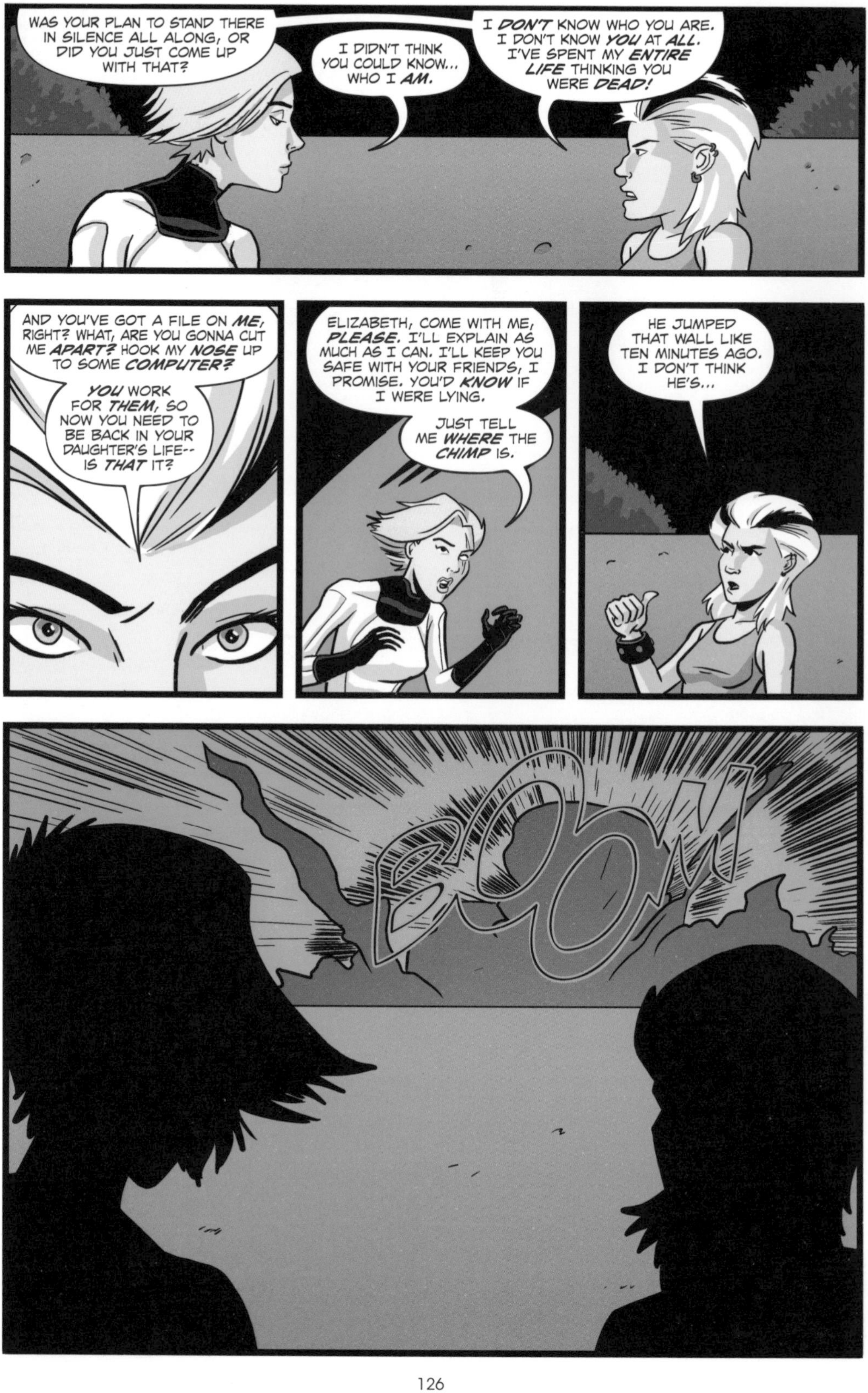
WAS YOUR PLAN TO STAND THERE IN SILENCE ALL ALONG, OR DID YOU JUST COME UP WITH THAT?
I DIDN'T THINK YOU COULD KNOW... WHO I AM.
I DON'T KNOW WHO YOU ARE. I DON'T KNOW YOU AT ALL. I'VE SPENT MY ENTIRE LIFE THINKING YOU WERE DEAD!
AND YOU'VE GOT A FILE ON ME, RIGHT? WHAT, ARE YOU GONNA CUT ME APART? HOOK MY NOSE UP TO SOME COMPUTER?
YOU WORK FOR THEM, SO NOW YOU NEED TO BE BACK IN YOUR DAUGHTER'S LIFE-- IS THAT IT?
ELIZABETH, COME WITH ME, PLEASE. I'LL EXPLAIN AS MUCH AS I CAN. I'LL KEEP YOU SAFE WITH YOUR FRIENDS, I PROMISE. YOU'D KNOW IF I WERE LYING.
JUST TELL ME WHERE THE CHIMP IS.
HE JUMPED THAT WALL LIKE TEN MINUTES AGO. I DON'T THINK HE'S...
BOOM

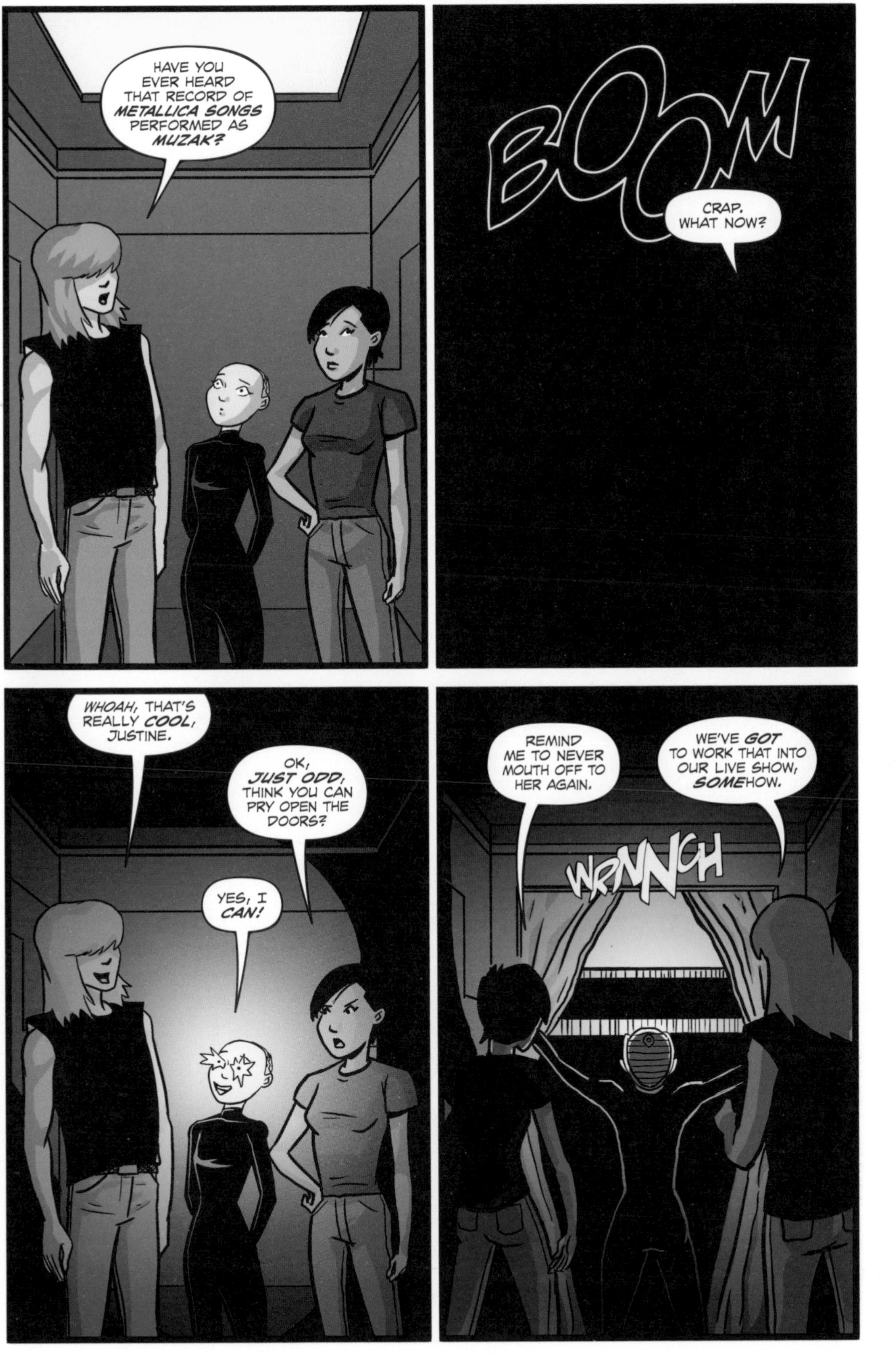
HAVE YOU EVER HEARD THAT RECORD OF METALLICA SONGS PERFORMED AS MUZAK?
BOOM
CRAP. WHAT NOW?
WHOAH, THAT'S REALLY COOL, JUSTINE.
OK, JUST ODD, THINK YOU CAN PRY OPEN THE DOORS?
YES, I CAN!
REMIND ME TO NEVER MOUTH OFF TO HER AGAIN.
WE'VE GOT TO WORK THAT INTO OUR LIVE SHOW, SOMEHOW.
WRNNCH

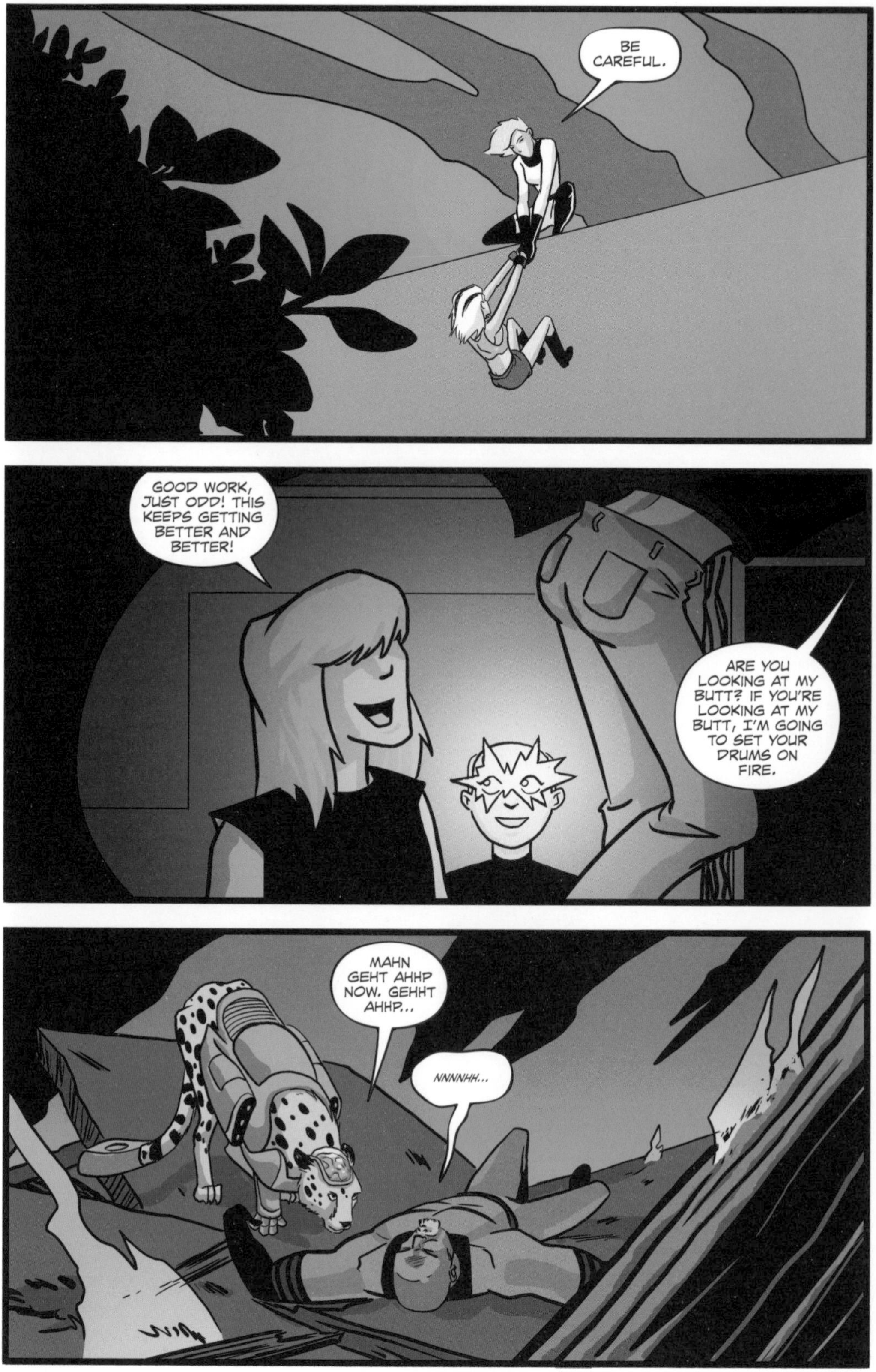
BE CAREFUL.
GOOD WORK, JUST ODD! THIS KEEPS GETTING BETTER AND BETTER!
ARE YOU LOOKING AT MY BUTT? IF YOU'RE LOOKING AT MY BUTT, I'M GOING TO SET YOUR DRUMS ON FIRE.
MAHN GEHT AHHP NOW. GEHHT AHHP...
NNNNHH...

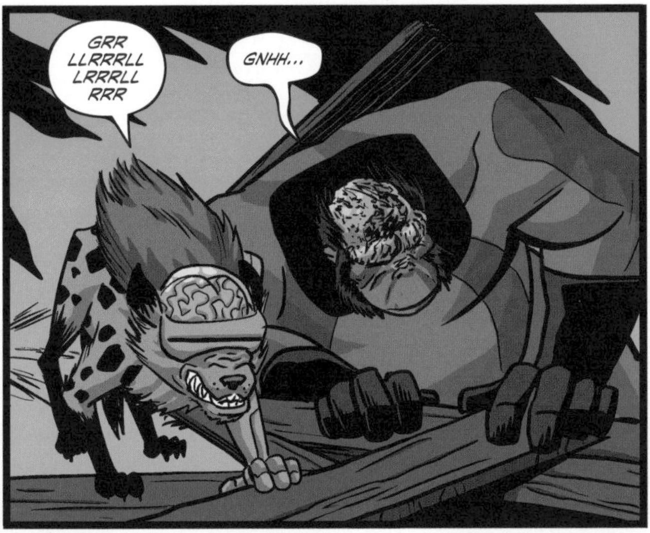
GRR LLRRRLL LRRRLL RRR
GNHH...

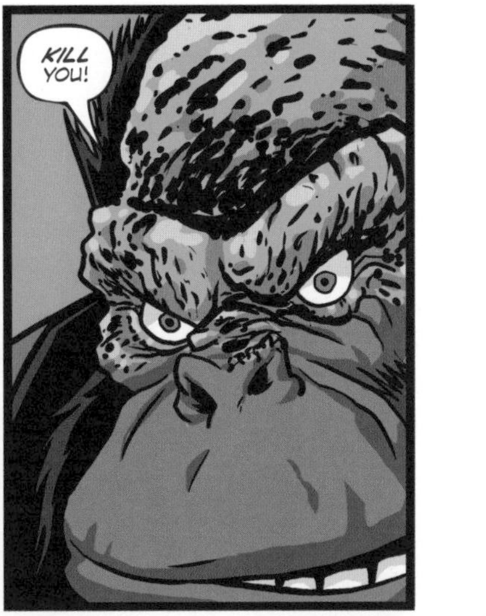
KILL YOU!

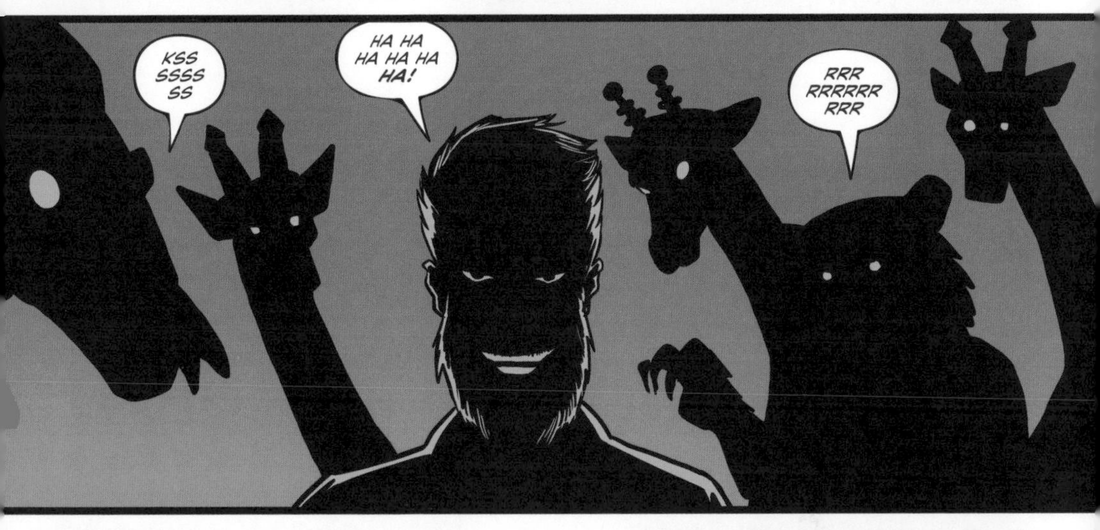
KSS SSSS SS
HA HA HA HA HA HA!
RRR RRRRRR RRR

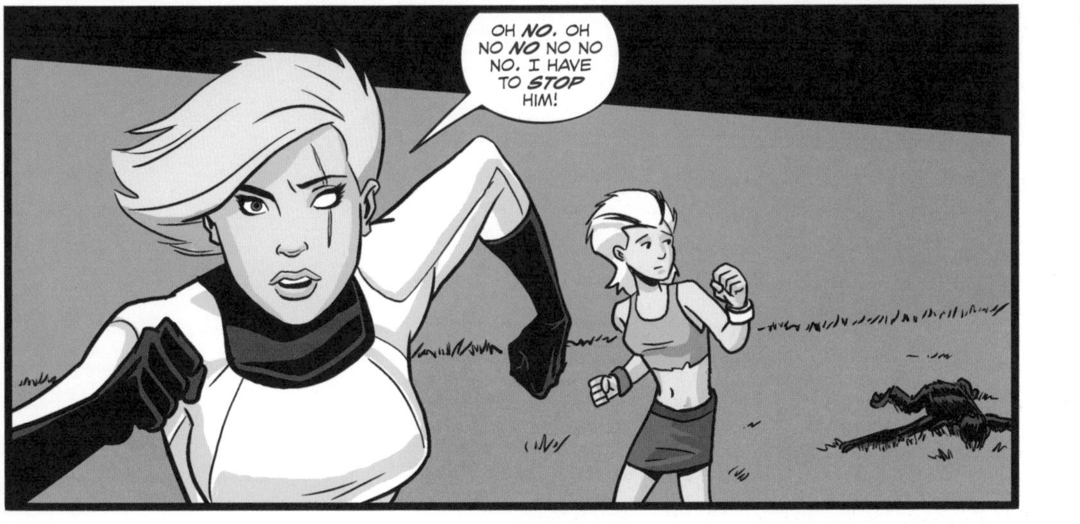
OH NO. OH NO NO NO NO NO. I HAVE TO STOP HIM!

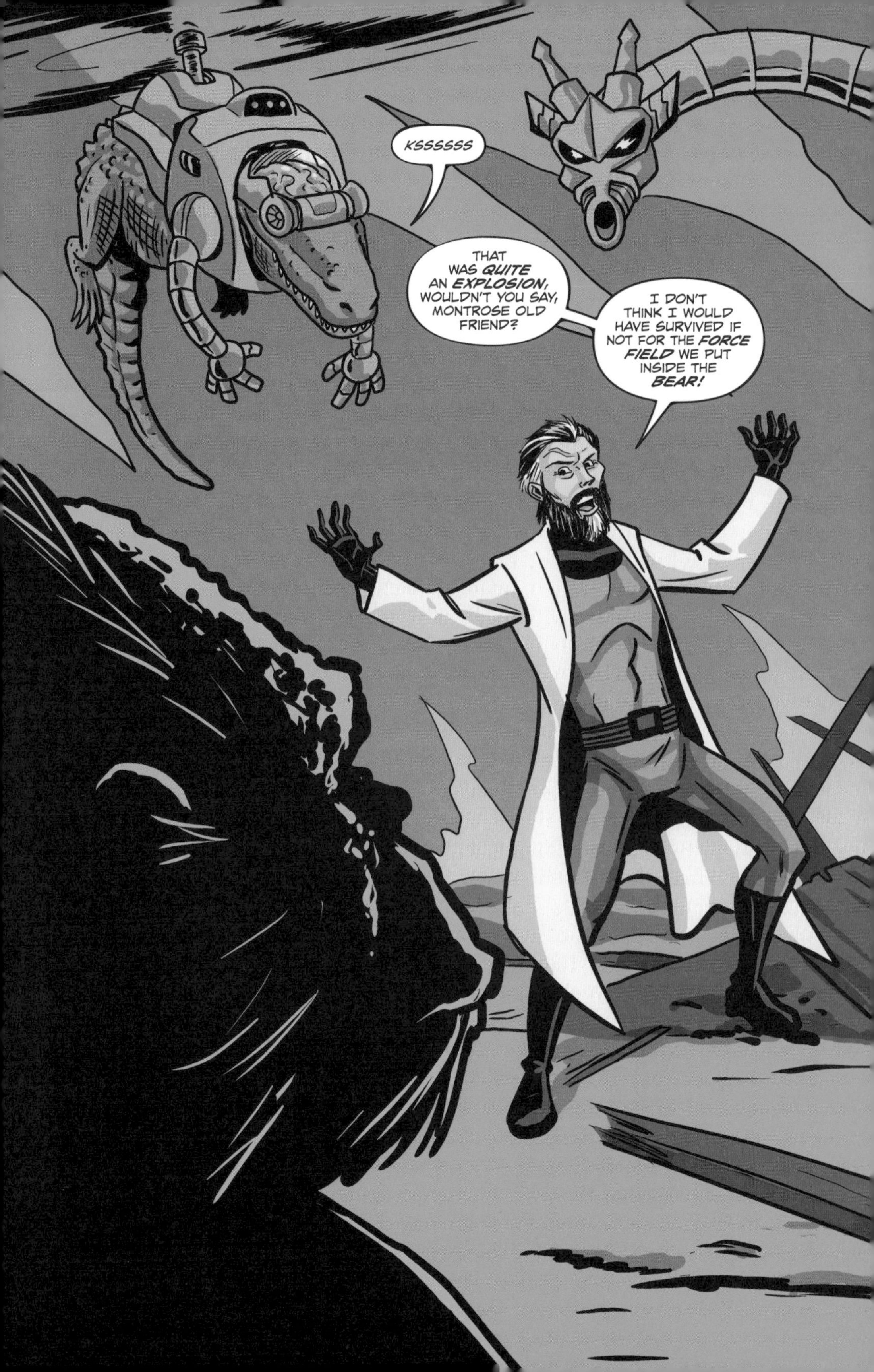
KSSSSSS
THAT WAS QUITE AN EXPLOSION, WOULDN'T YOU SAY, MONTROSE OLD FRIEND?
I DON'T THINK I WOULD HAVE SURVIVED IF NOT FOR THE FORCE FIELD WE PUT INSIDE THE BEAR!

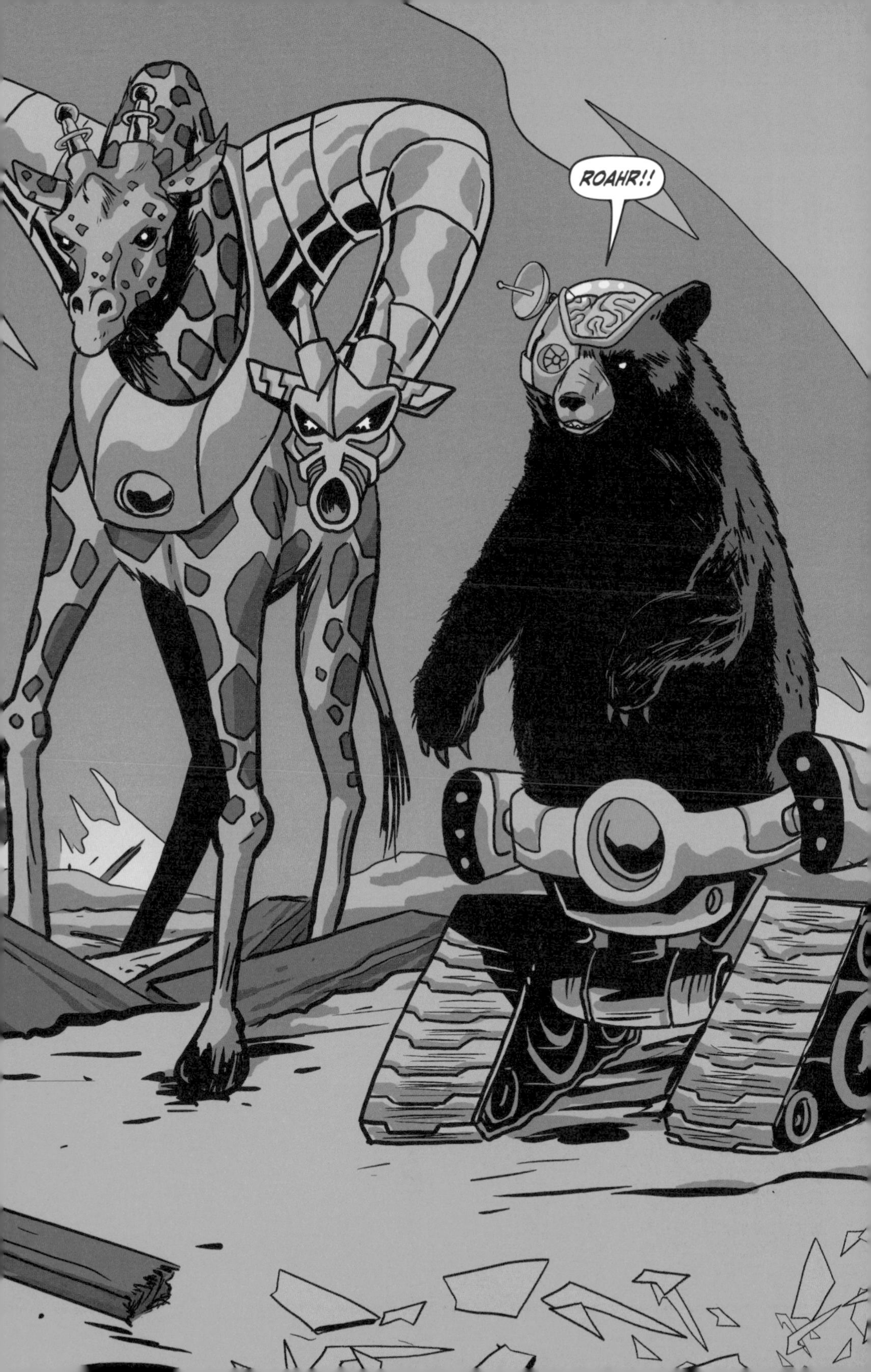
ROAHR!!

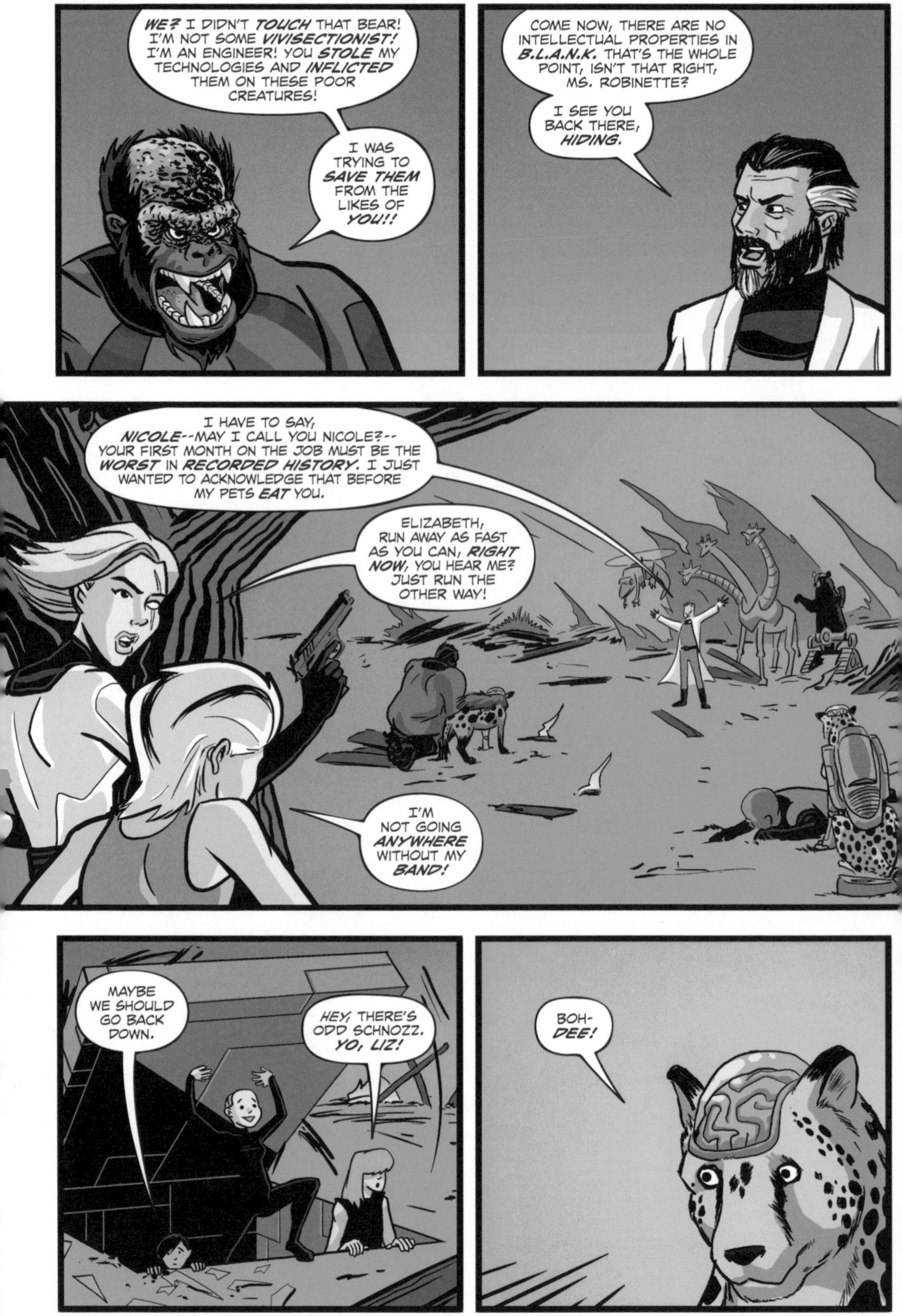
WE? I DIDN'T TOUCH THAT BEAR! I'M NOT SOME VIVISECTIONIST! I'M AN ENGINEER! YOU STOLE MY TECHNOLOGIES AND INFLICTED THEM ON THESE POOR CREATURES!
I WAS TRYING TO SAVE THEM FROM THE LIKES OF YOU!!
COME NOW, THERE ARE NO INTELLECTUAL PROPERTIES IN B.L.A.N.K. THAT'S THE WHOLE POINT, ISN'T THAT RIGHT, MS. ROBINETTE?
I SEE YOU BACK THERE, HIDING.
I HAVE TO SAY, NICOLE--MAY I CALL YOU NICOLE?--YOUR FIRST MONTH ON THE JOB MUST BE THE WORST IN RECORDED HISTORY. I JUST WANTED TO ACKNOWLEDGE THAT BEFORE MY PETS EAT YOU.
ELIZABETH, RUN AWAY AS FAST AS YOU CAN, RIGHT NOW, YOU HEAR ME? JUST RUN THE OTHER WAY!
I'M NOT GOING ANYWHERE WITHOUT MY BAND!
MAYBE WE SHOULD GO BACK DOWN.
HEY, THERE'S ODD SCHNOZZ. YO, LIZ!
BOH-DEE!

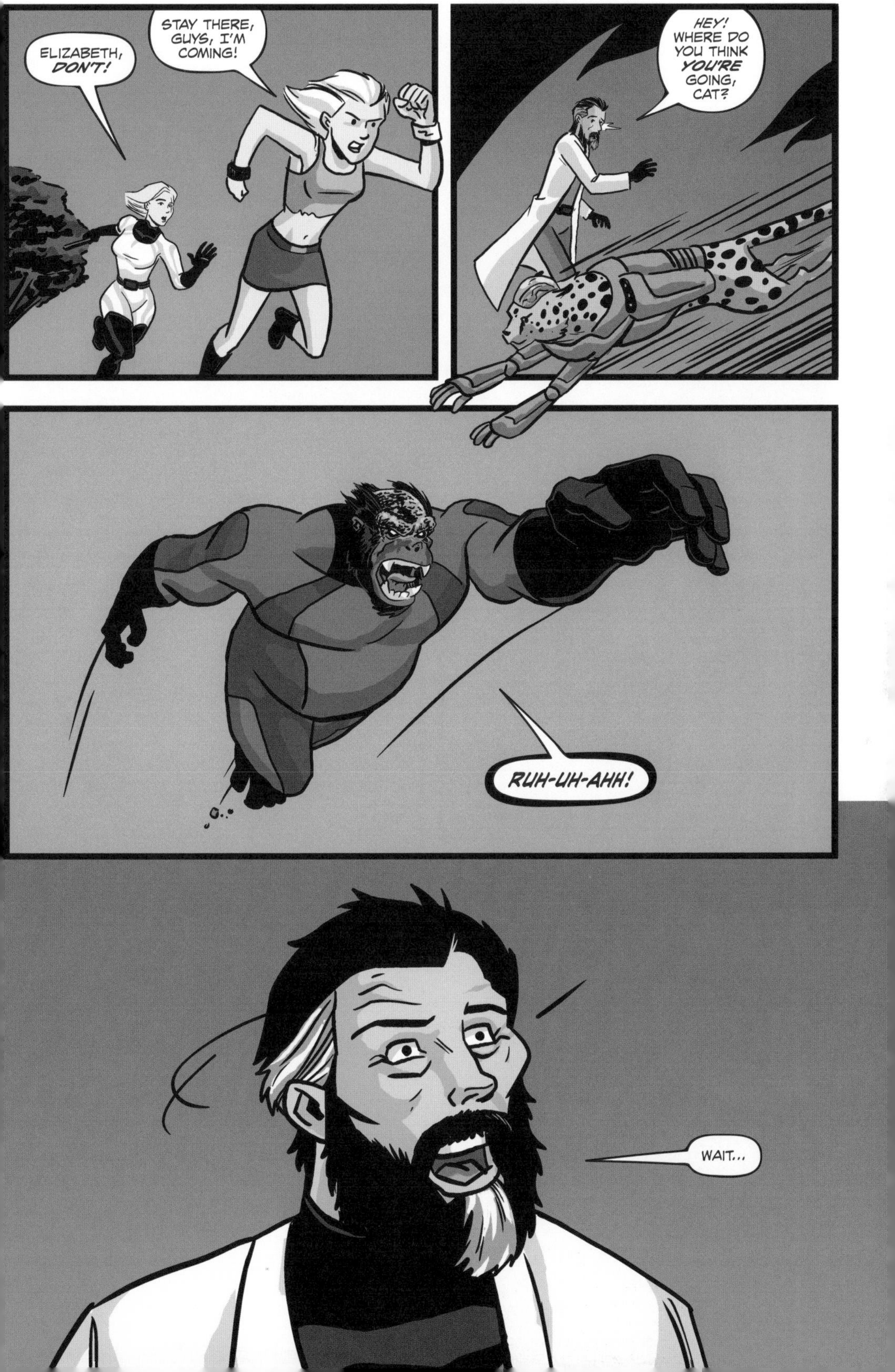
ELIZABETH, DON'T!
STAY THERE, GUYS, I'M COMING!
HEY! WHERE DO YOU THINK YOU'RE GOING, CAT?
RUH-UH-AHH!
WAIT...

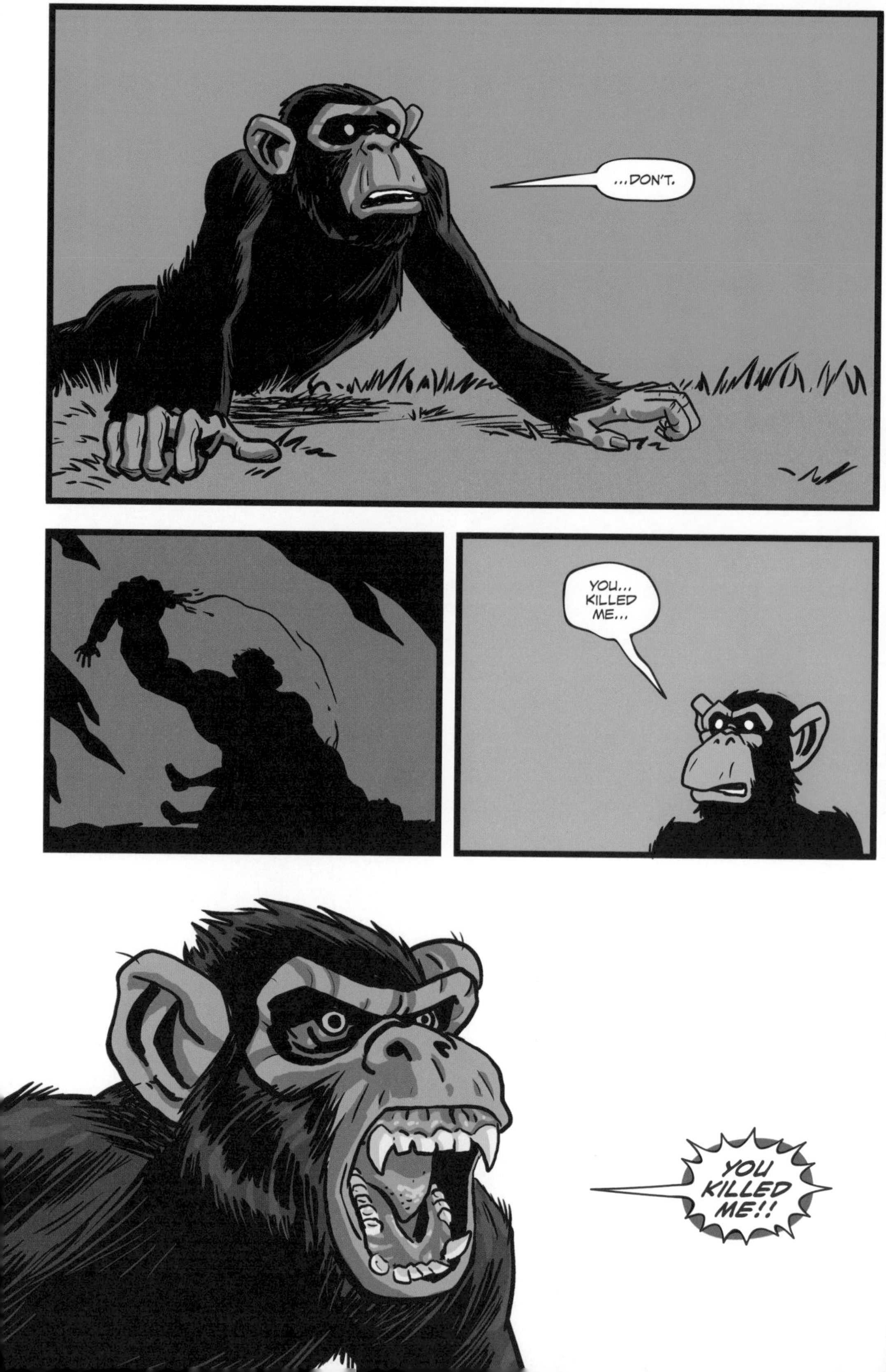
...DON'T.
YOU... KILLED ME...
YOU KILLED ME!!

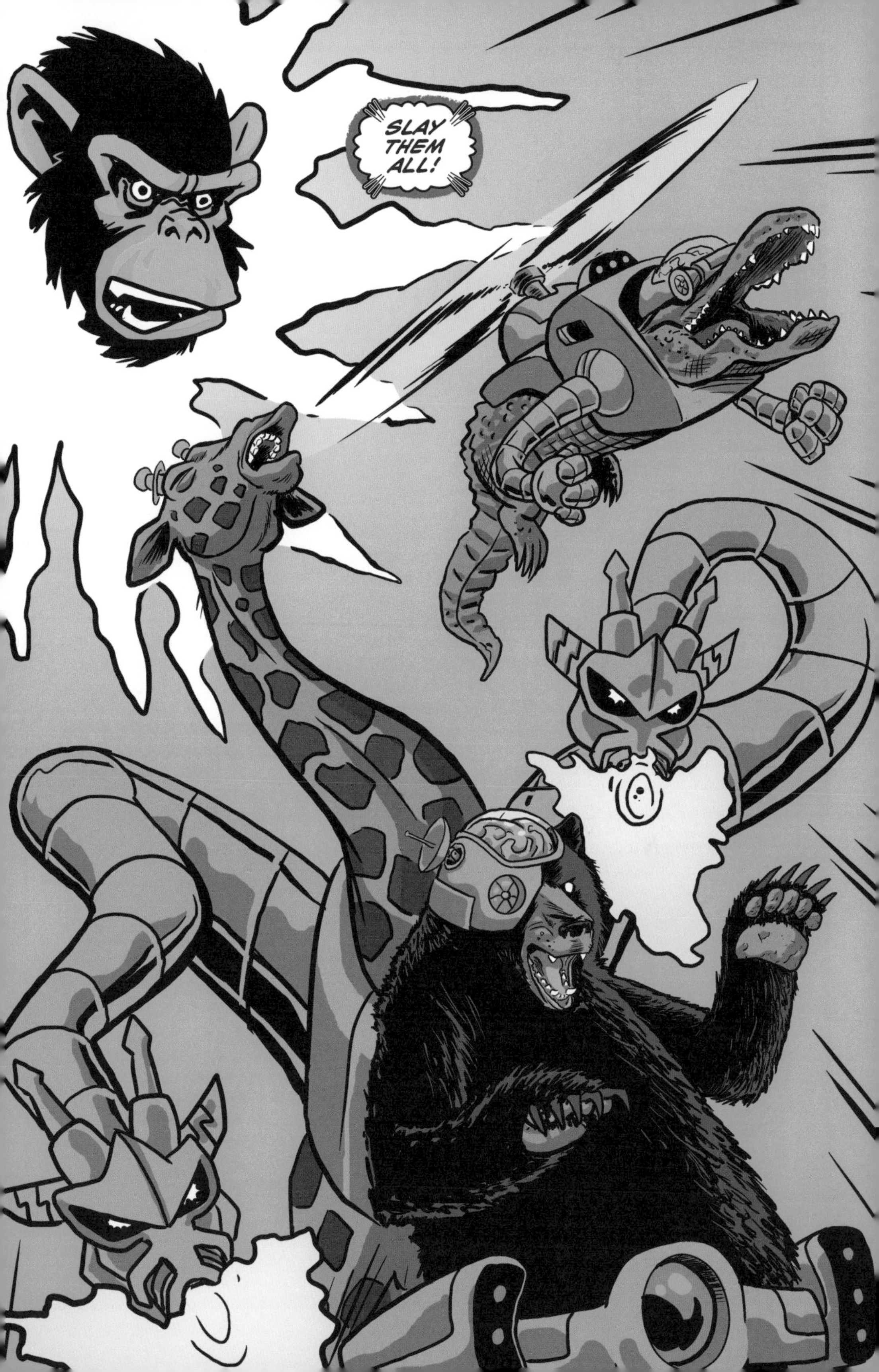
SLAY THEM ALL!

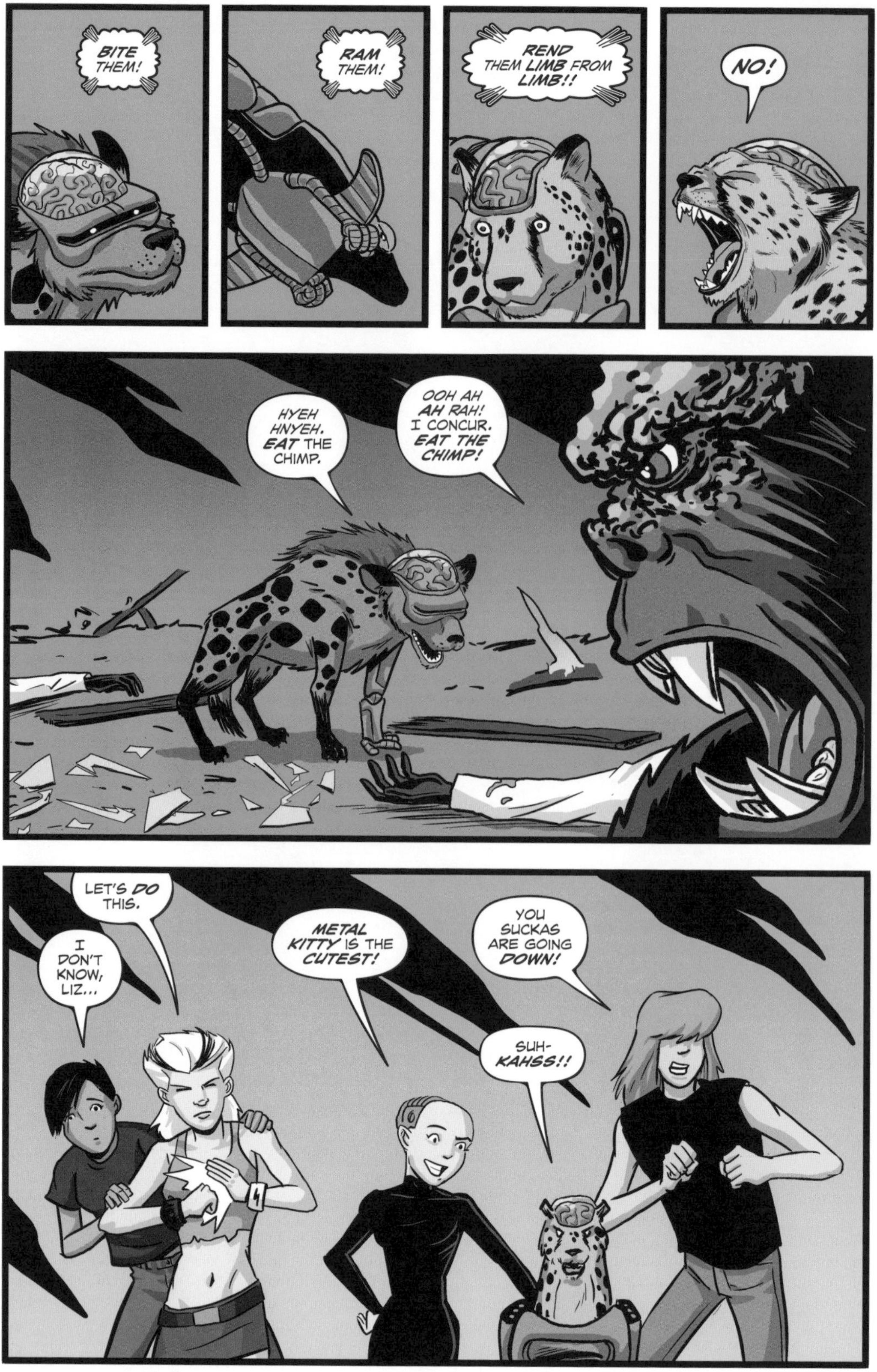
BITE THEM!
RAM THEM!
REND THEM LIMB FROM LIMB!!
NO!
HYEH HNYEH. EAT THE CHIMP.
OOH AH AH RAH! I CONCUR. EAT THE CHIMP!
LET'S DO THIS.
I DON'T KNOW, LIZ...
METAL KITTY IS THE CUTEST!
YOU SUCKAS ARE GOING DOWN!
SUH-KAHSS!!

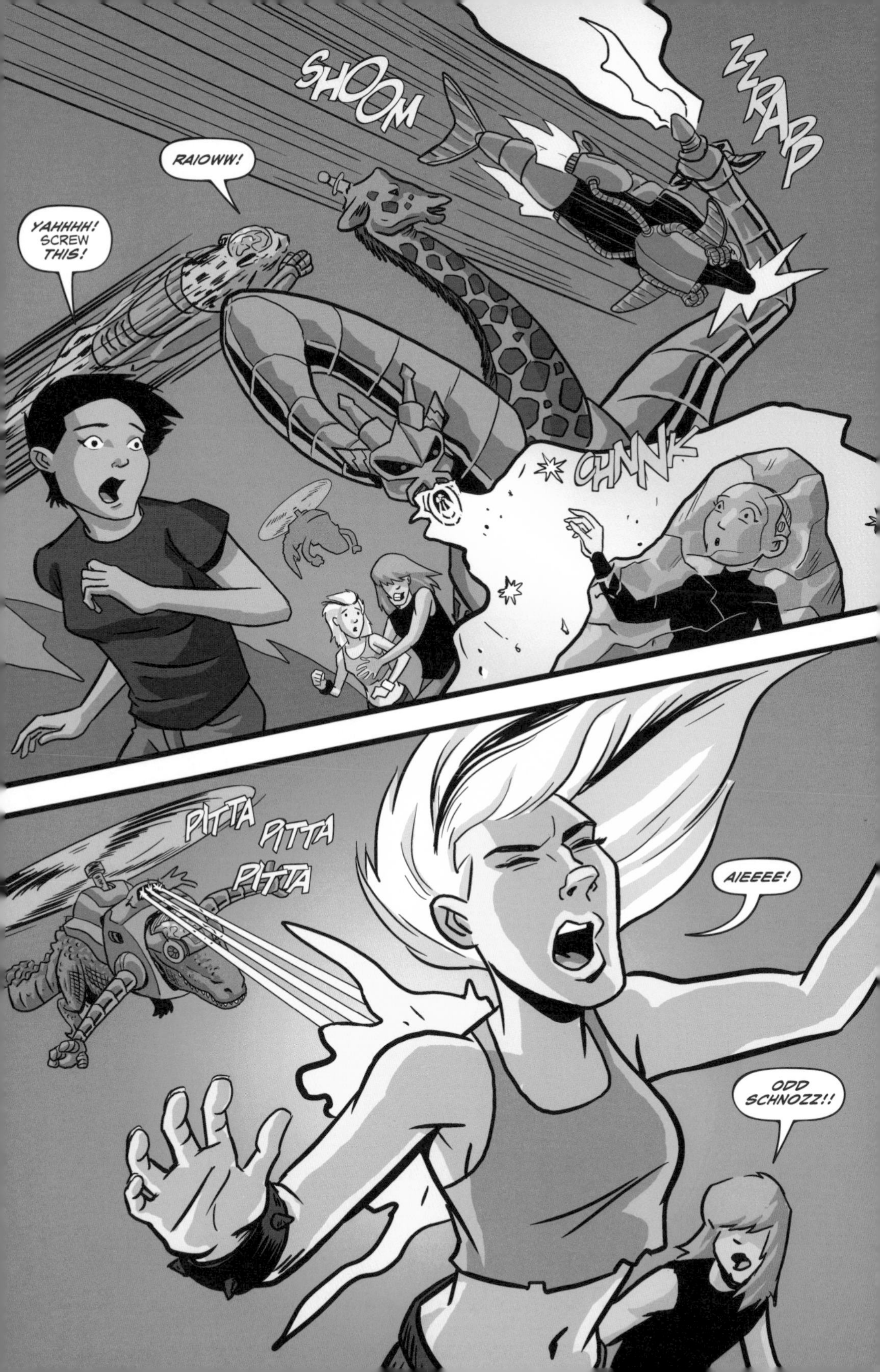
SHOOM
ZZZRAPP
RAIOWW!
YAHHHH! SCREW THIS!
CHNNK
PITTA
PITTA
PITTA
AIEEEE!
ODD SCHNOZZ!!

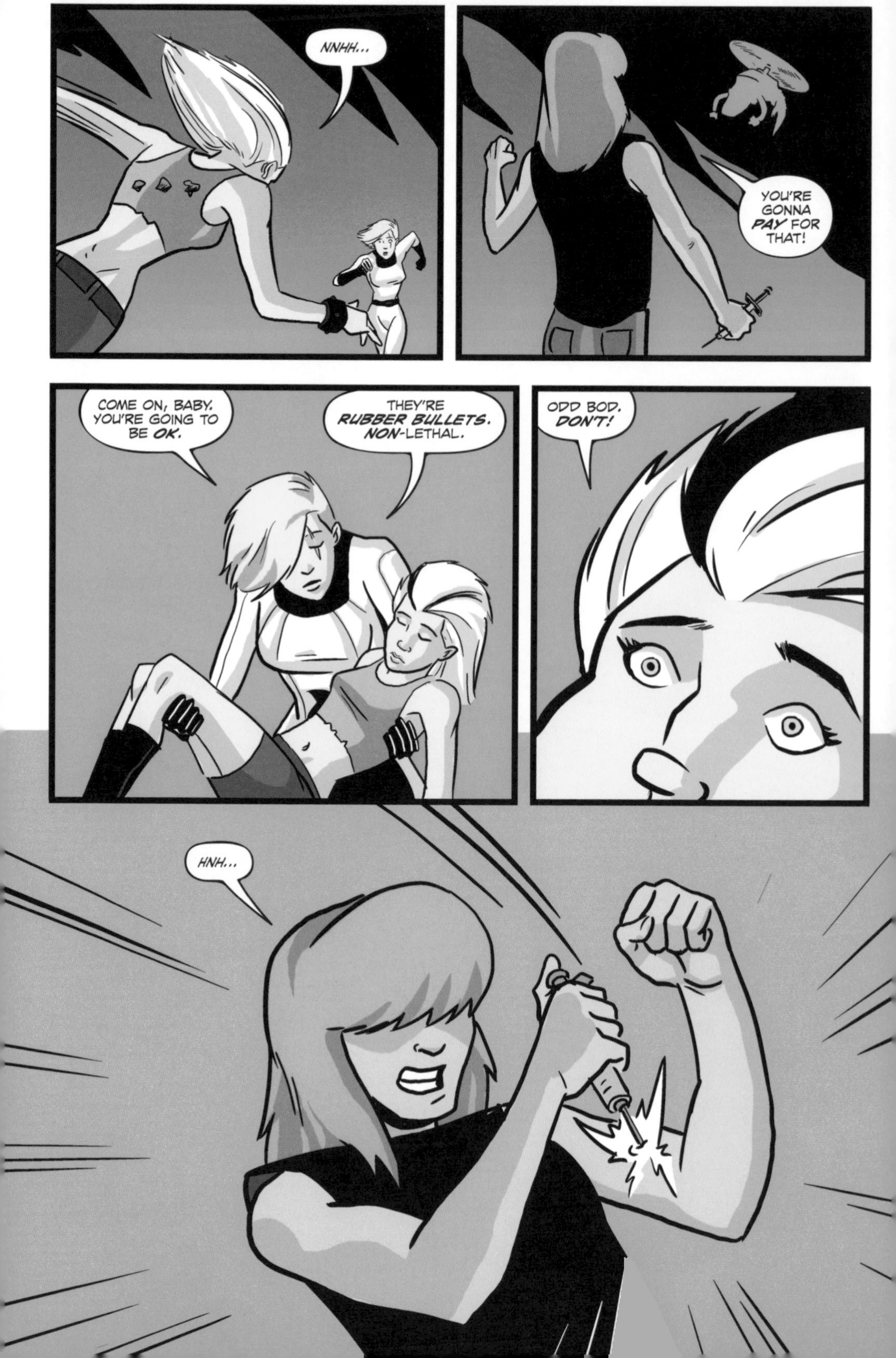
NNHH...
YOU'RE GONNA PAY FOR THAT!
COME ON, BABY. YOU'RE GOING TO BE OK.
THEY'RE RUBBER BULLETS. NON-LETHAL.
ODD BOD. DON'T!
HNH...

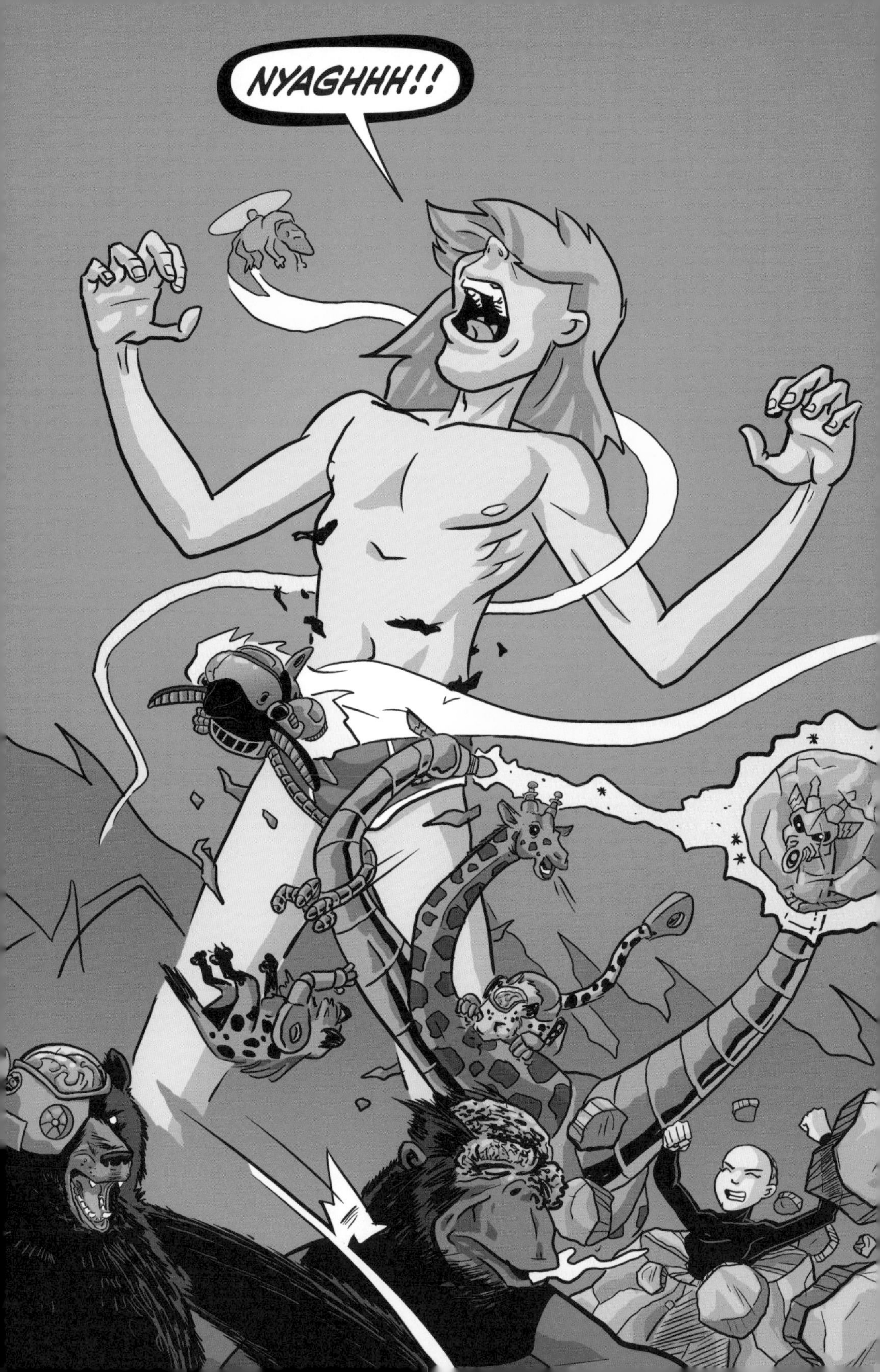
NYAGHHH!!

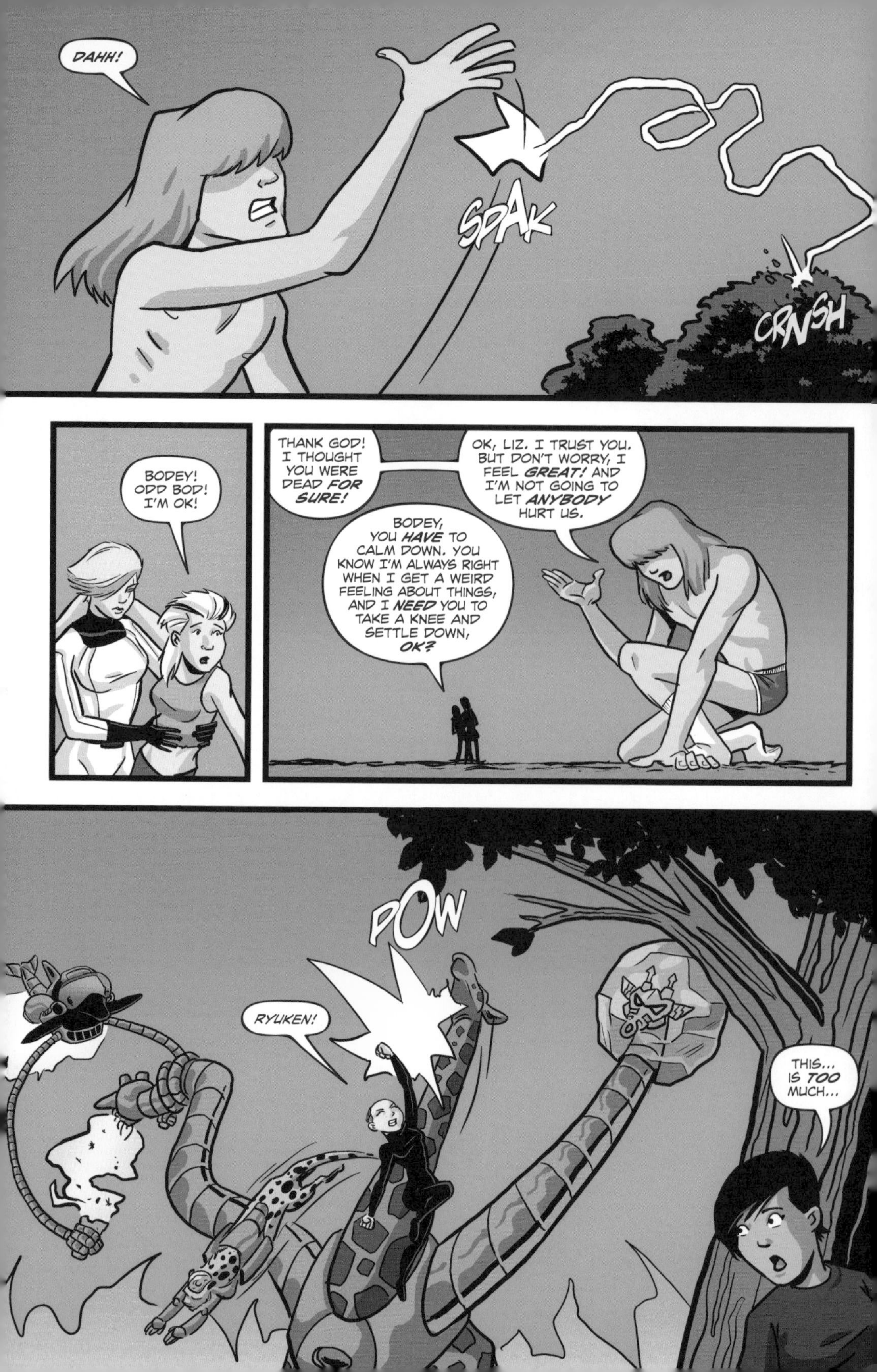
DAHH!
SPAK
CRNSH
BODEY! ODD BOD! I'M OK!
THANK GOD! I THOUGHT YOU WERE DEAD *FOR SURE!*
OK, LIZ. I TRUST YOU. BUT DON'T WORRY, I FEEL *GREAT!* AND I'M NOT GOING TO LET *ANYBODY* HURT US.
BODEY, YOU *HAVE* TO CALM DOWN. YOU KNOW I'M ALWAYS RIGHT WHEN I GET A WEIRD FEELING ABOUT THINGS, AND I *NEED* YOU TO TAKE A KNEE AND SETTLE DOWN, *OK?*
POW
RYUKEN!
THIS... IS *TOO* MUCH...

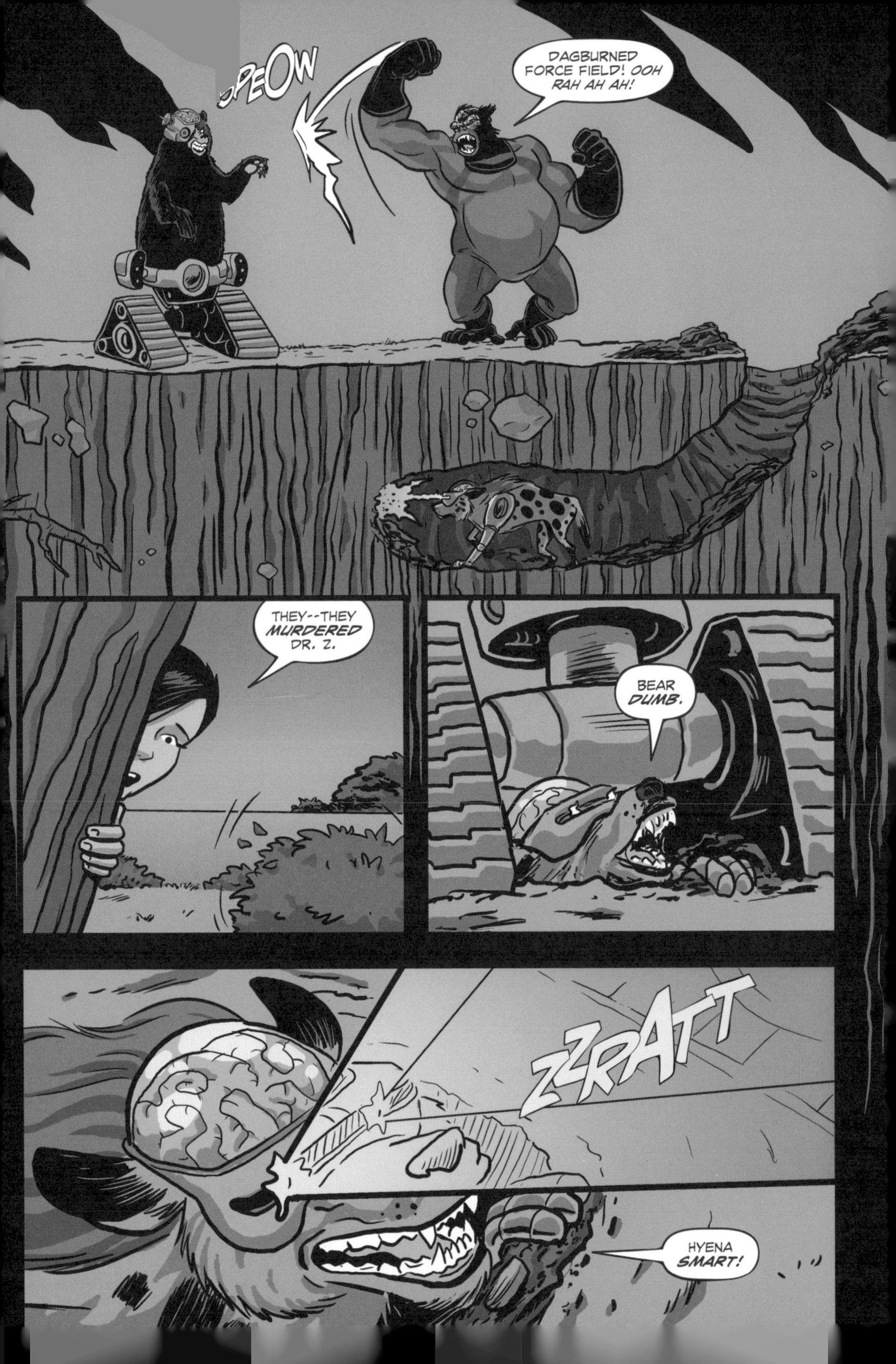

SPEOW
DAGBURNED FORCE FIELD! OOH RAH AH AH!
THEY--THEY MURDERED DR. Z.
BEAR DUMB.
ZZRATT
HYENA SMART!

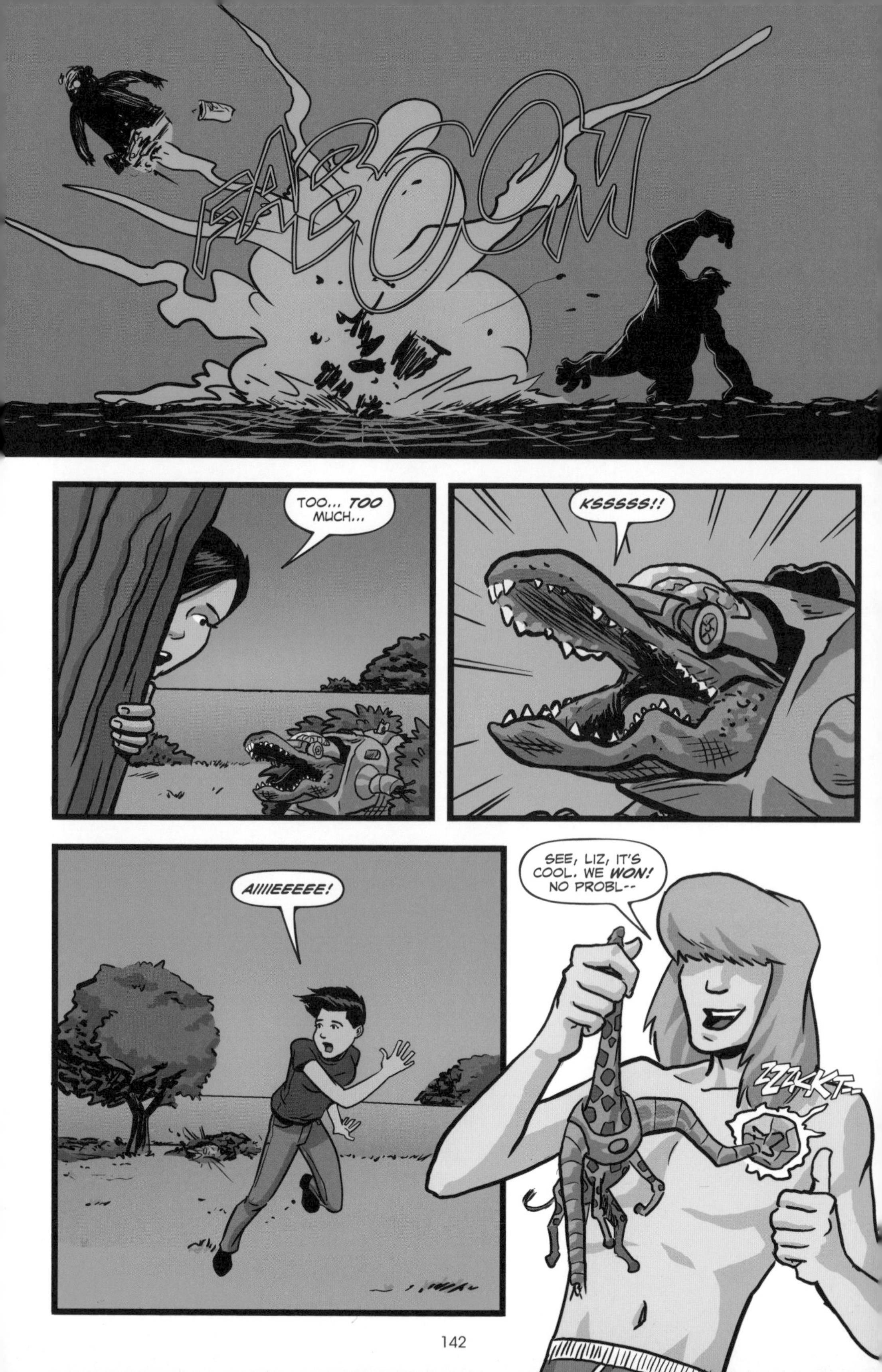
FABOOM
TOO... TOO MUCH...
KSSSSS!!
AIIIIEEEEE!
SEE, LIZ, IT'S COOL. WE WON! NO PROBL--
ZZZKKT--

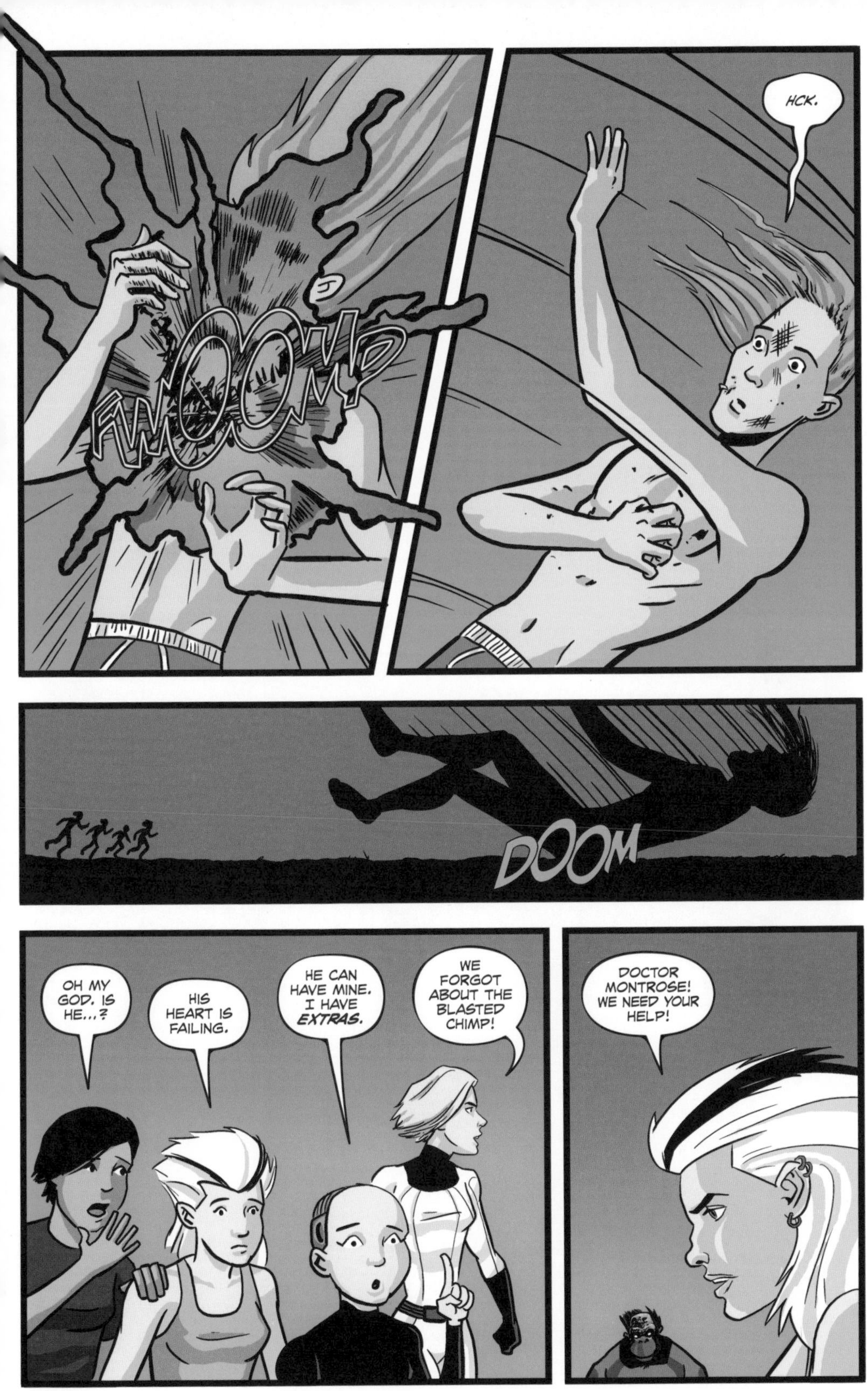
FWOOOMP
HCK.
DOOM
OH MY GOD. IS HE...?
HIS HEART IS FAILING.
HE CAN HAVE MINE. I HAVE *EXTRAS.*
WE FORGOT ABOUT THE BLASTED CHIMP!
DOCTOR MONTROSE! WE NEED YOUR HELP!

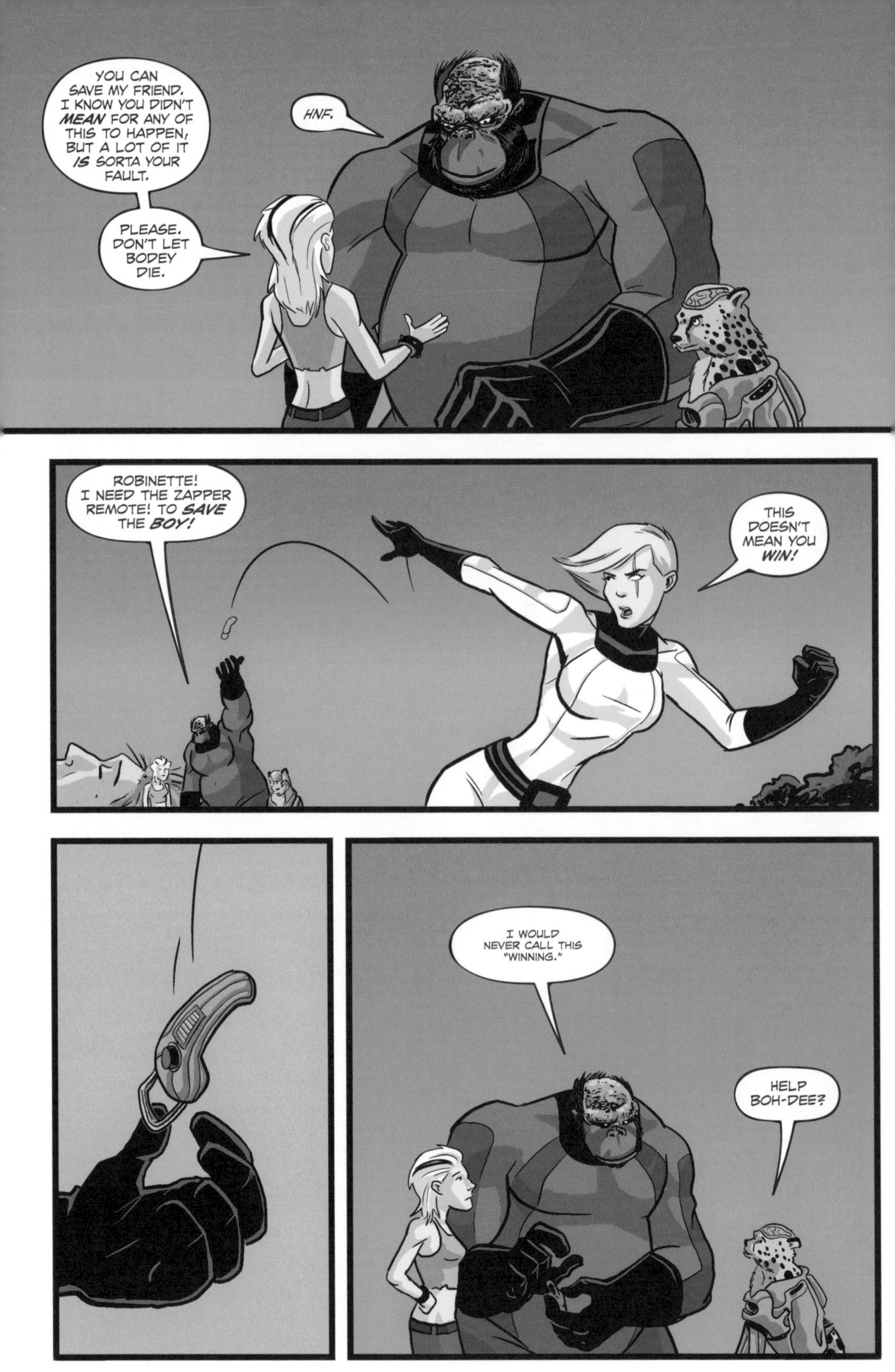
YOU CAN SAVE MY FRIEND. I KNOW YOU DIDN'T MEAN FOR ANY OF THIS TO HAPPEN, BUT A LOT OF IT IS SORTA YOUR FAULT.
HNF.
PLEASE. DON'T LET BODEY DIE.
ROBINETTE! I NEED THE ZAPPER REMOTE! TO SAVE THE BOY!
THIS DOESN'T MEAN YOU WIN!
I WOULD NEVER CALL THIS "WINNING."
HELP BOH-DEE?

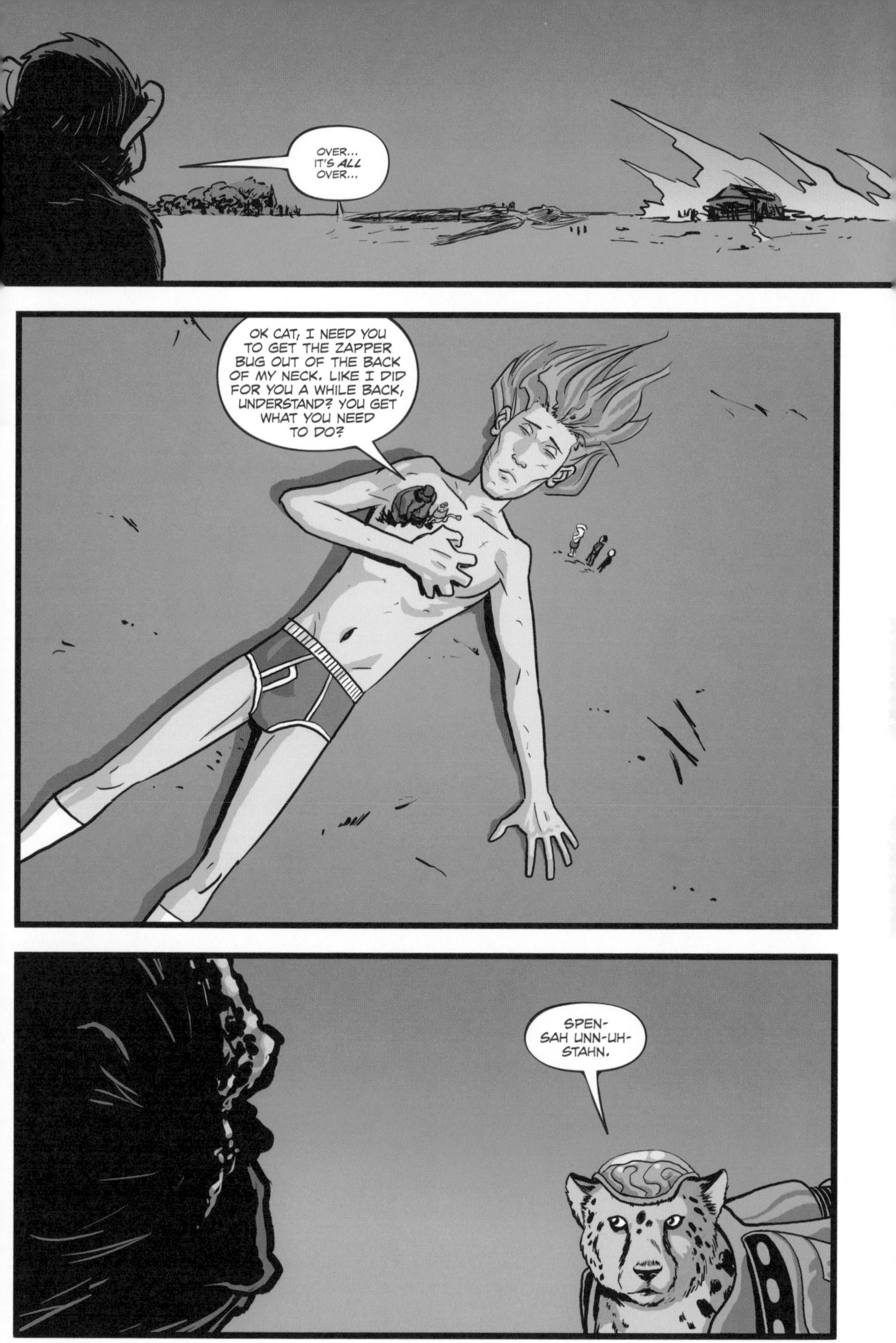
OVER... IT'S *ALL* OVER...
OK CAT, I NEED YOU TO GET THE ZAPPER BUG OUT OF THE BACK OF MY NECK. LIKE I DID FOR YOU A WHILE BACK, UNDERSTAND? YOU GET WHAT YOU NEED TO DO?
SPEN-SAH UNN-UH-STAHN.

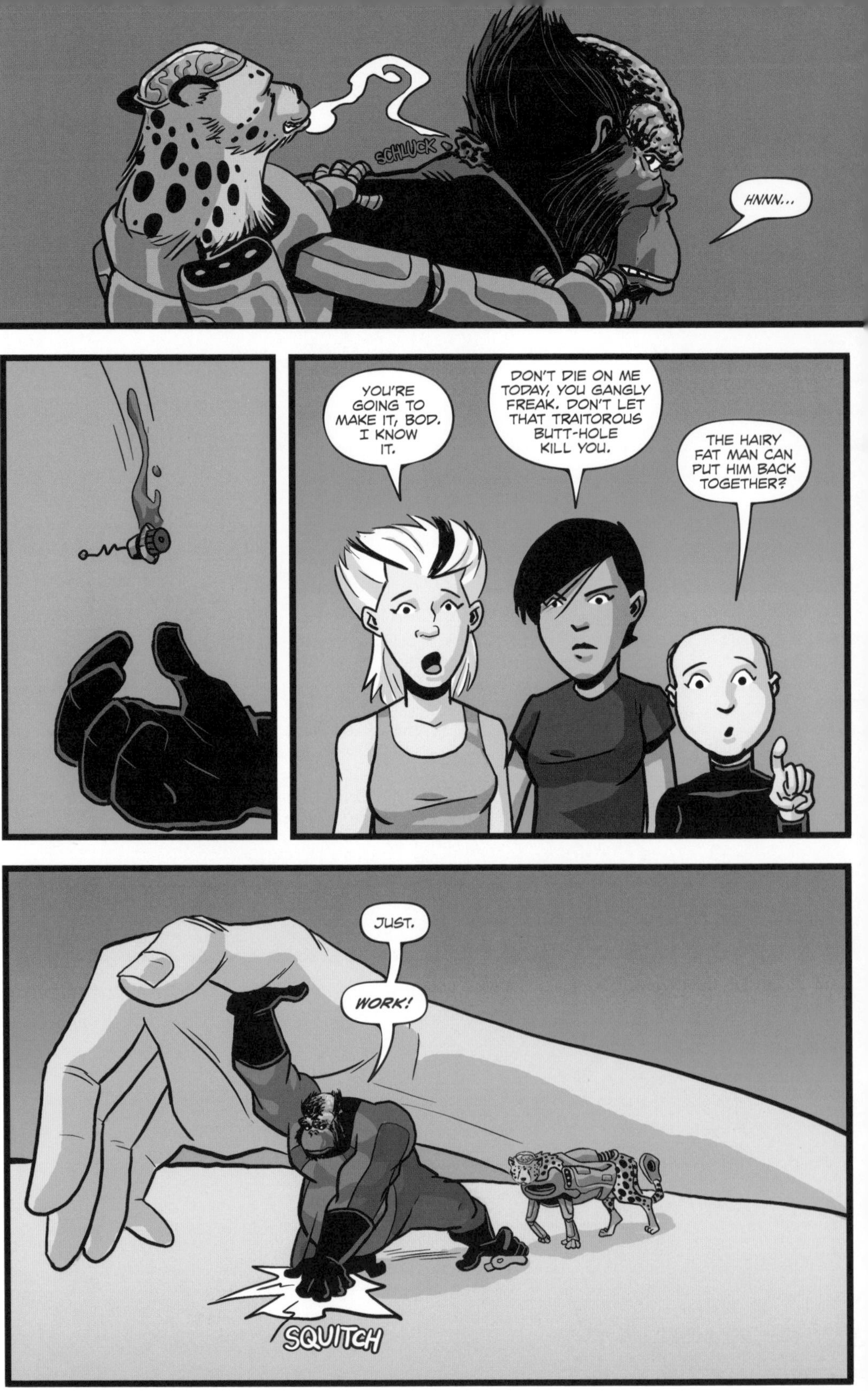
SCHLUCK
HNNN...
YOU'RE GOING TO MAKE IT, BOD. I KNOW IT.
DON'T DIE ON ME TODAY, YOU GANGLY FREAK. DON'T LET THAT TRAITOROUS BUTT-HOLE KILL YOU.
THE HAIRY FAT MAN CAN PUT HIM BACK TOGETHER?
JUST.
WORK!
SQUITCH

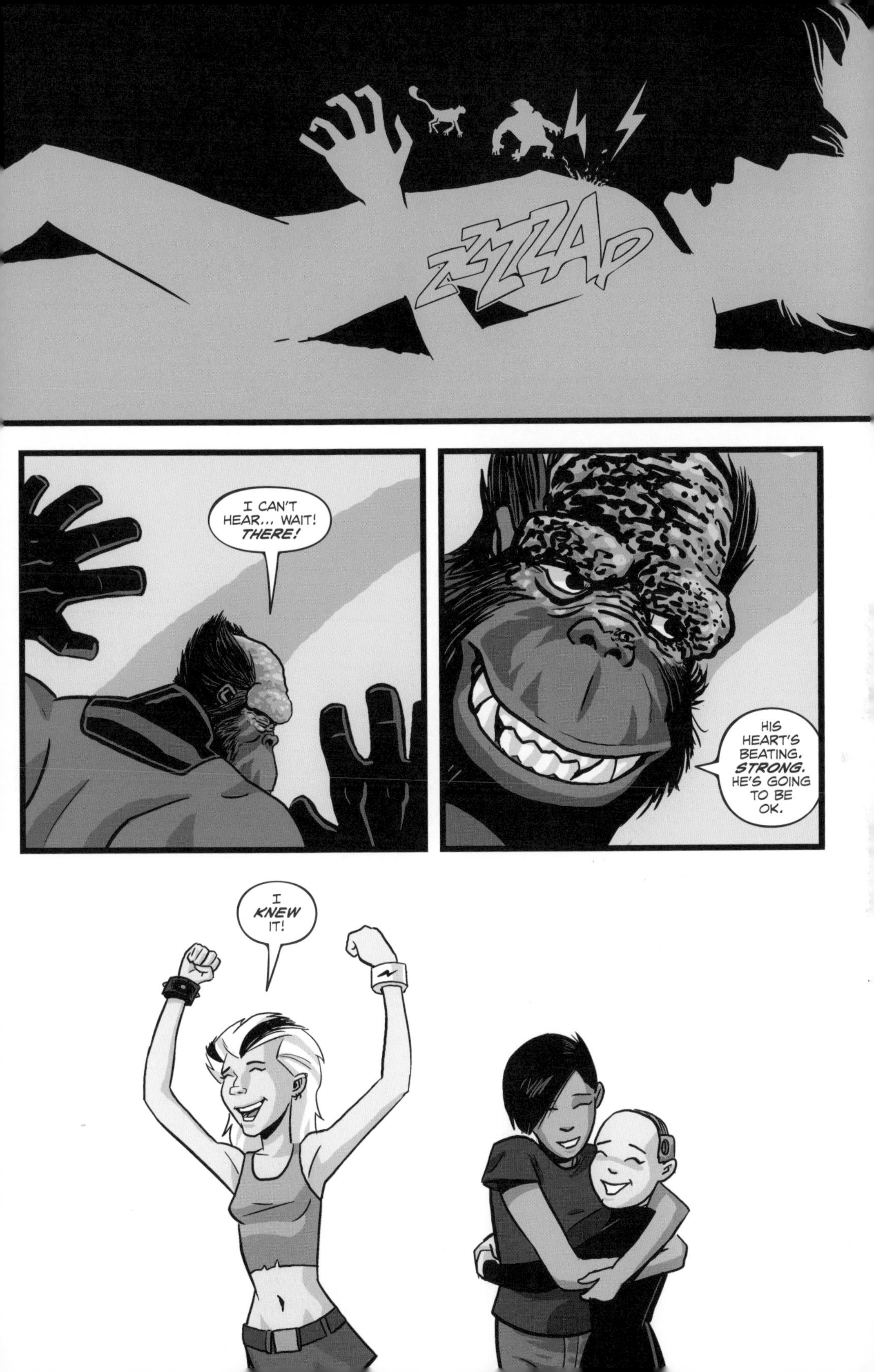
ZZZZAP
I CAN'T HEAR... WAIT! *THERE!*
HIS HEART'S BEATING. *STRONG.* HE'S GOING TO BE OK.
I *KNEW* IT!

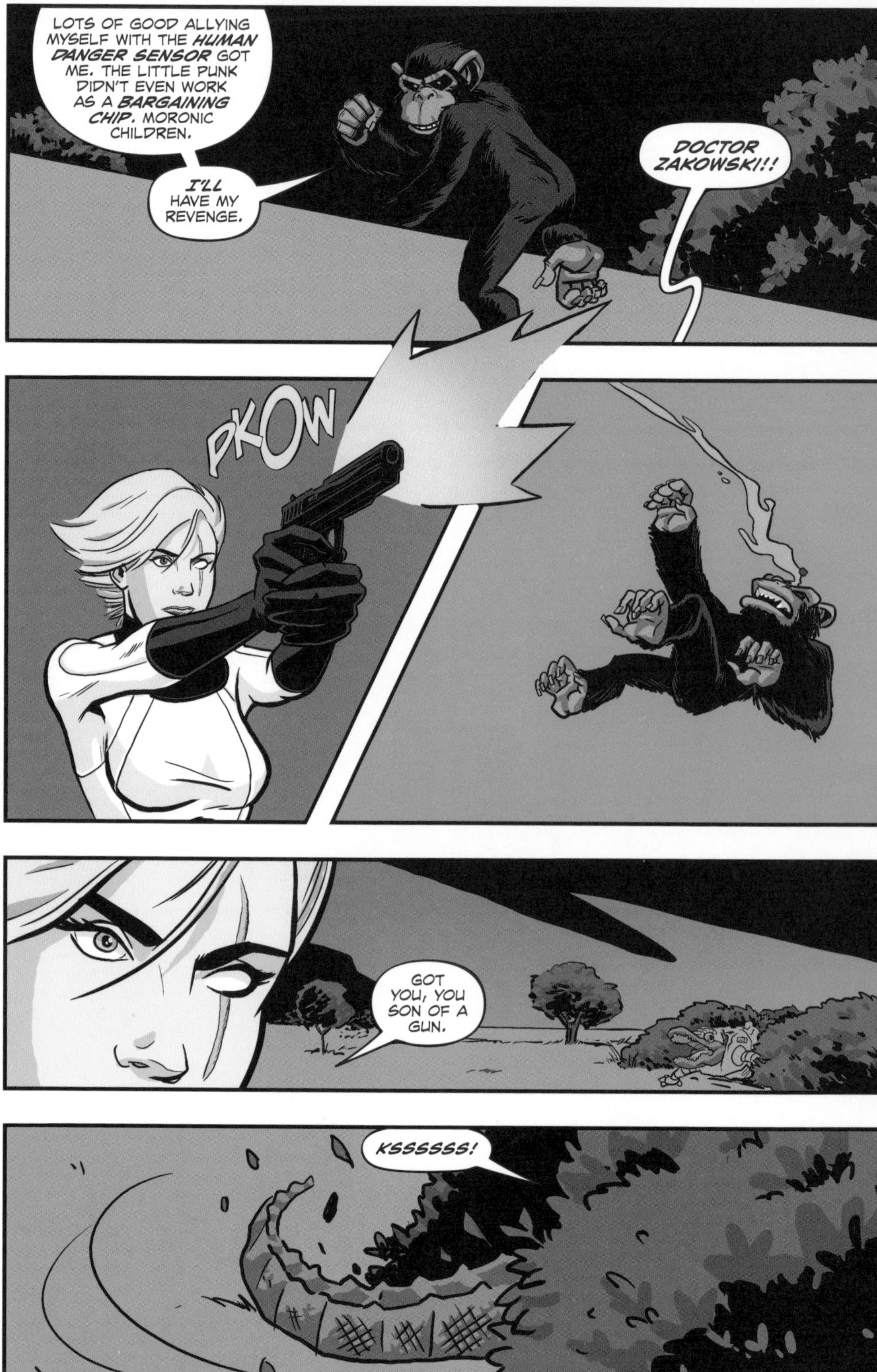
LOTS OF GOOD ALLYING MYSELF WITH THE HUMAN DANGER SENSOR GOT ME. THE LITTLE PUNK DIDN'T EVEN WORK AS A BARGAINING CHIP. MORONIC CHILDREN.
I'LL HAVE MY REVENGE.
DOCTOR ZAKOWSKI!!
PKOW
GOT YOU, YOU SON OF A GUN.
KSSSSSS!

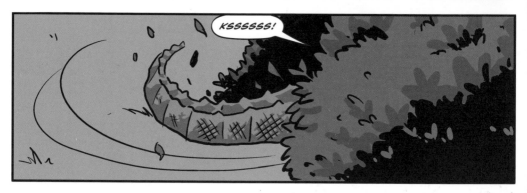

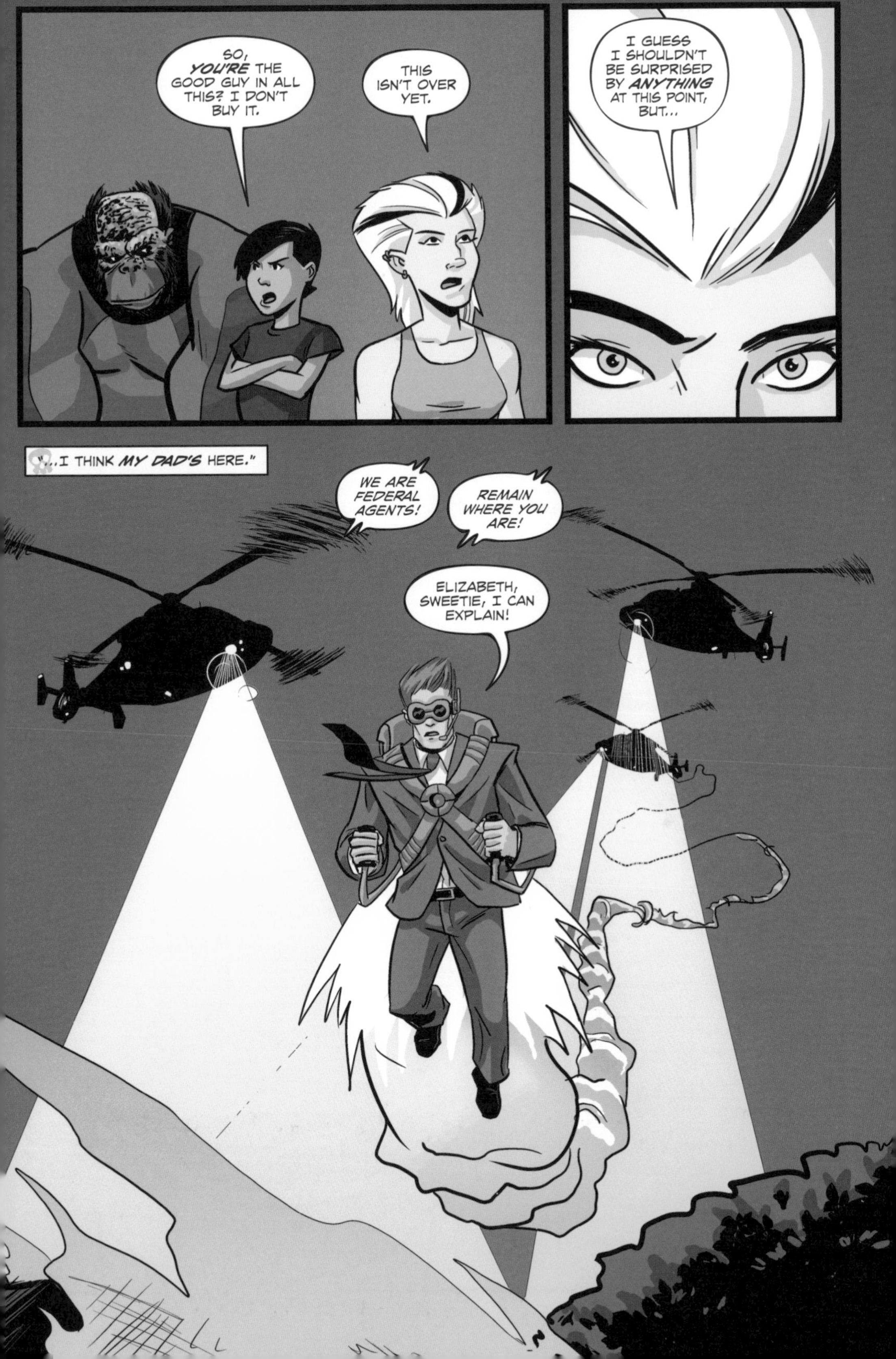
SO, YOU'RE THE GOOD GUY IN ALL THIS? I DON'T BUY IT.
THIS ISN'T OVER YET.
I GUESS I SHOULDN'T BE SURPRISED BY ANYTHING AT THIS POINT, BUT...
"...I THINK MY DAD'S HERE."
WE ARE FEDERAL AGENTS!
REMAIN WHERE YOU ARE!
ELIZABETH, SWEETIE, I CAN EXPLAIN!

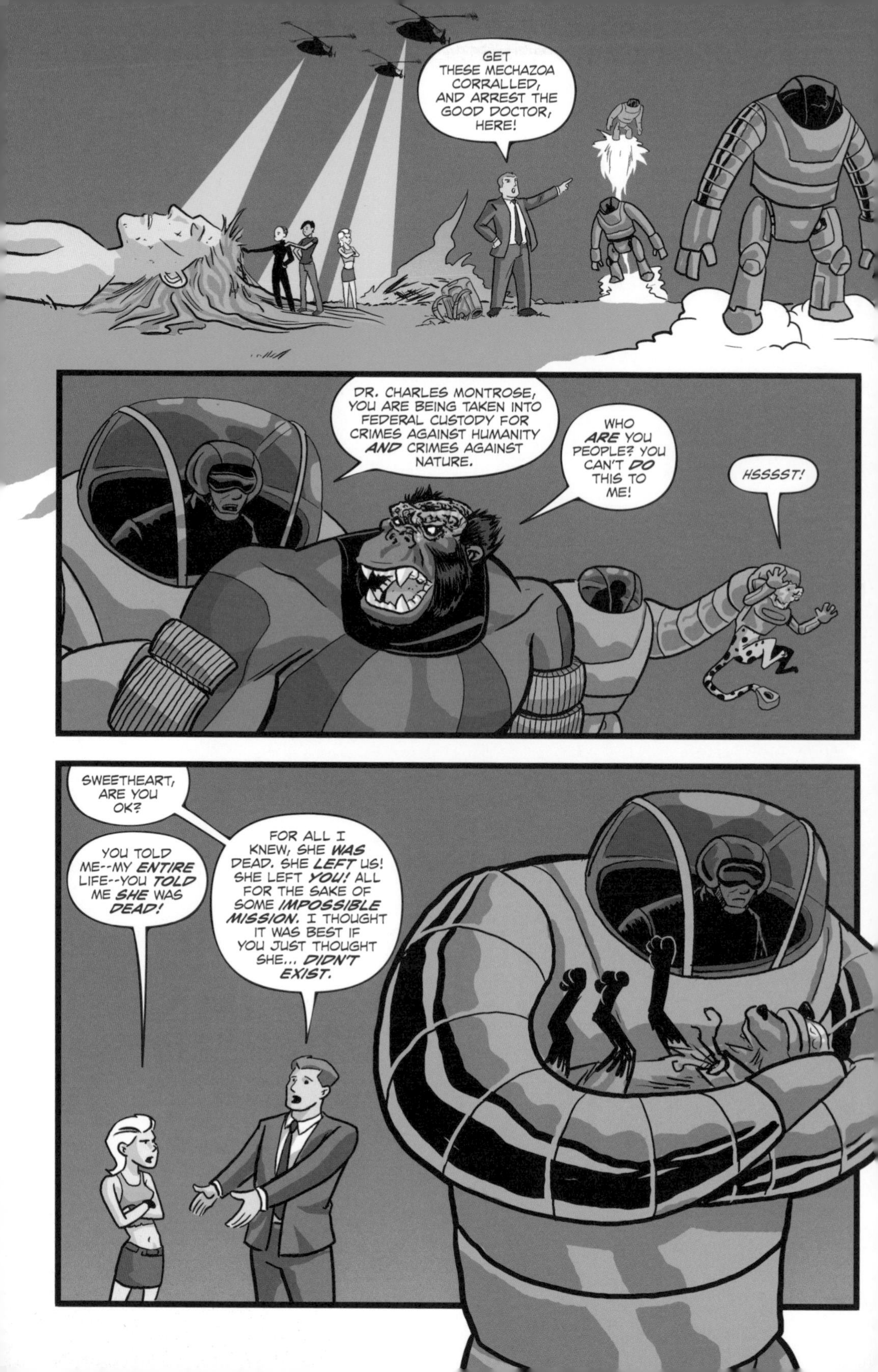
GET THESE MECHAZOA CORRALLED, AND ARREST THE GOOD DOCTOR, HERE!
DR. CHARLES MONTROSE, YOU ARE BEING TAKEN INTO FEDERAL CUSTODY FOR CRIMES AGAINST HUMANITY AND CRIMES AGAINST NATURE.
WHO ARE YOU PEOPLE? YOU CAN'T DO THIS TO ME!
HSSSST!
SWEETHEART, ARE YOU OK?
YOU TOLD ME--MY ENTIRE LIFE--YOU TOLD ME SHE WAS DEAD!
FOR ALL I KNEW, SHE WAS DEAD. SHE LEFT US! SHE LEFT YOU! ALL FOR THE SAKE OF SOME IMPOSSIBLE MISSION. I THOUGHT IT WAS BEST IF YOU JUST THOUGHT SHE... DIDN'T EXIST.

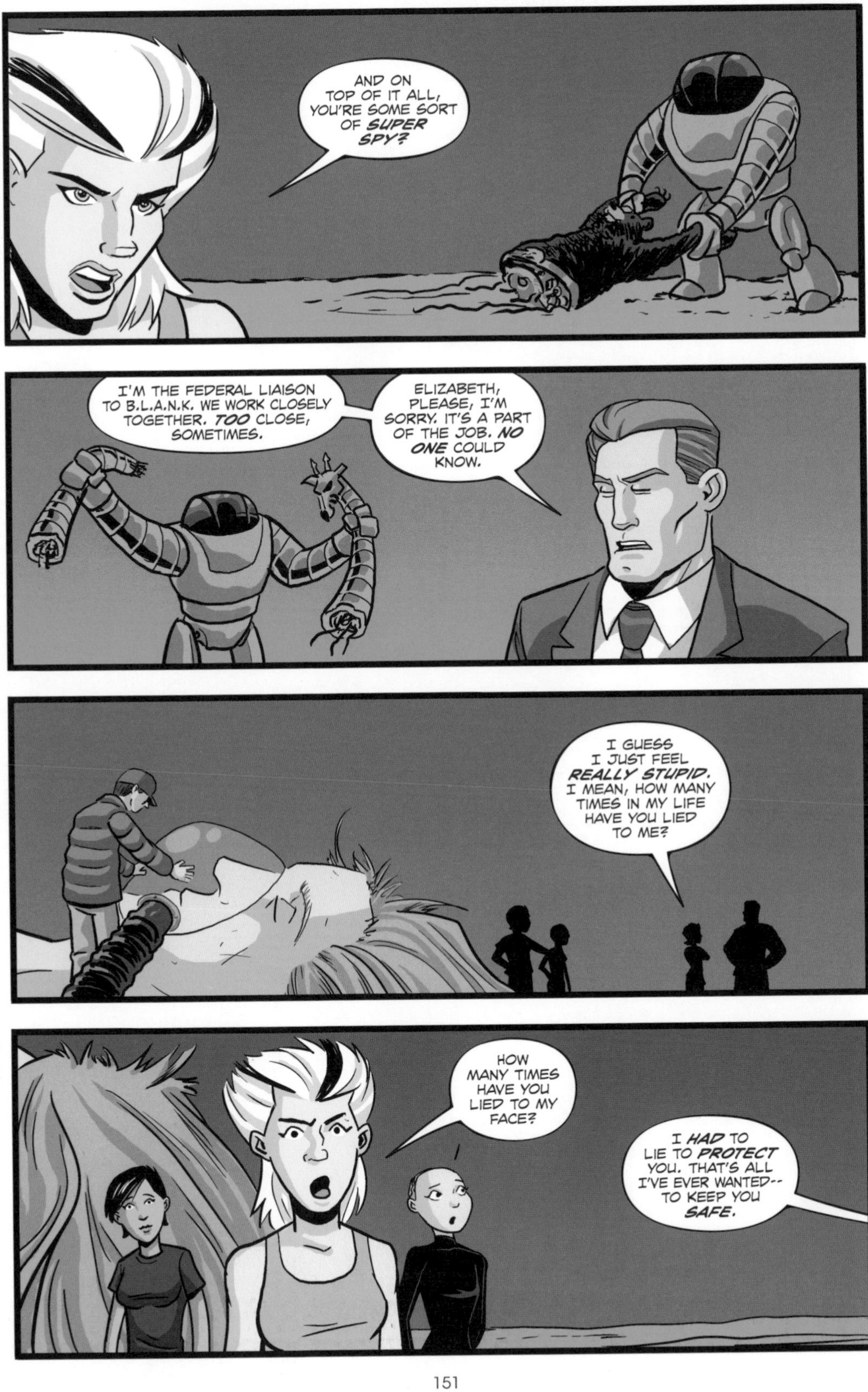
AND ON TOP OF IT ALL, YOU'RE SOME SORT OF *SUPER SPY?*
I'M THE FEDERAL LIAISON TO B.L.A.N.K. WE WORK CLOSELY TOGETHER. *TOO* CLOSE, SOMETIMES.
ELIZABETH, PLEASE, I'M SORRY. IT'S A PART OF THE JOB. *NO ONE* COULD KNOW.
I GUESS I JUST FEEL *REALLY STUPID.* I MEAN, HOW MANY TIMES IN MY LIFE HAVE YOU LIED TO ME?
HOW MANY TIMES HAVE YOU LIED TO MY FACE?
I *HAD* TO LIE TO *PROTECT* YOU. THAT'S ALL I'VE EVER WANTED-- TO KEEP YOU *SAFE.*

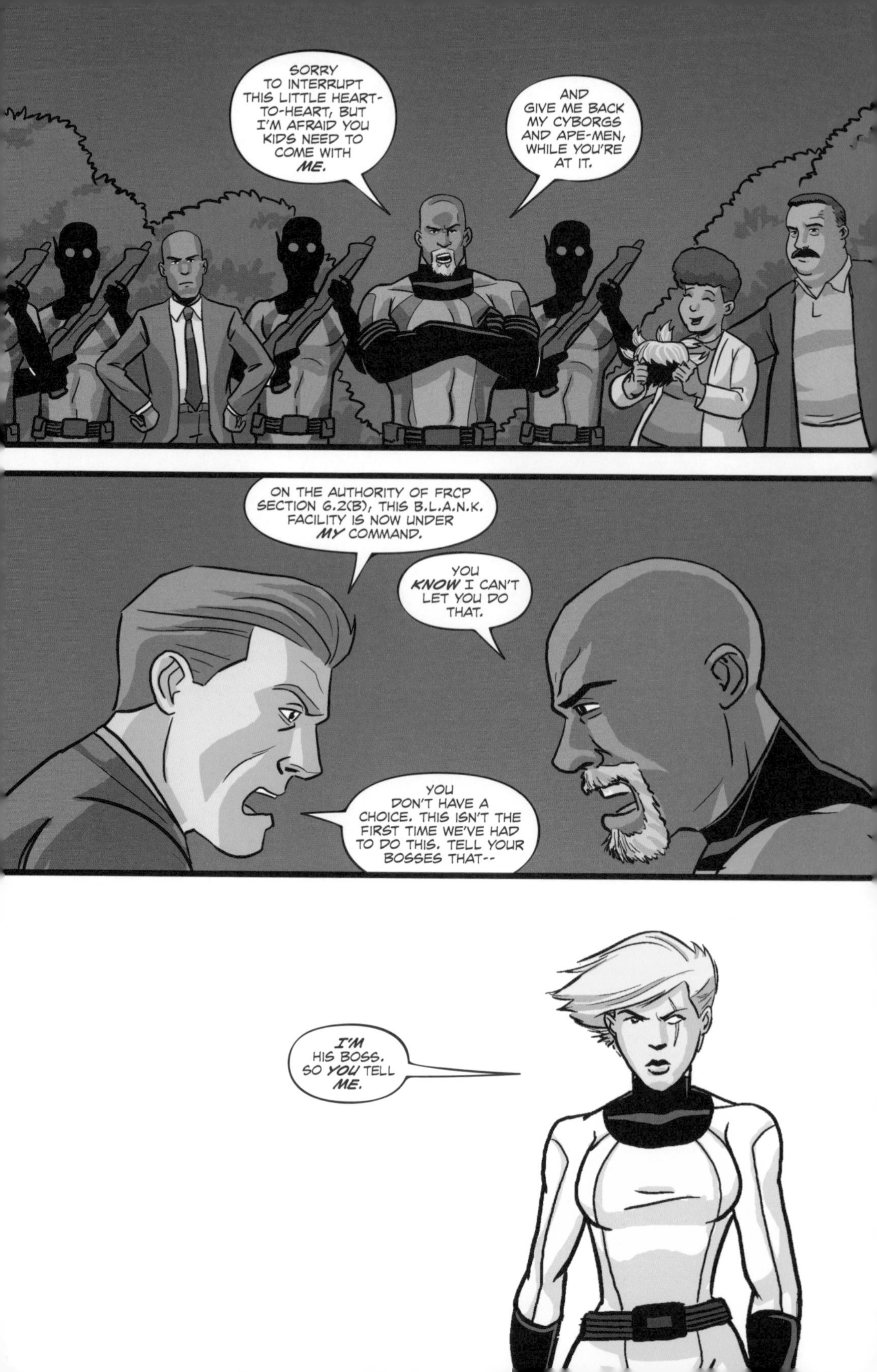
SORRY TO INTERRUPT THIS LITTLE HEART-TO-HEART, BUT I'M AFRAID YOU KIDS NEED TO COME WITH ME.
AND GIVE ME BACK MY CYBORGS AND APE-MEN, WHILE YOU'RE AT IT.
ON THE AUTHORITY OF FRCP SECTION 6.2(B), THIS B.L.A.N.K. FACILITY IS NOW UNDER MY COMMAND.
YOU KNOW I CAN'T LET YOU DO THAT.
YOU DON'T HAVE A CHOICE. THIS ISN'T THE FIRST TIME WE'VE HAD TO DO THIS. TELL YOUR BOSSES THAT--
I'M HIS BOSS. SO YOU TELL ME.

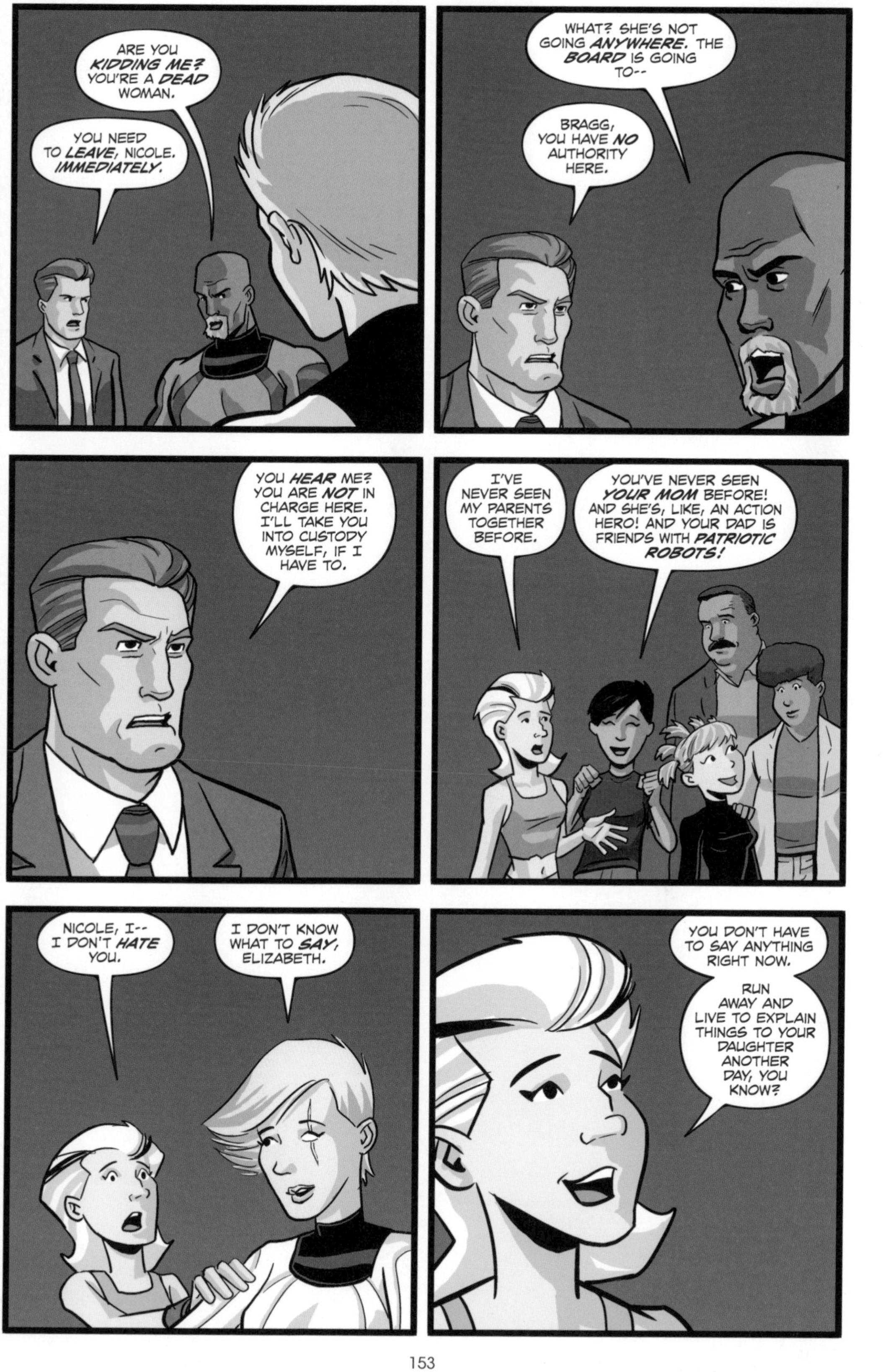
YOU NEED TO LEAVE, NICOLE. IMMEDIATELY.
ARE YOU KIDDING ME? YOU'RE A DEAD WOMAN.
WHAT? SHE'S NOT GOING ANYWHERE. THE BOARD IS GOING TO--
BRAGG, YOU HAVE NO AUTHORITY HERE.
YOU HEAR ME? YOU ARE NOT IN CHARGE HERE. I'LL TAKE YOU INTO CUSTODY MYSELF, IF I HAVE TO.
I'VE NEVER SEEN MY PARENTS TOGETHER BEFORE.
YOU'VE NEVER SEEN YOUR MOM BEFORE! AND SHE'S, LIKE, AN ACTION HERO! AND YOUR DAD IS FRIENDS WITH PATRIOTIC ROBOTS!
NICOLE, I-- I DON'T HATE YOU.
I DON'T KNOW WHAT TO SAY, ELIZABETH.
YOU DON'T HAVE TO SAY ANYTHING RIGHT NOW.
RUN AWAY AND LIVE TO EXPLAIN THINGS TO YOUR DAUGHTER ANOTHER DAY, YOU KNOW?

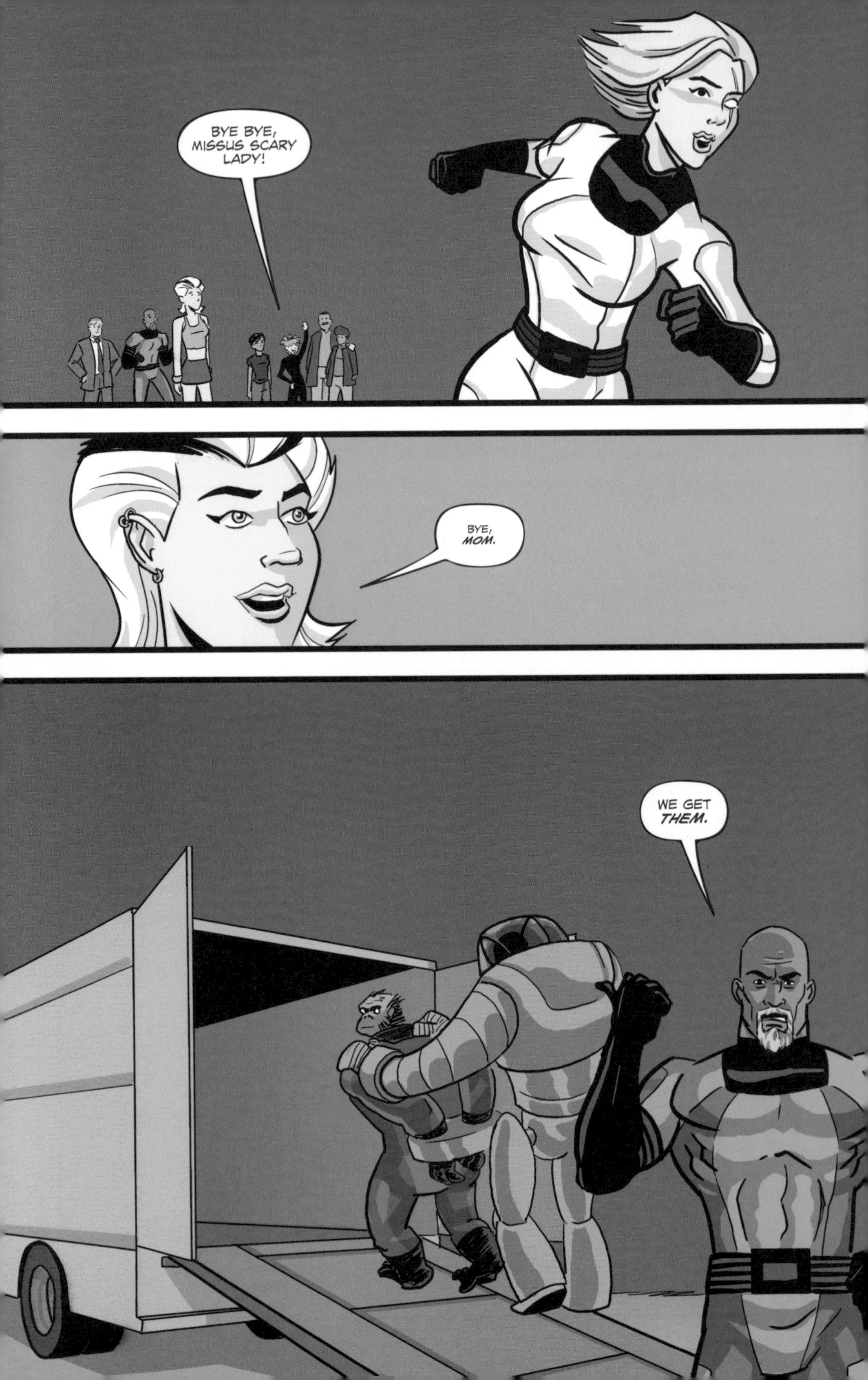
BYE BYE, MISSUS SCARY LADY!
BYE, *MOM.*
WE GET *THEM.*

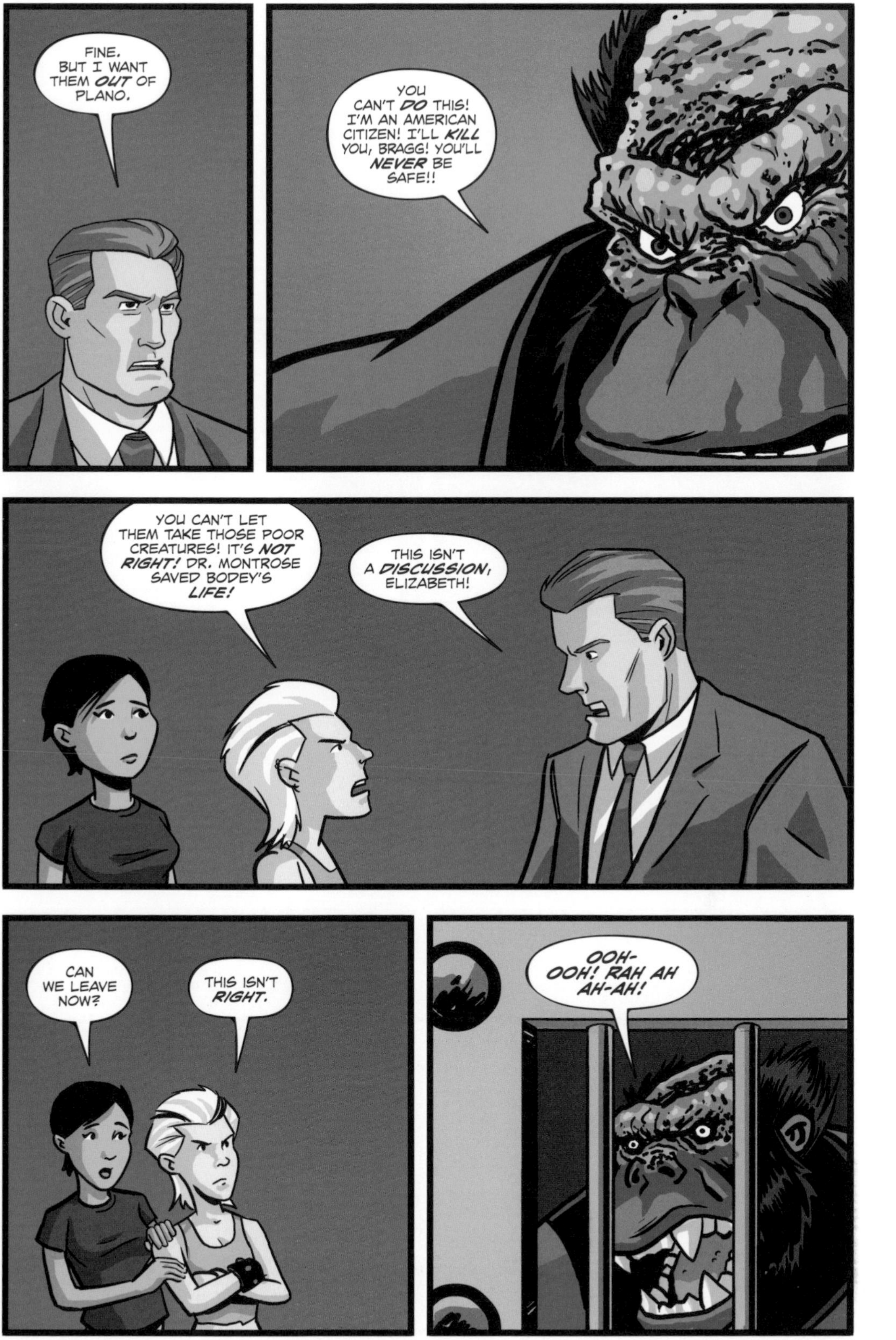
FINE. BUT I WANT THEM OUT OF PLANO.
YOU CAN'T DO THIS! I'M AN AMERICAN CITIZEN! I'LL KILL YOU, BRAGG! YOU'LL NEVER BE SAFE!!
YOU CAN'T LET THEM TAKE THOSE POOR CREATURES! IT'S NOT RIGHT! DR. MONTROSE SAVED BODEY'S LIFE!
THIS ISN'T A DISCUSSION, ELIZABETH!
CAN WE LEAVE NOW?
THIS ISN'T RIGHT.
OOH-OOH! RAH AH AH-AH!

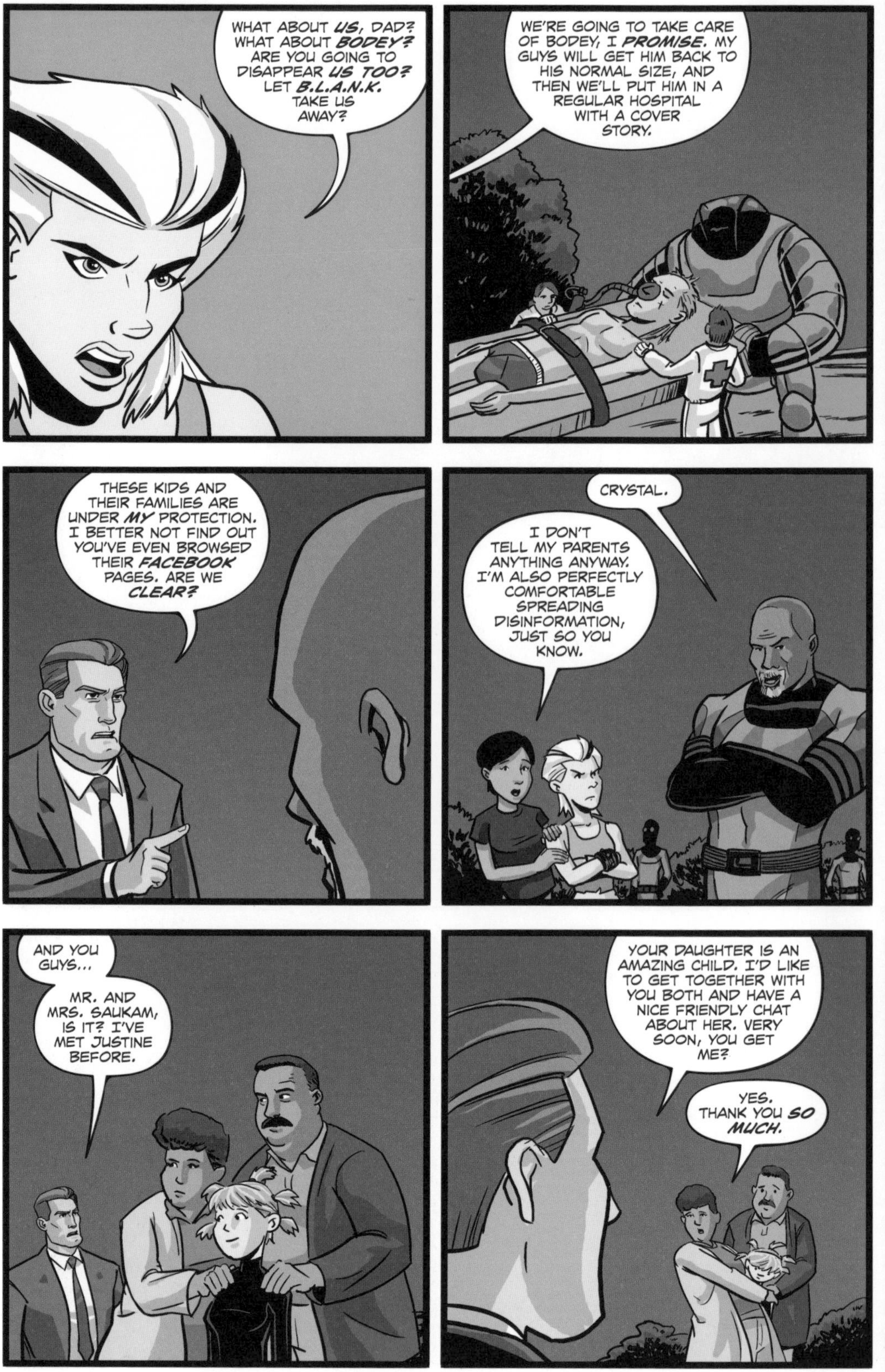
WHAT ABOUT US, DAD? WHAT ABOUT BODEY? ARE YOU GOING TO DISAPPEAR US TOO? LET B.L.A.N.K. TAKE US AWAY?
WE'RE GOING TO TAKE CARE OF BODEY, I PROMISE. MY GUYS WILL GET HIM BACK TO HIS NORMAL SIZE, AND THEN WE'LL PUT HIM IN A REGULAR HOSPITAL WITH A COVER STORY.
THESE KIDS AND THEIR FAMILIES ARE UNDER MY PROTECTION. I BETTER NOT FIND OUT YOU'VE EVEN BROWSED THEIR FACEBOOK PAGES. ARE WE CLEAR?
CRYSTAL.
I DON'T TELL MY PARENTS ANYTHING ANYWAY. I'M ALSO PERFECTLY COMFORTABLE SPREADING DISINFORMATION, JUST SO YOU KNOW.
AND YOU GUYS...
MR. AND MRS. SAUKAM, IS IT? I'VE MET JUSTINE BEFORE.
YOUR DAUGHTER IS AN AMAZING CHILD. I'D LIKE TO GET TOGETHER WITH YOU BOTH AND HAVE A NICE FRIENDLY CHAT ABOUT HER. VERY SOON, YOU GET ME?
YES. THANK YOU SO MUCH.

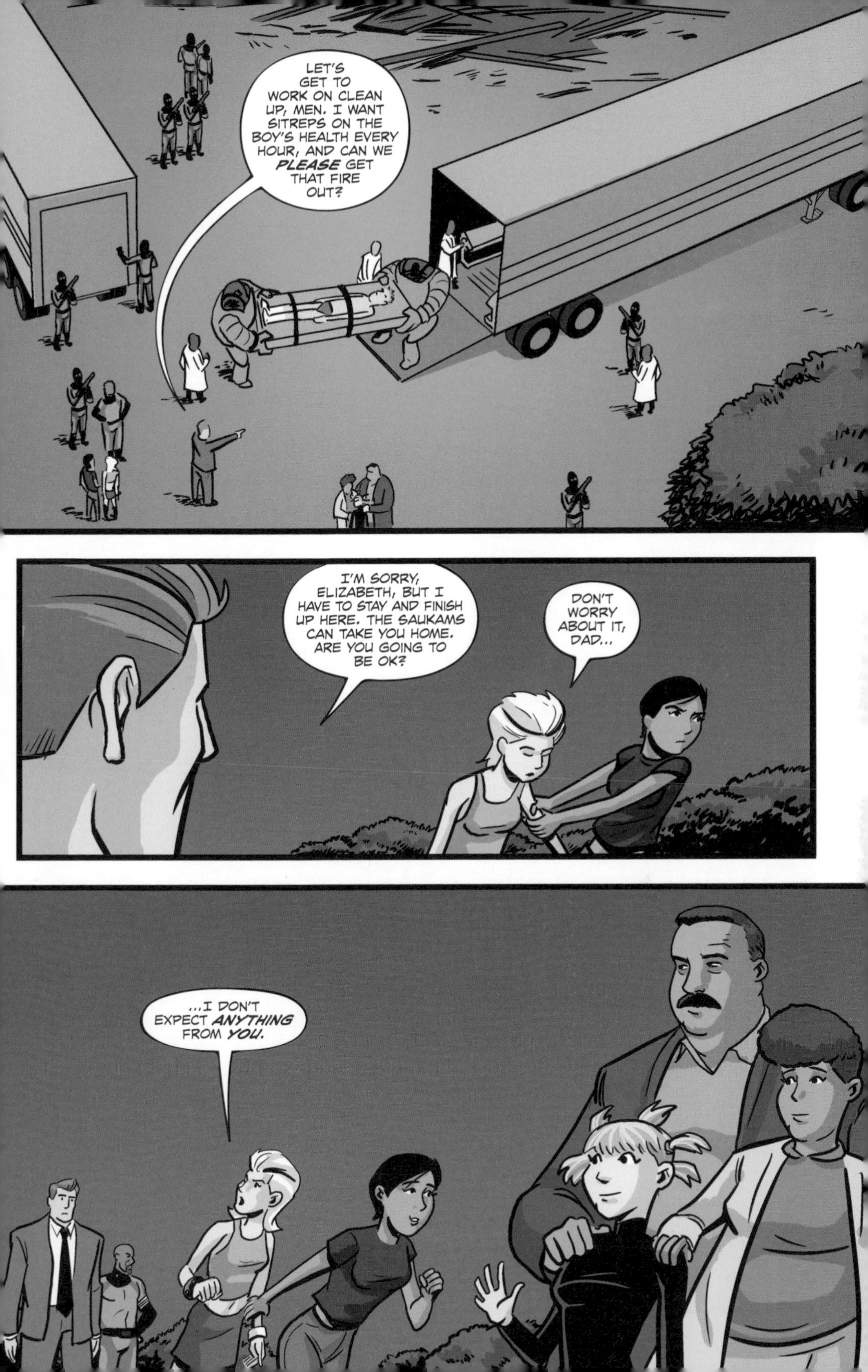
LET'S GET TO WORK ON CLEAN UP, MEN. I WANT SITREPS ON THE BOY'S HEALTH EVERY HOUR, AND CAN WE *PLEASE* GET THAT FIRE OUT?
I'M SORRY, ELIZABETH, BUT I HAVE TO STAY AND FINISH UP HERE. THE SAUKAMS CAN TAKE YOU HOME. ARE YOU GOING TO BE OK?
DON'T WORRY ABOUT IT, DAD...
...I DON'T EXPECT *ANYTHING* FROM *YOU*.

SO THAT'S HOW I FOUND OUT JUST EXACTLY HOW ODD PLANO REALLY IS, AND HOW I'M A *PART* OF THAT STRANGENESS.

I STARTED WRITING THIS JOURNAL SO I COULD MAYBE MAKE SOME SENSE OF IT ALL, BUT MOSTLY IT JUST FEELS GOOD TO GET STUFF OFF MY CHEST.

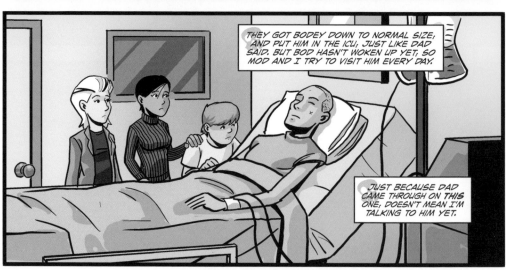

THEY GOT BODEY DOWN TO NORMAL SIZE, AND PUT HIM IN THE ICU, JUST LIKE DAD SAID. BUT BOD HASN'T WOKEN UP YET, SO MOD AND I TRY TO VISIT HIM EVERY DAY.

JUST BECAUSE DAD CAME THROUGH ON *THIS* ONE, DOESN'T MEAN I'M TALKING TO HIM YET.

MOD'S STEP-MOM LEFT HER DAD, AND SO HE AND MOD ARE MOVING IN WITH MOD'S *ABUELA* IN EAST PLANO.

MOD SEEMS PRETTY PSYCHED ABOUT IT ALL.

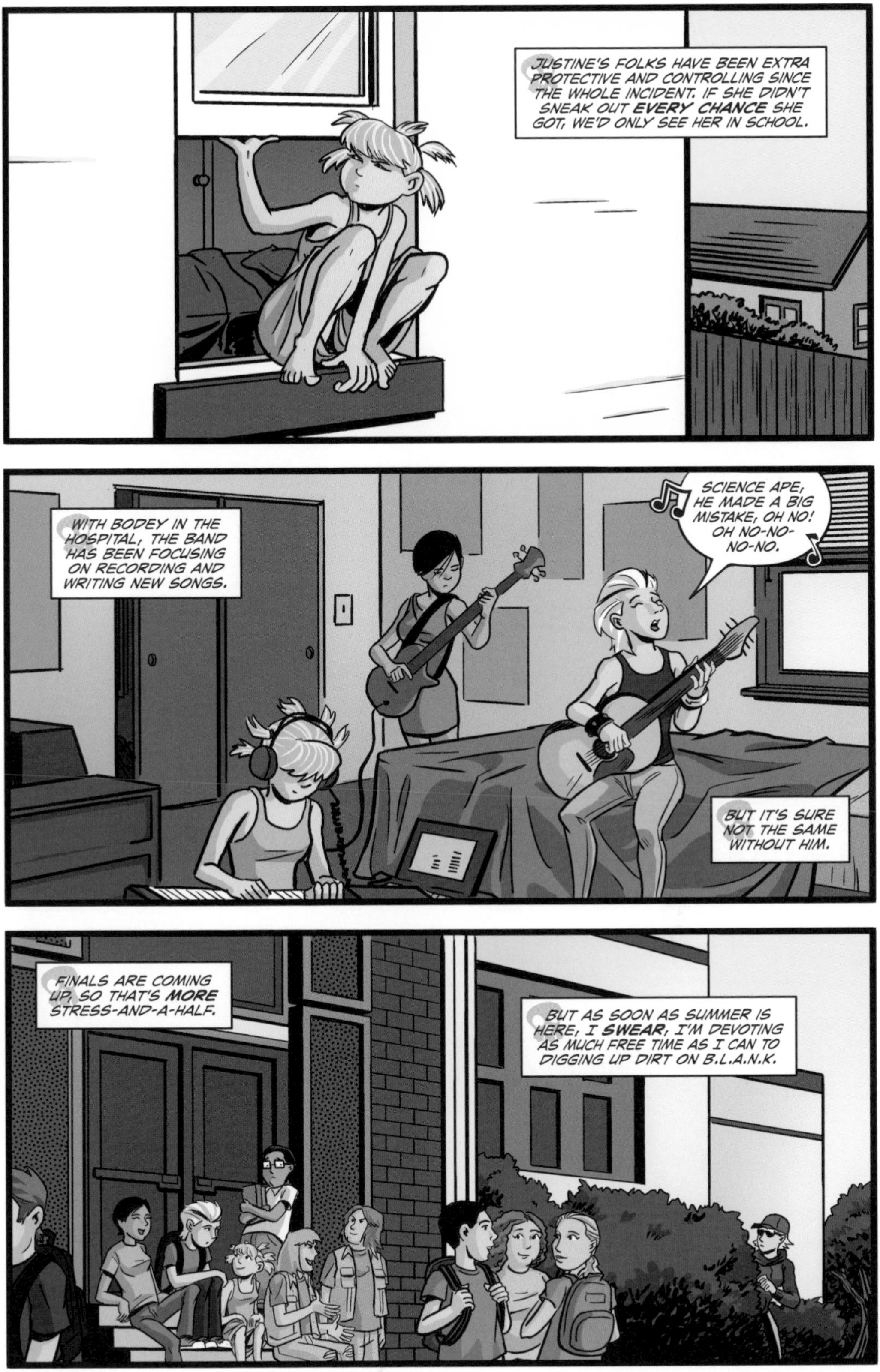
JUSTINE'S FOLKS HAVE BEEN EXTRA PROTECTIVE AND CONTROLLING SINCE THE WHOLE INCIDENT. IF SHE DIDN'T SNEAK OUT **EVERY CHANCE** SHE GOT, WE'D ONLY SEE HER IN SCHOOL.
WITH BODEY IN THE HOSPITAL, THE BAND HAS BEEN FOCUSING ON RECORDING AND WRITING NEW SONGS.
SCIENCE APE, HE MADE A BIG MISTAKE, OH NO! OH NO-NO-NO-NO.
BUT IT'S SURE NOT THE SAME WITHOUT HIM.
FINALS ARE COMING UP, SO THAT'S **MORE** STRESS-AND-A-HALF.
BUT AS SOON AS SUMMER IS HERE, I **SWEAR**, I'M DEVOTING AS MUCH FREE TIME AS I CAN TO DIGGING UP DIRT ON B.L.A.N.K.

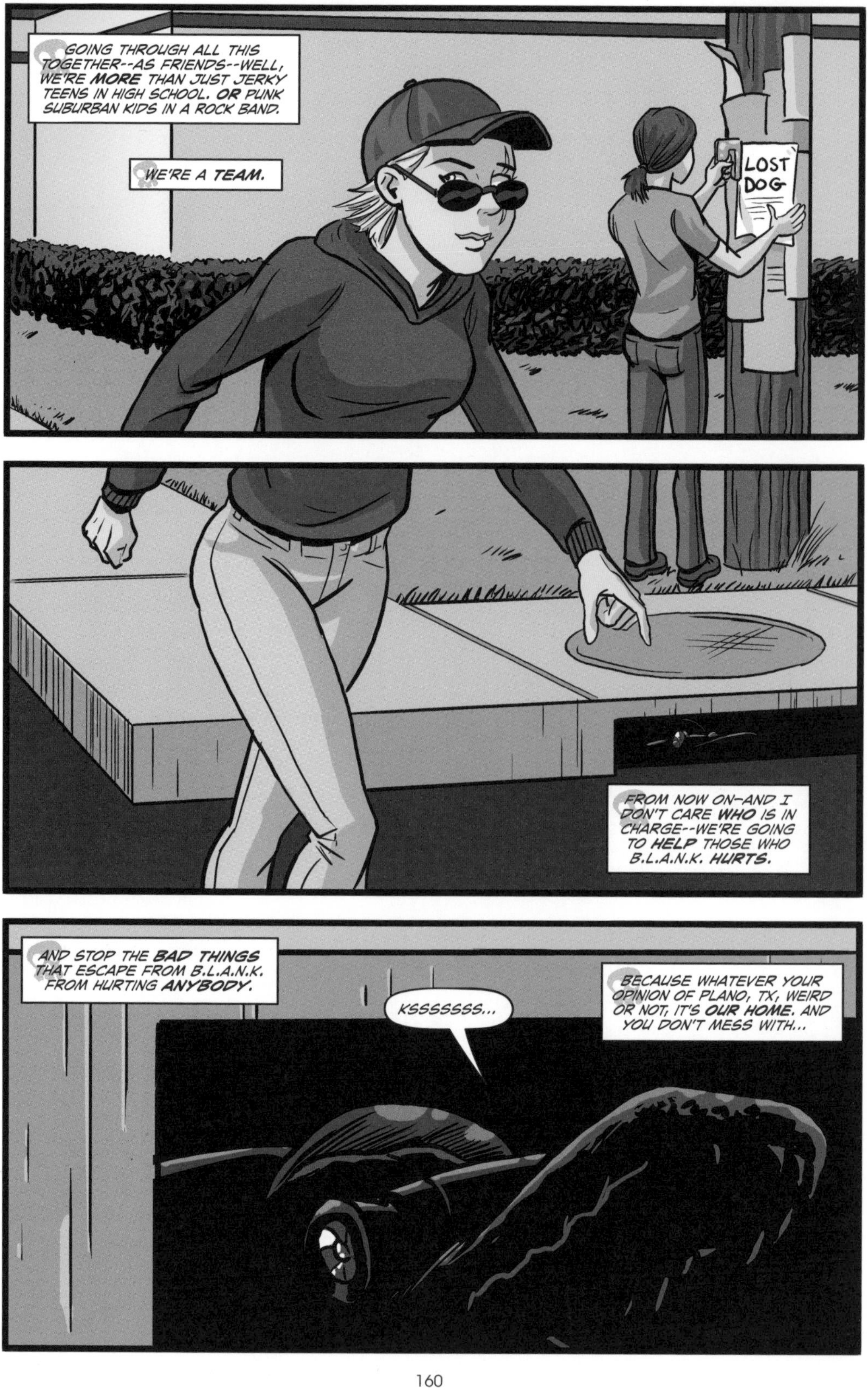
GOING THROUGH ALL THIS TOGETHER--AS FRIENDS--WELL, WE'RE MORE THAN JUST JERKY TEENS IN HIGH SCHOOL. OR PUNK SUBURBAN KIDS IN A ROCK BAND.
WE'RE A TEAM.
LOST DOG
FROM NOW ON—AND I DON'T CARE WHO IS IN CHARGE--WE'RE GOING TO HELP THOSE WHO B.L.A.N.K. HURTS.
AND STOP THE BAD THINGS THAT ESCAPE FROM B.L.A.N.K. FROM HURTING ANYBODY.
KSSSSSSS...
BECAUSE WHATEVER YOUR OPINION OF PLANO, TX, WEIRD OR NOT, IT'S OUR HOME. AND YOU DON'T MESS WITH...

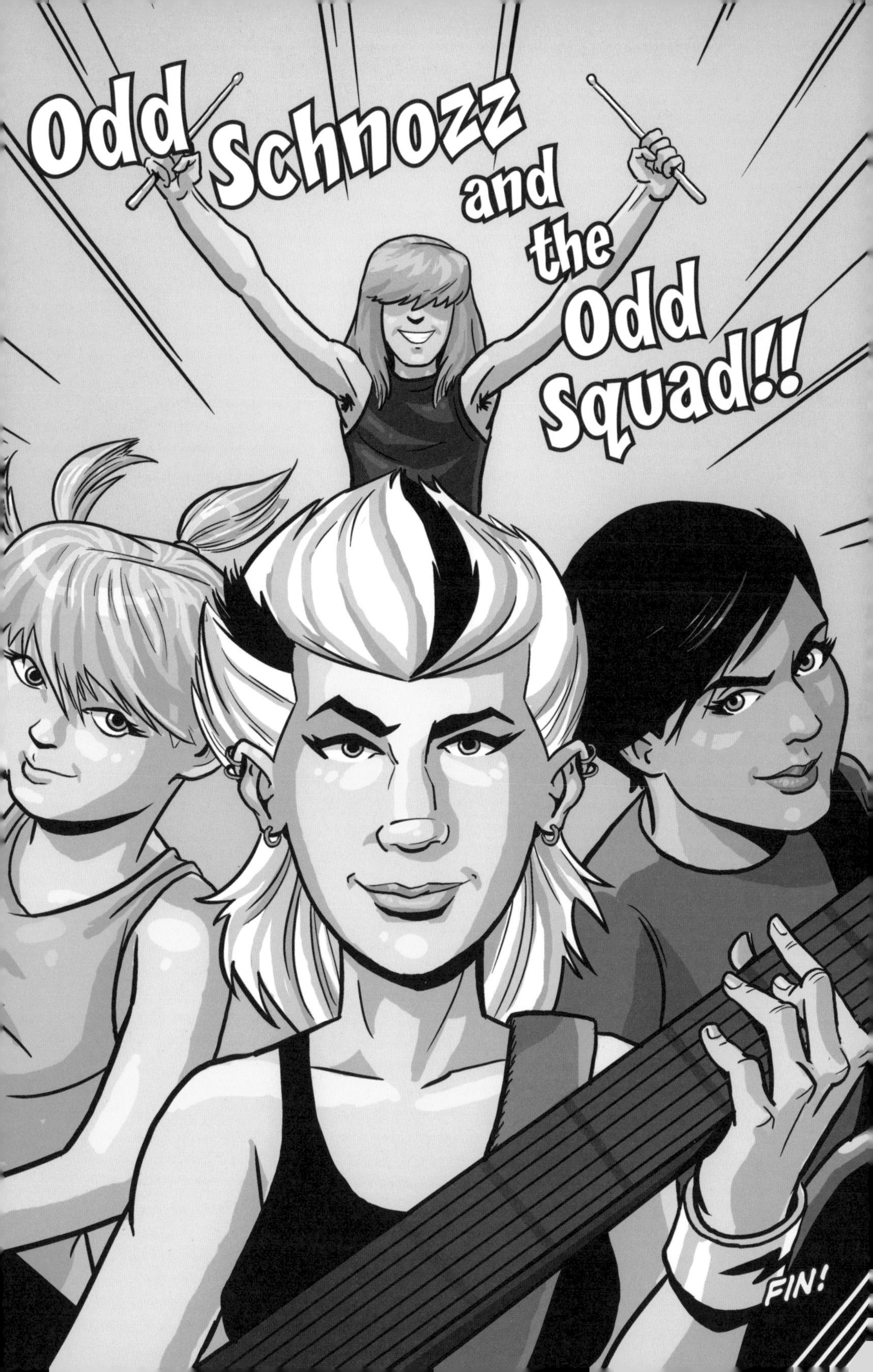
Odd Schnozz and the Odd Squad!!
FIN!

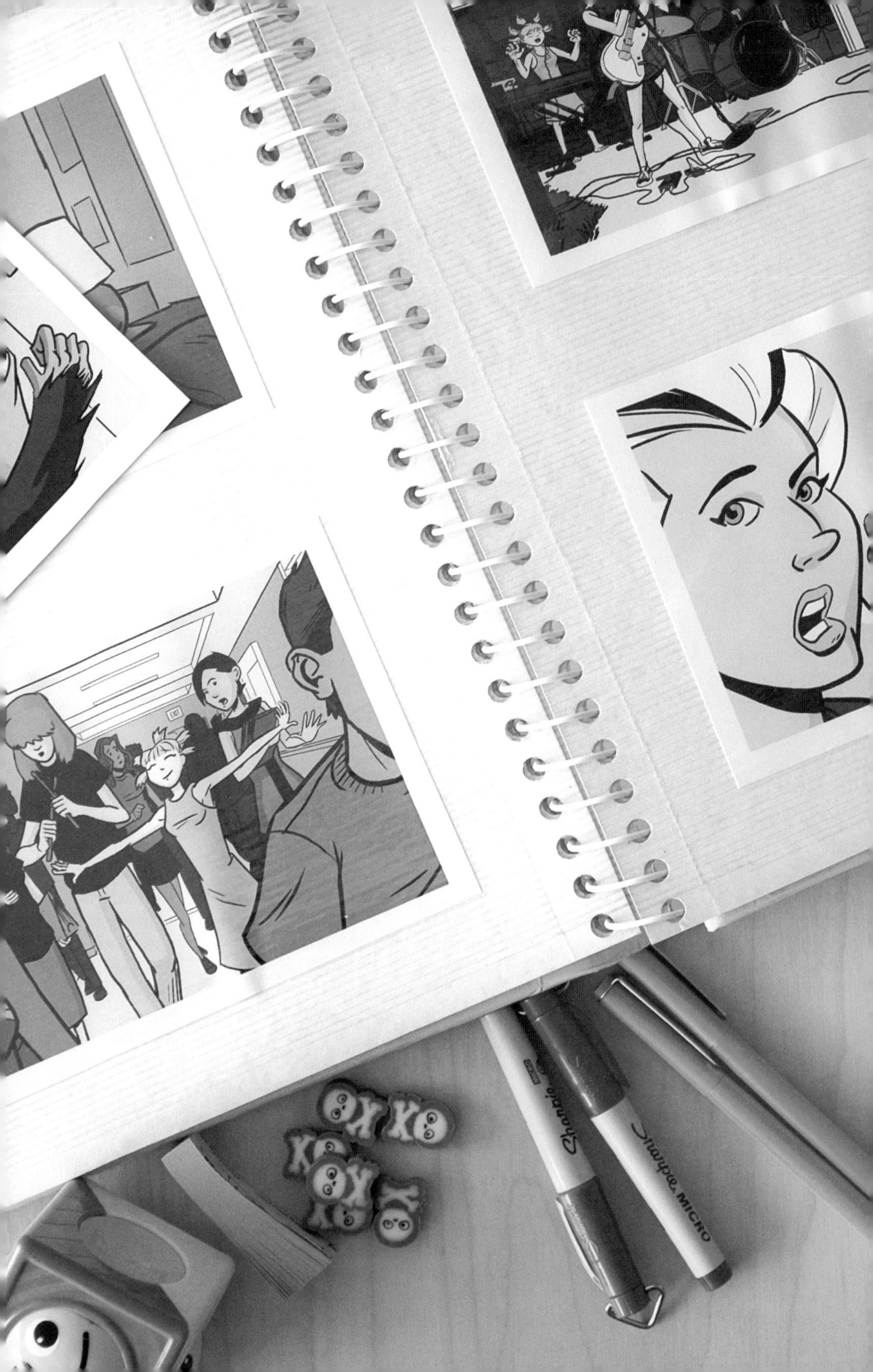
EXIT
Sharpie
Sharpie MICRO

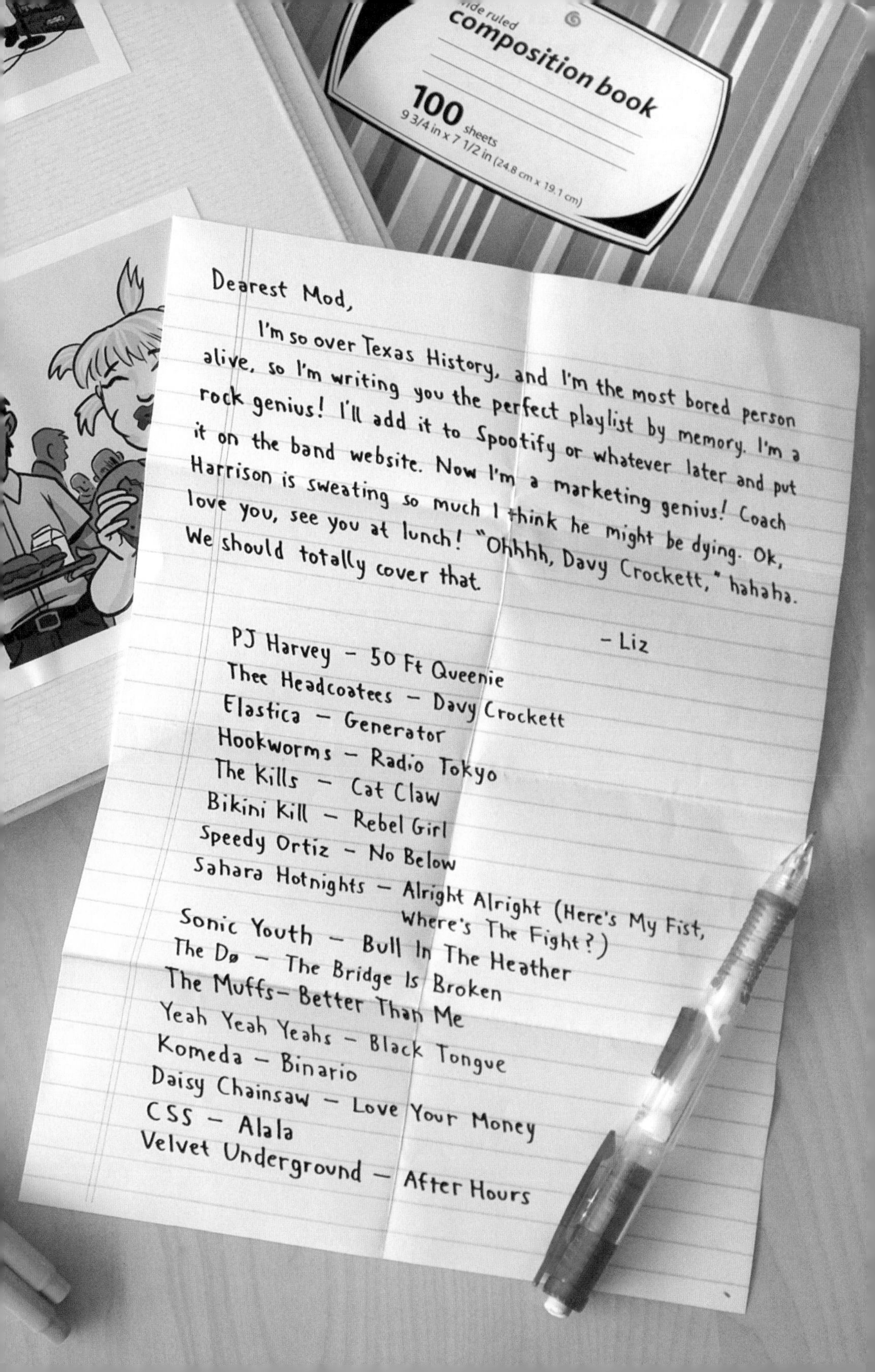
wide ruled
composition book
100 sheets
9 3/4 in x 7 1/2 in (24.8 cm x 19.1 cm)

Dearest Mod,

I'm so over Texas History, and I'm the most bored person alive, so I'm writing you the perfect playlist by memory. I'm a rock genius! I'll add it to Spootify or whatever later and put it on the band website. Now I'm a marketing genius! Coach Harrison is sweating so much I think he might be dying. Ok, love you, see you at lunch! "Ohhhh, Davy Crockett," hahaha. We should totally cover that.

– Liz

PJ Harvey – 50 Ft Queenie
Thee Headcoatees – Davy Crockett
Elastica – Generator
Hookworms – Radio Tokyo
The Kills – Cat Claw
Bikini Kill – Rebel Girl
Speedy Ortiz – No Below
Sahara Hotnights – Alright Alright (Here's My Fist, Where's The Fight?)
Sonic Youth – Bull In The Heather
The Dø – The Bridge Is Broken
The Muffs – Better Than Me
Yeah Yeah Yeahs – Black Tongue
Komeda – Binario
Daisy Chainsaw – Love Your Money
CSS – Alala
Velvet Underground – After Hours

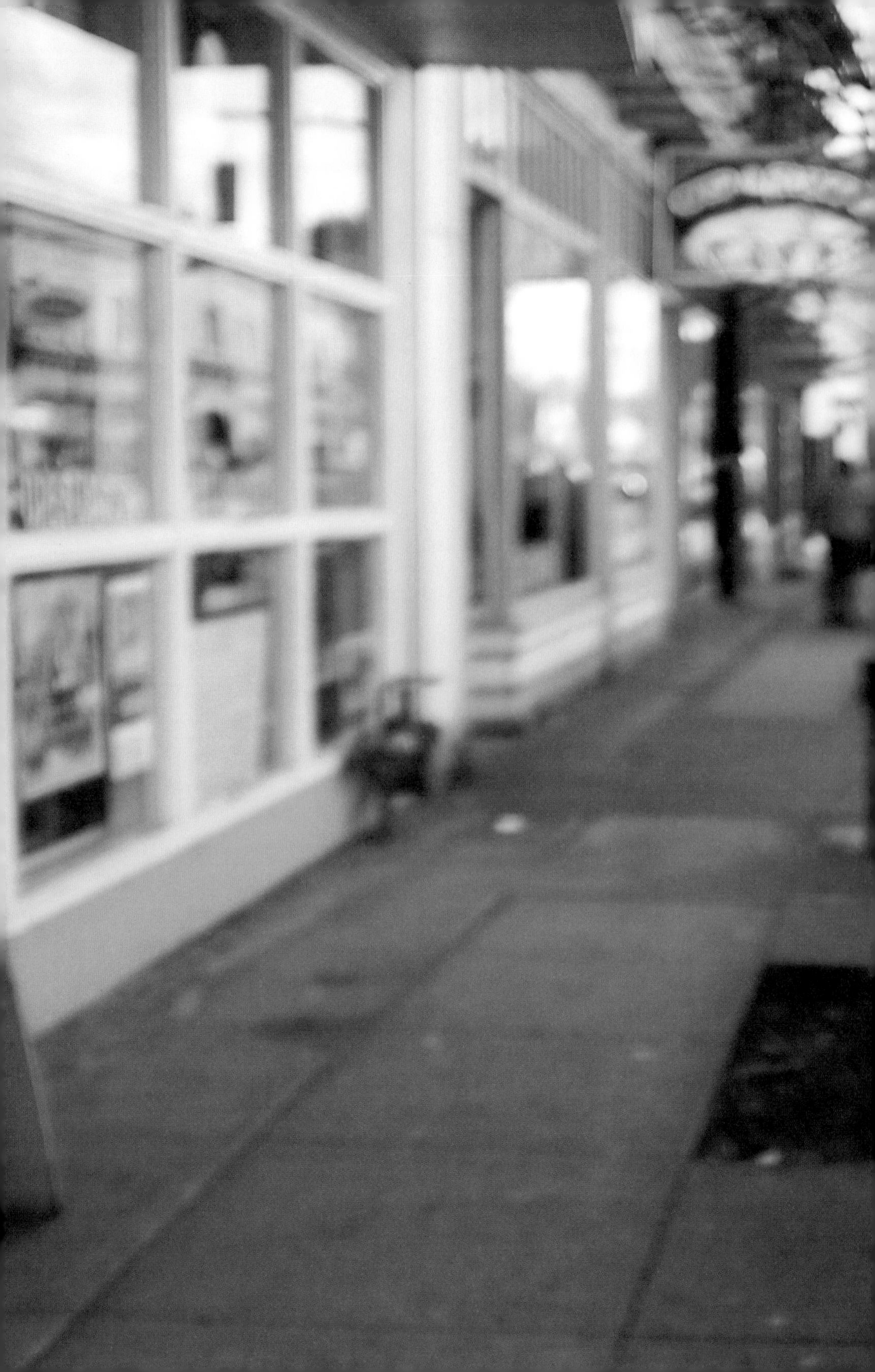

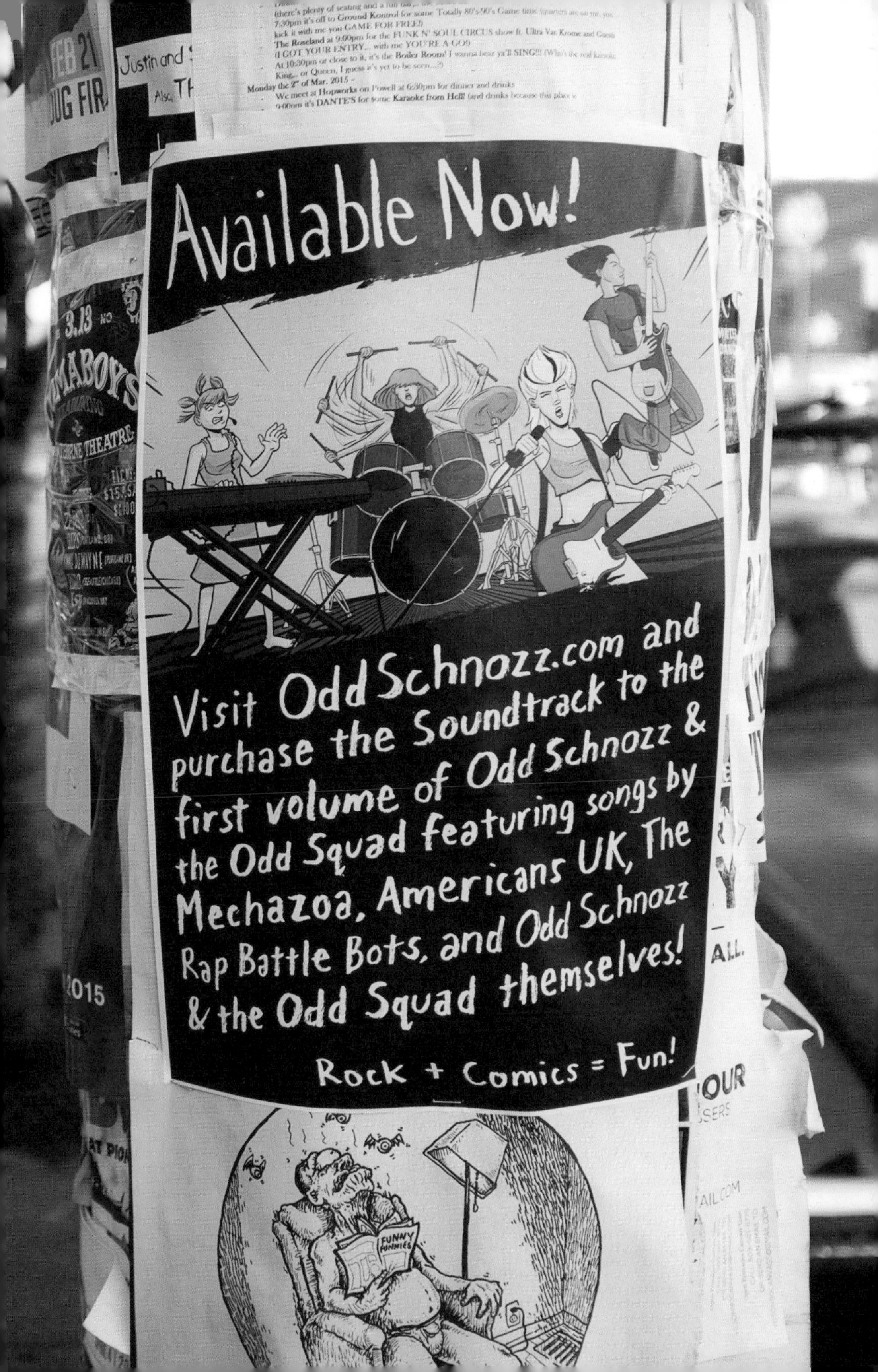

Available Now!
Visit OddSchnozz.com and purchase the Soundtrack to the first volume of Odd Schnozz & the Odd Squad featuring songs by the Mechazoa, Americans UK, The Rap Battle Bots, and Odd Schnozz & the Odd Squad themselves!
Rock + Comics = Fun!
FEB 21
DOUG FIR
FUNNY FUNNIES

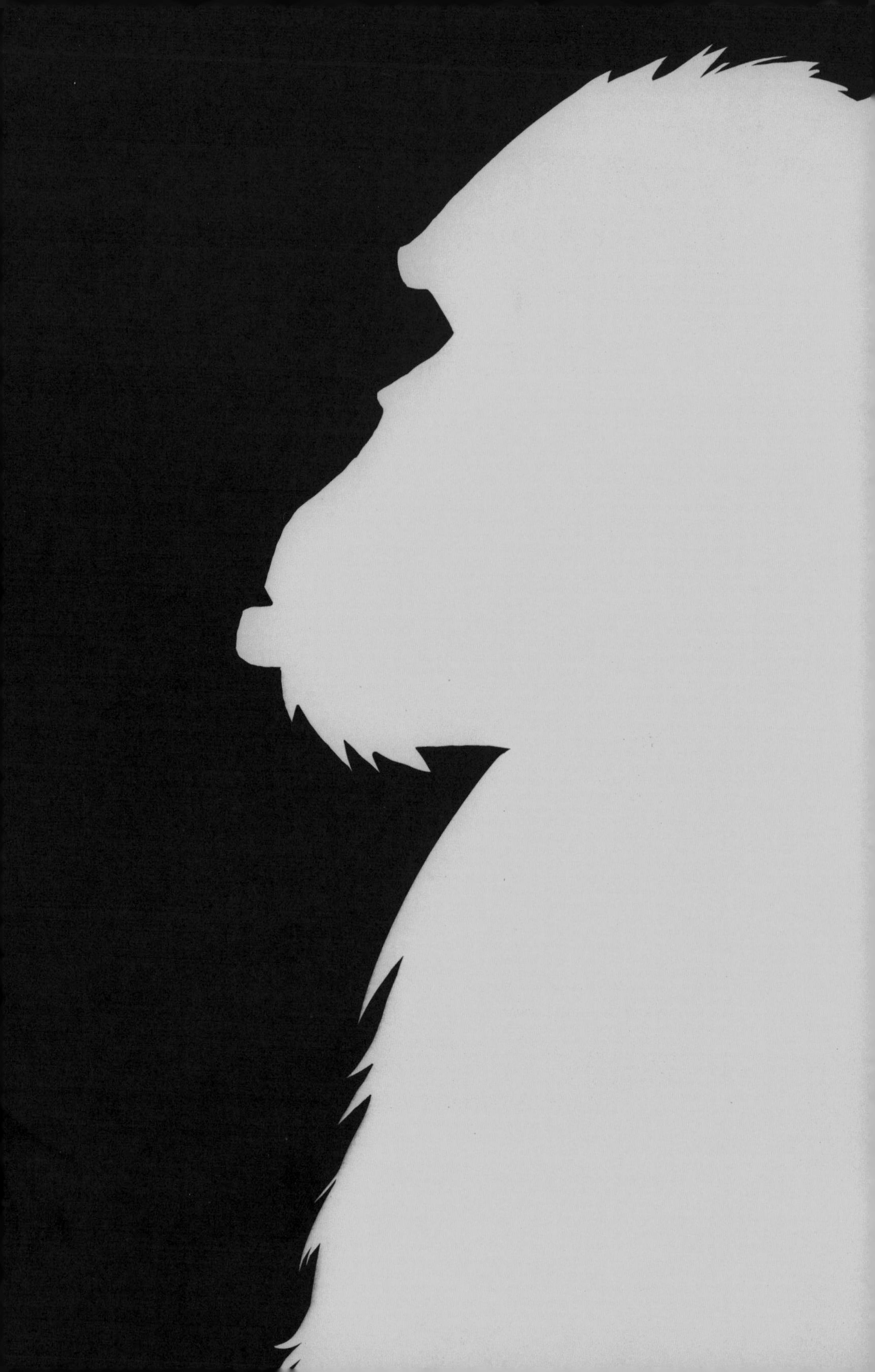